Religion and Politics in the Age of
the Counterreformation

The University of North Carolina Press Chapel Hill

ROBERT BIRELEY, S.J.

Religion and Politics in the Age of
the Counterreformation

Emperor Ferdinand II, William Lamormaini, S.J.,

and the Formation of Imperial Policy

© 1981 The University of North Carolina Press

All rights reserved

Manufactured in the United States of America

Library of Congress Cataloging in Publication Data

Bireley, Robert.
  Religion and politics in the age of the counterreformation.

  Bibliography: p.
  Includes index.
  1. Germany—History—1618–1648. 2. Thirty Years'
War, 1618–1648. 3. Counter-Reformation—Germany.
4. Ferdinand II, Emperor of Germany, 1578–1637.
5. Lamormaini, William. I. Title.
DD189.B54 943'.042 80-27334
ISBN 0-8078-1470-9

To My Fellow Jesuits

at Loyola University of Chicago

Contents

Contents

Illustrations

Preface

The Jesuit William Lamormaini served as the confessor of Emperor Ferdinand II from 1624 until the emperor's death in 1637. He must be counted among the major figures of the Counterreformation in Central Europe. Yet Lamormaini has been the subject of little scholarly attention. My own suspicion of his importance rose immensely when I discovered nearly one thousand letters in the Roman Archives of the Society of Jesus written by the superior general of the Jesuits to Lamormaini during his tenure as confessor in Vienna. To be sure, Lamormaini comes to the attention of anyone who reads a standard account of the Thirty Years War, such as those by C. V. Wedgwood or George Pagès. His name turns up in any treatment of the controversial general Wallenstein, as in the recent biography by Golo Mann. But the only major piece to appear on Lamormaini in the past fifty years is the account by Andreas Posch in the *Biographie nationale du pays de Luxembourg* published in 1953, which appeared in a slightly condensed form two years later in the *Mitteilungen des Instituts für österreichische Geschichtsforschung*.

When I first became interested in Lamormaini, I was engaged in research on the Elector Maximilian of Bavaria and the Jesuit Adam Contzen, who was his confessor for nearly the same span Lamormaini held the post in Vienna. The results, which I published in *Maximilian von Bayern, Adam Contzen, S.J., und die Gegenreformation in Deutschland, 1624–1635*, showed that religious or ideological motives often outweighed political ones with Maximilian and that Contzen, who had a major role in policy making, was partly responsible for this. This finding suggested that the same might be the case with Lamormaini and Ferdinand, who after Maximilian best incorporated the ideal of the Counterreformation prince in Germany and held a more exalted position. Indeed, the secondary literature pointed in this direction. My purpose in this book, then, is to study in detail the impact Lamormaini had on the policy of Emperor Ferdinand II. Obviously, this entails a careful look at the government in Vienna in action and at the complicated politics and foreign relations of the Thirty Years War. My hope is to make a contribution to the understanding of the ideological character of the war and the complex relationship between religion and politics during the Counterreformation. More generally, the story of Ferdinand and Lamormaini illustrates the extent to which ideas move men and make history.

A few remarks about procedure and usage are in order. All translations are my own. I have kept close to the text in order to preserve its flavor even at the occasional expense of readability. Often enough I have made use of the manuscript copy of published sources. This was necessary because the documents were not published in their entirety or because their handwriting was significant for my purpose. In such cases I have cited the manuscript and the published text. If a manuscript source has only been cited or referred to in a documentary collection, as is often the case in the *Briefe und Akten zur Geschichte des Dreissigjährigen Krieges*, I have not cited the collection if I have consulted the manuscript. In citing documents and especially letters, I have not indicated whether a document is an original, a register copy (as which the final draft usually served), or another copy, unless this seemed significant in the context. Often it is evident from the text. Nor have I indicated the place of origin of letters unless this was particularly noteworthy and not clear from the text.

The names of persons and places have caused me many a headache. My chief concern has been to employ the form that seemed most natural in the context. Usually this meant the anglicized form for rulers and major figures of the narrative, for example, *William* Lamormaini instead of *Wilhelm* Lamormaini, and the foreign form for others, *Heinrich* Philippi instead of *Henry* Philippi. Ranks and titles are given in the English form as are place names. In instances where there are two or more names for the same place, for example Pressburg, Pozsony, Bratislava, I have indicated the different names at the first mention in the text and tried subsequently to find a compromise between the name most familiar in the seventeenth century and to the reader of today.

The term *imperial* is used in two different but related senses. Usually it refers to the emperor and means the same as *kaiserlich*, as in "the traditional fears of imperial authority." Sometimes, however, it refers to the Empire or *Reich*, as in "imperial diet" or "imperial constitution." The use in each case is, I trust, clear from the context.

A substantial portion of chapter eleven was published in an earlier form as a demand article, "The Peace of Prague (1635) and the Counterreformation in Germany," by the *Journal of Modern History*, vol. 48 (1976), copyright 1976 by The University of Chicago Press. For the right to use this I am grateful to the *Journal of Modern History* and to The University of Chicago Press.

I am grateful to many people for the aid and support they have given me as I worked on this book. The National Endowment for the Humanities awarded me a Fellowship for Younger Humanists for the academic year 1972–73, during which time I did much of the basic research. A research fellowship from the American Council of Learned Societies enabled me to spend the spring and summer of 1979 bringing the manuscript into its final form. Grants-in-aid from the American Council of Learned Societies and the American Philosophical Society helped make it possible for me to spend most of the academic year 1975–76 preparing the rough draft of the manuscript and traveling in Europe to check further sources. The Loyola University of Chicago Committee on Research has been most helpful. It has made available several summer research grants, seen to the typing of the final manuscript, and provided a generous subsidy for publication. For this I am especially indebted to the university's research director, Dr. Thomas Bennett, and his predecessor, Rev. Matthew Creighton, S.J. Mrs. Arlene Ranalli did an outstanding job in preparing the typescript of the text. Mr. Lewis Bateman, executive editor of The University of North Carolina Press, has continually shown interest in my work. His regularly prompt response to communications is especially appreciated.

Of the many archivists and librarians to whom I owe thanks, deserving of special mention are Frau Doktor Anna Coreth, formerly director of the Haus-, Hof- und Staatsarchiv in Vienna, and Rev. Edmund Lamalle, S.J., Prefect of the Roman Archives of the Society of Jesus. My fellow Jesuits of the Istituto Storico della Compagnia di Gesù in Rome were always kind hosts during my extended stays there, as were Professor Doktor Alois Loidl, rector of the diocesan hostel Stephanushaus in Vienna, and the community there.

Above all, I want to express my gratitude to my fellow Jesuits of the Loyola University community for their support and understanding. To them I dedicate this book.

Religion and Politics in the Age of
the Counterreformation

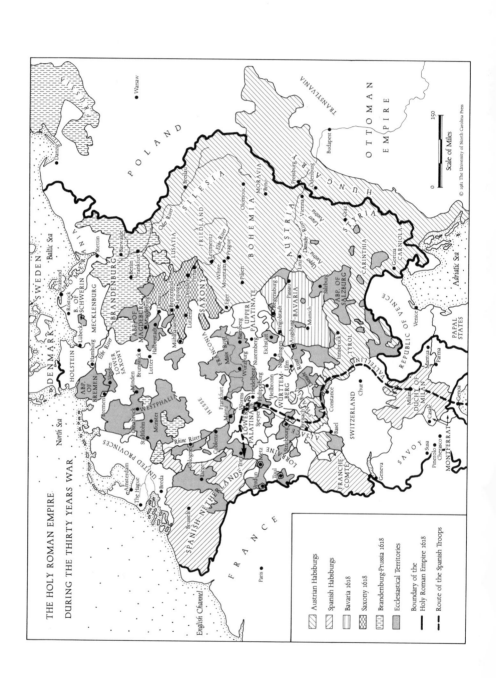

THE HOLY ROMAN EMPIRE

DURING THE THIRTY YEARS WAR

Austrian Habsburgs
Spanish Habsburgs
Bavaria 1618
Saxony 1618
Brandenburg-Prussia 1618
Ecclesiastical Territories
Boundary of the
Holy Roman Empire 1618
Route of the Spanish Troops

Scale of Miles

0   150

© 1981 The University of North Carolina Press

1. People and Policies to 1624

illiam Lamormaini published his Baroque classic, *The Virtues of Ferdinand II, Emperor of the Romans*, in 1638, the year after the emperor's death. Inside his personal copy he noted that it was on February 2, 1624, the Feast of the Purification of the Blessed Virgin Mary, that Ferdinand first approached him to confess his sins and receive absolution.[1] Thus did Lamormaini inaugurate his thirteen-year term of service as the emperor's confessor. This apparently insignificant event occurred between the entrances into European high politics by two figures who like Ferdinand and Lamormaini were to have a decisive impact on the fate of the Counterreformation in Central Europe and the outcome of the Thirty Years War. On August 6, 1623, Maffeo Cardinal Barberini had emerged from the conclave in Rome as the new pope and was soon crowned Urban VIII. In Paris on April 29, 1624, Armand-Jean du Plessis, Cardinal de Richelieu, entered Louis XIII's council of ministers, and he quickly came to dominate it.

At the start of 1624 what is often called the Bohemian phase of the Thirty Years War had ended, and the Danish phase had not yet begun. Ferdinand's attention was directed chiefly to the consolidation of his authority and the implementation of the Counterreformation in Bohemia and the lands that had joined with it after the rebellion of 1618 unloosed the war. That year, on May 23, members of an assembly of Bohemian Protestants meeting in Prague had marched into the Hradschin Palace and heaved three Catholic government officials out the window. Events following this Defenestration of Prague threatened disaster for the House of Habsburg in Central Europe. The Bohemian rebels convened the estates, established a government, and began to raise an army. The death of Emperor Matthias on March 20, 1619, further confused the situation. Protestant troops from Bohemia under Count Matthias von Thurn were on the brink of seizing Vienna in June 1619, and along with it Ferdinand himself, when a Protestant defeat in south Bohemia forced them to withdraw.

However, the respite was a brief one for Ferdinand. Ruler of Inner Austria since 1596, he had been recognized as King of Bohemia in 1617 and King of Hungary in 1618, and he was destined for the succession in the rest of the Austrian lands and in the Empire by a family agreement of the Austrian Habsburgs. But now the estates or representative bodies of

3

all the lands of the Bohemian crown (Moravia, Silesia, Upper and Lower Lusatia in addition to Bohemia proper) formed a confederation. They deposed Ferdinand as King of Bohemia and on August 26, 1619, elected in his place the youthful Calvinist Elector Palatine of the Rhine, Frederick V. His acceptance guaranteed the spread of hostilities into the heart of the Empire. That same month the estates of Upper Austria and the militant Protestant faction of the Lower Austrian estates allied with the Bohemian rebels. They coordinated their military efforts with the unpredictable Bethlen Gabor, Prince of Transylvania, who was the perennial rival of the Habsburgs for control of those parts of Hungary not held by the Turks. Bethlen's troops seized Pressburg (Pozsony/Bratislava), and by mid-October were advancing toward Vienna.[2]

Apart from his personal determination and courage, Ferdinand owed his triumph, indeed his survival, to his allies: his Wittelsbach cousin in Munich, Maximilian of Bavaria, his Habsburg cousin in Madrid, Philip III of Spain, and the Lutheran Elector John George of Saxony. He himself had few troops at his disposal. Despite his troubles, Ferdinand was chosen Holy Roman Emperor on August 28, 1619, in Frankfurt by the seven imperial electors. Homeward bound after his coronation, he stopped in Munich to conclude negotiations that assured him the assistance of the vigorous, competent Duke Maximilian, who was also the leader of the Catholic League, an alliance of west German Catholic states first formed at his initiative ten years before.[3] After careful preparations, the League army, under the direction of the outstanding general, the pious Belgian Johann Tserclaes von Tilly, overran Upper Austria in the summer of 1620. From the west troops of John George occupied the two Lusatias and marched into Silesia.

The crucial battle that established Habsburg domination in Bohemia for generations to come took place at the White Mountain outside Prague on November 8, 1620. There Tilly, assisted by imperial and Spanish troops, crushed the Bohemian rebels. League troops later followed up their victory, driving rebellious Protestant forces first from the Upper and then from the Lower Palatinate including Frederick's residential city, Heidelberg. Subsequently, Ferdinand, in accordance with his agreement with Maximilian, banned Frederick from the Empire and at the Convention of Deputies at Regensburg on February 25, 1623, publicly invested Maximilian, for his person but not his House, with Frederick's electoral title.[4] This signified a profound shift in the balance of power in the Empire. Only a few years before the Catholics had enjoyed a shaky four-to-three majority in the electoral college. A Protestant victory in Bohemia would have reversed this. Now the Catholics possessed a solid five-to-two majority, and the danger of the election of a Protestant to the imperial office had disappeared. The Calvinist Frederick, formerly a threat to the Catholic ecclesiastical states along the Rhine, sat in exile in The Hague. Ferdinand had agreed that Maximilian would hold as security the Upper Palatinate plus rich Habsburg Upper Austria until he was reimbursed for his war expenses. John George held the two Lusatias on the same terms. Maximilian also occupied provisionally the lands of the Lower Palatinate on the right bank of the Rhine. A principal goal of his policy from then on was to tighten his grip on the Palatinate electoral title and the Palatinate lands he held. Frederick, for his part, continually sought the support of European powers for his reinstatement. Thus was created the Palatinate question, which found final resolution only at the Peace of Westphalia.[5]

Unfortunately for Ferdinand and the German Catholics, the goals of Philip III and then Philip IV of Spain were scarcely compatible with those of Maximilian and the League. This state of affairs engendered much tension in Vienna during the coming years. Ferdinand was beholden to Spain as well as to Maximilian. The secret Oñate Treaty of 1617, negotiated with Ferdinand by the Spanish diplomat the Count of Oñate, helped prepare the way for what Madrid hoped would be close cooperation between the two branches of the House of Habsburg. Philip III renounced a claim to the Bohemian and Hungarian thrones and Ferdinand made certain commitments to Spain. He promised, once he became emperor, to foster Spanish interests in the disposition of imperial fiefs in Italy, and he agreed to cede to Spain territories in Anterior Austria (the Habsburg holdings in southwest Germany), which were then held by his uncle, the childless Archduke Maximilian, as soon as they fell to him or his progeny by inheritance.[6] More importantly, Spain lent Ferdinand decisive and generous support in his hour of need following the Bohemian rebellion. It contributed troops and subsidies for the Bohemian campaign as well as a Spanish army from the Netherlands that moved down the Rhine to hold Palatinate forces in check while the League army was active to the east. In 1624 Spanish troops still occupied the Palatinate lands on the left bank of the Rhine.

The Spanish perspective was European, Maximilian's essentially German. Even before the death of Philip III in 1621 and the ascent to power of the Count-Duke of Olivares under Philip IV, leading figures in the formation of Spanish policy, such as Oñate, looked to the reassertion of Spanish influence in Western and Central Europe. By this they understood above all victory over the stubborn Dutch, who had been in rebellion since the 1560s and were now a great power. Spain was realistic enough to see that it could not hope for complete subjection of the Dutch. What it desired was a favorable settlement with advantageous terms for the Spanish Netherlands.[7] But if Spain was to achieve this after the expiration of the Twelve Years Truce with the Dutch in 1621, it needed allies. Those that first came to mind were the emperor and the Catholic League. Once the Bohemian rebellion was quelled, Spain consistently urged peace in the Empire, even at the expense of major concessions to the Protestants, in order to free the emperor and the German Catholic princes to aid it in the Netherlands. But Maximilian and the princes regularly opposed intervention in the Dutch war for themselves or the emperor. For them it implied the subordination of German to essentially Habsburg interests and would only lead to a still greater conflagration that would imperil their gains and ravage their lands, close as many of them were to the Dutch border.

Spain needed secure means of communication with the Netherlands, either by sea around France and through the English Channel, or by land along the Spanish road from Milan across the Alps and on to Brussels. Spanish policy under Olivares oscillated. On the one hand, in order to win at least the tacit support of James I of England, Spain favored the restoration in the Palatinate of Frederick, who was James's son-in-law. Furthermore, a settlement with Frederick would contribute to the peace in the Empire necessary for German support in the Netherlands. But on the other hand, the Spaniards needed to protect the land route to the north. The provisions of the Oñate Treaty regarding the Anterior Austrian lands and the Italian principalities were dictated by this need. From this point of view the Spaniards preferred not to see Frederick reinstated. Their presence in the Palatinate greatly increased the security of the Milan-Brussels road, and it also served as a useful check on their main rivals for power in Europe, the French. War with France over a vital link of the Spanish lifeline, the Swiss Alpine pass of the Valtelline that connected Milan with the Austrian Habsburg lands, had only been avoided at the last minute in 1622,[8] and it did break out shortly after Richelieu's accession to power. Maximilian and the League were uneasy about the Spanish occupation of the Lower Palatinate because it involved a Spanish presence on German territory and served as a provocation to the French. Also, for fear of creating a French diversion on the Empire's western borders and the possibility of a disastrous expansion of the conflict, Maximilian and the League opposed any German intervention in the Valtelline.[9] Ferdinand was to find it increasingly difficult to satisfy the Spaniards and the Bavarians, both of whom had their supporters in Vienna.

When Lamormaini took up his office as confessor in 1624, the emperor's fortunes were still improving. In Germany no major Protestant army remained in the field to challenge the Catholic forces, which consisted largely of the League army fighting in the emperor's name. Tilly's resounding victory over the condottiere Christian of Halberstadt at Stadt-lohn near the Dutch border on August 6, 1623, had forestalled a plan to organize an anti-imperial alliance of German Protestant states hopeful of securing subsidies from the Dutch states, possibly England, and even France. Closer to home, troops of Bethlen Gabor did ravage southern Moravia and tied up a small imperial army until the Peace of Vienna on May 8, 1624. This agreement confirmed once again for the area of Hungary under Habsburg control a number of political and religious guarantees not enjoyed by other Habsburg territories but necessary to keep the Hungarians from stirring up trouble at the instigation of Bethlen. Of great importance for Ferdinand's whole reign was the twenty-year armistice of Zsitvatorok that Archduke Matthias had concluded with the Turks in 1606, ending the war begun in 1593. Largely because of pressure from the Persians, the Turks had agreed to this settlement more or less ratifying the status quo. Regularly renewed for nearly seventy-five years, the agreement meant that neither Ferdinand nor his son, Ferdinand III, had to face a serious Turkish threat. Had the Turks mounted an offensive during the Thirty Years War, it is hard to see how the emperor could have withstood it.[10]

Ferdinand's choice of a Jesuit as his confessor was to be expected. His father, Archduke Carl, son of Emperor Ferdinand I and founder of the Styrian Habsburg line, had summoned the Jesuits to open a college in his residential city of Graz in 1573, five years before Ferdinand's birth there on July 9, 1578. The fathers soon became important allies of Carl in his attempt to maintain and strengthen the precarious position of the Catholics in Inner Austria, which included Carinthia and Carniola as well as Styria.[11] When the college was raised to the status of a university in 1586, the eight-year-old Ferdinand was the first student to have his name inscribed in the book of matriculation.[12] However, Ferdinand does not seem to have had much contact with Jesuits during his early years when his devout mother, Maria of Bavaria, was the greatest influence on his life.[13] This changed when in 1590, the year his father died, he departed for the Jesuit University of Ingolstadt, in Bavaria, where he studied for five years. In 1597 Ferdinand selected as his confessor Bartholomew Viller, a Belgian and former provincial superior of the Austrian Jesuit Province, who resigned as confessor only after witnessing Ferdinand's imperial coronation in 1619. Succeeding Viller was Martin Becan, another Belgian, who during his years as professor of theology in Mainz and Vienna had become the most distinguished Catholic controversial theologian in Germany. He died in Vienna on January 24, 1624.[14]

Like his father, Ferdinand considered the Jesuits exemplary instruments for the defense and propagation of the faith. He came to form an extremely high opinion of the Society and more than once was heard to remark that if he were free, as his children were, he would enter the Society himself.[15] He admired in particular the work of the Jesuit colleges. They were in his opinion a leading means to spread and establish Catholicism. He founded, that is, completely endowed, six colleges and substantially contributed to the endowment of many more.[16] In a codicil to his will and testament drawn up on May 10, 1621, the emperor eloquently recommended the Society to his heir.[17]

> In the first place, with special concern we earnestly commend
> to you the well-deserving Society of Jesus and its priests. Through
> their skill, their instruction of our dear youth, and their exem-
> plary manner of life, they do much good in the Christian Catholic
> Churches and more than others loyally work and exert themselves to
> maintain and propagate the Catholic religion not only in our Inner
> Austrian lands but in all our kingdoms and territories and throughout
> Christendom. In this ungrateful and perverse world they encounter
> more hatred and persecution than others and so are more in need
> of protection, help, and assistance.

Born in 1570 near Dochamps in Belgian Luxembourg, Lamormaini was Ferdinand's senior by eight years. Young William attended the Jesuit college in Trier. His parents had planned to send him to the Jesuits in Cologne for further study when at the last moment events intervened. William's uncle, a cook at the court of Emperor Rudolf II, passed through in the entourage of the Spanish ambassador to the emperor, who was en route to the court in Prague. He suggested that his nephew could study with the Jesuits in Prague as well as in Cologne. William's parents agreed, and when the ambassador moved on, William was a member of the party.

Lamormaini entered the novitiate of the Society of Jesus on February 5, 1590, at Brno (Brünn) in Moravia. His theological studies were made in Vienna from 1592 to 1596, so that by the time of his First Mass in the college church in Vienna on May 5, 1596, he was well acquainted with the two pivotal cities of the Austrian Habsburgs, Prague and Vienna. After a brief stint in the college in Prague, Lamormaini came to Graz in 1598, two years after Ferdinand assumed the full powers of government in Inner Austria. There apart from short interruptions Lamormaini remained until 1621, first as professor of philosophy, then professor of theology, and finally as rector of the university from 1613 to 1621.[18]

Ferdinand and Lamormaini became close friends during Lamormaini's long years of activity in Graz. Once during Lamormaini's term as confessor, when his enemies were making a concerted effort to have him dismissed, Ferdinand summoned Lamormaini and reassured him in words that surely referred to their years in Graz as well as in Vienna: "So long, my Father, have we been companions through life, no one will separate us from each other."[19] Lamormaini's surviving correspondence with three of Ferdinand's sisters, Maria Christina, Eleonora, and Maria Magdalena, and especially with his brother, Archduke Leopold, Bishop of Passau and Strasbourg and later Governor of Tyrol and Anterior Austria, shows that he was on familiar terms with the archducal family.[20] After the death in 1617 of his first wife, Maria Anna of Bavaria, Maximilian's sister, Ferdinand consulted with Lamormaini about his future marital plans. In order to facilitate Ferdinand's election to the imperial title, Cardinal Melchior Khlesl, Emperor Matthias's controversial minister, urged marriage with the Lutheran widow of Elector Christian II of Saxony. Even some Jesuits favored the match, Lamormaini later wrote disapprovingly, but he himself opposed a Protestant marriage; Ferdinand did not remarry until 1622, when he took Eleonora of Mantua, a Gonzaga, as his second wife.[21]

Even after Ferdinand took up residence in Vienna, he continued to seek Lamormaini's advice. At the meeting of the Lower Austrian estates in Vienna in the spring of 1620, the Protestant nobles in the majority refused to do homage to Ferdinand as their new territorial ruler unless he first renewed the free exercise of the Confession of Augsburg granted them by Matthias. Ferdinand's refusal was likely to drive them more completely into the hands of the Bohemian rebels. Johann Ulrich von Eggenberg, Ferdinand's director of the privy council, journeyed to Graz, where he laid the matter before Lamormaini and the theologians there. Lamormaini judged the concession could be made on two conditions. First, there must exist "an insuperable necessity and a virtually clear future danger that should it not be made and promised, the Catholic religion would either perish or suffer much greater evils." Second, the concession should be so worded that it could not be construed as extending beyond the period that the state of necessity actually existed. But Lamormaini then went on in a manner anticipatory of his later views to set the standard for a state of necessity so high that it was difficult to admit one was ever at hand. Ferdinand did yield, largely on the basis of Becan's slightly less rigid position, and a good number of the Protestant nobles then joined the Catholics in the act of homage.[22]

Following the conclusion of his term as rector in Graz, Lamormaini traveled to Rome, where he arrived on October 16, 1621. The main purpose of his trip seems to have been to rest and then to consult about ecclesiastical affairs in the north with Mutio Vitelleschi, superior general of the Society of Jesus, and officials in the Roman Curia. With him he brought for the Curia a memorandum he had drawn up on the reform of the Church in Bohemia, a document that already showed his special interest in the conversion of neighboring Saxony.[23] During his rectorate in Graz complaints about his government had reached Rome. Some felt that he was too political and somewhat pompous; others, that as a religious superior he was curt and not sufficiently available to his subjects. Vitelleschi called this criticism to his attention and bade him reflect on it. While in Rome Lamormaini made contacts with members of the Curia and was proposed, it appears, for the cardinalate.[24] After his return to the north, he was named rector of the Jesuit college in Vienna on February 19, 1622, a position that brought him once again into the immediate circle of Ferdinand.[25]

The principal problem Lamormaini inherited in Vienna was the relationship between the Jesuit college and the university. Tension had long existed between the two as a result of the decline of the university and the consequent loss of students to the college, where lectures in philosophy and theology were held. In 1617 Cardinal Khlesl had forced an agreement on both sides that satisfied neither, but his fall and the death of Matthias had prevented its implementation. Undoubtedly, one reason for the appointment of Lamormaini was the hope that his influence with Ferdinand would facilitate a solution to the problem.

Ferdinand was determined to unite the college with the university but on terms much more favorable to the Society than those of Khlesl. Chief architects of a basic agreement approved by the emperor in 1622 were Eggenberg, Lamormaini, and Joannes Argenti, another Jesuit. But it, too, ran into objections. Vitelleschi, alerted by Becan among others, warned the Jesuits in Vienna lest the emperor's beneficence stir the resentment of others and in the long run prove counterproductive for the emperor and the Society. Lamormaini was admonished for his high-handed manner in the negotiations and was told to surrender some of the Jesuits' claims, including any pretense to the rectorship of the university.[26] Further talks finally produced another agreement that incorporated the college into the university and gave the Society a predominance that would make the Jesuits chiefly responsible for the institution's successes and failures during the next century and a half. They took over the faculties of arts, philosophy, and theology with the provision that members of other religious orders would continue to hold professorates in theology. The status of the faculties of law and medicine remained untouched, except that the Jesuits could exercise a veto over the admission of students. The old college building was to be converted into a Jesuit residence, and a new building plus a church was to be erected on the grounds of the university.[27] One of Lamormaini's main concerns during the coming years was the construction of the new buildings and especially of the church, whose Baroque facade still dominates Ignaz-Seipel-Platz below.[28]

When Becan died, Ferdinand's choice of a confessor fell naturally upon Lamormaini. His appointment seems to have been taken for granted. Argenti, now the provincial superior in Vienna, notified Vitelleschi that Ferdinand had provisionally selected Lamormaini as his confessor. Vitelleschi, with some hesitation, approved. Lamormaini himself was at first reluctant, but when it became evident that Ferdinand wanted him for the post permanently, Vitelleschi encouraged Lamormaini to accept, and he did.[29]

During the coming years a voluminous correspondence was to develop between Lamormaini and Vitelleschi, a native Roman who served as superior general of the order from 1615 until his death in 1645 at the age of eighty-two.[30] Unfortunately, the bulk of the letters from Lamormaini to Vitelleschi has been lost, but a good number survive, as do nearly one thousand letters Vitelleschi sent Lamormaini during his thirteen years as imperial confessor. Vitelleschi's primary concerns soon emerged from the correspondence: the maintenance of peace and harmony within the Society and the formation of a united front among the Catholic princes, including the pope, in support of the Counterreformation throughout Europe. These goals were to be difficult to achieve.

Responding to Lamormaini's request for guidelines as he took up his new office, Vitelleschi called his attention to the instruction "On the Confessors of Princes." This was a document issued by Vitelleschi's predecessor, Claudio Acquaviva, in 1602 and confirmed in 1608 by the General Congregation, the highest legislative authority of the Society.[31] It dealt with matters of religious discipline, such as the requirement that the confessor reside in the local Jesuit house and be subject to the superior there. But from the first paragraph there came into sharp focus the dilemma created for the Society by the requests of princes for confessors. The Jesuits did not want to forego the influence they could exert for the advancement of the Church's interests through men close to the centers of power. Nor could requests for Jesuit confessors from generous benefactors and patrons of the order be turned down without causing ill-feeling and perhaps losing valuable support. But there were disadvantages. Inevitably the popular mind associated the Society, through the confessor, with unpopular or questionable policies, such as an increase in taxes; this burdened the Society's pastoral activity.[32] Still greater liabilities were involvement with factions in government and entanglement in rivalries among princes.

Acquaviva's directives sought to secure the benefits while avoiding the liabilities associated with the office of court confessor. The confessor was to shun even the appearance of the exercise of power through the prince. Nor was he to procure favors for individuals nor allow himself to be used to convey orders or, worse, reprimands from the prince to his ministers. The most important passage of the instruction, to which Vitelleschi explicitly alerted Lamormaini, displayed confusion and ambivalence. "Let the confessor take care," it read, "lest he become involved in external and political matters. . . . Let him devote himself to those matters only that pertain to the conscience of the prince, or are related to it, and to certain other pious works." But did not "external and political matters" concern the conscience of the prince? In an attempt at clarification, the General Congregation considered examples of these to be "treaties between princes, the rights of kingdoms and the succession in them, matters pertaining to war, civil and foreign."[33] Yet all these instances had a moral aspect, and in the seventeenth century they often had an explicitly religious one too. They were matters of conscience. Neither the instruction nor the clarification suggested the useful distinction between general principles and their application. Some contemporaries felt that the role of the confessor or consultant theologian was to enlighten the ruler about principles but to leave their application to him and his ministers. Lamormaini rejected this view, as we shall see.

The position of confessor to a Catholic ruler was a court rather than a government office. Beyond the regular hearing of the prince's confession, the confessor's function was not clearly delineated. His influence depended largely on his personality and the personality and method of government of his princely penitent. In the case of Ferdinand and Lamormaini one would expect from the start that the confessor's voice would be consistently heard. The advice Lamormaini gave his penitent during his weekly confession is closed to us because of the secrecy of the confessional, but it is unlikely that it differed from the counsel he gave at other times. In effect, Lamormaini was a resident expert for the moral and religious aspects of policy. Protestant princes of the day sometimes had advisers or preachers who while not hearing their confession, counseled and advised them in a similar fashion, such as the well-known Hoé von Hoénegg, chaplain and preacher to Elector John George of Saxony.[34] Ferdinand occasionally convoked a council of theologians to discuss especially difficult or critical decisions, a procedure called for by the instruction "On the Confessors of Princes."

"Time always passed quickly for him when engaged in three activities, divine liturgy, the council, the hunt."[35] So ran a contemporary dictum about Ferdinand. Religion was the dominant force in his life. According to Lamormaini, each morning upon rising he devoted an hour to meditation before he attended two Masses in his private chapel, the second always offered for the soul of his first wife. In the course of a normal day, another hour was spent in either mental or vocal prayer. Besides this, on Sundays and feast days he participated in the Solemn Mass in the court chapel in the morning and in vesper services in the afternoon. Approximately once a week he went to confession and received Holy Communion. In his private life the emperor's morality was above reproach, but he was not a puritan, as his passion for hunting and hawking and his delight in music attested. His general good nature and his ability to make those of high or low station feel at ease with him were well known.[36] In fact, his affability and trusting nature led him to be easy going and permissive with his ministers and officials. Esaias Leuker, the Bavarian agent in Vienna, noted the contrast between the lazy work habits and broad consciences of the ministers there and the orderly, disciplined regime in Munich.[37]

As a territorial ruler Ferdinand represented a form of paternalistic absolutism that was characterized by moderation and a strong sense of responsibility for his subjects.[38] The brief instructions in his testament of 1621 revealed the ideal for which he strove.[39] He impressed on his son that he was to govern for the advancement of God's glory and the temporal and eternal welfare of his subjects, not for his own private advantage. The Lord would call him to account for this. The even-handed administration of justice was the ruler's obligation. He was to govern according to the law of the land and always to respect the rights of his subjects. Ferdinand's careful efforts to take inflation into account when repaying his debts represented only one instance of his desire to be fair.[40]

But clearly the primary element in the welfare of his subjects was their religious well-being. The codicil to the testament of 1621 dealt with this. Ferdinand saw as his first obligation the preservation of country and people (*Land und Leut*) in the Catholic faith, an obligation that was reinforced and extended, analogously, to the Empire by the oath he swore to defend the Church at the time of his imperial coronation.[41] He undertook a thorough reformation of religion in Inner Austria shortly after he took up the government there, with the result that thousands returned to the Catholic faith, and he expected his son to continue in this spirit. Ferdinand's concern for religion led him to descend to detail. The instructions for commissioners appointed to look into the state of religion in Carinthia directed them, among other things, to check the observance of the fasting laws and the quality of care for the poor.[42] Obviously, Ferdinand's zeal had a political side. Widely accepted contemporary wisdom asserted that unity of religion was essential to civil peace and that heresy was the chief stimulus to rebellion. But there can be little doubt that with Ferdinand the religious motive predominated. According to Lamormaini, Ferdinand "often asserted both in writing and orally that he would give up his provinces and his kingdoms more readily and more gladly than knowingly neglect an opportunity to extend the faith; that he would rather live on bread and water alone, go into exile with his wife and children equipped only with a staff, beg his bread from door to door, be cut to pieces and torn apart for nothing rather than suffer any longer the harm done to God and the Church by the heretics in the territories under his rule."[43]

"To those fighting a just fight goes the crown" (*Legitime certantibus corona*). This motto that Ferdinand early made his own[44] displayed a basic conviction that was given lengthier and more specific expression in the codicil to the testament of 1621. In carrying out the reform of religion, he wrote for his heir, "you should not allow yourself to be scared off or hindered by anything, but rather keep in mind that this is God's work and thus there can be no doubt of his divine assistance and blessing. Thus with the divine help we persisted in this work of reformation in the face of no little difficulty and brought it along successfully despite the dangerous situation and circumstances that confronted us." The emperor's firm belief he was doing God's work, especially in implementing the Counterreformation, and the consequent conviction the Lord would care for him accounted in large part for his courage, steadfastness, and equanimity in face of chaos and seemingly imminent collapse.

Ferdinand possessed a profound sense of mission that was confirmed by several crucial experiences. The first was his decision in the second year of his government in Graz to expel from Inner Austria the Protestant preachers and schoolteachers of the city. He issued a decree to this effect against the advice even of some Catholic councilors, who assured him it would lead to serious civil unrest. In the words of a contemporary, "nearly a miracle" took place.[45] The expulsion went off without incident. When this was reported to the young prince, he exclaimed in the words of the Psalmist, "not to us, O Lord, not to us, but to your name give glory." He immediately withdrew to his room, knelt down, and humbly gave thanks to God.[46] The outcome strengthened him in his resolve to carry out his religious program in Inner Austria.

Catastrophe confronted Ferdinand and his whole House in the wake of the Bohemian rebellion. His recovery, and especially several dramatic moments in it, further strengthened his conviction that God's providence watched over him. In June 1619 when Thurn endangered Vienna, Father Viller, coming upon Ferdinand unannounced, found him in his room prostrate before the crucifix in prayer. "I have weighed the dangers that approach from all sides," he explained to his confessor, "and since I know of no further human aid, I asked the Lord for his help. But if it should be the will of God that I go under in this struggle, so be it." Thurn then gradually began to retire, compelled, as we have seen, by a Catholic victory in southern Bohemia. This sudden change of fortune indicating God's special care for Ferdinand was for a long time reenacted annually in Vienna in a highly embellished form, and there soon developed a legend that Lamormaini refused to confirm or deny in *The Virtues of Ferdinand II, Emperor of the Romans.* According to it, Christ had said from the crucifix, "Ferdinand, I will not desert you."[47] The Battle of the White Mountain, where the Catholic troops unexpectedly humiliated the Bohemian rebels, was perhaps the outstanding instance where the arm of the Lord seemed to be fighting on Ferdinand's side in defense of Catholicism. Catholics generally interpreted this victory as a triumph bestowed upon Ferdinand by the Lord.[48]

Ferdinand's sense of a godly mission cannot be reduced to the simplistic notion that God assured him success in all his efforts on behalf of the Catholic religion. To be sure, when carried away by his victories, Ferdinand did seem sometimes to lose sight of the possibility of defeat in this world, but this never lasted for long. As his remark in the crisis of 1619 showed, he was well aware that the Lord might permit the humiliation of those on his side. The good did not always win in this life, Ferdinand well knew, though they did in the next. Lamormaini attributed profound sentiments to him in 1616 when the imperial succession was still uncertain.[49] "All mortal things have their own time; to be born, to grow, to pass away; it may be that the rule of the Austrians is included in this; and if this should seem good to God, he would not only not resist but not be sad that God chose by his will to distribute empires and kingdoms now to these people, now to those. Human resources and power are at his disposal, and He gives them and takes them away as He will." Thus adversity did not induce Ferdinand to lose his belief in God's providence. What is important is that he saw God's hand in the events of his rule. His successes and triumphs seemed explainable only in terms of divine aid, especially since the odds were often heavy against him. Ferdinand and many close to him eventually interpreted his victories as a divine summons to a still broader mission, the restoration of Catholicism in the Empire. Here Lamormaini's influence was to be paramount.

Ferdinand took an active personal role in the government. All the sources attest to his diligence in studying government papers and correspondence and his frequent attendance at sessions of the privy council. No major decision was made without his approval; yet Ferdinand relied heavily on his advisers, and the charge has been made that he did so excessively. Father Viller had impressed upon him that "it was safer to follow the advice of one's councilors, even if this occasionally led to a mistake, than to be governed by one's own judgment."[50] Clearly there was in Ferdinand's makeup a reluctance to make decisions that resulted, it seems, from a combination of factors: his acute awareness of having to answer to God for his actions; his delicate and occasionally scrupulous conscience; and the apparent moral dilemmas he faced. Ferdinand's most trying moments were not those requiring courage and perseverance in the face of ill fortune but those compelling him to choose between options firmly supported by trusted ministers and, especially, between different policies advocated by his two closest advisors, Lamormaini and Eggenberg.

The orientation of Ferdinand's policy was toward greater control from Vienna, and under his rule there was considerable movement toward the development of a Habsburg state in Central Europe. For the first time since Ferdinand I divided the inheritance in 1564, rule over all the lands of the Austrian Habsburgs, except the Tyrol and Anterior Austria, came into the hands of one person in Ferdinand. In his testament of 1621 he expressed his intent to pass on to his heir all his territories and kingdoms as an indivisible, hereditary monarchy. The previous year he had created in Vienna an Austrian chancery, distinct from the imperial chancery, with competence for Upper, Lower, and Inner Austria. Chanceries for Bohemia and Hungary were also located in Vienna. Most of the historical units were governed in Ferdinand's name by appointed governors, one of whom was the influential Cardinal Franz von Dietrichstein, Governor of Moravia from 1621 to 1636.[51] In Hungary the estates retained a crucial role in the government even after the Bohemian rebellion; and they shared in the selection of Ferdinand's representative there, the Count Palatine, an office that carried much less authority than the governors possessed elsewhere.[52] Archduke Leopold, Bishop of Passau and Strasbourg, had been named Governor of the Tyrol and Anterior Austria following the death of Archduke Maximilian in 1618. After Leopold's resignation of his ecclesiastical dignities and subsequent marriage, Ferdinand agreed to a settlement in 1625 that made Leopold ruler of the Tyrol and two-thirds of Anterior Austria and founder of a Tyrolean Habsburg dynasty that lasted until 1665. Ferdinand acted with the consent of the King of Spain, who thus accepted an indefinite postponement of the Oñate Treaty's implementation in Anterior Austria.[53]

The principal organ of government for all Ferdinand's lands as well as for the Empire was the imperial privy council. Though occasionally Ferdinand bypassed it in favor of consultation with one or two ministers, the normal procedure was to have it discuss all major matters. The power of decision rested with the emperor alone. Important decisions of other councils, such as the war or treasury council, went to the privy council for further consideration before coming to the emperor himself if he had not attended the council's session. The privy council numbered about fourteen, the majority drawn from the nobility of the Austrian lands and Bohemia, but business was often conducted with many fewer present. A practice that developed during Ferdinand's reign was the formation of committees to prepare reports or position papers for the whole council. To these committees or deputations were often added representatives of the sphere of government with which the report dealt, such as members of the war council in military matters. They, then, would be present at the privy council meeting at which the report was discussed and its recommendations voted upon.[54]

Director of the privy council and Ferdinand's most important minister was Eggenberg, whom Ferdinand named to this post as soon as he became emperor, and in which Eggenberg remained until his death in 1634. Born in 1568 of a Lutheran family in Graz, where his father had been mayor, Eggenberg became a Catholic sometime during his youth. Except for a year spent at the University of Tübingen in 1583, his career until 1597 is obscure. Then, a year before Lamormaini came to Graz, Eggenberg appeared at court there; he soon became a favorite of Ferdinand's mother, Maria of Bavaria, and of the young archduke, twelve years his junior. Ferdinand and Eggenberg became good friends, and one can perhaps see in Eggenberg, as in Lamormaini, a father figure for the prince who lost his own father when he was only twelve. Eggenberg accompanied Ferdinand on the pilgrimage he made to Loreto and Rome in 1598 shortly after his assumption of the government in Inner Austria. Named to the Inner Austrian privy council in 1604, Eggenberg soon became Ferdinand's most trusted councilor. The archduke leaned heavily on his advice, and it was Eggenberg who negotiated the Oñate Treaty with Spain. During two diplomatic journeys to Spain in 1598–99 and 1605, Eggenberg had developed an inclination toward things Spanish; a copy of Cervantes's *Don Quixote* as well as a complete edition of the plays of Lope de Vega with many annotations in his own hand were later found in his library. For years Madrid considered him the one man in Vienna in whom it could place complete trust, and the Spanish government paid him a generous pension.[55]

Ferdinand rewarded Eggenberg lavishly for his services, and he became an extremely wealthy man. After the death without heirs of the Bohemian magnate Peter Wok von Rosenberg, Eggenberg was given his estates at Krumau in 1622. Later he was elevated to the status of an imperial prince and made Duke of Krumau. In 1625 Ferdinand appointed Eggenberg Governor of Inner Austria, where he also had acquired vast lands. Out-

side Graz he began to construct a magnificent Renaissance palace which
showed the stylistic influence of the Escorial. As one of the city's show-
pieces, it still testifies today to his self-consciousness and his taste. The
post in Inner Austria plus his affliction with gout kept Eggenberg away
from court for extended periods, but Ferdinand rarely made a decision
without consulting him. Couriers traveled regularly between Vienna and
Graz when he was away from court.[56]

The evidence indicates that Eggenberg and Lamormaini were on close
terms from their days in Graz together. Lamormaini was Eggenberg's
confessor, and he remained his confessor long after serious differences
between them began to come to light following Lamormaini's appointment as imperial confessor in 1624. As late as April 1631, Eggenberg in a
letter to Ferdinand referred to Lamormaini as one "to whom I have
entrusted my soul for many years."[57] But it is difficult to determine what
this relationship meant for Eggenberg, especially once he and Lamormaini became rivals in the formation of policy.

After the privy council, the most important governmental body in
Vienna was the imperial aulic council (*Reichshofrat*). Its basic function
was to assist the emperor in his role as the highest judicial instance in the
Empire. Unclear and frequently disputed was its relationship to the imperial cameral court (*Reichskammergericht*) in Speyer, a rival imperial
court under the control of the princes which, however, virtually ceased to
function during the long war. Decisions of the aulic council were subject to review by the privy council, and a reversal was not uncommon.
Though fundamentally a judicial body, the aulic council was often called
upon for an opinion on imperial political issues; judicial and political
affairs were hard to separate. There were thirty aulic councilors in 1636,
twenty of them nobles and the rest professional jurists, though the aulic
council also often operated with considerably less than a full contingent.
As with the privy council so with the aulic: the tendency under Ferdinand
was to make more appointments from the Austrian and Bohemian lands
and fewer from the rest of the Empire.[58]

Leading member of the aulic council was Peter Heinrich von Stralendorf, who was appointed its vice president (*Reichshofratsvizepräsident*)
by Ferdinand in 1620 and held the post until his death in 1637. Named
to the privy council in the early 1620s, he long served as the principal
liaison between the two bodies. In the absence of the president, who had
to be an imperial prince, he presided over the aulic council. Much more
importantly, as acting vice chancellor of the Empire from 1623 and vice
chancellor (*Reichsvizekanzler*) from 1627 until his death, Stralendorf
directed the imperial chancery through which passed the affairs of the
aulic council and the political correspondence with states of the Empire

and foreign princes.[59] The numerous surviving drafts of reports, proposals, and letters in his hand attest that he was a tireless worker. The son of Leopold von Stralendorf, who had risen in the service of the Elector of Mainz and himself served as imperial vice chancellor from 1607 to 1612, Peter Heinrich was born in Vienna in 1580. In 1605 he first entered the aulic council, where he sat as a baron with the nobles.[60] Of Ferdinand's chief ministers, Stralendorf was most consistently responsive to the position of Maximilian of Bavaria, a fact perhaps explained by the association of his family with Mainz and the orientation toward the Empire of the offices he held.

Along with Eggenberg and Stralendorf, the ministers who exerted the most influence in Vienna were Anton Wolfradt, Abbot of Kremsmünster and later Bishop of Vienna, and Maximilian von Trautmannsdorf. Born in Cologne in 1581, Anton Wolfradt entered the Cistercian Order at Clairvaux in 1604. Following theological studies in Rome, he was named Abbot of Wilhering in Upper Austria in 1612. The next year, on the recommendation of Emperor Matthias, he was made Abbot of Kremsmünster in Upper Austria, a change which required his transfer to the Benedictines. From his first year as emperor, Ferdinand employed Abbot Anton for political and diplomatic missions and for the conduct of Upper Austrian affairs. In 1623 he became president of the treasury council (*Hofkammerrat*). This was a thankless position, given Ferdinand's excessive bounty in rewarding his servants and friends, his generosity to the church, and the enormous costs of the war.[61] The comprehensive plan Abbot Anton soon produced for financial reform did little to bring order into the confused and even chaotic state of Ferdinand's finances. In 1624 he became a member of the privy council, where he remained until he died in 1639. Only after his repeated requests did Ferdinand relieve him of his treasury duties in 1630, and he then named him the first Prince-Bishop of Vienna.[62] Ferdinand's desire to secure the cardinal's hat for him was frustrated by staunch opposition in Rome, explained, it seems, by Abbot Anton's close association with the pro-Spanish policy of Eggenberg, for whom he frequently stood in as director of the privy council after 1630. Moreover, Ferdinand already had three cardinals: Dietrichstein; Peter Pazmany, Archbishop of Estergom (Gran) and Primate of Hungary; and Ernst von Harrach, Archbishop of Prague.[63]

Maximilian von Trautmannsdorf has been called the greatest diplomat in Austrian history.[64] His outstanding achievement, the negotiation of the Peace of Westphalia, would come under Ferdinand III, but he played a key role under Ferdinand II. Although a native of Graz and convert to Catholicism like Eggenberg, he never seems to have been a close associate of Eggenberg, much less to have owed his advancement to him. His

father served as president of the Inner Austrian war council from 1589 to
1601. Young Trautmannsdorf came to Vienna in 1609 at the age of
twenty-five to assume a position on the imperial aulic council, where he
remained until he entered the privy council in 1618. Ferdinand frequently
called on him for diplomatic missions and made him an imperial count in
1623, but Trautmannsdorf was a man of mild personal ambitions, whose
contemporaries rightly respected him for his integrity as well as his negotiating skills.[65] Lamormaini's involvement in preparing the testament of
his brother, Sigismund Frederick, suggests that he knew the family from
his days in Graz.[66]

Lamormaini himself was deeply conscious of the responsibilities that
his new office of confessor imposed on him. His initial hesitation to
accept the post does not seem to have been merely a formality. The Lord
would require an account from him as well as from Ferdinand. To him,
the confessor, had been committed the salvation of the emperor "on
whose perfection and zeal depended innumerable thousands of souls and
all the progress of the Catholic religion in Germany," he wrote in his
private notes.[67] This was indeed a heavy burden. As imperial confessor,
Lamormaini set three goals for himself. The first was that he live his life
as completely as possible for the Lord. His performance as confessor, he
realized, depended upon the quality of his own religious life. He was well
aware, for example, that frequent contact with important persons at
court could lead to pride and haughtiness, and he resolved to avoid this.
However, he was not always successful. His second goal was for Ferdinand to grow personally in the Christian life to the highest point attain-
able by him. As his third goal, Lamormaini envisioned "that the Catholic
religion with the help and authority of this emperor be completely restored in the two Austrias [Upper and Lower], the Kingdom of Bohemia, Hungary, and in the Roman Empire," and there especially in those
imperial cities where the practice of Catholicism had been prohibited.[68]

From the start Lamormaini conceived of himself both as a father to
Ferdinand and as a prophet urging the interests of God with the emperor.
Ferdinand was his "adopted son."[69] As the instruction "On the Confessors of Princes" required of rulers who desired a Jesuit confessor, Ferdinand consented to listen patiently to his confessor "as to a spiritual
father" whenever Lamormaini had anything to say which he judged
necessary "for the security of both their consciences and the fulfillment of
his office." In fact, Ferdinand encouraged Lamormaini always to advise
him of any opportunities to advance the faith.[70] Lamormaini drew up
guidelines for himself. "When it is a matter pertaining to the soul of the
Emperor, his conscience, or religion," he wrote, "deal and act with modesty but fearlessly, either as a legate of God or as the advocate of the

divine honor." If the question required further consideration, he noted, request more time. "When the issue at hand is of itself indifferent or of such a nature that it concerns the majesty of the Emperor, his dignity and advantage or that of his House, either keep silence or so speak that it can be noted that the matter does not concern you, that you are not worried about it."[71] But in the concrete there were for Lamormaini few matters that were not related to the emperor's salvation or the advancement of religion.

At Lamormaini's assumption of office, Ferdinand renewed his commitment to the restoration of Catholicism. On March 25, 1624, the Feast of the Annunciation, in the imperial chapel and with Lamormaini present, the emperor vowed that "he would undertake whatever the circumstances seemed to permit" for the good of religion, "not only gladly but with great pleasure and joy." Eggenberg joined him in the vow, at Ferdinand's explicit request. Several months later Lamormaini wrote to the influential Cardinal Francesco Barberini, nephew of Pope Urban, in whose name the official correspondence of the papal secretariat of state was conducted. "It is perhaps necessary that the Pope know about this [the vow] so that he realize that great things can be accomplished by this Emperor and perhaps even all Germany be led back to the old faith, provided that united in soul and intention and joining all their forces together, having supplicated the benevolent God, these two supreme lights of the world [pope and emperor] take up the matter vigorously and see it through with persistence."[72] Lamormaini's hopes were not without foundation.

2. Conflicts among Counterreformers, 1624–1626

he position of the Catholic forces in the Empire was strong in early 1624. But in the course of the year a new threat appeared in the form of Danish intervention backed in various degrees by dissident German Protestants, the Protestant powers Holland and England, and Catholic France, where Cardinal Richelieu assumed the control of foreign policy. After causing some anxious moments, the new menace receded following Tilly's defeat of Christian IV of Denmark at Lutter in Lower Saxony on August 27, 1626. The result was a still more pronounced Catholic predominance. But during this span their own initiatives generated for the Catholics new problems that would eventually become serious. Meanwhile, Ferdinand moved to tighten up his rule and establish the Church more firmly in his own lands. Serious differences over the procedure to be followed, especially in Bohemia, stirred opposition to Lamormaini and the Jesuits that soon found the sympathy of Eggenberg and support from Rome. From the very start Lamormaini encountered Catholics opposed to his vision of the Counterreformation.

Richelieu's rise to power meant the return of France to a foreign policy aimed at weakening the Habsburgs. In June 1624 the French, English, and Dutch concluded a defensive alliance and began to encourage Christian of Denmark and unhappy German Protestants to take up arms against the emperor. In addition to defending Protestantism and the liberties of the German princes as he professed, Christian hoped to expand his influence in north Germany by acquiring several prince-bishoprics for his son. To the south Richelieu revived a French alliance with Venice and Savoy, both wary of Habsburg expansion in Italy, and in December the French seized control of the crucial Valtelline pass. The marriage the next May of France's Princess Henrietta Maria with the young Prince Charles of England seemed to point to long-term cooperation between the French and English, directed inevitably against the Habsburgs.

Hostilities broke out in Germany in July 1625, when Tilly crossed into the Lower Saxon Circle[1] to disperse the army Christian was assembling there. Attempts at a negotiated settlement failed and the issue was finally settled militarily. The newly appointed imperial general, Albrecht von

Wallenstein, defeated the Protestant condottiere Ernst von Mansfeld at Dessau on the Elbe River in April 1626, thus preventing Mansfeld from proceeding to the southeast to a projected union with the ever restless Bethlen. Next came the triumph of Tilly at Lutter. France had been forced to draw back earlier because of a Huguenot revolt in the spring of 1626. Disagreement over the treatment of Huguenots in France and Catholics in England led to a break between France and England and soon to open war. France and Spain then came to a vague agreement over the Valtelline in the Treaty of Monzon of March 5, 1626, that seemed to permit free passage of Spanish troops along this important route. Richelieu needed his soldiers at home. Until the fall of the Huguenot stronghold La Rochelle in late October 1628, the cardinal would have to be extremely cautious about foreign ventures.[2]

By the winter of 1625–26 two ominous problems began to surface for the Catholics. The first originated with the commission given the energetic and enigmatic Bohemian nobleman Wallenstein to raise an imperial army. It was issued by the emperor on July 25, 1625, with the encouragement of Maximilian of Bavaria to help meet the danger posed by Christian of Denmark. Tension soon developed between Maximilian and Wallenstein. Sharp personality differences combined with different strategic conceptions and competition for recruits and resources to create misunderstanding. Most basic was the shift in political balance that Wallenstein's appointment gradually brought about. Until this time the emperor had been heavily dependent upon the Catholic League. The creation, rapid expansion, and success of Wallenstein's army greatly increased the real power of the emperor and lessened that of Maximilian and the League. The stuff for conflict was there.[3]

Second, as the Catholic position in the Empire grew stronger, a struggle began to develop within the Catholic camp over the way to exploit their advantage. The more militant spirits discerned in the Catholic triumphs a divine summons to roll Protestantism back still further, as well as a pledge of divine aid. They looked upon any compromise with the Protestants as a pusillanimous lack of confidence in God, and they sometimes referred with disdain to their rivals as *politici*, a term that for them frequently connoted lack of religious principle much as the word "politician," unfortunately, often suggests dishonesty today.[4] More moderate figures were inclined toward a peace settlement that would consolidate Catholic gains even at the expense of some concessions to the Protestants. For them, to prolong the war was only to overextend the resources of the Catholics, to imperil the gains already made on behalf of Church and Empire, and to visit still more woe on the long-suffering population.

Both sides represented a theological as well as a political position, as will become evident. It was not a contest between religion and politics, although the militants tended to conceive it as such.

As militants like Lamormaini came to the fore in Vienna, it became increasingly difficult to retain the allegiance of Protestant states hitherto loyal to the emperor, such as the electorates of Saxony and Brandenburg. Saxony was key because of its size and location in the center of Germany, its leadership among the German Lutheran states, and its traditional loyalty to the imperial House. At the time of the Bohemian rebellion, besides making promises to Saxony about the two Lusatias, Ferdinand had joined the Catholic states in offering reassurances to the Protestant princes of the Upper and Lower Saxon Circles, including the two electors. In March 1620 at Mühlhausen the Catholics promised not to attempt to regain by force imperial church lands in the two circles, which they felt had been secularized illegally, without first giving the Protestants in possession a legal hearing or opportunity to present their case. This promise, or Mühlhausen guarantee as it came to be called, was given on condition that the Protestants loyally support the emperor against his enemies. Only Saxony seems positively to have responded to it.[5] Perhaps the other princes felt it offered them too little to warrant a commitment on their part. Nor were they in any particular peril at the time. In the years immediately following the rebellion, Ferdinand hesitated to carry through the Counterreformation rigorously in his own lands for fear of alienating Saxony, who along with Brandenburg was being courted by the emperor's enemies. As the emperor resorted to sterner measures in his territories and the Catholics seemed inclined to a more militant policy in the Empire, the danger of disaffection in Dresden and Berlin increased proportionately.

Two plans to exploit the upper hand of the Catholics were suggested in 1624–25, but the Danish intervention forced postponement of their serious consideration. The first of these was put forth by the Spanish minister Olivares in April 1625. Its ultimate goal was the reduction of the Dutch. Olivares intended to upset and even destroy Dutch trade in the Baltic through the creation of a Spanish-German trading company and an aggressive imperial control, or at least predominant influence, in the Hanseatic cities on the north coast of Germany. Eggenberg showed great enthusiasm for the plan, on condition that the Hanseatic cities themselves first form the company with the Spanish and then request imperial protection, so that the German princes would have no cause for complaint. In a postscript to his position paper of May 30, 1625, he urged that the project be kept a tight secret, to be shown only to Lamormaini for his opinion, "since in view of his piety, his prudence and experience, and his ability to keep a secret, this [his opinion] can only help."[6] What Lamormaini had to say about the project is not known.

To understand the second expansionist proposal one must first return to the Religious Peace of Augsburg of 1555. This fundamental agreement had restored peace to the Empire after the years of civil unrest and war that followed the Reformation. Two confessions or religious parties had been accorded the right of existence within the Empire: the Catholic and the Lutheran, that is, those subscribing to the Confession of Augsburg. Within this framework, the prince was granted the right to determine the religion to be practiced in his territory according to the formula later enunciated by the jurists, "whose the region, his the religion" (*cujus regio ejus religio*). In the imperial cities, the status of 1552 was frozen so that the exclusive practice of either religion or the practice of both might be legal.[7] Territorial church lands—those subject to the political authority of a territorial prince or city—that had been confiscated by the Protestants up to that time were surrendered permanently by the Catholics on condition that the Protestants seize no more. The Ecclesiastical Reservation, an element of the Peace, concerned imperial church lands, the ecclesiastical states subordinate politically only to the emperor. Should a prelate who governed such a state, usually as prince-bishop or prince-abbot, accept Protestantism, it required that he forfeit his territory and all the privileges accruing to it. This provision was intended to prevent the heretics' acquisition of the widespread imperial church lands of west and northwest Germany, including the three electorates of Mainz, Trier, and Cologne.[8]

Although the settlement of Augsburg succeeded in bringing a period of peace to a Germany weary of strife, it also contained unclear provisions, often left purposely so by negotiators despairing of complete agreement. Each of the two groups soon developed its own understanding of the Peace in accordance with the norm of interpretation it accepted. The Protestant party understood the Peace in terms of the parity of the two confessions. They claimed equality with the Catholics. This was the actual future course of things. The Catholics, on the other hand, looked upon the concessions to the Protestant party as exceptions to the general law of the Empire, a temporary suspension that in no sense established equality between the two parties. They looked forward to the day when the unity of faith proper to the Empire would be restored. In doubtful instances and in cases not covered by the Peace, the Catholics wanted decisions rendered according to the traditional imperial and canon law, whereas the Protestants appealed to a growing custom in their favor.[9]

Four points at issue were of special importance. Territorial church lands secularized prior to the settlement had been ceded by the Catholics;

but, Protestants argued, did not the principle "whose the region, his the religion" allow for the further confiscation of church lands subject to the prince's territorial jurisdiction and located within his territory? On the basis of this argument many territorial church lands had been subsequently seized by the Protestants. The Ecclesiastical Reservation stipulated that a Catholic prelate who converted to Protestantism surrender his dignity and lands, but did it also prohibit a cathedral chapter from electing an adherent of the Confession of Augsburg to a prince-bishopric? A number of imperial church lands, especially in the Lower Saxon and Westphalian Circles in northwest Germany, passed into the hands of Protestant "administrators" by such election. Who was to interpret authentically the Confession of Augsburg of 1530? It seemed that many Protestant states, especially the Calvinist ones, had departed from the sense of the Confession and thus overstepped the limits set by the Peace. Lastly, did the imperial cities and ecclesiastical princes enjoy the same right of reformation as the secular princes? Many cities acted as if they did. Ferdinand I in what came to be called the Declaration of Ferdinand had secretly assured the Lutherans freedom of belief in the ecclesiastical territories, but this guarantee was not incorporated into the Peace and never became imperial law.[10]

From the ambiguities of the Peace of Augsburg sprang conflicts that eventually helped produce the Thirty Years War. Increasingly in the 1580s, after the generation that had concluded the Peace passed from the scene, the divergent interpretations of it provoked not only prolonged litigation but political and military confrontation. In 1583, for example, the announced intention of the Archbishop of Cologne to convert to Protestantism and still retain his see generated the short-lived War of Cologne. Spurred on by Rome, Duke William of Bavaria intervened decisively and with the help of Spanish troops from the Netherlands prevented the loss of the rich Rhenish electorate and the formation of a Protestant majority in the electoral college. Upon the heels of the fight for Cologne there began a conflict over the imperial Bishopric of Strasbourg that dragged on for more than twenty years. At the Diet of Regensburg in 1603, the Palatinate delegates were determined to make money grants contingent upon religious concessions. Finding themselves in the minority, they rejected the application of the majority principle to tax measures. Five years later they walked out of the diet after both sides firmly refused concessions on the Religious Peace. The central organs of government, first the courts and then the diet, broke down in the face of intransigence on the part of militant Calvinists and Catholics.[11] The Bohemian rebellion then put the match to the tinder.

After the victory of the White Mountain and the triumphs in its wake,

Catholics began to see the opportunity to realize a goal many had long had in mind, the restoration to the Church of secularized church lands, not only in the emperor's territories and the Palatinate but in the rest of Germany too. The new papal nuncio in Vienna, Carlo Carafa, who arrived in 1621, brought with him instructions to work actively for the restitution of church lands. In 1623, after the death of the Protestant incumbent, the Catholic faction in the cathedral chapter of Osnabrück secured the election of Cardinal Eitel Friedrich von Hohenzollern to that see, which the Protestants had held since at least the 1590s. Catholic prelates began to petition the imperial aulic council for the return of more Catholic lands.[12]

At first, cases for restitution were brought individually to the council and a decision sought in each instance. Then gradually some Catholics came to envision a general restitution of all church lands. The idea seems to have originated at the court of the Elector of Mainz, Johann Schweikardt, possibly with his confessor, the Jesuit Reinhard Ziegler.[13] Associated with it was a conviction that was to become a theme of the militants: God in his providence had presented the Catholics with this opportunity to restore justice in the Empire, that is, the Catholic interpretation of the Religious Peace. In early September 1625, about two months after Tilly's march into the Lower Saxon Circle, Mainz dispatched Ziegler to Munich and Vienna to present his proposal. The military situation favored the Catholics, Mainz affirmed, citing among other things the difficulties the French were having in the Valtelline. The Catholics were now strong enough to remedy their grievances. In the words of the proposition given Ziegler for Maximilian,[14] "it almost has the appearance that the good God wants to furnish us with a suitable opportunity and circumstances to seek this [the return of church lands] more suitably and to obtain it more easily. This chance we cannot justly pass up; rather we must diligently take advantage of it." The proposed forum for such far-reaching changes was an imperial diet, where Mainz safely assumed a Catholic majority. Meanwhile, Tilly should seize the wealthy and strategically important Archbishopric of Magdeburg along with the Bishopric of Halberstadt, both then held by Duke Christian William, brother of the Elector of Brandenburg, who by supporting the King of Denmark had forfeited any guarantees made him. Saxony should be given secret assurances that no action was intended against him, since the three bishoprics he held had allegedly been confiscated before 1555 and thus were not subject to restitution.[15] So Mainz hoped to split John George from the other Protestants.

Mainz's proposal did not find acceptance in either Munich or Vienna. Both Maximilian and Ferdinand evaluated the military situation much more pessimistically than Mainz. They also felt that an imperial diet was too clumsy and time-consuming to be feasible under the circumstances. The time was not yet ripe for such an aggressive initiative. Ferdinand and Lamormaini both seem to have had some doubts about the legality of the suggested measures. They were uncertain about their reconcilability with the Peace of Augsburg, which by virtue of his coronation oath Ferdinand was bound to uphold. Besides, only the previous June the emperor had renewed the Mühlhausen guarantee first given in 1620, and it appeared to preclude any precipitate action.[16] Ziegler was in Vienna from October 2 to 6, where he had an audience with the emperor and Eggenberg. Though he indicated in his reports that he had received support in Munich from Maximilian's confessor, Adam Contzen, there was strangely no mention of Lamormaini in the account of his stay in Vienna.[17]

Much of Ferdinand's attention during these years was directed to the consolidation of his authority and the implementation of the Counter-reformation in his own lands. Lamormaini played an important and often determinative role in these efforts at the reformation of religion. There seemed to be no part of the Habsburg lands where he was not involved. In February 1625 he gave up his position as rector of the college in Vienna, partly as a result of renewed complaints about his government but principally so he would have more time for his many duties as confessor.[18]

Habsburg Hungary, as we have seen, constituted a special case among the Habsburg territories, where legal and political considerations imposed particular restrictions on the emperor's freedom of action. Moreover, since it lay outside the Empire, he could not invoke there the right conceded imperial princes by the Peace of Augsburg to order religion in their territories. At the time of his coronation as King of Hungary in 1617 and again at the Peace of Vienna of 1624, Ferdinand confirmed for Hungary the concessions first granted it by Archduke Matthias in 1606. These included the free exercise of religion and associated privileges, such as the construction of churches.

The original intentions of the Vienna government at the Hungarian Diet at Ödenburg (Sopron) in the fall of 1625 did not comprise the election of the emperor's son, the seventeen-year-old Archduke Ferdinand, as King of Hungary. The initiative for this came from the Hungarian magnates themselves, who saw in it a means to peace and stability in the kingdom. There was disagreement among the advisers of Ferdinand about whether young Ferdinand should accept the election at this time and if so, whether he should go ahead with the coronation. Some felt the election would prejudice the claim to hereditary succession. But most of the opposition stemmed from the desire to avoid another confirmation of the concessions of 1606. According to the nuncio Carafa, he himself, Lamormaini, and Eggenberg at first opposed the confirmation, chiefly on grounds of conscience. The imminent danger to the state that alone had justified it earlier for the archduke's father no longer existed, and there was strong likelihood that the improving military and political situation might soon make such an explicit confirmation unnecessary. Virtually all the other ministers, however, disagreed, asserting that postponement would only stir suspicions among the Hungarian nobles and might create serious obstacles to the succession. In particular, the Spanish ambassador, the Marquis of Aytona, insisted that the proposed marriage of the archduke with the Spanish Infanta could not take place until he was crowned and the succession guaranteed. Eventually, then, it was concluded that there was justification to confirm the privileges. The decision was made easier by the reasoning of the newly elected Count Palatine, the Catholic Nicholas Esterhazy. Once there was a firm Catholic majority in Hungary, he argued, the situation could be changed legally. So the election took place on November 27 and the coronation on December 8.[19]

Carafa indicated no significant dissent from this decision, and he strongly implied his own agreement. Thus Lamormaini apparently concurred, a conclusion bolstered by the enthusiasm he showed in a letter to Vitelleschi describing the mood at the diet. He contrasted the Hungarians' attitude toward the election of young Ferdinand with their attitude toward his father's election eight years previously. Then they had been sullen and hostile; after all, as Archduke of Styria, Ferdinand had expelled the Protestant preachers from his Inner Austrian lands. Now they gave the emperor a joyful and enthusiastic reception. "The finger of God is certainly here," he concluded, especially since many Protestant refugees from other Habsburg territories had settled in Hungary.[20]

Fortunately for the Catholics, the Church in Hungary possessed a vigorous and creative champion in Peter Pazmany, a former Jesuit and colleague of Lamormaini in Graz, who had been made Archbishop of Estergom and Primate of Hungary in 1616 and would become a cardinal in 1629. In 1623 he established a seminary in Vienna to be conducted by the Jesuits for the education of Hungarian priests. The foundation of a college in Pressburg, the capital of Habsburg Hungary, followed in 1626, and in 1635 the elevation of the college at Tyrnau (Nagyszombat) to the rank of an academy. As such it would become the intellectual center of the Counterreformation in Hungary.[21]

Lamormaini supported with vigor Pazmany's efforts, especially those for the foundation of colleges,[22] but there were differences between them. They seem to have counseled Ferdinand in different directions at the

Hungarian Diet of 1625, where Pazmany was from the start in favor of the election of Archduke Ferdinand.[23] Pazmany complained that measures taken against the Protestants in Vienna, supported by Lamormaini, meant that more Protestant refugees fled to Hungary and made his work more difficult. He also felt the Jesuits were receiving too many young sons of the Hungarian nobility into the Society. They could do more for the Church in the diet and on their estates. Sufficient vocations to the religious life could be found among the townspeople.[24]

Ferdinand could invoke the Peace of Augsburg in support of his program in the Austrian and Bohemian lands. To be sure, in 1609 Archduke Matthias had reaffirmed and expanded concessions made earlier by Emperor Maximilian II to the Upper Austrian nobility regarding the free exercise of religion. That same year Emperor Rudolf had made more far-reaching concessions to the Protestants of the Bohemian lands, and Ferdinand himself had confirmed them at the time of his recognition as King of Bohemia. But Ferdinand insisted that these privileges were forfeit as a result of the estates' participation in the rebellion following the Defenestration of Prague. He now held these territories by right of conquest, and he was free to reorganize church and state as he desired.[25]

This was not the case in Lower Austria. There in 1620 he had confirmed the free exercise of religion first granted by Matthias for those Protestant nobles who had refused to join in the Bohemian rebellion. Ferdinand was to interpret this promise more narrowly and controversially as time went on and his position grew stronger. But his decree of March 20, 1625, had a solid legal basis. It was the one about which Pazmany complained, and it ordered all non-Catholic citizens of Vienna to begin instructions in the Catholic faith within three months or leave the city. The measure also urged Catholics to attend the instructions to learn more about their faith. Lamormaini strongly supported it.[26]

Upper Austria posed a much more difficult problem. There of all the Austrian lands Protestantism had struck the deepest roots not only among the nobility but also in the towns and among the peasantry. Though there is no direct evidence for Lamormaini's influence behind the emperor's hard line in Upper Austria at this time, one can reasonably infer it from the policy he generally advocated. Ferdinand retained sovereignty over the territory during the Bavarian occupation, and in the fall of 1624 he issued a decree expelling from Upper Austria all Protestant preachers and schoolteachers despite the hesitation of Maximilian, who preferred a less aggressive policy. Soon the inhabitants faced severe pressures to convert. These measures were the main cause of the great Upper Austrian peasants' rebellion that broke out in May 1626. It was of potentially serious danger to Ferdinand, since the leaders looked to both

Christian of Denmark and Bethlen for assistance, and they in turn hoped to profit from it. Not until well into the fall was the rebellion completely suppressed. Fortunately for Ferdinand, much of the onus for the Counter-reformation policy as well as for the rigorous measures taken against the rebels fell on the Bavarian administration rather than on the government in Vienna. Though Ferdinand was generous in pardoning offenders, he still made no compromise on the religious issue.[27]

In the 1620s the most profound changes were taking place in the lands of the Bohemian crown, especially Bohemia proper and Moravia. Silesia got off easily largely because of Ferdinand's desire to conciliate John George of Saxony and to avoid trouble in a territory so strategically located. John George held the two Lusatias provisionally, and as Ferdinand's representative he received the homage of the Silesian estates after the rebellion. In 1621 Ferdinand confirmed the privileges granted Silesia by Emperor Rudolf in 1609, which included the free exercise of religion for adherents of the Confession of Augsburg.[28] For the Czechs and Moravians these years marked a turning point in their history. The large-scale confiscation and redistribution of rebel lands combined with the intro-duction of absolutism and the full force of the Counterreformation to alter the face of the land. The process was well under way when on March 29, 1624, less than a week after the vow of March 25, Ferdinand issued a royal patent declaring Catholicism to be the only religion per-mitted the inhabitants of the cities and the peasants in Bohemia. A similar decree for Moravia followed on April 9. This left untouched only the nobility that had not participated in the rebellion. But implementation was another matter. A substantial majority of the population, especially in rural areas, was composed of Protestants of different types, Lutherans, Calvinists, Bohemian Brethren. Besides, the Hussite tradition remained strong.[29]

Carafa lobbied consistently for more effective Counterreformation measures in Bohemia. In the spring of 1624 there was considerable op-position to this among the imperial councilors, even among those Carafa counted "good Catholics" as opposed to the "politici." They feared un-rest in Bohemia and, above all, they did not want to risk stirring up John George of Saxony before a meeting of electors that summer when he was expected to sanction formally the appointment of Maximilian to the electoral college. Both Maximilian and Mainz counseled moderation in Vienna. Carafa, who accepted the need to go slowly in Hungary, thought that the time had come for a firm policy in recalcitrant Bohemia. He sought out the newly-appointed Lamormaini, whom he characterized "a most zealous man, very wise and prudent," and he found that Lamor-maini was already trying to move Ferdinand in the same direction but finding him "a little fearful." Lamormaini then suggested to Ferdinand that he pray over the matter for several days, asking the Lord to enlighten him as to the right course of action. When Lamormaini returned four days later, the emperor reported "that after communion God had inspired him to do whatever His Paternity said without any question or contradiction."[30] Shortly afterwards decrees were issued expelling anew all Protestant preachers from Bohemia and Moravia. According to Carafa, at least one thousand of them were still in Bohemia. A reformation commission was soon set up to oversee the implementation of this and other measures. The event vindicated Carafa and Lamormaini when despite the action taken, the Elector of Saxony approved Maximilian's entrance into the electoral college.[31] Bold action along with trust in God had paid off.

New differences soon arose over the method and pace of the Counterreformation in Bohemia. At the heart of them all was the issue concerning the proper role of the emperor and the Jesuits. The first point of contention was the future of the Charles University in Prague, the Empire's oldest university, whose origins traced back to 1348. The conflict over the reorganization of the University of Vienna was but a squabble compared to the long and bitter dispute over the new form the university in Prague ought to take. Here Lamormaini ran into opposition from the brilliant but one-sided and erratic Capuchin, Valeriano Magni, who came to see himself as the champion of the other religious orders and the Archbishop of Prague against the exaggerated claims of the Jesuits.[32] Eventually the quarrel escalated to one between emperor and pope over the ultimate control of the university, and it merged with allied disputes over the program for the conversion of Bohemia and the disposition of the recovered ecclesiastical lands of the kingdom. Together they contributed to a resentment among other Catholic groups toward the Jesuits; this ill feeling would appear much more openly later, in the conflict over the fate of ecclesiastical lands regained in the Empire by virtue of the Edict of Restitution.

Long before the rebellion, Catholics in Bohemia had recognized the need for a thoroughly Catholic institution of higher learning in the kingdom. The ancient university had become a center of heresy infecting all of Bohemia through the many lawyers, notaries, teachers, and government officials it graduated. During the rebellion the rector and faculty had supported the rebels with such enthusiasm that some imperial councilors favored the complete suppression of the university.[33] But this solution was considered too radical, and in the course of negotiations in 1622 and 1623 a provisional agreement between the Jesuits and the imperial authorities was reached, which Ferdinand then approved. It called for the expansion into full-fledged faculties of the theological and philosophical courses taught at the Jesuit college in Prague. The *Ferdinandea*, as the courses were called after Ferdinand I, who established them at the same time he founded the college, the *Clementinum*, were then to be united with the medical and law faculties of the Charles University in a new university, the *Universitas Carolo-Ferdinandea*. It was to be under the direction of the Jesuits and was expected to be a center of orthodoxy for all Bohemia. Jesuit superiors would appoint both the chancellor and the rector; no longer would they be elected by the faculty. All non-Jesuit professors would be banned from the theological faculty, a measure considered necessary to insure doctrinal correctness and the avoidance of theological wrangling. The censorship of books for the whole kingdom would be in the hands of the Jesuit rector. The landed endowment of the old university would pass to the control of the new institution, that is, to the Jesuits.[34]

There was a great deal of dissatisfaction with these arrangements. Members of other religious orders resented the complete control of the theological faculty given the Jesuits. Their chief representatives were Casper von Questenberg, Abbot of the Premonstratensian Abbey of Strahov on the Hradschin in Prague, and especially Magni, now guardian of the Capuchin convent on the Hradschin and provincial superior of the Capuchins in Bohemia. More important still were the objections of the newly appointed Archbishop of Prague, Ernst von Harrach, son of Karl von Harrach, a trusted imperial privy councilor and an intimate of Wallenstein.[35] In 1623, at the age of twenty-five, he succeeded to the administration of the huge archdiocese that comprised all Bohemia. Magni and Questenberg were his principal advisers and allies. The papal bulls establishing the university, Harrach claimed, stipulated that the chancellorship and with it ultimate authority in the university belonged to the archbishop. The Council of Trent accorded him the right to approve the members of the faculty of theology. The administration of the censorship in the kingdom, he protested, was his right. Another point of friction was the transfer of the university's endowment. All in all, Harrach along with Magni and Questenberg appeared as the defenders of ecclesiastical rights against the imperial government, which with Ferdinand's well-known preference for the Society tended to expand the role of the Jesuits. This was a cause of embarrassment to Vitelleschi, if not to Lamormaini.[36]

On March 2, 1624, Harrach officially presented his objections to the Governor of Bohemia in Prague. The Bohemian chancery then prepared a further outline of the union and returned it to Harrach, having taken virtually no cognizance of his position. Harrach next threatened both the governor and the emperor with excommunication if they went through with the plan, and he ordered the Jesuit rector to suspend all granting of degrees until agreement was reached. At the behest of the emperor negotiations continued, but without success. Finally, on September 9, the rector defied the archbishop and approved the conferral of degrees.[37]

Lamormaini now entered the picture with a proposal drawn up at the request of Eggenberg. But its new elements were more formal than real. Charles University, because of its role in the rebellion, was to be suppressed. The Ferdinandea was to be expanded into a new university, to be called simply the University of Prague, in which the Jesuits would retain control of the faculties of philosophy and theology. The lands of the old university were to be transferred to the Jesuits to pay the salaries of the lay professors of law and medicine. Privileges accorded the Society, the projected agreement asserted explicitly, were not to be construed as prejudicing the rights of the archbishop. Admittedly, this solution solved the legal problems connected with the rights and privileges of the old university and undermined the archbishop's reliance on the papal bulls. But it raised new problems. Could the emperor, on his own, suppress an institution of papal foundation? What were his rights with respect to the properties of the university? Then there remained the fundamental question, who was to have the final say in the university, the Jesuits or the archbishop?[38]

In a long letter to Vitelleschi Lamormaini explained that Ferdinand was determined to have the Jesuits in control of the university, and he insisted that this would not stir up the ill will toward the Society the superior general feared. The emperor did not approve the modesty of those Jesuits who wanted to compromise, Lamormaini wrote, since this would benefit neither Church nor state. His grandfather, Ferdinand I, had brought the Jesuits to Prague when the Church there was collapsing, and they had stemmed the tide of heresy largely through the Clementinum and the Ferdinandea he had founded. The present Ferdinand wanted the Jesuits to continue this work effectively. For this reason the Society must have firm charge of the university. Moreover, Lamormaini went on, according to Ferdinand it was the Jesuits who had turned back heresy in Germany. Only the previous day Ferdinand had remarked spontaneously, "If there had been no Society, there would be no trace of the Catholic religion in Germany today." To the Jesuits belonged the credit for the reform of the other orders since the Reformation. Eggenberg, Lamormaini added, went so far as to say that without the Jesuits the other orders would revert to their old ways.[39] Such views were not calculated to be popular with Magni and Questenberg.

Archbishop Harrach came to Vienna for renewed negotiations in November 1624, and surprisingly accepted in substance Lamormaini's proposal. Undoubtedly, he faced great pressure from the emperor and his councilors. On November 27 Harrach, Eggenberg for the emperor, Carafa for the Holy See, and Gregor Rumer, provincial superior of the Bohemian Jesuits, for the Society, all signed the agreement. Vitelleschi had given his approval in advance.[40] The matter appeared settled.

Unfortunately, this was only the beginning of the long struggle over the structure of the university in Prague. The agreement still had to be ratified in Rome, where Pope Urban VIII turned it over to the newly-created Congregation for the Propagation of the Faith, or *Propaganda*.[41] Rome hesitated. Resentment had been building up in Roman circles, and especially at the Propaganda, about what were felt to be usurpations by the Prague Jesuits. Even some Jesuits in Rome shared this feeling, including the rector of the German college.[42] Harrach's awareness of the sentiment in Rome plus the pressure from opponents of the plan once he returned to Prague convinced him to reverse his position. In a letter of June 28, 1625, to the Propaganda he repudiated the agreement. Carafa then, increasingly fearful of the growing influence in Vienna of the Jesuits and especially Lamormaini, followed suit in September. He undertook to obtain a papal decree compelling the Jesuits to yield to the archbishop. The Propaganda refused to ratify the agreement and informed the Jesuits that under no circumstances were they to assume the chancellorship of the university which with final control over the institution belonged to the archbishop.[43] Lamormaini urged the emperor to stand firm against the "little dogs" (*cuniculos*) who were causing trouble in Rome, and he did.[44]

The matter dragged on. In August 1627 the Propaganda forbade the Jesuits to confer degrees. They obeyed, and new talks began. Magni became more and more involved, accusing Lamormaini of intrigue against him at court and intimating to Rome that he ought to be sent away from Vienna. His assertion that the Jesuits aimed at the control of all the Catholic universities in Europe was wide of the mark, but his contention that "the father [Lamormaini] supposes that [the interests of] the House of Austria and the Society are identical" was not.[45] Harrach and Magni were determined that the archbishop would have the last word in the university, and Rome consistently supported them. The contest was a frequent topic of the nuncio's reports. The pope made some concessions in 1629 and 1630, but any agreement foundered on the chancellorship.[46] The Jesuits eventually tried to extricate themselves from the affair, reducing their interest to their own institutions and leaving the Charles University to the emperor. But the dispute remained a source of friction between emperor and pope and of anti-Jesuit feeling. Only in 1654 under Emperor Ferdinand III did the conflict find a final resolution, to which, however,

Rome never gave its formal blessing. The Ferdinandea was joined with the Charles University in a new entity, the Universitas Carolo-Ferdinandea. Though some concessions were made to the archbishop, the emperor along with the Jesuits emerged as the victors.[47]

But to return to 1626, the related issue of the general procedure to be followed in the reform of religion in Bohemia had arisen to divide Lamormaini and his opponents. That spring the Danish threat peaked and in May the revolt in Upper Austria broke out. Mainz and Saxony both warned Ferdinand that continued prosecution of the Counterreformation in Bohemia might drive Saxony and Brandenburg into the arms of the enemy. The Catholics, for their part, were disappointed with the results of their efforts at conversion. Their measures were poorly organized, too hasty and stern. Abuses had undoubtedly taken place, such as the misbehavior of troops quartered on a town or the exile of Protestants for the sake of their property. A more gradual and thorough reform was desirable. Consultations were held in Vienna to find a method that would be effective without further alienating the German Protestants. Among those participating were Eggenberg, Abbot Anton, and Dietrichstein, whose reform procedures in Moravia had met with much success. Suggestions were prepared and sent to Harrach in Prague in April, and he traveled to Vienna in November to present his views, which were based substantially on a paper of Magni. Before coming to a decision, however, the councilors wanted to hear from the imperial theologians. So Lamormaini, assisted by Heinrich Philippi, Jesuit confessor of the young King of Hungary, drew up a plan that was approved by the faculty of theology at the University of Vienna.[48]

The most fundamental divergence between the two programs concerned the role of the emperor in the elimination of heresy in Bohemia and thus the relationship between prince and Church. For Magni the reform of religion was the task of the archbishop, whom the emperor should support and assist when called upon.[49] The latter's role was a subordinate one. According to Lamormaini, the Christian prince had the obligation to purge his lands of heresy "directly by reason of his office," not only when requested by episcopal authority. Indeed, the bishop had the duty of teaching and leading the faithful, but at the same time the primary task of the Christian prince was the advancement of religion. "And so complete reformation depends upon both powers, the lord [Domini] and the father [Patris]." Unless compelled to do so by circumstances, which was not then the case in Bohemia, "the king ought not to tolerate in his kingdom a profession of faith other than the Catholic. The pastor ought to instruct the heretics, so that their conversion is genuine." Lamormaini pointed to the example of Ferdinand's Habsburg predecessors. He was more influenced by his vision of the history of the Catholic response to the Reformation in Germany than by theoretical considerations about the relationship between the temporal and the spiritual power. The German upper clergy had, for the most part, sat back and watched while the Habsburg and Wittelsbach princes with their allies, the Jesuits, had taken energetic and vigorous measures to combat heresy and revive Catholicism. The princes and the Jesuits had saved the Church in Germany, and they would continue the work of restoration together. Magni, on the other hand, stood for the tradition of ecclesiastical independence and strict respect for ecclesiastical rights and privileges. His later remark that according to Lamormaini the archbishop "had no other right in the reform except to administer the sacraments and preach the Word of God" contained more than a grain of truth.[50]

"Piety can only be restored in Bohemia by a powerful authority," Lamormaini wrote. He recommended the use of the reformation commissions already employed in the Austrian lands. Teams of two reformation commissioners were to tour the kingdom. One would be appointed by the king, the other by the archbishop, but both would appear in the king's name, since the heretics did not recognize the authority of the archbishop. When it was considered necessary for the preservation of order and the protection of the commissioners—in rural areas especially hostility could be expected—a band of soldiers would accompany them. Upon arriving in a parish or on an estate, the secular commissioner would read to the assembled people the imperial decree enjoining conversion, explain to them the advantages to be gained by it, and advise them of the time they would be allowed to make a decision. Then the ecclesiastical commissioner would begin instructions in the Catholic faith and introduce the missionaries who were to continue the work of preparing the people for reception into the Church. Together the commissioners would take steps to revive the parish; they would, for example, report on the condition of the church building and take an inventory of revenues. Ideally, one of the missionaries would remain as pastor. After the lapse of the determined time, which varied according to the nature of the individual community, the commissioners would return. Then, if necessary, pressures to convert would be placed on the inhabitants, such as the denial of Christian burial, a disciplined quartering of troops, and finally, exile.

Lamormaini looked to the long-term establishment of the Church in Bohemia. He was intent on winning the youth. He advocated the foundation of Catholic schools for boys and girls in urban and rural areas. The schoolteachers would be trained at the newly reformed university in Prague, a plan that helps explain his firmness on the university question.

The foundation of Jesuit colleges was important to Lamormaini; nine of them in Bohemia and Moravia owed their foundation or significant expansion to him.[51] But he did not discuss them in this paper, perhaps for political reasons. Lamormaini insisted on the education of devout, zealous, and competent diocesan priests, as did Magni, and he called for the establishment of a seminary to accommodate two hundred native Bohemians. The priests must speak Czech well, he noted, and not with the Polish accent the people ridiculed. His interest in the long term inclined Lamormaini to allow Protestant nobility to remain in the country, provided they kept no preachers and recalled their children from heretical foreign schools. In the cities, obnoxious Protestants should be expelled immediately, but others treated with patience. Peasants could not be allowed to emigrate, since most would leave in pursuit of freedom. They were to be brought "to embrace the faith by penalties moderately and prudently applied." The most dangerous situations existed where both lord and peasants were Protestants. Here great prudence had to be exercised lest unrest develop.

Implicit in Lamormaini's program were two basic presuppositions. One was the widely held view that if over a long enough time an individual was gently compelled to perform certain good acts, such as attending Mass on Sundays, he would gradually take on the proper interior attitude.[52] This psychological principle was especially applicable to youth, and it was perhaps a factor in his concern to found colleges and schools. Another presupposition was a position Lamormaini had defended while he was a professor in Graz, namely, that the Church had the right to compel the obedience of heretics if necessary through the use of the secular arm. This was not an undue violation of freedom, he affirmed, drawing on a long medieval tradition. Heretics differed from Jews or nonbelievers inasmuch as they were baptized and thus subject to the jurisdiction of the Church. Just as a prince could compel men endowed with reason to obey the natural law and punish them for not doing so, the Christian prince could force the baptized to obey the Church's law and punish the failure to do so. Besides, for Lamormaini any heretic who did not acknowledge the clear truth of the Catholic faith once it had been properly presented to him was simply of bad will.[53]

Magni opposed Lamormaini's program on several counts. Apart from seminaries, he showed little interest in education. He wanted the archbishop to divide the country provisionally into districts and to appoint a commissioner for each one. The commissioner would then begin the task of reformation by taking an inventory of the parishes in his district and recruiting diocesan and religious priests for missionary work. Subsequently, the commissioners would meet with the archbishop and prelates of the country in a synod. There with the cooperation of the political authority, they would clarify the ecclesiastical laws of the realm and determine the site for four new bishoprics, each to have its own seminary. The results of the synod would be sent to Rome for approval. Magni stressed the importance of the four bishoprics, to be subordinate to the Archbishopric of Prague. Only with more bishops could one hope to carry out the necessary supervision of the reform and visitation of parishes called for by the Council of Trent. Also the bishoprics, along with the chapters to be created later, provided positions for the nobility and thus made it possible to bind the interests of this social class to the Church.

Magni urged a spirit of mildness. He did not conceive the Protestants as a political danger and source of turbulence to the extent Lamormaini did. The use of direct pressures, he felt, would easily bring about false conversions, stimulate resentment, and in the long run prove counterproductive. What was to be gained, he queried, from a policy of exile? It would only lose the exiles for the faith and depopulate the country. Heretics should be tolerated in Bohemia, to be won over by example and preaching, he argued, though he did indicate that the king should reserve special privileges for Catholics. Lamormaini's program, he protested, tried to accomplish too much too rapidly. Nor did he accept Lamormaini's argument that the amount of time granted the people to recognize the truth of the Catholic faith would prevent simulated conversions. Subsequently, Magni himself did incline to more rigor, since both the Propaganda and Harrach thought it necessary; the ridicule and even assault experienced by the missionaries seemed to render it advisable.[54]

Lamormaini and the imperial theologians also clashed with Magni and Harrach on the future of the church lands recovered from the Protestants. Discussion of this issue had begun almost immediately after the defeat of the rebels. Harrach's predecessor laid claim to all the lands taken from the Church since the Hussite wars, or to equivalent compensation. Though the Governor of Bohemia made it clear to Harrach from the start that this was not possible, both the archbishop and the Propaganda maintained the claim, since they counted on the restored lands to finance the reconstruction of the Church in Bohemia. A commission including Harrach and Magni was set up to study the question, and in November 1626, a provisional solution was reached. It stipulated that for the next thirty years the Church would receive as compensation one-quarter gulden on every vat of salt imported into the kingdom.[55]

Lamormaini challenged this in the position paper of the imperial theologians. He opposed the salt tax as being too high already and a burden on the poor. But his attack focused not so much on the solution itself as on the assertion of the commission that the emperor was obliged in conscience to make restitution. To Lamormaini any such obligation was unrealistic. Many claims were invalid by virtue of prescription. In other cases the king had transferred lands or secularized them with papal approval. To clarify now what lands had once belonged to the Church would be impossible. Lamormaini turned to history for his chief argument, which was based on the efforts of Ferdinand and his predecessors for the Church. They had generously endowed it. Ferdinand himself had fought a costly war, at the explicit urging of the pope, for the Palatinate, and he had sold to Catholics at greatly reduced prices many lands confiscated from the rebels and thus had taken a loss himself in order to strengthen the Church in Bohemia. As King of Bohemia Ferdinand had the duty to support the reform financially, and this he did with great openhandedness, but he was under no obligation in conscience to honor the claims of ecclesiastics for restitution.

As early as 1621, Lamormaini had espoused this position in principle and sought papal approval for it.[56] In 1623 his predecessor, Becan, had approved Ferdinand's disposition of ecclesiastical lands after the rebellion and so had quieted his conscience. But Becan had suggested that in order to avoid scandal and a possible blemish on his reputation, the emperor might seek Rome's consent for his action. Lamormaini made this opinion his own in 1625.[57] In the present paper he passed over completely the matter of papal consent. Nor should one lose sight of the fact that insistence on the emperor's obligation to restitution meant that compensation would go to the archbishop, to finance reform as he intended it, whereas the more Ferdinand's liberty was stressed, the more likely it was that funds would go to the Jesuits. It looked to some, as it was reported to the Propaganda, that "while the Society is established, the establishment of the Catholic faith is neglected."[58]

Lamormaini personally read the plan of the imperial theologians to Harrach in Vienna in mid-December 1626. The archbishop told Ferdinand that he was, generally speaking, in agreement with it, but that he had reservations about the denial of any obligation to restitution or compensation. Lamormaini now seems to have agreed to the salt tax, provided the proceeds were used principally to maintain the seminary he envisioned, which was to be conducted by the Society, and to finance the work of the commissioners as foreseen in his plan. Finally, on February 5, 1627, new instructions were issued for the reformation commissioners that embodied in general the views of the imperial theologians, though the archbishop was assigned a somewhat larger role than the theologians had advocated.[59] But the restitution issue remained. With Lamormaini stood the emperor himself, the majority of the councilors, and the Jesuits. With Magni were aligned Eggenberg, Dietrichstein, Harrach, the Capuchins, and soon the Propaganda, which rejected the salt tax as inadequate.[60] Negotiations continued for three more years, though Lamormaini seems to have taken no further part in them. Finally, on March 8, 1630, an agreement was signed in Vienna by representatives of Ferdinand, by Harrach, and by the new nuncio, and it was then ratified in Rome. The salt tax was extended to all salt consumed in Bohemia, whether imported or mined there, and the provision that the revenues from it were to go to the Church was written into the permanent law of the land. In return, the Church surrendered any further claim to restitution or compensation for confiscated ecclesiastical lands. The agreement called for the foundation of four new bishoprics in Bohemia, but lack of funds prevented this. At first, the revenue from the salt tax proved disappointingly low.[61]

Both Eggenberg and Carafa opposed Lamormaini on the restitution issue in late 1626. The chief minister seems to have first become wary of Lamormaini's growing influence in the fall of 1625, when he advised Wallenstein not to make any arrangement with him about the disposition of Magdeburg and Halberstadt.[62] This was just after Carafa reversed his position on the university question. In his report to Rome of November 25, 1626, when the program for reform in Bohemia was under discussion, Carafa vented his feelings against the Jesuits in general and Lamormaini in particular. With Lamormaini as confessor the influence of the Jesuits in Vienna had become intolerable. They exploited their favor with the emperor, he affirmed, not only to secure a position superior to other orders but to exclude them completely from matters in which the Society had a spiritual or political interest. Even the imperial ministers needed Jesuit support. Privately Eggenberg told him, he wrote, that the power the Society enjoyed under Ferdinand would in the long run be its undoing. According to Carafa, Lamormaini was "little well disposed to the Roman Curia." Magni had recently recounted to him a visit he had paid Lamormaini, who was ill. He had gone to inform the confessor of progress in the discussions on the reform in Bohemia. Lamormaini had advised him there was no need to communicate the news to Carafa. The nuncio carried little weight with Ferdinand, Lamormaini allegedly said, "since the German princes are correct in their opinion that the nuncios are sent into these parts only to increase and expand apostolic [papal] jurisdiction and to reduce that of the princes, and for no other reason." Carafa ended his report emphasizing the need to find a way to deal with Lamormaini and the Society in Vienna.[63]

Carafa's remarks about Lamormaini's attitude toward Rome and especially the account of his conversation with Magni were received in Rome with skepticism. A marginal notation by the secretary of state, Cardinal Lorenzo Magalotti, about the well-known anti-Jesuit sentiment of Magni made this clear.[64] That Lamormaini ever said what Magni attributed to him is unlikely, though he may have thought it. Generally speaking, he attempted to act according to the periodical admonitions of Vitelleschi to respect the wishes of the Holy See and to foster relations between Rome and Vienna. Especially as his plans for the restoration of religion grew, he became more aware of the need for papal support for their success. Rome had stymied his designs for the university in Prague.

But at times Lamormaini was clearly out of tune with Rome. There were several underlying reasons for this. Lamormaini assigned a positive role and initiative to the prince in the pursuit of the religious welfare of his subjects. This corresponded to a long imperial tradition and to the more recent history of firm Habsburg support for the Counterreformation. Both Ferdinand and Lamormaini took seriously the oath the emperor had sworn at his coronation to administer justice and uphold the rights of the Empire; it imposed a profound obligation in conscience. Urban, for his part, emphasized his determination to maintain the ecclesiastical and papal rights entrusted to him by establishing a special congregation to deal with questions of ecclesiastical immunity.[65] He did not want to go down in history as a pope who yielded church rights. Thus both pope and emperor tended to be intransigent in the legal disputes that filled the correspondence of the nuncios. One of these disagreements, of course, was over the university in Prague. Another was the drawn-out conflict over the right of appointment to the Patriarchate of Aquileia, whose jurisdiction lay half in imperial and half in Venetian territory. Of lesser importance was the dispute over the succession in the two tiny north Italian imperial fiefs, Bardi and Campione, a case that lay before the imperial aulic council in the fall of 1626. For a time Lamormaini succeeded in delaying the execution of a decision unfavorable to the papacy, but Ferdinand himself then impressed upon Carafa his duty to uphold the "reason of the empire," and Lamormaini concurred.[66]

Pope Urban's priorities often did not suit Lamormaini or Vienna. He did pursue the long range goal of peace among Catholic princes in the interest of a united front against the heretics. In the second year of his pontificate he dispatched his nephew Francesco to Madrid and Paris in an effort to mediate the differences between Habsburg and Bourbon.[67] But Urban shared the traditional papal fear of Habsburg domination in Italy and in Europe. Consequently, he tended to tilt slightly toward France in his efforts to promote cooperation among Catholic princes. During his years as nuncio in Paris, Urban had acquired an inclination toward things French, and Richelieu subtly exploited it. Under Urban the nepotism of the Renaissance was again at home on the Tiber. Enormous sums found their way into the coffers of the Barberini family, and great amounts were spent on monumental art that would enrich Rome and glorify the Barberinis. Urban was concerned to aid the Counterreformation in Germany, but it did not have the priority it enjoyed under his predecessor, Gregory XV, who had immediately recognized the opportunity presented by the victory at the White Mountain and had assisted Ferdinand and Maximilian with generous financial, diplomatic, and military aid. Once Urban ascended the papal throne, the subsidies conceded by Gregory dried up.[68]

As early as 1624, Lamormaini tried through Vitelleschi to support imperial efforts to have the subsidies renewed, but he was unsuccessful. One reason the pope did not act, Vitelleschi responded, was the allegation of financial mismanagement in Vienna. Lamormaini thought it wiser not to mention this in Vienna, and he then gently criticized the pope's priorities in his answer to the superior general.[69] Under Urban VIII the militant spirit of the Counterreformation no longer predominated in Rome.

3. Restoration in the Empire, 1626–1627

o the triumphant victor, the most good and most powerful God, Emperor Ferdinand II has raised this monument in memory of the Blessed Virgin Mary and Saints Ignatius and Francis Xavier." So reads today in downtown Vienna the inscription across the facade of the Jesuit Church built under Lamormaini's direction. It bears the date 1627 and gives expression to the sense of a triumphant crusade that inspired the militants in Vienna at the conclusion of the Electoral Convention of Mühlhausen that autumn. Ferdinand was fighting the battles of the Lord. God's assistance brought victory, and to Him belonged the glory of the triumph. Ferdinand's principal allies were the Jesuits, represented on the facade by statues of their two greatest figures, Ignatius Loyola and Francis Xavier, both canonized in 1622.

Protests reaching Vitelleschi that the emperor would do better for himself and the Society if he would pay off his creditors instead of building expensive churches showed that not everyone, not even every Jesuit, shared Lamormaini's enthusiasm.[1] There was opposition within the government to the increasingly expansionist policy of Ferdinand, but with the triumphs of 1627 it grew mute. The victory at Lutter the previous year had established Catholic military predominance in the north. Tilly and Wallenstein continued to advance throughout the campaign of 1627, and by year's end they occupied nearly all the Lower Saxon Circle, including Mecklenburg plus Pomerania to the east. The Empire had been practically cleared of hostile troops. Negotiations continued with Christian of Denmark until the Peace of Lübeck on July 7, 1629, but after late 1627 he was no longer a serious military threat despite his efforts to recover. The Huguenots still kept Richelieu busy at home, and the growing aggressiveness of parliament in England seemed to guarantee that Charles I would not be a factor on the continent for a time. Besides, France and England were still at war with each other. After another treaty with Bethlen, the Peace of Pressburg on December 20, 1626, and a renewed understanding with the Turks the following year, the Hungarian front remained quiet.[2]

The victories of 1626–27 encouraged Ferdinand to continue his program of religious reformation and political consolidation in the Austrian and Bohemian lands. Ferdinand never formally revoked the privileges he had confirmed for the loyal Protestant nobility of Lower Austria in 1620. But he did take measures that seemed to many to contravene the spirit if not the letter of his agreement with them. Lamormaini, for his part, defended the emperor's action. The Protestant nobles, he alleged, abused their privileges by permitting, for example, the attendance at services of people clearly not authorized to be there and by keeping Calvinist ministers and teachers. Thus all Protestant preachers and schoolteachers were ordered to leave Lower Austria on September 14, 1627. This was a victory for Lamormaini over unidentified figures in the government who feared the measure would unleash civil unrest. According to Vitelleschi, who certainly mirrored Lamormaini's view, such decisive action would win divine support for Ferdinand's other endeavors and confound those who relied on human, as opposed to divine, prudence. As it worked out, the decree was implemented with little difficulty. Further measures were taken to pressure the Protestant nobility to convert, but the emperor never went so far as to expel those who refused to do so.[3]

This was not to be the case in Inner Austria, where the nobility were the one group to have escaped the full rigor of Ferdinand's earlier measures. Here he could make a strong legal argument for his position, since his father, Archduke Carl, had always denied having made any permanent concessions to the Protestants. Ferdinand moved against the Protestant nobility in 1628. They connived, he felt, at opposition to his religious policy, and in any event, they had not shown themselves as receptive as he had hoped to measures intended to incline them toward conversion. On August 1 Protestant nobles were given one year to convert or go into exile. Over 750 of them took leave of the land.[4]

By the late autumn of 1626 the peasant rebellion in Upper Austria had been effectively suppressed, at great cost in life and property. The following June after the execution of eighteen ringleaders, Ferdinand issued a general pardon. But no religious concessions were offered. The emperor did not attempt to reorganize the state here as he did in Bohemia, but he made it abundantly clear that the privileges permitted the estates were due to his grace. An imperial patent gave the provincial nobility three months to convert or emigrate. After the withdrawal of the Bavarian occupation and the reversion of Upper Austria to full Habsburg control in May 1628, new measures were taken to ensure the departure of all non-Catholics except the peasants, who were not given the option to leave. Lamormaini advocated these measures in the face of opposition from some councilors, who he felt considered the matter from an exclusively human perspective. Again the short-term event seemed to vindicate him. All went smoothly. But another less serious peasant uprising in August 1632 showed that Protestant sentiment remained strong in Upper Austria.[5]

All in all, under Ferdinand II approximately one hundred thousand inhabitants picked up their stakes and departed from the Austrian territories, most of them heading for Germany or Hungary.[6] Lamormaini must bear a major share of the responsibility for this harsh policy that cost the Austrian lands a large number of economically and culturally productive people.

Ferdinand's program of reform proceeded apace in the Bohemian lands. Silesia succeeded in holding on to the free exercise of religion for adherents of the Confession of Augsburg, but the estates saw their position weakened by the introduction of a governmental council directly dependent upon the emperor. The changes in Bohemia and Moravia were far-reaching. A new constitution was issued for Bohemia in May 1627, and a similar one followed the next year for Moravia. Bohemia became, in effect, an absolute monarchy, hereditary in the male Habsburg line. Supreme judicial and legislative authority was vested clearly in the king. The estates were not abolished, but the rights of this traditionally strong body were greatly reduced; the principal one they retained was to approve taxes. The clergy was restored to the first place in the estates from which it had been completely excluded since the Hussite era. The leading social group in the kingdom remained the nobility with their strong position in the estates and their rights as landlords. But they were now a nobility closely bound to the ruler. Many nobles owed their status to the emperor's favor at the time of the redistribution of rebel property, and the new constitution gave to the king the exclusive right to elevate to the nobility, a right he formerly had shared with the estates. Imperial decrees in 1627 and 1628 expelled the remaining non-Catholic nobles from Bohemia and Moravia. Altogether during the 1620s, the two territories saw the departure of about one-fourth of the nobility and well-to-do citizenry.[7]

Meanwhile, Lamormaini accompanied Ferdinand to Prague in the autumn of 1627, where the emperor held court until late into the spring. On November 21, amid elaborate ceremonies, Ferdinand's wife, Empress Eleonora, was crowned Queen of Bohemia. A few days later his son Ferdinand was crowned king, thus assuring the succession in Bohemia as well as in Hungary. Indeed the emperor's position in the Bohemian lands was growing secure.[8]

The general purpose of the convention of electors in the Thuringian town of Mühlhausen in October 1627 was to search for a stable peace in the Empire. This meant the Palatinate question and the terms of settlement with Christian of Denmark would be on the agenda. A major reason for the meeting was the growing threat the electors felt from Wallenstein. As we have seen, friction had been quick to develop between Maximilian and the general. The growth and success of the imperial army alarmed the electors, of whose rights Maximilian had become the foremost champion. They suspected Wallenstein aimed to enhance the emperor's position at their expense and that of the traditional constitution. They feared that the competition for resources and recruits was weakening the League army, which they had come to consider the ultimate guarantee of their rights. Wallenstein's accumulation of titles, his establishment of a virtually independent principality in Friedland in Bohemia, and his maintenance of a court in the grand style all pointed to pretensions. His disregard and occasional scarcely veiled contempt for the electors were bound to fester, especially in the highly self-conscious Maximilian. To the Catholic electors the large number of Protestants in Wallenstein's army seemed to imply he did not take the religious goals of the war as seriously as they did.[9]

Magni was responsible for greatly heightening Maximilian's suspicions of Wallenstein in early 1627. The Capuchin had conceived a hatred for the general. One can only speculate this was due to Wallenstein's initially good relations with Lamormaini and the Jesuits or to Magni's sensing that Wallenstein's ascent guaranteed increasing power for Ferdinand, which implied growing influence for the Jesuits. Perhaps both. Precisely at this time Magni and Lamormaini were clashing over the Counterreformation in Bohemia. Magni may have seen greater independence for the electors as a healthy but Catholic check on Ferdinand and the Jesuits. In any event, in a report from Vienna Magni outlined for Maximilian the program that Wallenstein had purportedly advocated in a conference with Eggenberg at Brück in November 1626. Though it was not said in so many words, from Magni's assertions one could easily infer that Wallenstein intended to make Ferdinand an absolute monarch in Germany.[10]

Magni's report scared Maximilian. Whether the Capuchin's information could be checked out or not, it seemed to fit the pattern of Wallenstein's actions. Catholic successes in the north had already revived the plans for a Habsburg fleet in the Baltic and talk of League intervention against the Dutch.[11] Maximilian called a meeting of the Catholic League for February 1627 in Würzburg. Beforehand, he circulated a summary of Magni's paper among the ecclesiastical electors. At Würzburg the two main points of discussion were the Wallenstein danger and the maintenance of the League army, and at the end of the meeting a delegation was dispatched to Vienna to describe the misdeeds of Wallenstein's soldiers and to complain about his quartering of troops. In their restricted discussions at Würzburg, Maximilian and the three ecclesiastical electors agreed on the need for an electoral convention to discuss the affairs of the Empire including the status of Wallenstein. They preferred a convention of electors to a convention of deputies or a diet, since in the first-named the influence of the emperor would be considerably reduced. Subsequently, they obtained the support of Saxony and Brandenburg, who also felt threatened by the general. So an electoral convention was scheduled for the autumn in Mühlhausen.[12]

Lamormaini and Wallenstein started out on good terms. The confessor had encouraged the appointment of Wallenstein, who was a generous if occasionally difficult benefactor of the Society. In 1622 he had undertaken the foundation of a Jesuit college at Gitschin (Jičín), the center of his Bohemian possessions. His influence with Archbishop Harrach was instrumental in securing for the Jesuits permission to open a residence on the Hradschin in Prague. This was another of Lamormaini's projects, and Magni's efforts to hinder it were in vain. Later, in 1628 Vitelleschi named Wallenstein a Founder of the Society, a title reserved for outstanding benefactors, which granted them a special share in the prayers of the Society. By then Wallenstein's gifts included the beginnings of new colleges in his recently acquired territory of Sagan and at Troppau, both in Silesia.[13] At one point, Magni wrote Munich asserting that Wallenstein had won Lamormaini's support with the emperor by his promises to found colleges. Consequently, "the Emperor, relying on the confessor who has assured him of the faithfulness of the personage [Wallenstein], believes no one else. . . ."[14]

Before Wallenstein first took the field, perhaps even before his formal appointment, Lamormaini had arrived at an understanding with him that was to cause trouble with Maximilian. Apparently acting on his own, without even telling the emperor, Lamormaini had agreed that Magdeburg and Halberstadt should be given to Archduke Leopold William, Ferdinand's twelve-year-old son, who had been made Bishop of Passau and Strasbourg earlier that year. The legal basis for this was the law of conquest, not the Peace of Religion, the incumbent Christian William of Brandenburg having been guilty of rebellion. Wallenstein's interest in this plan lay in his hope of obtaining the revenues and resources of the territories for his army.[15] But Maximilian and Tilly had their eyes on Magdeburg and Halberstadt for the same reason. The dispute over them was part of the rivalry between the League and imperial armies for revenues and winter quarters.

Almost certainly as a result of his association with Wallenstein, Esaias Leuker, the Bavarian resident in Vienna, accused Lamormaini the next year of causing dissension between Maximilian and Ferdinand. Maximilian's confessor, Contzen, duly passed Leuker's complaint on to Vitelleschi, who then raised the matter tactfully with Lamormaini. In the meantime, Lamormaini learned of the accusation from another source and cleared himself with Maximilian.[16] But his resentment toward Leuker remained; it only increased when he learned that on the basis of rumors circulating in Vienna, the Bavarian resident had reported to Munich that Ferdinand had proposed Lamormaini for the cardinalate. To this he was especially sensitive, since it seemed to imply a violation of his Jesuit vow not to seek ecclesiastical office. Even a personal meeting between the two in December 1626 failed to calm Lamormaini. He wrote Raphael Cobenzl, superior of the professed house in Vienna where he lived, that no more serious charge could be leveled against a Jesuit and a confessor of the emperor "than that he was sowing seeds of discord between the emperor and the elector, most pious princes bound to each other by the closest ties of every type, on whom depend today in the judgment of the whole world the Catholic Church in Germany and the Catholic religion and to both of whom as well as to their distinguished Houses our Society is forever obligated."[17] Lamormaini promised in the future to treat Leuker in a Christian manner, but he affirmed his intent to protect his reputation.

Lamormaini was deeply conscious of the need for unity among the German Catholic princes if his plans for the restoration of Catholicism were to be successful. Therefore he was eager to help prevent any disagreement between Maximilian and Ferdinand when the two delegates of the Catholic League arrived in Vienna on May 10, 1627. His first move away from Wallenstein was dictated by the desire to preserve harmony between the two pillars of the Counterreformation in Germany, not by any hostility to the general. Only later did he realize Wallenstein did not share his goals. Lamormaini's attitude seems to have been that it was obviously preferable to resolve any difficulties between Maximilian and Wallenstein, but should this prove impossible, then it was wiser to yield to the elector and reduce the position of the general, rather than to risk a rift between Ferdinand and Maximilian. Lamormaini helped prepare the delegates for their interviews with Eggenberg and Ferdinand, and he advised them to be frank in their talks with Wallenstein himself. He was present at a meeting where Wallenstein assured one of the League delegates that he did not want to give the electors any cause for complaint. The reassurances the delegates received in Vienna eased the suspicions of the electors and helped blunt their attack on Wallenstein at Mühlhausen.[18] Later that summer, heartened by their experience, Maximilian and Mainz agreed to make use of Lamormaini in the future to bring their grievances against Wallenstein to the emperor's attention.[19]

A clear settlement of the Palatinate question remained a presupposition for any permanent peace in the Empire. In 1624 Saxony had finally recognized Maximilian's personal tenure of the electorate but not the permanent retention of it in his House. Brandenburg had not done even that much. Foreigners meddling in the Empire could always pose as defenders of the rights of Frederick, who was even less inclined to compromise than Maximilian. Ferdinand and Maximilian had corresponded about possible terms of an agreement in 1625, when the Danish threat was materializing and it appeared a convention of deputies might be held at Ulm, but the convention was canceled.[20] Ferdinand had to be wary of exerting pressure on Maximilian lest he alienate his chief ally, who still held Upper Austria as surety for the war debts Ferdinand owed him. Any compromise Maximilian made with Frederick at Ferdinand's behest would make it that much more difficult to get him out of Upper Austria. Nor was Ferdinand himself inclined to view with equanimity the reinstatement of the militantly Calvinist Frederick. Still, urged on by members of the council, Ferdinand continued to pursue a peaceful solution to the problem. In early 1627 he requested Duke Charles of Lorraine to serve as a go-between in secret negotiations between his representatives and Frederick's.

Ferdinand asked Lamormaini to draw up a paper on the stance to be adopted by the imperial negotiators, and the confessor reiterated for the most part the position he and Becan had taken jointly back in January 1624. One condition on which he insisted for the restoration of Frederick to any of his lands was Frederick's or his son's conversion to Catholicism.[21] This was not included in the instruction for the imperial negotiators drawn up in June by Stralendorf and Eggenberg. Desirable as Frederick's conversion was, Stralendorf countered, one could not postpone peace for it. But the emperor's proposals were still certain to be unacceptable to Frederick. Besides formal submission to the emperor and the renunciation of any claims to Bohemia, they included the retention of Catholicism where it had been restored by Maximilian in the Palatinate and financial compensation for Ferdinand's war costs. This would enable Ferdinand, in turn, to redeem Upper Austria from Bavaria and the Lusatias from Saxony. Most importantly, Frederick would have to come to a satisfactory agreement with Maximilian about the electoral title; this meant, in effect, he would have to give it up. Frederick, on the other hand, expected in return for his renunciation of Bohemia full restoration to his lands in the Palatinate and at least the alternation of the electoral dignity between himself and Maximilian until the latter's death, when it would revert to himself or his heirs. Nor was Frederick ready to grant more than token toleration of Catholicism in the Palatinate. Neither of the interested parties was ready for substantial concessions, the negotiations showed. When the Duke of Württemberg subsequently approached Ferdinand to intercede for Frederick, the emperor referred him to the coming electoral convention at Mühlhausen.[22]

Tilly's triumph at Lutter once again encouraged hopes for a widespread restitution of ecclesiastical lands. Only a week after news of the victory reached Brussels, two Bavarian diplomats reported enthusiastically a conversation there with the nuncio assigned to Cologne, Pier Luigi Carafa. As with his confrère in Vienna, Carafa was given a principal charge to foster the return of church lands, especially prince-bishoprics, to the Church. The three men talked about the projected restitutions in the Lower Saxon Circle, where the Catholics were expected soon to be in complete control. Surprisingly, according to the account of Johann Christoph von Preysing, one of the diplomats, Carafa agreed that for a time, perhaps ten years, the income from the recovered lands would have to be applied for the most part to the support of the Catholic armies.[23]

In September 1626, Pope Urban congratulated Ferdinand effusively on his victories and went on to declare that "all nations believe that the heavenly power guides the affairs of Your Majesty and affirm that it is a great crime to oppose the imperial legions. . . . " Urban expected more triumphs, "by which not only the armies of the heretics but their very name would be destroyed."[24] Again, in early February 1627, Urban vigorously urged the emperor to use his military advantage to return to the Church her lost bishoprics and affirmed that Ferdinand was championing the interests of God.[25] "Certainly there is no lack of voices encouraging Your Majesty to undertake this [the restitution of church lands]; you have so served God's cause that from your triumphant virtue other victors over the enemy can draw an example of piety. However, now that with the help of the Lord of Hosts the victorious arms of Your Majesty have driven the impious Dane from many usurped churches, we know that you will diligently take care that the Catholic religion will be restored to its rightful possession of them." Such papal language could only confirm Ferdinand's conviction that he was an instrument of divine providence for the restoration of Catholicism in Germany.

However, as Carlo Carafa reported from Vienna on March 3, 1627, there was still significant opposition at court to an aggressive policy of restitution.[26] The reasons came out clearly in a long memorandum drawn up by imperial councilors the previous autumn, after Christian of Denmark's defeat at Lutter but with the Upper Austrian peasants' rebellion fresh in mind and before the Peace of Pressburg with Bethlen in December.[27] The paper showed that its authors were seriously concerned for the long-term good of religion but that they conceived it differently from the militants. It pointed out the impossibility of conducting war on two fronts, that is, against Bethlen, whom the councilors feared the Turks would soon join, and against Denmark in the Lower Saxon Circle. Their clear preference was for an eventual campaign against the traditional enemy, the Turks. This would serve both religious and political goals, the liberation of Christians and the increase of the emperor's territory in Hungary. The attraction of a crusade against the Turks was still strong in Vienna, but for this, peace in the Empire was a prerequisite. Peace was also necessary if the emperor's efforts to consolidate his hold on the hereditary lands were to continue to be successful. For the councilors, Ferdinand's priority lay in his own lands.

To be sure, the report went on, the war in the Empire promoted religion, but one had to be careful not to use irreligious means to foster religion. Some councilors, at least, had reservations about the legality of an aggressive policy of restitution. Though they may have raised these doubts to cloak political objections, there did seem to be some uncertainty in Vienna about the legal situation. Ferdinand had sworn at his coronation to uphold the imperial constitution including the Religious Peace, the report asserted, and only recently he had renewed the Mühlhausen guarantee of 1620. The councilors favored the return of former church lands to the Church, but they wanted this goal pursued in a gradual manner, the legality of which would not be open to challenge by the Protestants. Especially did they want to avoid the appearance of a religious war, which would alienate the Protestant states, in particular Saxony. Nor did they feel Tilly's victory at Lutter had completely finished Denmark. Tilly himself had warned against assuming this. Even if the emperor did win a complete victory over his enemies in Germany, there were foreign powers who would not tolerate the situation and would certainly intervene against him; here the councilors obviously had France in mind. It would be better now to conciliate the states of Lower Saxony and split them from Denmark, then after forcing Christian's withdrawal from the Empire, to make peace with him and seek a solution of the Palatinate question. This plan would lead to peace in the Empire, create good will toward the emperor, allow for the piecemeal restitution of church lands, and prepare the way for a campaign in the east.

The Peace of Pressburg with Bethlen weakened somewhat the argument of the position paper, but the hesitation about policy regarding restitution remained. Lamormaini's stance at this time is not known. Carafa soon saw gains for the militants.[28] The successes of the campaign of 1627 helped dissipate many reservations.

Meanwhile, to the south several Swabian monasteries that had survived throughout the previous century renewed their endeavors to recover monastic foundations secularized by the Duke of Württemberg and other Protestant princes of the area. Heinrich von Knöringen, Bishop of Augsburg and a zealous Catholic militant, took up their cause. On February 21, 1627, the Bishop of Constance brought before the imperial aulic council the case against Württemberg for the restitution of the Abbey of Reichenbach in Hesse. An imperial decree of July 3 ordered restitution by the duke. To this decision was appended a list of seven other south German abbeys claimed by the Catholics and a request that the duke respond with his side of the question within two months. Before rendering a decision having such broad implications, however, Ferdinand wanted the advice of the Catholic electors. This he sought in a letter to them, also of July 3.[29]

During the summer of 1627, the preparations for the convention of Mühlhausen were in progress. The military picture improved consistently. As a result, both the emperor and the Catholic electors significantly escalated their goals in the weeks immediately preceding the convention. Now in the offing was the Edict of Restitution, Ferdinand's most fateful action during his reign as emperor.[30]

Stralendorf was selected to be the imperial representative at the coming convention. In late July the emperor still had reservations about the wisdom of an ambitious policy of restitution. The procurator of the Bursfeld Congregation of Benedictines had now come forward with a request having more ramifications than the case already pending of the seven south German monasteries. He sought the restoration of all the Benedictine monasteries lost to the Protestants in the dioceses of Lower Saxony since 1555. Writing to Stralendorf, Ferdinand indicated that those he had consulted had agreed that to honor the request was legal, that is, consonant with the imperial constitution. But he feared such action might be interpreted as a violation of the guarantee he had given at Mühlhausen as well as other assurances he had given the Protestants. This could make the achievement of peace more difficult. Stralendorf was instructed to raise the matter at Mühlhausen, at least with the delegates of the Catholic electors.[31] When he arrived there shortly before September 17, only the Bavarian delegation was on hand. Saxony, besides Mainz the only elector to appear in person, was awaiting the arrival of the other delegations in a small town several miles away. As more people turned up, Stralendorf could not help noticing the nervousness and fear Ferdinand's military strength generated in the Protestants.[32]

Then Stralendorf received from Vienna new instructions dated October 4.[33] The Catholic forces had fought for nine years, Ferdinand pointed out, above all for the glory of God, with little to show for it. Now that their victories had given them a clear advantage, the time had come to consider remedying the violations of the Religious Peace the Catholics had long endured, as well as restoring all the lands illegally taken from them.[34] This the emperor held to be "the great gain and fruit of the war." Ferdinand directed Stralendorf to explain this to the Catholic participants at Mühlhausen and to inquire what they considered the most suitable means to exploit the present God-given opportunity to right the long-standing wrongs done the Catholics. He was to inform them that "just as up to now we [Ferdinand] have never thought to let pass any chance to secure the restitution of church lands, neither do we intend now or in the future to have to bear the responsibility before posterity of having neglected or failed to exploit even the least opportunity." The instructions showed Ferdinand ready for action. Clearly he now had no doubts about the constitutionality of a vigorous restitution program; he did not mention the Mühlhausen guarantee.

Stralendorf in his response praised the emperor's zeal for the welfare of the Empire and the good of religion, and he expressed his confidence in divine assistance.[35] His enthusiasm was a little surprising, inasmuch as up to this point he seemed to be wary of Ferdinand's overplaying his hand. Only a few days before, he had encouraged the emperor to play down the religious element in his dealings with the states of the Lower Saxon Circle.[36] On October 22, four days after the convention formally opened, Stralendorf communicated the emperor's message confidentially to Mainz.[37]

Almost simultaneously, a similar shift toward a more activist policy took place in Munich and Mainz. Queried by Mainz concerning a common response by the four Catholic electors to the emperor's letter of July 3, Maximilian replied on September 7 that Ferdinand should order the restitution of the Swabian monasteries. "We think the opportunity presented us by God should be accepted and the course pointed out by him continued," he wrote. To the chagrin of some of his privy councilors, Maximilian was strongly influenced by his confessor, Contzen, who argued that the recovery of the lands was one of the goals of the war. Since they were fighting for God's cause, Contzen affirmed, the Lord would protect the Catholics from any enmity their action might stir among the Protestants. The new Archbishop-Elector of Mainz, Georg Friedrich von Greiffenklau, who had replaced the deceased Schweikardt, then made a decisive change in the common opinion of the electors. Going beyond the case of the seven Swabian monasteries, he advocated in the response he drew up for Ferdinand dated September 20, that the emperor render a decision regarding all the illegally confiscated church lands in the Empire. In the long run, peace could be attained only through a return to the

observance of the imperial constitution, which meant the Catholic interpretation of the Peace of Augsburg.[38]

No one in Munich showed any surprise at this substantial new development. Maximilian dispatched the opinion to Vienna on October 19,
his signature added to that of Mainz, Cologne, and Trier. His action was
easily explained. Only five days before he had sent new instructions to
Mühlhausen. His delegates there were told to initiate secret discussions
with the other Catholics about the method to recover all the church lands
secularized since 1555, not merely those in the Lower Saxon Circle with
which a prior instruction had dealt. Now was the providential moment,
Maximilian declared once again, to restore Catholicism to the place it
once enjoyed in the Empire. Neither Maximilian nor Mainz showed any
hesitation about the juridical propriety of their action. Both felt imperial
law including the Peace of Augsburg was on their side. The earlier Bavarian instruction had also outlined a position on the Mühlhausen guarantee.
According to it, the guarantee applied only to Saxony. Most other states
of the Lower Saxon Circle had forfeited it by taking up arms against the
emperor.[39] Implicit acceptance of this position, which would become a
common one, may explain the emperor's failure to mention the guarantee
in his instruction of October 4 for Stralendorf. Nor should it be forgotten
that the Mühlhausen guarantee was severely limited. It afforded protection only against the forceful restoration of imperial church lands, without a prior hearing, and only to those Protestants of the two Saxon
circles who had remained faithful to the emperor.

Thus, at almost the same time, the emperor, Maximilian, and Mainz
all arrived at the conviction that the time had come to implement the
Catholic view of the Peace of Augsburg and in so doing to reestablish
justice in the Empire. It was in Germany that the initiative for a policy of
general restitution originated, not in Rome with the pope or Vitelleschi.
All three princes saw God's providence clearly pointing in this direction
through the victories bestowed on the Catholic forces. Such a conver-
gence of views can scarcely have been an accident. Certainly it was
helped along by the news that the armies of Tilly and Wallenstein had
met on September 1 in Lauenburg and were preparing to march into
Denmark.[40] But we can speculate that the three confessors, Lamormaini,
Contzen, and Ziegler, had a hand in the development.

Lamormaini always claimed for himself a major role in the promulgation of the Edict,[41] but there appears to be no documentation for his
activity on its behalf this early, in contrast to his advocacy of individual
restitutions. As we have seen, in early 1626 he seems to have had some
reservations about the juridical correctness of a policy of general restitu-

tion. During the late summer and early autumn of 1627 Bohemian affairs engaged his attention. His subsequent ardent support of the Edict inclines one to believe that he supported it at this time and that his support was reflected in the instructions for Stralendorf; it seems doubtful, however, that the idea for the Edict originated with him.

Contzen and Ziegler probably played more important parts in the origins of the policy; the initiative for the Edict came from the states of the League. A response by Vitelleschi to Contzen's letters of August 29, September 2, and September 9 indicates that Contzen had sought support in Rome. Vitelleschi promised to do what he could to encourage the pope to stir the princes to undertake the restoration of the churches "in the manner you have suggested."[42] Contzen boldly urged the aggressive restitution of church lands. Two years previously he had done the same when Ziegler had come to Munich to propose Mainz's plan for a general restitution. It was in Mainz that the demand for the return of all illegally seized church lands was inserted into the common opinion of the Catholic electors. At Mühlhausen, then, accompanied by Ziegler, the new archbishop-elector championed the cause of a general restitution of ecclesiastical lands.[43]

Ziegler evaluated the outlook for a militant policy in a letter to nuncio Carafa in Cologne, dated October 18, the day the convention opened.[44] He did not display the same confident enthusiasm of either Maximilian's statements or the emperor's instruction. For Ziegler the policy was an obligation to be undertaken and was not without its risks. It was likely to unite many Lutheran princes under Saxony, who would then join forces with the Calvinist rebels and so prolong the war and suffering. On the other hand, wrote Ziegler hopefully, John George was an honest prince, who perhaps would eventually acknowledge the justice of the Catholic cause and who certainly recognized the danger implicit for all if agreements, in this case the Peace of Religion, were to be violated with impunity. "Finally, it consoles me that even if our resources are exhausted, we Catholics cherish a just cause. May God protect it. And if so great an evil is to be feared, nevertheless we must hope for this much good, that should we be compelled to take up arms by such pernicious arrangements [between Lutherans and Calvinists], John George having taken sides against a most just cause, we will finally see the elimination also of the Lutheran heresy from this earth and then a more secure triumph of the Catholic religion." He closed plaintively with the prayerful hope that with divine assistance the princes at Mühlhausen would find a way to peace and security for "our Germany."

At the conclusion of the Mühlhausen Convention, all the electors joined in four communications to the emperor in Prague. Besides, at

Stralendorf's request, the Catholic electors in separate, confidential communications stated their positions on issues on which they disagreed with Saxony and Brandenburg.[45] Their hand strengthened by the campaign of 1627, the Catholic electors won the consent of the two Protestants for the recommendation that Ferdinand render a decision on the mutual complaints of Catholics and Protestants on the outstanding ecclesiastical issues. The permanent peace of the Empire required that these complaints be settled according to the imperial constitution and the Peace of Augsburg. To this recommendation, however, was added at the insistence of Saxony and Brandenburg the unclear and controversial phrase, "to the extent and inasmuch as submission is made."[46] They were unwilling to turn the matter over to the emperor in a manner that would permit him to make decisions without some further, undefined cooperation of the imperial diet and/or the parties involved. In their confidential message to the emperor, however, in accordance with their still secret plans for restitution, the Catholic electors urged vigorously the restoration of all church property seized by the Protestants since 1555. For them the juridical case was closed. They wanted the emperor to act.[47]

All the electors recommended jointly that Frederick of the Palatinate be restored to a portion of his lands, provided he submitted formally to the emperor, consented to pay the war costs, and renounced his electoral title and lands, his Bohemian claims, and all alliances hostile to the Empire. But Saxony and Brandenburg would make no commitment on the fate of the electoral title and lands after the deaths of Frederick and Maximilian. Therefore the Catholic electors in a confidential memorandum for the emperor insisted that the electoral title remain permanently in the Munich line of the Wittelsbachs and that the recent gains of the Catholic religion be safeguarded in any lands restored to Frederick. All the electors agreed that the emperor should be entrusted with the preparation of the peace terms for Denmark, but they wanted at least some electoral participation in the negotiations.[48]

Needless to say, the above resolutions showed that the Catholic electors were willing to subordinate traditional fears of imperial authority to the interests of the restoration. This was also the case in their treatment of the Wallenstein issue, where they shared a common interest with the Protestant electors. The original draft of a joint electoral communication to Vienna called for the appointment of a new general, and it contained a veiled threat to take up arms against Wallenstein if matters were not remedied. When word of this reached Prague, Ferdinand dispatched a courier to Mühlhausen warning the electors not to infringe on his authority.[49] Maximilian himself felt the statement too strong, and at his initiative the two objectionable points were eliminated. The communication became just another complaint about the conduct of Wallenstein's army. Maximilian and the Catholic electors realized that a Catholic expansionist policy required the backing of a formidable military force. Moreover, a falling out with the emperor over Wallenstein was to be avoided if at all possible, since it would split the Catholic front at a time when unity was essential.[50]

Because the results of Mühlhausen had not completely satisfied him, Maximilian sent Preysing on a secret mission to Ferdinand in Prague in December to urge specific Bavarian goals. Maximilian sought the complete and final exclusion of Frederick from the electoral title. Secondly, he put forward a measure that would eventually find its way into the Edict in a modified form, the formal prohibition of Calvinism in the Empire. This, of course, would make any restoration of Frederick even more difficult. There was no legal problem involved, Preysing's message for the emperor read, since the Peace of Augsburg permitted only the Confession of Augsburg. Recent history in England, Holland, and France demonstrated that the Calvinists were a continual source of unrest in any land. So long as they were tolerated, there would be no genuine peace in Germany. Realizing that the other Catholic states might not be as enthusiastic as he was in this regard, Maximilian urged Ferdinand to present them with a fait accompli. Thirdly, Preysing repeated the demand for the restitution of church lands. It would increase the resources of the Catholics at the same time it fostered the cause of the Church. His message then added a new recommendation, the restoration of the Catholic religion in the imperial cities to the status it had enjoyed at the time of the Peace of Augsburg. Since then, many cities had prohibited the exercise of Catholicism or severely restricted it.

Maximilian rejected the Protestant claim that matters touching the Religious Peace could not be decided either by the emperor, a majority vote in the imperial diet, or the imperial cameral tribunal in Speyer, but had to be agreed upon by the parties involved. Negotiations had been conducted interminably. Now was the time for action. Otherwise the Catholics would repeat the mistake of Charles V, who had wrongly thought a conciliatory policy after the War of the League of Schmalkalden would lead to agreement.[51]

Vienna was highly pleased with the outcome of Mühlhausen. The outstanding differences between Ferdinand and especially the Catholic electors seemed to have been eliminated or at least greatly reduced. The way appeared open for a much freer exercise of imperial authority in the interest of Church and Empire as Vienna understood it. Still a note of caution remained in the position papers prepared in January for the emperor by Stralendorf with the collaboration of Trautmannsdorf and

Abbot Anton.[52] They did favor an activist policy. They admitted that God's power had enabled Ferdinand to obtain victories the political councilors could never have foreseen. But they quietly warned that a dangerous war could result if Ferdinand attempted precipitously to secure the objectives outlined by the Catholic electors. They advocated moderate terms for Denmark and cautioned against pursuing "absolute victory." New triumphs would always call forth new enemies hostile to the growth of imperial power. Vienna's first priority must be a firm guarantee of the imperial succession for the King of Hungary, and Ferdinand must be careful not to alienate Saxony and Brandenburg, certainly not before the succession was assured. There was also need for a clearer commitment from the Catholic electors to support Ferdinand should war ensue when he attempted to carry out the projected decree regarding church lands. Meanwhile, in the opinion of the three, the aulic council should begin work on the decree by looking into the grievances over the observance of the Religious Peace and by investigating the legal situation. Ferdinand himself had already assigned this task to the council.[53]

Lamormaini was exultant over the results of Mühlhausen, but he was careful to keep his thoughts from Carafa, who was also in Prague. Carafa reported the satisfaction of the court with the outcome, but he only slowly acquired specific information. He noted the increase in authority Mühlhausen meant for the emperor, and he remarked that there was little thought of peace in Prague.[54] The nuncio puzzled over remarks Lamormaini made to him shortly before Christmas. More encouragement from the pope would be an inspiration for both emperor and Catholic princes, Lamormaini asserted, thus taking up a theme familiar to Carafa. Carafa countered by explaining the difficult financial situation of the pope and his many obligations. Lamormaini then made it clear that it was not so much a matter of money or troops but of some clear sign that the pope as well as the emperor stood behind the German Catholics in their "*gloriosa impresa*," a term, incidentally, reminiscent of the Spanish Armada. Carafa pointed to the zeal of the pope but did not know precisely at what Lamormaini was driving.[55]

In his dispatch of December 22, Carafa included a message of Lamormaini for Barberini that gave expression to the confessor's enthusiasm but still did not reveal directly what he was after. "The one and only thought of the Emperor," Lamormaini wrote, "is to return his provinces, his kingdoms, and all Germany to the Catholic faith and the Catholic Church." In time, Lamormaini continued, he would bring to Rome's attention the means envisioned to this goal. Lamormaini wanted the pope to have a major share in Ferdinand's design for the glory of God and the Roman Church, "for whose authority we struggle with beasts in these northern parts." The words embodied the spirit of the new Jesuit Church in Vienna. But Lamormaini did seem a little unsure of his plan. He asked for prayers.

> Some have judged my zeal for the House of the Lord to be a passion and less ordered affection. May God be propitious to us and direct all to the honor of his Most Holy Name and the confusion of the demon of darkness. He who knows his [the demon's] innumerable deceits is wise, he who escapes them is humble and holy, he who knows them but cannot elude them because of the evil of the times but bears them nevertheless and protects himself with the help of divine grace, that person is patient and prudent. O wisdom, come to teach us.[56]

Lamormaini seemed to hope that he was included in the third category of persons. The prayer to divine wisdom would come naturally to his lips since it was a theme of the liturgy as Christmas approached.

Lamormaini sought to organize Jesuit resources for a venture into new territory. He asked Vitelleschi to order prayers throughout the Society for a major decision to be made by the imperial council in the course of the winter. He requested that priests be prepared for missionary work in the areas soon to be recovered in Lower Saxony, and he promoted, unsuccessfully, the construction of a new Jesuit novitiate in Prague that would help meet the need for more men. Vitelleschi had to remind him in his zeal not to recommend men to the emperor for assignments without first consulting the provincial superior. Already Lamormaini had worked out a program for the spread of Jesuit colleges in Lower Saxony.[57]

Carafa turned to the subject of the restitution of church lands in his report of February 9. Surprisingly, he did not show much enthusiasm for the proposed measures about which he was not fully informed. He had told privy councilors that he would like to see them extended to those lands secularized before 1552, that is, those protected by the Peace of Religion. What seemed to concern Carafa most was the emperor's alleged intent to apply part of the recovered lands to the payment of his war costs. To this idea, the nuncio reported, he had shown himself firmly opposed.[58] The contrast with his colleague in Cologne was noteworthy.

In the meantime, Barberini had instructed Carafa to find out from Lamormaini what the pope could do to satisfy the emperor and improve relations. Rome now had new reason for harmony with Ferdinand. Upon being approached anew by the nuncio, Lamormaini treated him with what Carafa called his customary reserve and referred him to Vitelleschi. But this did not satisfy the nuncio. Finally, after further prodding, Lamormaini frankly told Carafa what ought to be done to dispel the widespread impression, so harmful to the necessary Catholic unity, that the pope and emperor were not on good terms. Urban should send a papal brief to Ferdinand praising the emperor's zeal and piety, promising "to protect and support him in such glorious undertakings (*Imprese così gloriose*), and furthermore, showing that he wished to defer to him in the arrangements that would be necessary after the recovery of so many ecclesiastical principalities and lands." This was still too vague for Carafa, so Lamormaini spelled it out. Ferdinand wanted to use the revenue of those recovered church lands "for whom the titleholder was not known" to found colleges and support religious orders in the regained ecclesiastical principalities.[59] In other words, Ferdinand and Lamormaini wanted the pope to support the Edict explicitly and to allow them to use some of the recovered revenues to endow Jesuit colleges. One can well understand Lamormaini's reluctance to say this clearly to Carafa. The dispute over the university in Prague and the disposition of the Bohemian church lands was still very much alive.

A Carafa dispatch in mid-February revealed one reason for Rome's increased interest in good relations with Ferdinand. The Patriarch of Aquileia had died, thus rekindling a controversy involving the emperor, Venice, and the Roman Curia that dated back to the fifteenth century. Since that time, when the patriarchate had lost its secular jurisdiction, it exercised ecclesiastical jurisdiction in Austrian as well as Venetian territory. The Austrian rulers resented the regular appointment of a Venetian noble to the patriarchate. Archduke Carl, Ferdinand's father, had succeeded in obtaining the erection of a relatively independent archdiaconate in Gorizia but not the bishopric he desired. Ferdinand now ordered his officials not to allow a new patriarch to exercise any functions within imperial territory until all imperial rights were recognized. Carafa sought assistance from Lamormaini. He wrote Barberini that the only way the problem could be resolved was through an appeal to the emperor's conscience, which depended upon the Jesuits and especially upon Lamormaini. The matter of Aquileia was to remain a point of friction with the Curia during the rest of Ferdinand's reign. The emperor secured the elevation of Gorizia to a nearly autonomous vicariate of Aquileia, but not the creation of a bishopric.[60]

But in North Italy a more serious crisis had arisen. On Christmas Day 1627, Vincenzo Gonzaga, ruler of Mantua and Montferrat, imperial fiefs, died without leaving any direct heir. Spain and France would both soon support their own candidates for the strategically crucial territories. Here the papacy had a major interest. The dispute over the Mantuan lands, that is Mantua and Montferrat, would greatly influence the papal attitude toward the emperor, not to mention the career of Carlo Carafa.

4. New Commitments, 1628–1629

erdinand's power peaked in the spring of 1628. The imperial and League armies dominated the north of Germany, where enemy troops were scarcely to be found. At Mühlhausen the previous autumn the electors, especially the Catholic electors, had deferred to the emperor to a surprising degree. He achieved a much-desired goal in February 1628 when he redeemed Upper Austria by granting Maximilian the Upper Palatinate and the Lower Palatinate east of the Rhine as compensation for his war costs and by promising explicitly to bestow the electoral title on his heirs.[1] Until late spring Ferdinand resided in Prague, where Wallenstein also spent much of the winter. Both were elated by the triumphs of the last two years. During the winter of 1627–28 plans for Habsburg domination of the Baltic were again on the agenda, and there was talk of an eventual crusade against the Turks. Lamormaini was enthusiastic. His scenario for a Catholic restoration seemed to be moving toward realization.

But the scene was about to change. The unity among Catholic princes considered so necessary for the restoration was soon to receive two setbacks. As the figure of Wallenstein loomed larger and larger, the electors led by Maximilian again grew alarmed and remounted their campaign against him. Then the disputed succession in Mantua and Montferrat stirred up the seemingly eternal conflict between Spain and France and soon dragged the emperor into it. Lamormaini's efforts during 1628 were directed as much to the avoidance of war in Italy as to the promotion of the Edict of Restitution. The fate of two cities pointed to the course of future events. Ominously aided by Sweden, the crucial city of Stralsund on the Baltic coast resisted imperial troops until Wallenstein was forced to raise his siege in July. This gave heart to the Protestants and made clearer than ever the intent of Sweden to intervene in the Empire. On October 28, 1628, French forces finally took the Huguenot stronghold of La Rochelle, thus freeing Richelieu to assist the French claimant in Mantua and to return to a vigorous anti-Habsburg policy. To the northeast in Poland and to the northwest in the Netherlands were further disturbing developments. By late March 1629, when the Edict of Restitution was promulgated, the political outlook was much less favor-

able for the German Catholics than it had been in the aftermath of
Mühlhausen.

During 1628 plans went ahead for the restoration of church lands.
Trautmannsdorf was dispatched to Munich in February to obtain a pledge
from Maximilian that League troops would assist the emperor in the
implementation of the Edict should this prove necessary. Maximilian
gave Trautmannsdorf the desired assurance while adding a stipulation
that vexed Vienna: provided Wallenstein's soldiers did not exhaust the
available resources. While in Munich Trautmannsdorf revealed some
hesitation about policy when he suggested it might be wiser to postpone any decision about the Religious Peace until after the conclusion of
peace with Denmark. Maximilian rejected the idea, and there was no
follow-up.[2]

Some at court favored rapid action in the Lower Saxon Circle. According to Carlo Carafa, writing in early February, Wallenstein proposed to
seize the bishoprics there, evict the Protestant canons, and with the consent of the Holy See, appoint new bishops. Lamormaini, it seems, shared
this view, and both of them continued to advocate the nomination of
Leopold William to Halberstadt and Magdeburg.[3] Pier Luigi Carafa, the
nuncio in Cologne, urged the proscription of the incumbents of the Lower
Saxon bishoprics; they all had participated in rebellious activity, he affirmed, and he stressed the need for haste. A diet was in the offing, he
thought, and should it decide to pardon offenders, the recovery of the
lands might be out of reach.[4] His report, combined with Lamormaini's
forceful request for papal support conveyed through Carlo Carafa, may
well have prompted Urban's remarks in a brief to the emperor recommending the claims of the clergy of the Bishopric of Basel.[5] "Not only
does the Catholic religion triumph in your victories, but the ecclesiastical
order finds in them its firmest support. The churches of Germany hope to
regain their former extent and endowment now that the Emperor Ferdinand is victorious. One word from the imperial authority is able to extort
from the belly of heretical impiety the sacred riches which it devoured
with such rapacity."

The privy council wanted to proceed with caution. There were still
doubts about legality. Some councilors, including Eggenberg according
to Carlo Carafa, thought it wise to attempt to deal first with the cathedral
chapters. Indeed, the intimidated chapter of Halberstadt did elect Leopold William bishop on January 3, 1628.[6] Generally, the councilors
preferred to wait until the emperor was ready to take action on the policy
of restitution called for by the Catholic electors at Mühlhausen. Acting in

concert with them, he would be assured of their support and obviate any suspicions they had of imperial policy.[7] Tension with Maximilian was already rising over recovered bishoprics. During Preysing's visit to Prague in December, Ferdinand and Carlo Carafa had assured him that the Archbishopric of Bremen was reserved for a Bavarian candidate; however, during the summer at the behest of Vienna the Curia promised it to Leopold William. Maximilian was upset at what appeared to be a grab for power by Vienna.[8] Complications with Saxony threatened when, to forestall the appointment of Leopold William, the chapter of Magdeburg postulated August of Saxony, John George's son, as the new administrator, and he accepted.[9] Aggressive action was liable to alienate Saxony.

The work of the aulic council preparing the Edict remained shrouded in secrecy, lest the Protestants suspect what was in process. In April, Jakob Löffler, vice chancellor of Württemberg, arrived in Prague to make the duke's case for the retention of the monasteries claimed by the Catholics. His argument impressed the council, and he secured the postponement of a final decision except in the case of Reichenbach itself, which had to be surrendered. Lamormaini, he felt, was his chief adversary. He also sensed that some form of general restitution was in the offing.[10] But the council was having legal scruples. They reported on June 15 that they needed more documentation before they could recommend a decision. The emperor and privy council approved their writing for legal help to Mainz, who kept the imperial archives, and to Leonhard Götz, the Bishop of Lavant in Inner Austria, who had served as Ferdinand's chancellor in Graz. But Ferdinand insisted the council continue working on the decree themselves in the meantime. Neither source proved fruitful.[11]

Wallenstein had returned to Bohemia in mid-December 1627. The emperor, accompanied by Lamormaini, went out to meet him at Brandeis.[12] A sense of triumph filled emperor and general. Great plans were in the air. The previous May Ferdinand had bestowed the Duchy of Sagan, in Silesia, on Wallenstein. Now in Prague, with Eggenberg's support, Wallenstein sought for himself the imperial Duchy of Mecklenburg, partly on the grounds that this would assure him a firm base of operations in the Baltic. Ferdinand startled the imperial princes on February 1 by conferring the duchy conditionally on Wallenstein as a pledge of payment for the enormous sums the general had advanced for the imperial army. The next year Wallenstein would become full-fledged Duke of Mecklenburg. Thus Ferdinand in a questionable exercise of imperial authority transferred the duchy from the two incumbents, Dukes Adolf Friedrich and Johann Albrecht, who shared the inheritance, to one who was in the eyes of the imperial princes a newcomer, an upstart, and increasingly a threat. Vienna justified the deprivation of the two dukes by pointing to the aid they had tendered Christian of Denmark despite a warning from the emperor. Sources at court unfriendly to Wallenstein— one thinks of Magni—contended that ecclesiastics supported his pursuit of Mecklenburg because he promised them the restitution of church lands and the foundation of colleges.[13]

Negotiations with Spain had revived in the summer of 1627 toward the creation of a Habsburg fleet in the Baltic and North Seas. It was to be employed against the Danes and especially against the Dutch, and the hope was eventually to bring the commerce of the area into Habsburg hands. Talks were initiated from the imperial side with the Hanseatic cities, whose cooperation remained a prerequisite for any such venture. On April 21, Ferdinand named Wallenstein "General of the Oceanic and Baltic Seas"; the title pointed to grandiose intentions even after Spain lost interest in the project because of the Catholic electors' opposition to involvement in war against the Dutch. A week later Wallenstein received the designation "Supreme Captain-General" of the imperial armies and with it unprecedented control over the troops, including the right of appointment to many offices usually reserved to the emperor's selection. Some in Vienna including Wallenstein and Lamormaini were projecting a campaign against the Turks once German affairs were in order.[14]

Once again, Magni was responsible for intensifying Maximilian's suspicion of Wallenstein, this time in the so-called Capuchin Relations he sent to Munich in April and May 1628. Undoubtedly exaggerated, his reports were plausible, and they possessed some foundation in fact. Magni painted Wallenstein as a man devoid of any religion, clever, deceitful, and characterized above all by an insatiable lust for power. He had won over Lamormaini and the Jesuits by his benefactions to the Society. His final goals were the establishment of an absolute monarchy in Germany and after the death of the present emperor, the imperial crown for himself. Already, according to Magni, he controlled policy at the imperial court, where no one dared oppose him openly. The only check to his designs was a strong, dependable army in the hands of the League.

Upon reception of the Relations, Maximilian, instinctively distrustful of Wallenstein, alerted Mainz and Tilly to the danger. War between the imperial and League armies seemed possible, and a League convention was summoned for Bingen on the Rhine in late June to discuss the situation. Even before learning of the Relations, Mainz had written the emperor that the electors certainly would not fix the succession on young Ferdinand by electing him King of the Romans unless the excesses of the imperial army were checked. Maximilian sent his high chancellor, Joachim von Donnersberg, to the imperial court to emphasize how desperate the quartering of imperial troops was making many German states.

Donnersberg was to do this, however, in a manner typical of Maximilian. He was to make it clear that he only brought forward the complaints of others, not Maximilian's. At Bingen Maximilian and Mainz seriously laid plans to turn the League army against the imperial troops unless their demands for a reduction of the latter were met, and they agreed to invite Saxony and Brandenburg to join them. The Catholic electors now envisioned the dismissal of the general.[15]

Maximilian sought to enlist Lamormaini's aid in his efforts to tame Wallenstein. Donnersberg was to seek him out and impress upon him the danger Wallenstein represented for the Catholic cause. Maximilian also tried to bring influence to bear on Lamormaini through Contzen and Vitelleschi. Vitelleschi wrote Contzen that he had been "terrified" by his letters of early June.[16] "We would hope that the Emperor in his prudence and piety, once he has been alerted to the situation, will dispel every danger and that Father William Lamormaini will not fail in his duty. Still, we cannot even call to mind without shuddering how near lies the treacherous rock on which the fruit of so many victories could quickly be shattered and dashed." Vitelleschi promised to make strenuous efforts to prevent a disastrous split among the Catholics. After trying unsuccessfully to bring the matter to Lamormaini's attention through an unidentified third party, he raised it in a manner typical of his dealings with Lamormaini.[17]

> At the end of my letter I cannot but communicate to Your Reverence what a trustworthy man, well-versed in German affairs, has written us about rumors circulating there concerning Your Reverence and others close to the Emperor as the exasperation of many increases amid the public disasters of Germany. I know for sure that these things are not true and that they are repeated about Your Reverence and others without basis in fact. Yet it is of great importance to the Catholic cause and to that of His Imperial Majesty himself that the causes of such suspicions and grievances, which seem to be nothing other than the suffering which such a large army imposes on all Germany, [be dealt with]. Thus I wanted to inform you of these rumors in nearly the same words they came to me, so that you can consider whether your efforts might be able to remedy these public ills. Please read the material on the attached page. But I beseech you not to think that I consider it true or that as a result of it I am suspicious of you or any other persons.

The accompanying paper is missing, but its content was certainly reflected in two subsequent letters of Vitelleschi to Contzen affirming that

Wallenstein's army burdened unbearably the lands of Germany and was feared equally by Catholic friend and Protestant foe.[18]

There is no direct evidence of any response of Lamormaini to either the letter of Vitelleschi or the efforts of Maximilian. Obviously, he had an interest in keeping quiet any action he undertook. Ferdinand did compel Wallenstein to reduce significantly the troops he had under arms, especially in Upper Germany. At the end of September Contzen asserted, perhaps too optimistically, that the difficulty had been met. The extent to which this was due to Lamormaini or to the more direct pressures from Maximilian and Mainz is not clear.[19]

"Not for a few months but for years, Mantua was the name that occurred most often in the papers of the European chanceries."[20] The Mantuan inheritance included the Duchy of Mantua to the southeast of Milan, and to the southwest, lodged between Milan and the Duchy of Savoy, the Marquisate of Montferrat, on whose territory stood the imposing fortress of Casale dominating the Upper Po Valley. The dispute that broke out over the succession in the Mantuan lands quickly escalated into a European power struggle and became the focus of attention for the imperial court. Lamormaini would readily have agreed with the historians who have seen Ferdinand's greatest mistake in allowing himself to be sucked into the vortex of the Mantuan problem.[21] Certainly, Ferdinand's intervention in the affair distracted him from his program in Germany and created another source of dissension with the Catholic electors, who saw in it his pursuit of Habsburg rather than imperial interests.

Two chief claimants quickly appeared for the inheritance of Duke Vincenzo Gonzaga, who had died childless Christmas night 1627. The first was Duke Charles of Nevers, a member of the French branch of the Gonzagas, whom Vincenzo on his deathbed had designated his heir. As a French vassal, Nevers was opposed by Spain because he was almost certain to become a vehicle for French influence in Italy. Spain intended to divide Montferrat with its short-term ally, the Duke of Savoy, who had a remote claim on the marquisate, and then to place a friendly prince in Mantua. This would further consolidate its position in Northern Italy and so strengthen the whole Spanish empire. For this reason Spain supported its Gonzaga client, Ferrante, Duke of Guastalla, a small Italian principality. He had a less direct claim than Nevers but contended his rival had forfeited his claim by assisting the emperor's enemies for a time. Since the two territories were still fiefs of the Empire, both sides at least initially looked to the emperor for favorable adjudication. Through the years Spain had generously aided Ferdinand in Germany but had never succeeded in obtaining his assistance in the war against the Dutch, mostly because of the opposition of the German princes. Now, in the matter of Mantua and Italy, Spain made it clear that payment was due.[22]

Charles of Nevers, who had been forewarned of the impending death of Duke Vincenzo, arrived in Mantua on January 17, 1628, with a small band of troops, and he quickly gained control of the government. The very next day he dispatched the Bishop of Mantua, Vincenzo Agnelli-Soardi, to plead his case with the emperor in Prague. One of the allies he could count on there was the Empress Eleonora, herself a Gonzaga and sister of the deceased duke. Before Agnelli-Soardi's arrival, Ferdinand assured the permanent Mantuan resident at his court that he would not permit any preemptive action against Nevers. But the Spanish ambassador, the Marquis of Aytona, pushed Ferdinand either to sequester the disputed territories until a decision was reached or to permit the occupation of Montferrat by a joint Spanish-Savoyan force that would forestall further action by Nevers. Philip IV wrote Ferdinand that Don Gonzalo de Cordoba, Spanish Governor of Milan, had been ordered to assist in the implementation of an imperial sequester and should Nevers not accept it, to support Guastalla against him. Guastalla's son, Don Cesare, arrived in Prague on February 13 to represent his father. He claimed to respect imperial authority, which had been disparaged by Nevers' precipitate seizure of power in Mantua. Acting on the recommendation of the aulic and privy councils, Ferdinand decreed a sequester of the two territories on April 1 and soon sent an imperial commissioner to Mantua, where he arrived on May 2. In the meantime, Don Gonzalo, without explicit instructions from Madrid and without imperial approval, occupied a portion of Montferrat in the emperor's name and began the siege of Casale. Nevers refused to obey any imperial commissioner until these forces withdrew. So matters stood.[23]

Upon his arrival in Prague, Agnelli-Soardi reported that one of the first to visit him was the nuncio Carafa, who assured him of papal support. Indeed, Pope Urban had a profound interest in the Mantuan question. Because of his fear of Habsburg domination in Italy, he favored Nevers' candidacy and secretly promoted it. Above all, he feared the outbreak of war in Italy with its ravages and horrors plus the infection of heresy that a large influx of imperial troops would bring. Memories of the Sack of Rome the previous century were still alive. Thus the first goal of papal foreign policy became the peaceful solution of the Mantuan issue in favor of Nevers.[24] This called for intensive diplomatic activity at the imperial court.

On April 15 an extraordinary nuncio, Giovanni Battista Pallotto, was dispatched to Prague. The Curia realized the importance of Lamormaini, for whom Pallotto brought a special brief, and it was well aware of his friction with Carafa.[25] Vitelleschi alerted Lamormaini that Carafa's reports had convinced many in the Curia that the confessor was responsible for Ferdinand's failure to act more favorably in the matters of Mantua and Aquileia, and he encouraged Lamormaini to aid Pallotto in every way possible. Vitelleschi noted the new nuncio's partiality for the Society, and he declared that he himself could not have chosen a more suitable man for the post. In great confidence, he went on to inform Lamormaini that in all likelihood Pallotto would remain as permanent nuncio and Carafa would be recalled.[26] This turned out to be the case. Carafa departed for the south in September, victim of his inability to work with Lamormaini.[27]

Urban in his brief implored Lamormaini to urge the emperor to employ his arms for the subjugation of heresy in the north and not to bring fire and sword into Italy. "What devotee of the Heavenly Kingdom would [not] be tormented to see those arms bathed in Italian blood that could quickly be run through the throats of the terrified supporters of impiety? ... What greater glory in the Christian Commonwealth could be compared with that of the Austrian princes than if their triumphant power be decorated by these two titles and they be remembered by history as conquerors of heresy and guardians of the peace?" As his confessor, Lamormaini himself would share in the glory of Ferdinand.

Such an appeal corresponded to Lamormaini's own ideas. Moreover, he may have reasoned that the situation in Mantua could be used to secure greater papal support for his own plans. Pallotto was pleased with the warm reception he received from Lamormaini, who visited him on May 26, the day after he arrived in Prague. Lamormaini assured him of his assistance, Pallotto reported, and he guaranteed him that no imperial soldiers would be sent to Italy. Lamormaini also spoke to him of the campaign against the Turks then being talked about in Prague, to which Lamormaini hoped imperial troops would be diverted after the conclusion of matters in Germany. Implicit was a request for papal support. Barberini recognized this and honored it with a vague expression of willingness to help, communicated through Pallotto.[28]

Lamormaini's intentions became clearer in his formal response to Rome on July 15. He wanted above all unity between pope and emperor. He assured Urban he would do all he could consonant with his state and office to keep imperial troops out of Italy and to have them employed against the German heretics.[29] But the pope would also have to do his part. This was evident in Lamormaini's letters to Cardinal Barberini and Francesco Paolucci, Secretary of the Congregation for the Interpretation of the Council of Trent and an important figure in the Curia for German affairs. Lamormaini evidently knew him from his stay in Rome. To Barberini, Lamormaini emphasized the desire of all the privy councilors for peace. But for this, he added, it was necessary that Nevers accept the sequester and recognize the emperor's right to decide the dispute. For Lamormaini the basic issue in Italy was increasingly the recognition of imperial authority. Strongly implied in the letter was the pope's obligation to secure the submission of Nevers. Once this was obtained, "all will be forced back into the bottle whence it had come."[30]

The theme of the letter to Paolucci was again the need for cooperation between pope and emperor.[31] Lamormaini stressed the importance of a favorable solution to the controversy over the university in Prague. Those hostile to it were merely jealous of the Jesuits. Responding to Roman criticism, he disclaimed responsibility for the emperor's position in the Aquileia affair; it had originated before he became confessor and lay outside his competence. Helpful also would be papal acquiescence in the emperor's plans for the disposition of recovered church lands. Nothing could so impede the restoration in Germany like a feeling among the Germans that pope and emperor were not in harmony.

> All Catholics and non-Catholics as well, even the obdurate, witness the Emperor's nearly continual, miraculous victories and the wonderful manner in which the Lord frustrates all the designs and schemes conceived against him and reduces them to nothing (many are unaware of the full extent of these designs, but in time all will know of them and marvel). As a result, they have concluded that it is impossible for the Emperor not to be most beloved and most acceptable to God. Should they [pope and emperor] fall out, they would conclude the contrary about the Roman Pontiff. But we ought to establish his authority in the innermost hearts of all, if we desire to lead them back to the Catholic Church, the sheepfold of Christ, as we ought.

The "one and only consideration" that kept him at court was his desire to assist the emperor in seizing the opportunity to restore the faith in Germany. Yet Lamormaini again revealed some hesitation about the righteousness of his course. "But this war, savage, boundless, interminable, devours everything. Unless after such great suffering in Germany there follows a restoration of the Church and religion, I will grieve to have lived in these times and to have seen the devastation which I see around me and about which people write me from every side."

The following month, at Pallotto's behest, Lamormaini drew up for Barberini a list of imperial requests to which the emperor felt the pope had not responded.[32] Besides the expected decision on the university in

Prague and the recognition of imperial rights in Aquileia, several directly religious matters appeared on Lamormaini's list. The emperor had petitioned in 1625 that the still controversial doctrine of the Immaculate Conception of the Blessed Virgin Mary be declared a dogma of the faith. Both Ferdinand and Lamormaini saw in this a way to thank the Blessed Mother for her assistance in his victories.[33] Ferdinand had asked that the veneration of a number of saints for whom he had special devotion be extended to the whole Church; all had a particular significance for his Counterreformation activity and included the Jesuits Ignatius Loyola and Francis Xavier, King Stephen of Hungary (975–1038), and the Bohemians Adalbert (956–997) and Wenceslaus (907–929). Nothing was said about the disposition of church lands, presumably because the pope had just agreed to the appointment of Leopold William to Bremen and the application to the war effort of ten years' revenues from the Palatinate monasteries.[34] Several months later, Rome also consented in principle to the bestowal of Magdeburg on Leopold William, a move Lamormaini interpreted as another sign of papal good will.[35]

However, there were limits to what Urban could and would do to conciliate the emperor. Barberini protested it was beyond the power of Rome to secure the obedience of Nevers. The pope had attempted to do so, he wrote Pallotto for Lamormaini, but without success. Rome would not yield in the dispute over the university in Prague, since it was a matter of conscience and church law. Nor, Barberini continued, could the pope oblige the emperor in questions of dogma, which really did not concern him. And where would it all end if every ruler wanted to insert five new saints into the universal liturgical calendar?[36]

Throughout 1628 Lamormaini pursued a consistent policy in the Mantuan question. He enunciated it for Pallotto in July and elaborated it further for the benefit of the Spanish court early the next year.[37] He made no attempt to decide the merits of the case for either Nevers or Guastalla, he advised Pallotto. That lay beyond his competence. It was Ferdinand's task to determine where justice lay. His purpose, Lamormaini asserted, was to convince both sides to refrain from hostilities and to await the emperor's decision. For this reason he had tried, at the emperor's behest, to convince the Bishop of Mantua that Nevers should obey the sequester. To the same end, he had written the rector of the Jesuit college in Mantua, urging him to influence Nevers himself. Lamormaini left no doubt about his condemnation of the invasion of Montferrat, undertaken ostensibly in the emperor's name by the forces of de Cordoba and the Duke of Savoy. This was clearly unjust, because they were taking the law into their own hands before Ferdinand rendered a decision. "If someone kills another in the middle of the town square, and this is obvious to all, still the assailant may be executed justly only by the authority of a judge after his case has been heard and decided. How am I able to declare they die justly who fall by the sword in this war, when the judge has not yet decided on whose side justice is to be found? . . . "

Lamormaini's notion of justice took on a typical twist in the communication he prepared to satisfy his critics in Madrid. He declared openly that he had told Ferdinand that he could justly intervene militarily in the dispute only on condition that theologians affirmed the war to be just in terms of divine law. It was not enough that jurists and political councilors judged the war to be just from the perspective of human law, since there were many actions considered just in the eyes of men that were not so in the eyes of God. Even if the war should be judged necessary and just, Lamormaini went on, he had besought the emperor to pursue the resolution of the conflict through peaceful means. In this he was only following the example of many saints and religious persons who had convinced Christian rulers to battle infidels rather than one another. War among Catholics would only destroy the common front against the heretics and cost the Catholics the blessing of God, which had brought them so many victories. It was the devil himself, the source of all heresy, who fomented conflict among Catholics in order to prevent the restoration of Catholicism in Germany.

Both Pallotto and Agnelli-Soardi recognized the success of Lamormaini's efforts. In July Pallotto attributed to him the failure of Ferdinand to place Nevers under the ban or to send troops to Italy.[38] Against the Spanish party led by Eggenberg stood Lamormaini and Empress Eleonora, whom he urged to show the fortitude of the Old Testament heroine Esther.[39] The Spaniards grew angrier with him as it became evident that Ferdinand's hesitation increased the likelihood of active French intervention once Richelieu finished with the Huguenots at La Rochelle. Time was on Richelieu's side. In mid-July Lamormaini had a stormy interview with the Spanish and Savoyan ambassadors. He told them outright their action was unjust. Aytona was furious. "A cleric is supposed to pray and not to meddle in such matters," he shouted. Eggenberg threatened to resign. Ferdinand refused to consider this and asked his minister to admonish Lamormaini. The confessor maintained his position, affirming that he did not act as confessor but as a Christian man who was obliged to do all he could to prevent injustice. He told Pallotto "that since His Majesty and Prince Eggenberg had entrusted their souls to him, he would not have satisfied his obligations as a human being toward peace and morality, if in such serious matters he had permitted them to run to the precipice without warning them." Both genuinely feared God, he continued, and were serious about the salvation of their souls. They would be angry for a time, but his words would have their effect.[40]

Despite the hopes that remained alive in Vienna, gradually it became evident that Nevers would not submit to an imperial decision, especially after he received assurances of support from France in early June.[41] This weakened Lamormaini's position. On October 28 La Rochelle fell, and this made war appear inevitable to Vienna. By mid-January 1629, in the depths of the winter, French troops were on their way over the Alps to Italy, with Richelieu and the king himself at their head. They raised de Cordoba's siege of Casale in March, forced Savoy to abandon Spain in favor of an alliance with France, and then waited. In April imperial troops departed to clear the way for an invasion through the Swiss Alpine passes. They went with Lamormaini's blessing, since Ferdinand could not allow the French to dictate to him.[42] But there was still hope to forestall a direct military confrontation.

Lamormaini's vigorous opposition to Spanish policy in Italy during 1628 earned him the enduring hostility of Madrid. In November of that year Olivares accused him through Franz Christoph von Khevenhiller, the imperial ambassador there, of unduly interfering in Italian affairs and of speaking and writing against the King of Spain. Particularly insulting had been his words to Aytona. Lamormaini in his response protested his loyalty to the king as a subject—he was a native of Spanish Luxembourg—and as a member of the Society of Jesus, which stood greatly in his debt.[43] But he defended his hostility to imperial intervention in Italy for reasons we have already seen, the need to await a judicial decision and to preserve a united Catholic front. War had to be avoided. Barberini and Urban VIII himself were pleased with his answer, and they let him know this through Pallotto.[44] Vitelleschi found the letter "prudently and religiously written," but because he feared reprisals against the Spanish Jesuits, he begged Lamormaini to be more cautious in his language. Rumors of his alleged outbursts against the King of Spain and de Cordoba were circulating in Rome.[45]

Olivares took it upon himself to answer Lamormaini through Khevenhiller. He acknowledged Lamormaini's good will but claimed he was simply uninformed, and it was the duty of a confessor to be well informed. There was justification for war. Spanish jurists and theologians had approved the Spanish action in Montferrat, he argued, thus repeating a point Ferdinand himself had already made with Lamormaini. The true enemies of heresy were the Spaniards, who kept it far from their borders. Once the French established roots in Italy, heresy would inevitably follow, since the major part of the French nation was Calvinist. How could the Jesuits permit this? In his most telling argument, Olivares reminded Lamormaini of the disobedience of Nevers, his refusal to recognize imperial authority.[46] Lamormaini wanted to respond once again, but fearful of a drawn-out polemic that would benefit no one, Ferdinand forbade it.[47]

Meanwhile, in September 1628 a joint letter to the emperor from five south German prelates, the bishops of Bamberg, Würzburg, Eichstätt, Constance, and Augsburg, had moved forward the plans for the restitution of church property.[48] The bishops lamented the exhaustion of their land and people by the heavy quartering of troops. Only the hope for the restoration of church lands had enabled them to put up with it thus far, and now that prospect was dimming. Time and souls were being lost. The bishops, who were not officially privy to the request made by the electors at Mühlhausen, urgently recommended a general decision requiring the restitution of all church lands confiscated since 1552. For the aulic council to deal with cases individually would take forever. Now was the time to act.

Asked for an opinion by Ferdinand, the aulic council responded favorably to the bishops' petition, but the privy council hesitated.[49] The main question was political: whether the time was opportune to undertake the restitutions. The aulic council took for granted the Catholic interpretation of the Peace of Augsburg. The Protestant claim that the provisions of the Peace regarding mediate church lands were in need of further interpretation was simply false, they asserted. Protestant seizure of such lands after 1552 was obviously illegal. The time had arrived to redress the grievances the Catholics had protested since the days of Maximilian II. Ferdinand possessed the necessary military force. As emperor he was bound to protect the interests of the exploited, as Defender of the Church, to protect its rights. His election capitulation stipulated that he uphold the Peace of Augsburg, and the Catholic electors affirmed his authority to act.

The privy council, however, felt there should first be more discussion of the papers submitted by the electors at the conclusion of Mühlhausen. Aware as they were of the tension with the electors over Wallenstein and the prospect of imperial aid to Spain in Italy, they were evidently concerned to involve the Catholic electors in the decision as much as possible and to guarantee the emperor their effective support. One can only surmise that the hesitation of the privy council was also due to some further doubts about the timeliness of the measure. Still, on September 23 Carafa, whose source was Trautmannsdorf, expected a decision any day.[50] Georg Schönhainz, a Premonstratensian in Vienna looking after the interests of his order, wrote on October 20 that Lamormaini had assured him there was no longer any doubt about a general restitution.[51] But before acting it was decided once again to procure the opinions of the two most prominent Catholic electors, Maximilian and Mainz. On October 25 a tentative draft of the Edict was sent to them for their evaluation along with covering letters from Stralendorf and Ferdinand.[52]

The preamble of the text affirmed the now familiar position that the emperor's God-given victories enabled him to restore peace in the Empire and, beyond that, to uproot the source of so much civil strife through a return to the observance of the Peace of Augsburg. The responsibility of his office left him no alternative. The text then turned to the legal case for the decree. It asserted a position certainly not shared by Saxony or Brandenburg when it declared, without noting any qualifications, that at Mühlhausen the electors had recommended that the emperor restore the observance of the imperial constitution and the Religious Peace. Moreover, as early as the imperial diet of 1576 the Protestant party had acknowledged the emperor's right to act on his own to pacify the Empire, that is, they had submitted.[53] But then, as if there were still some doubt about his right to render a decision, the text went on to make a point that would be frequently repeated in the coming years, namely, that Ferdinand intended only to enforce those provisions of the Peace of Augsburg which were so clear as to be beyond dispute. In this way he obviously hoped to circumvent the prohibition written into the Peace itself against either party's assuming the right of interpretation.

There followed a lengthy explanation of the three points of the Peace the emperor intended to implement. It reflected the longstanding Catholic understanding of the Peace. Then came the core of the decree. All territorial church lands seized since the Treaty of Passau in 1552 were subject to restitution. Second, prelates who had left the Catholic Church could not hold imperial church lands. In other words, according to the Ecclesiastical Reservation even the vote of a cathedral chapter could not deprive the Church of imperial church lands. Third, the ecclesiastical states had the same right to enforce uniformity of religion as did other states, that is, the Declaration of Ferdinand was invalid. As to implementation, imperial commissioners were to be dispatched to hear the claims of the despoiled, and upon their demand, lands were to be surrendered.

In his accompanying letter Ferdinand once again affirmed his obligation not to let slip the providential opportunity to establish permanent peace in the Empire.[54] Then he put two important questions to the electors. Were they willing to supply effective assistance for the enforcement of the decree should this prove necessary? Where should implementation begin? The emperor clearly wanted to start with Magdeburg, for which the chapter had postulated August of Saxony. Lamormaini strongly favored this course.[55] But it would increase the chances of a clash with John George of Saxony. Stralendorf raised two further points in his letter, one of which was also related to Saxony.[56] Should imperial church lands confiscated prior to Passau also be reclaimed, as some were urging? Should the prohibition of Calvinism in the Empire be reaffirmed, as Maximilian wanted? Stralendorf seemed to hope for a negative answer in both cases, since this would render both Saxony and Brandenburg more amenable. There was some evidence that the three bishoprics Saxony held, Meissen, Merseburg, and Naumburg, were, in fact, imperial lands seized before 1552.[57] George William was a Calvinist in a state populated mostly by Lutherans.

While the imperial ministers in Vienna were working on the Edict, Bishop Knöringen of Augsburg took important action in support of it. In June 1628, when the aulic councilors appeared a little unsure of the Catholic legal stance, Knöringen commissioned Paul Laymann, Jesuit professor of moral theology and canon law at the University of Dillingen, to write a defense of the Catholic interpretation of the Peace of Augsburg. The resultant book, *The Way to Peace* (*Pacis Compositio*), which was published anonymously, came to be known as "the Dillingen book" because of its place of publication. It was a rigidly Catholic commentary on the Peace of Augsburg and was to the Edict of Restitution as theory to practice. Laymann argued forcefully and with great clarity the Catholic understanding of the Peace, but he did so in a low key free of all polemical passion and thus much more effectively.[58]

The fascicles of the book began to come off the press in early January 1629. They were then shipped to Johann Grenzing, an aulic councilor in Vienna, for distribution to other councilors there. Grenzing was a member of the prince-bishop's council in Augsburg and his representative in Vienna. He had been admitted to the aulic council in April 1628 and to full-fledged membership in August.[59] During the following fall and winter he took part in many sessions of the council dealing with the restitution issue, and there can be little doubt that Knöringen planted him there to advance the bishop's position. Stralendorf subsequently showed great enthusiasm for *The Way to Peace*, partly because of its value as a "white book" for the Edict. Another reason, we can surmise, was that the arguments of Laymann, communicated to Vienna first through Grenzing and then through the book, helped to remove any remaining hesitation about the legality of the Edict. Vienna could honestly claim that it was merely the "clear letter" of the Peace of Augsburg. Ferdinand need have no scruple that his policy of restitution was in conflict with any obligation he had undertaken to uphold the imperial constitution. On the contrary, the Edict answered to his duty to administer justice in the Empire. There is no reason to doubt Lamormaini's annotation in his copy of *The Virtues of Ferdinand II, Emperor of the Romans*, that Ferdinand considered his efforts to restore Catholicism in the Empire to be in accord with its constitution.[60]

The responses of Maximilian and Mainz arrived in Vienna about January 11, and they were the subject of a session of the aulic council almost immediately. The council was satisfied with the assurance of League support in the event the Edict met with resistance. The two electors suggested but did not urge the publication of a list of all the ecclesiastical lands that would be affected by the decree. This the council rejected. The virtue of the coming decree was precisely that it was a general solution chosen to obviate the delays and disputes that would arise in the treatment of individual cases. To draw up such a list before the issuance of the Edict would postpone it indefinitely. Neither elector felt the time was ripe to move for the restoration of imperial church lands confiscated before 1552. Though a strict interpretation of the Peace of Augsburg according to Laymann would have justified this, they and the emperor held back, largely out of fear of Saxony's reaction. Maximilian initially was reluctant to begin enforcement with Magdeburg for the same reason, but against his better judgment he acquiesced in Mainz's desire to go along with the emperor.[61]

Two further recommendations of the electors, neither of them new, required more time for deliberation: that Calvinism be expressly prohibited in the Empire and that the Edict be extended to the imperial cities. There is no clear evidence indicating where Lamormaini stood on these two points. But a hard line and specifically the application of the Edict to the cities was consistently advocated by the new aulic councilor, Justus Gebhardt, a native of Upper Lusatia who became a Catholic in 1627 under Lamormaini's influence and subsequently remained close to him.[62] In any event, the aulic council opposed the prohibition on political and legal grounds. It would stir up more resistance and would make it appear as if the emperor were doing more than just returning to the observance of the Religious Peace, since many Calvinists showed no hesitation in subscribing to the Confession of Augsburg. But Maximilian had written to Stralendorf specifically to urge this prohibition, and in spite of the council's position, the vice chancellor inserted it into the Edict in a weakened form. It was stated explicitly that only the Confession of Augsburg was permitted in the Empire and all other sects were forbidden.

Both political and legal considerations also carried weight in the discussion of the recommendation that the Edict encompass the cities too. The argument was put forth that the cities themselves did not possess direct territorial jurisdiction (*jus territorii*) and consequently could not

regulate religion in their area; only the emperor could do this. Laymann
had asserted this position.[63] But Stralendorf himself argued that the
Peace of Religion had not dealt clearly with the cities. Since their status
could not be determined by an appeal to its obvious intent, the Edict
should leave them aside. Nor could the emperor afford to alienate a large
number of cities at once. It would be wiser to deal with them individually.[64] On March 6, then, the privy council approved the decision of the
aulic council to take no action on the cities in the coming Edict.[65]

The emperor made the final decision to issue the Edict of Restitution at
that same privy council session.[66] The only major change in the text sent
the two electors the previous fall was that regarding Calvinism. The
sessions of the aulic council for the rest of the month dealt with the
promulgation and enforcement of the Edict. Under date of March 6, it
was finally published on March 25, precisely the date on which a large
number of copies of *The Way to Peace* were placed on sale at the annual
Frankfurt book fair. Early in March Stralendorf had ordered them for
Frankfurt. He counted on Laymann's book to win popular support for
the imperial government's position that the Edict merely implemented
the obvious intent of the Peace of Augsburg.[67]

Lamormaini immediately notified Cardinal Barberini of the publication of the Edict, "a deed truly worthy of this Emperor."[68] The confessor
was jubilant to see his plans for Catholicism in the Empire take this step
toward realization. "No Roman Pontiff since the time of Charlemagne
has received such a harvest of joys from Germany, so that we can call
Urban VIII blessed since he witnesses such gains for the Catholic religion." Lamormaini was confident Ferdinand would lead all Germany
back to the faith, provided a propitious Lord gave Ferdinand ten more
years of life and enabled him to keep peace in Italy. A month earlier
Lamormaini had written to Cardinal Dietrichstein, "Now is the time to
lead back souls into the storehouse of the Church, to bring back into the
sheepfold the sheep that have been astray for over a century."[69] If the
effort was to be successful, there could be no involvement in new wars.
Lamormaini's letters to Vitelleschi breathed the same enthusiasm when
he spoke of "a much different type of Empire in the future." The superior
general shared his hopes, but he could not prevent from creeping into his
response the fear that the emperor was overextending himself, precisely
in view of the troubles in Italy.[70]

There was no serious, open opposition in Vienna to the Edict's main
thrust, the recovery of church lands. But neither was there great enthusiasm for it among the leading figures at court apart from Lamormaini.
The initiative and the principal momentum for it came from the Catholic
electors and the ecclesiastical princes. Stralendorf's support was cautious

and perhaps strongly encouraged by Maximilian's advocacy of the Edict. Trautmannsdorf, as we have seen, showed some reservations about policy on his mission to Munich in February 1628. The only individual to warn Ferdinand clearly about the dangers of the coming Edict was Ramboldo Collalto, a privy councilor and president of the war council since 1624, who gave his opinion at Ferdinand's request. His stance was the obverse of Lamormaini's and corresponded to the Spanish position once they learned of the measure Ferdinand planned. Collalto warned that the Edict would only stir up hostility to the emperor in Germany and eventually incite a religious war. This would undermine the emperor's authority and distract him from Italy, where Collalto strongly advocated imperial intervention.[71]

Eggenberg appears to have been unhappy with the Edict, but this does not mean he actively opposed it. Illness forced him to cut down on his activity in the winter of 1628–29, and he was not present at the privy council session of March 6, when Ferdinand gave his formal approval to the Edict. In mid-March he complained to the Bishop of Mantua that Ferdinand had not consulted him recently as he usually did even when he was indisposed, and he spoke of retirement.[72] At the time Ferdinand had not yet committed troops to Italy, so that Lamormaini was winning on that issue too. Probably Eggenberg and perhaps other privy councilors felt that Ferdinand had made up his mind on the Edict and it was useless to resist. Lamormaini's influence was predominant.

Wallenstein's position is more difficult than usual to ascertain for the period from July 1628 to July 1629, when he was much occupied with the reorganization of his new acquisition, the Duchy of Mecklenburg.[73] In the summer of 1628 he began to draw back from the expansionist policy envisioned the previous winter in Prague. This was due, it seems, to an increasing awareness of the limitations of imperial power plus a desire to consolidate his own position in Mecklenburg. Wallenstein was sensitive to the danger posed by Protestant Sweden from the northeast, where the ambitious Gustav Adolph had been at war with Poland since 1621. As early as March 1627, Wallenstein had sent a contingent of troops to assist King Sigismund of Poland and help keep Gustav Adolph busy in the east; he dispatched a small army to Poland in June 1629 under his finest general, the Protestant Hans Georg von Arnim. Meanwhile, Sweden had come to the assistance of Stralsund, the Protestant city on the Baltic that had successfully defied Wallenstein during the campaign of 1627. In July 1628 after a long siege, Wallenstein was compelled to withdraw in what was a great victory for the Protestants. Shortly afterward the Hanseatic cities finally rejected the plans for imperial naval and commercial expansion in the Baltic. They had never been enthusiastic about them anyway. To the northwest, the position of the Spaniards deteriorated in the course of 1628. That autumn the Dutch captured the annual Spanish treasure fleet for the first time. Wallenstein viewed the situation with alarm when the Dutch, going over to the offensive, began the siege of the great fortress of 's Hertogenbusch in April 1629.

By late 1628 the changing political situation had convinced Wallenstein of the need for a compromise peace with Denmark. He became the prime mover on the imperial side for the Peace of Lübeck, which was concluded with King Christian in late May and soon ratified by Ferdinand. Christian retained his kingdom intact. Imperial troops withdrew from the Danish territory they had occupied, and no indemnity was demanded. Christian, for his part, renounced his claims and those of his sons to prince-bishoprics in Lower Saxony, and he promised not to meddle in imperial affairs.[74]

Wallenstein's awareness of the need to retrench was one reason he dissented from Lamormaini on the Edict and except for a brief span, agreed with him on Italian policy. From the start Wallenstein had advocated the recovery of bishoprics in Lower Saxony from princes disloyal to the emperor. These territories he considered bases of imperial power and sources of revenue. But he did not favor any attempt to seize church lands from Protestant states that had remained faithful to Ferdinand. That would only encourage Protestant resistance, especially at the grassroots level, cause trouble among his own Protestant officers, and generally embitter the conflict. Thus he did not favor the Edict. But he made no effort to hinder its issuance, and the extent to which his view was known in Vienna is unclear.[75] In late May 1629, Wallenstein assured Lamormaini of his interest in locating recovered church foundations suitable for the endowment of Jesuit colleges. "For I realize that such are a means to the glory of God and the advancement of the Catholic religion,"[76] he wrote the confessor. Such a message was not an endorsement of the Edict, but Lamormaini was likely to read it as such and Wallenstein may well have realized this.

From the first outbreak of the dispute over the Mantuan succession, Wallenstein appears to have differed with Eggenberg and opposed imperial intervention, though as we shall see later, he took pains to keep his opposition from becoming public. He felt the cause of Nevers to be just. Above all, he feared France. Ferdinand's interference in Italy would only provoke France and so garner him another enemy, a powerful one at that. During the winter of 1628–29, Spanish promises of a principality in Venetian territory lured Wallenstein briefly into support of a campaign against Venice, which was allied with Nevers. But by April he had returned to a policy of nonintervention.[77]

What stance did Rome assume toward the Edict of Restitution? To answer this, a distinction must be made between papal policy as it was in reality and as it was quite understandably perceived in Vienna. It does seem that Urban never consciously gave the Edict explicit support. On the other hand, one can easily understand the exasperation of Ferdinand and the imperial court when after the Edict's manifest failure, Urban disclaimed any responsibility for it. Rome had steadily encouraged Ferdinand to exploit his victories to recover ecclesiastical lands, especially the bishoprics in Lower Saxony. In March 1628 when the aulic council was working on the Edict, Urban expressed in vigorous language his hope for the restoration of the churches in Germany "to their former extent and endowment."[78] Pallotto and Pier Luigi Carafa, on the scene in Germany, tended to be much more favorable to imperial policy than the Curia and consequently gave the impression of greater papal support for the Edict than was merited. Lamormaini for one was only too glad to receive this impression. Thanks to the adroit diplomacy of the two nuncios the differences that arose between pope and emperor over the disposition of the recovered ecclesiastical lands never reached a crisis. Both nuncios genuinely sympathized with the goals of Ferdinand and Lamormaini and were concerned to avoid any papal-imperial confrontation that might obstruct their achievement. Pallotto, in addition, looked to Lamormaini as the main force in Vienna for peace in Italy, and thus was inclined to accommodate him on other issues.

As preparations for the Edict became known in Rome, both Cardinal Giovanni Bandini, Prefect of the Propaganda, and Barberini wanted to appoint papal commissioners who would oversee the restitution of ecclesiastical property.[79] On February 17, 1629, Barberini informed Pallotto that the pope had decided to entrust Pier Luigi Carafa with the authority to supervise the restitutions and that he and Pallotto should work together.[80] Neither nuncio was happy with this arrangement, and both told Rome so. Pallotto thought that in the circumstances it would only stir suspicions and generally cause trouble.[81] Vienna considered the Edict essentially a temporal affair and foresaw implementation by imperial commissioners. Hence Pallotto considered it "absolutely necessary" to await publication of the Edict and then when problems arose in the disposition of the lands, to insinuate the need to assign a papal representative to resolve them. From Cologne Pier Luigi Carafa, who was highly sensitive to the political situation, complained that the role assigned him would require long journeys and prolonged absence from the courts of

Cologne and Liège, where he was needed to defend papal privileges.[82]
Later an unknown correspondent advised the Curia to grant broad faculties including the authority to transfer ecclesiastical property to Franz
Wilhelm von Wartenberg, the energetic cousin of Maximilian who had
succeeded the deceased Cardinal Hohenzollern as Bishop of Osnabrück
and was one of the imperial commissioners for the area. After praising
Wartenberg's zeal and devotion to the Holy See, the author argued that
the papal representative had to be a German, since the Germans suspected Italians and feared being deceived by them. This was one reason
why Cardinal Cajetan had failed in his effort to win back Luther at the
Diet of Augsburg in 1518.[83]

Shortly after the promulgation of the Edict, Pallotto informed the Curia
that Vienna expected the pope to make "some notable demonstration of
joy" at Ferdinand's heroic and generous action on behalf of the faith.[84]
For Vienna the issuance of the Edict overshadowed the conquest of La
Rochelle, which Urban had celebrated by attending in person a solemn
Te Deum of Thanksgiving in the French church in Rome. We can only
speculate that Lamormaini had his hand in this or, as Barberini himself
suspected,[85] in Ferdinand's claim to the right of presentation to all secular benefices—bishoprics, canonries, prelatures—the first time they were
awarded after their recovery by virtue of the Edict. Toward this demand
Pallotto reported he had taken a conciliatory line indicating that such a
pious emperor would certainly nominate only candidates whom the pope
would have no trouble approving.

Barberini's reply was not enthusiastic. He let Pallotto know that Urban
would dispatch "an affectionate and laudatory" brief to Ferdinand and
would praise his zeal and magnanimity in the next consistory.[86] But to
celebrate as at the fall of La Rochelle would be to celebrate at the start
rather than at the end of the campaign. An important reason for papal
reserve was juridical. The papacy had never approved the Peace of Augsburg with the recognition and concessions it granted the heretics. The
pope would not now sanction "either in words or deeds" any measure
that even implicitly acknowledged the validity of the Religious Peace, as
did the Edict. Particular care would be given to this, Barberini continued,
in the composition of the brief for Ferdinand.

Nor would Barberini hear of allowing Ferdinand's claim to the presentation of benefices or of guaranteeing approval of imperial appointments.
Gradually, then, Pallotto worked out an understanding with Vienna.
First Eggenberg let him know that Ferdinand would not claim the right
of presentation to all the recovered benefices. Pallotto then told the emperor that the pope would give Pier Luigi Carafa the broad faculties
necessary to decide cases involving the assignment of benefices and would

instruct him to cooperate with the imperial commissioners. Nothing was said about the title of papal commissioner for the restitution of church lands. Pallotto made this commitment before he had final approval from Rome, but the pope ratified it.[87] Still, difficulties persisted about the disposition of benefices. Pallotto advised Rome to give Ferdinand satisfaction on appointments while not yielding on the principle, a procedure that suited Rome's concern for juridical form. Eggenberg confirmed that the emperor did not seek the recognition of a right. What he did expect was "that the said churches be provided with apt and well-deserving subjects, whom His Majesty will propose and for whom he will intercede." The emperor's merits and the genuine welfare of the Church in Germany required as much.[88]

Papal policy on the Edict was subtle, complex, and sometimes simply unclear. Among those formulating and implementing it, the right hand did not always know what the left hand was doing. Urban certainly wanted the restitution of church property, but he was anxious not to compromise the Church's juridical position. He was not the one to surrender ecclesiastical rights, though he had no intention of openly challenging the validity of the Peace of Augsburg, as some extremists wanted.[89] Urban's reluctance to support the Edict wholeheartedly may also have come from the realization that it was a vast overextension of imperial power that was bound to provoke a reaction no less extreme. A number of Catholics feared precisely this. Enthusiastic, unqualified support for the Edict would have morally committed the pope to generous subsidies, especially if things went badly. Urban had other uses for papal funds. He feared the expansion of Habsburg power in Italy and Europe. The successful implementation of the Edict would have meant an enormous increase in imperial power and prestige. Urban's efforts to secure the recognition of ecclesiastical rights in the distribution of recovered lands was dictated in part by his unwillingness to allow the emperor control over so much property.[90]

However, Urban did have to make a demonstration of support for the Edict. In a brief of May 5, 1629, in which he later claimed an enthusiastic secretary may have exaggerated his feelings, Urban wrote,[91]

> Our soul has been filled with a marvelous joy by the recent Edict of Your Majesty which orders the sectaries to return to the priestly estate the ecclesiastical lands they have long held and in which are contained other provisions (which we bless) that remove obstacles that have up to now held back the Catholic restoration. When we reported these developments in secret consistory [of the cardinals] the apostolic senate rejoiced and praised your well-deserving piety,

desirous that the reward of your noble action will be [more] victories. Thus heresy will have learned that the gates of hell do not
prevail against the church which legions of angels and the arms of
powerful Austria so happily defend. How closely you have thereby
bound the soul of the pontiff to yourself . . . our nuncio will declare
to Your Majesty in a more magnificent fashion.

The Scriptural reference to Christ's promise to Peter that "the gates of
hell will not prevail against it," that is, the Church (Matt. 16:18), emphasized the pope's association of Ferdinand's arms with the divine protection promised the Church; pope and emperor were united, the emperor
championing the Church led by Urban, Peter's successor. Barberini sent a
letter in the same tone.[92] Pallotto reported that the emperor was happy
with the letters from Rome and the events in consistory.[93] Indeed, it
would have taken a mind of unusual subtlety not to see in them firm
papal support for the Edict.

5. Complications, 1629–1630

he Edict of Restitution soon became the central issue of German politics. Though rumors of a general reformation had been rife, the Edict caught the Protestants by surprise as it was meant to do. Immediately, loyal Protestant states began to protest and implicitly to threaten their defection if the emperor and Catholic princes persisted in their design. Thus there came into sharper focus still the problem for the Catholics of how to conciliate the moderate Protestant princes, especially Saxony, without compromising the program for a Catholic restoration. The Edict came at a time when the emperor had to fear the Catholic electors' deepening discontent with Wallenstein, when he could expect new threats from the Dutch and especially the Swedes, and when he was becoming increasingly involved in Italy at the risk of war with France. Some Austrian historians have, in fact, insinuated that the initiative for the Edict came from Richelieu, who intended it precisely to sow disruption and division in Germany.[1] By the middle of 1629, both the emperor and the Catholic electors had come to feel that an electoral convention in which the emperor would also participate would be the best means to deal with the problems faced by the Empire and to establish a stable peace. But the parties had widely different conceptions of specific solutions. Finally, in March 1630, Mainz summoned the convention for June 3 in Regensburg.[2]

In the concrete, the Edict pointed to a massive transfer of property from the Protestant party to the Catholic. First, there were the imperial archbishoprics and bishoprics in the Lower Saxon and Westphalian Circles. Magdeburg, Bremen, and Halberstadt had already been assigned to Leopold William by emperor and pope. Minden and Verden were also liable to restitution, the principal claimant being Franz Wilhelm von Wartenberg, Bishop of Osnabrück.[3] Schwerin was already incorporated into Wallenstein's Mecklenburg.[4] The fate of Ratzeburg, Lübeck, and Kamin, the last-named in Pomerania in the Upper Saxon Circle, was still uncertain, but they were subject to restitution according to the terms of the Edict. The Mühlhausen guarantee seemed to protect Saxony's bishoprics, Meissen, Merseburg, and Naumburg, at least for the time being. Brandenburg's three bishoprics appeared to lie outside the reach of the

Edict, having been mediatized and confiscated before 1552, but even they stood on at least one list in Vienna of bishoprics to be reclaimed.[5]

Scarcely less important were the nearly five hundred territorial ecclesiastical foundations, particularly monasteries and convents but also churches and other benefices, encompassed by the Edict. Many of these had been fully integrated into the states in which they were located, so that their loss threatened serious disruption. Especially hard hit was Württemberg in the southwest, where the Catholics quickly claimed fourteen large monasteries and thirty-six convents, and took rapid and rigorous measures to enforce their claims. In the north, Brunswick-Wolfenbüttel in Lower Saxony was most seriously affected.[6]

But to appreciate the full impact of the Edict, we must consider not only the lands it directly affected and the enforcement actually undertaken but also the forebodings it aroused among the Protestants should the emperor retain the upper hand. For this Laymann's *The Way to Peace* is of major importance. There was little Catholic sentiment in Germany for the overthrow of the Peace of Augsburg itself, but the militant interpretation of the Peace found in Laymann's book was enough to strike fear in Protestant hearts. Later it was said that Gustav Adolph wanted to hang three men whose names began with *L*, Lamormaini, Laymann, and Laurentius Forer, who assisted in the writing of the Dillingen Book.[7] For the Catholics the book became a storehouse of further claims, some of which, as we have seen, were discussed in Vienna prior to the issuance of the Edict. As his principle of interpreting the Peace of Religion, Laymann took the dictum "whatever is not found to have been granted [explicitly] ought to be considered forbidden." This was the case because the Catholics enjoyed free exercise of religion in the Empire by virtue of the ancient and general law, the Protestants merely by virtue of privilege and particular law. In all doubtful instances the Catholics were to be favored. Thus, even if the Protestants had not consented to the Ecclesiastical Reservation as some claimed, they were still bound to surrender all imperial church lands, whether confiscated before or after 1552, because this corresponded to the general law of the Empire, and the Peace made no further provision about imperial church lands.[8] Laymann conceded that the territorial church lands taken by the Protestants before 1552 were to remain with them. However, he then asserted the far-reaching claim that in these areas the ecclesiastical jurisdiction of the bishops remained in effect in all matters not directly concerned with the points of the Confession of Augsburg; thus, for example, Catholic marriage law was still valid there.[9] Such a claim undermined the jurisdiction over ecclesiastical affairs acquired and developed by the Protestant states since the Reformation.

The likelihood of war in Italy plus the persisting state of war with

Denmark suggested to Vienna the desirability of a special arrangement with Saxony even before John George had the chance to react to the Edict. On April 3, 1629, Ferdinand wrote Maximilian and Mainz that Saxony might be urging his claim to Magdeburg merely to trade it off for renewed guarantees for the three bishoprics that long ago had been integrated into his crown lands. Should some kind of accommodation be proposed to him?[10] Maximilian, who was often more rigid than Ferdinand, hesitated, fearful of further Protestant demands for special consideration that this settlement might stimulate. Shortly afterwards he complained to Ferdinand, not for the last time, about security in Vienna. Somehow it had leaked out that the Catholic electors had approved the Edict before its publication. This could only cause them difficulty, he lamented.[11] While Maximilian was as firmly committed to the Edict as Ferdinand, he expected the emperor to bear the full onus of its unpopularity among the Protestants. Such an attitude did not endear him to Vienna.

Before the two electors could respond to the emperor's query, Saxony's first protest, written immediately upon his reception of the Edict, arrived in Vienna. The Edict was illegal, John George affirmed. The electors at Mühlhausen had never empowered the emperor to make a decision about the grievances regarding the Religious Peace and then to enforce it without any further reference to them. Everything he possessed, John George contended vigorously, he possessed with a clear legal title. He was neither a robber nor a spoliator. No complaints had ever been lodged against him. Was he now to be condemned without a hearing? This prospect seemed to excite him the most. Alluding to the Bohemian rebellion, John George reminded Ferdinand that he had come to the aid of the House of Austria in its hour of need, at considerable cost to himself. Was this his reward? Shortly afterwards he sent on to Vienna a detailed defense of his legal position. Similar protests went to Mainz and Maximilian, warning them that instead of serving as a foundation for peace, the Edict was liable to ignite a conflagration that would not easily be put out.[12]

The imperial councilors, in an opinion prepared the following month, rejected Saxony's legal case and any general compromise on the Edict while recommending indulgence toward the elector himself.[13] The legal arguments, they felt, had been more than sufficiently aired. Ferdinand had no intention of introducing a new Religious Peace or even interpreting the present one. He was merely enforcing the Peace as it stood. Nearly everyone now agreed, they thought, that "the words of the Religious Peace [were] so clear that from them alone a decision could be made about the grievances." The councilors then turned to political considerations. They realized that the Edict might not lead to peace and that it might cause considerable suffering. "Nevertheless, Your Imperial Majesty is sworn to Justice and for its sake has God given you Crown and Scepter. It must prevail. Injustice cannot be allowed to run its course." Ferdinand's honor and reputation, the obligations of his office, his conscience all counseled firmness on the Edict, including the refusal to suspend it until an imperial diet could be held, as had been suggested.

But the councilors advised special consideration for Saxony where this could be given without sacrificing principle. The emperor should reassure John George that he had no intention of departing from the Mühlhausen promise of 1620. This guaranteed there would be no attempt to enforce the Edict in the case of church lands he long held (which excluded Magdeburg) without a prior legal process. In fact, the councilors recommended that Ferdinand refrain in practice from any attempt to apply the Edict to Saxony. This would help retain the loyalty of John George, split him from the other Protestants, and facilitate enforcement elsewhere. John George should also be reassured that Ferdinand had no intention of extirpating Protestantism in Germany, as the Edict apparently led him to fear. But Ferdinand should indicate that he expected John George to uphold the Edict just as he had always firmly supported the Religious Peace. The councilors closed by suggesting that Ferdinand send a special emissary to Dresden to explain the imperial position and to encourage John George to attend in person the electoral convention that the emperor hoped would soon be called.

A group of theologians were then asked for their views on the response to Saxony. These were four Jesuits, Lamormaini, Heinrich Philippi, Lukas Fanini, confessor of the Empress Eleonora since 1624, and Michael Sumerckher, professor of theology and Lamormaini's successor as rector of the college in Vienna. In their joint paper they affirmed their allegiance to the Peace of Augsburg.[14] They thought as did Laymann that the reformation of religion could be carried out within its bounds; consequently they consciously opposed the position on the Peace of "some Catholics," meaning perhaps the Propaganda in Rome and possibly the Bishop of Augsburg, whose stand will soon be examined. Ferdinand could promise John George in good conscience that he would neither propose nor undertake anything contrary to the Peace at the anticipated electoral convention. He had promised as much at his election to the imperial dignity. The theologians stated that Ferdinand could keep and confirm explicitly the promise made to Saxony in 1620 in order to prevent the unrest and disruption the Catholic electors feared if he did not do so. Provided no new promises were made "that conflicted with justice, the Catholic religion, the emperor's office or obligations," Ferdinand could legitimately suspend any steps to implement the Edict against Saxony. That the theologians had their eye on the eventual restitution of the three Saxon bishoprics was clear. They reasoned that the enforcement of justice could be postponed to a more opportune time should it involve serious dangers, as in the present case. "A short time is taken for no time," they noted.

After consultation with Mainz and Maximilian, Ferdinand dispatched Trautmannsdorf to Dresden on June 28. The response he carried to John George was substantially what the councilors had recommended.[15] Trautmannsdorf was to make a particular effort to convince Saxony to come in person to the projected electoral convention. His absence would make considerably more difficult the achievement of one of the emperor's chief goals for the convention, the election to King of the Romans of young Ferdinand. But Saxony was not at all satisfied with Trautmannsdorf's mission. John George wanted further guarantees for the three bishoprics. When he complained that Magdeburg was to be snatched from his son, he raised a subject Trautmannsdorf had been instructed to avoid unless he was compelled to defend the emperor's position. John George's second major grievance was the burden of supporting imperial troops. As long as his complaints about the Edict and the soldiers were not remedied, the elector would not attend the convention in person.[16]

Upon his return, Trautmannsdorf made several recommendations, all but one of which the committee of councilors approved. He advised immediate enforcement of the Edict against Magdeburg, since he thought it certain Saxony would not resist. But the councilors were not so sure and feared in particular the city of Magdeburg. Some efforts, they agreed, were to be made to ease the pressure of the troops on Saxony. But unable to see how Saxony might be given further guarantees for the bishoprics, they advised querying Maximilian and Mainz once again.[17] But the two electors had little to suggest beyond a greater solemnization of the Mühlhausen promise.[18]

Meanwhile Wallenstein let a Saxon delegation know in August that he did not share the plans for restitution of Lamormaini and, he added, Eggenberg. He assured delegates of the Hanseatic cities they had nothing to fear from the Edict. His views were now certainly known in Vienna. Even Pallotto noted in March 1630 his efforts to moderate the Edict for Saxony and Brandenburg.[19] Once he established headquarters in Memmingen in south Germany that spring, he did not energetically attempt to enforce the Edict in Württemberg as had been expected of him.[20]

Saxon protests to the emperor and remonstrances with the Catholic electors continued right up to the opening of the electoral convention. But they had little effect. John George showed that he could not be isolated from other Protestants when he increasingly took up the cause of

the Lutheran citizens of Augsburg, with whom he particularly sympathized, as they tried to ward off a rigorous Counterreformation. In December 1629, Ferdinand assured Saxony that he had every intention of
observing the imperial laws and implementing them in such a way that
no one would have cause for complaint, but this was little consolation.[21]
The Catholic electors did not weaken in supporting Ferdinand on the
Edict, even though they saw themselves gradually pushed in the direction
of Saxony by the Wallenstein and foreign policy issues.

The four Jesuit theologians also gave their opinion, in the paper already mentioned, on two other matters related to the Edict. In the first
case they turned out to be more liberal than their Bavarian colleague,
Contzen. The question was whether Ferdinand could show special consideration to the administrators of Bremen and Minden, Duke Johann
Friedrich of Holstein and Duke Christian of Brunswick-Lüneburg, respectively. Both had demonstrated their loyalty during the Danish war,
according to the imperial councilors. The theologians readily agreed to
the proposal that the two dukes be granted a pension from the revenues
of the lands, provided they surrendered them voluntarily. "For it all
works to the good of the Church, which the dukes serve wittingly or
unwittingly by remaining with Ferdinand and fighting on his side." Subsequently, Ferdinand requested an opinion from Maximilian, going so
far as to suggest a separation of the spiritual from the temporal administration and the retention of the latter by the dukes until they died.
This his councilors had recommended, Ferdinand wrote, without men-
tioning the theologians. Both dukes were elderly, as was Duke August
of Brunswick-Lüneburg, Administrator of Ratzeburg, who was also
included in the proposal now. They could not be expected to live long.[22]

Acting on the advice of Contzen, Maximilian rejected any separation
of temporal from spiritual administration out of hand, and he couched
his agreement to the payment of pensions in all sorts of restrictions. It
had to be the last means to avert disorder and had to be sanctioned by the
pope. Typically, the elector was careful to keep his response secret. He
communicated it to Stralendorf in a letter the privy councilor was directed to burn immediately after reading.[23] In an imperial resolution of
February 11, 1630, Ferdinand did allot a generous pension to Johann
Friedrich, and the emperor expressed his regret that he could not dispose
of the lands singlehandedly, implying that if he could, the duke would
have retained them.[24] As far as can be seen, no concessions were made to
the other dukes despite the sympathy for them in Vienna.

The Mühlhausen guarantee was not brought up in the discussion of
the case of the three dukes, as one might have expected. To be sure,
Minden lay outside the Lower Saxon Circle, but Bremen and Ratzeburg

did not. The answer seems to lie in Vienna's explicit acceptance of the Bavarian position on the Mühlhausen guarantee, given at a conference of Bavarian and imperial councilors in Vienna in late May. There it was agreed that strictly speaking the Mühlhausen guarantee applied to Saxony alone. The other states of the Saxon Circles had either forfeited the guarantee by aiding the emperor's enemies or they had not received the guarantee in the first place. In any event, the burden of proof lay with them.[25] As a matter of fact, despite the statement of the imperial councilors, Duke Johann Friedrich of Holstein had allied for a time with Christian of Denmark.[26] Whereas some Protestant holders of imperial church lands in the Saxon circles may have held off from joining with the enemy, it does seem that only Saxony had made a positive commitment to the emperor.

The other question put to the four theologians concerned the procedure for implementing the Edict. According to the instructions for the imperial commissioners, they were to listen first to the claims of bishops and representatives of religious orders; then they were to deal one at a time with the properties in question. The holder was to be cited and given the opportunity to present his side. But the principal point of the hearing was to determine the question of fact, did the property at issue belong to the Catholic Church in 1552 or not? If it did, it was to be surrendered to the commissioners, who would then return it to the aggrieved or hold it in sequester, depending upon the situation. Certain objections to be expected from the present holders were to be dismissed out of hand, such as the claim that the emperor was exceeding his authority; should the holder offer an objection of merit, the case was to be referred to Vienna. In the event of minor resistance, the commissioners were to summon aid from the nearest imperial or League commander; if serious resistance appeared likely, recourse was to be had to Vienna before any action was taken.[27]

The specific case out of which the inquiry for the theologians arose cannot be determined, but it involved a difficulty that could logically have been expected and may have been related to an anticipated protest from representatives of the Franconian Circle, especially Württemberg, which was finally lodged on July 20.[28] The theologians were asked: if the holder requested more time to prove his possession of the property in 1552, should the lands be left with him pending a decision? The answer for the theologians was merely an application of Laymann's position. Where there was a doubt of fact, the property was to be returned to the Catholics, since the presumption was in their favor. Nothing was said about an appeal. But Ferdinand does seem to have hesitated to act on this. The protest of the Franconian estates called for a suspension of the Edict until the convocation of a diet. This of course was completely rejected, since the emperor had only acted on the "clear letter" of the Peace of Augsburg. However, on the recommendation of the aulic council, the commissioners in the Franconian and Swabian Circles were instructed to proceed to implementation only in notorious cases; in others they were to undertake an investigation and send the results to Vienna for decision. The burden of proof still lay with the heretics; on the other hand, Ferdinand wanted no one to be able to claim reasonably that he had not been given a hearing or that he had been treated illegally.[29]

Lamormaini was now active for the improvement of the Catholic position in many cities of the Empire, including Nuremberg, Strasbourg, and Hamburg.[30] But nowhere did the status of Catholicism so profoundly concern Lamormaini and Ferdinand more than in the wealthy imperial city of Augsburg, where even the forceful intercession of Saxony on behalf of his Lutheran compatriots did not much avail them.[31] As early as 1622 the emperor had requested a report about the condition of religion there. Little came of this. Then in January 1628, Ferdinand entrusted two commissioners, his brother Archduke Leopold and the Bishop of Eichstätt, with the task of bringing the religious situation in Augsburg into line with the provisions of the Religious Peace. The commission began hearings in Augsburg in May, but they were surprised to find that the Catholics, who according to their report constituted about one-tenth of the citizenry, had few complaints to make. In late June the commission departed, unable to establish any serious violations of the Peace.[32]

But this was not the end. The city fathers soon learned that Bishop Knöringen had further designs on the city that he was urging at court, whither he had sent Grenzing. The bishop now argued that he was not bound in his diocese by the Peace of Religion itself, and so he could proceed unchecked in carrying out the Counterreformation in his whole diocese, including the city of Augsburg. To demonstrate this was a second main purpose of Laymann's *The Way to Peace*. In making his point, Laymann turned a familiar Protestant argument against the Protestants. Many Protestant authors affirmed that the Peace of Religion was a treaty, not a law, and consequently could not be altered without the approval of all involved. No majority decision in the imperial diet could touch it. But Bishop Knöringen had discovered that Cardinal Otto von Truchsess, Bishop of Augsburg in 1555, had in juridical form solemnly and persistently protested against the Peace. Thus, Knöringen now claimed, he was not bound by the Peace and enjoyed a free hand to reform religion in the city and the whole diocese.[33] The bishop also based his right to proceed with the Counterreformation in the city on a treaty concluded between the city and his predecessor in 1548 and allegedly confirmed in 1582.

Drawn up at the time of Catholic ascendancy after the victory of Charles V at Mühlberg, it recognized the bishop's ecclesiastical jurisdiction in the city, so that he now possessed the right to regulate religion there.

Whether Lamormaini subscribed to the position of Laymann is uncertain, but he did believe the treaty of 1548 clearly spoke for the bishop. This he told Dr. Georg Theissen, himself a Catholic, whom the city sent to Vienna to protect its interests. To Theissen Lamormaini admitted that he had written the rector of the Jesuit college in Augsburg encouraging him to stir up support for the bishop. "Then just as the emperor has his prosecutor in earthly matters, so has God his prosecutors in matters spiritual," Lamormaini told him. "He was one of them, and it was incumbent on him to secure respect for what belonged to God." The evidence supports Theissen's assertion that the aulic council was on the verge of deciding in favor of the city in December 1628 when Lamormaini and Grenzing succeeded in having the matter brought before the privy council. Justus Gebhardt, Lamormaini's convert and ally in the aulic council, was also influential in the matter. The aulic council voted eight-to-five in favor of the city, with Stralendorf voting for the city and Gebhardt against it. But the privy council decided on the need for more information about the treaty of 1548 and on the desirability of seeking the views of Mainz and Maximilian.[34] The two electors replied in May and June 1629 that they preferred not to take a position on the Laymann theory but that the treaty of 1548 justified the bishop's proceeding with his plans.[35]

Ferdinand issued a rescript on July 20 declaring that the bishop possessed ecclesiastical jurisdiction in the city. This was promulgated officially in Augsburg on August 8. Saxony's intervention with the emperor had no effect. The next day a list of the bishop's demands was presented to the city officials. Among them were the expulsion of all noncitizen preachers and the prohibition of the ministry for citizen preachers, the prohibition of heretical books, the future extension of citizens' rights to Catholics only, and the requirement that Protestants attend Catholic services, at least for a time. The city officials stalled, however, in implementing these extreme measures, hoping still for the successful intercession of Saxony. Lamormaini himself visited the city in June 1630, just before the opening of the electoral convention in Regensburg, in order to get a first-hand view of the situation.[36] Again the committee of councilors dealing with Augsburg wanted to obtain the opinion of Mainz and Maximilian before going ahead with vigorous implementation. Lamormaini agreed that they should be consulted, but at his behest the implementation was not held up until they responded. An imperial decree issued on July 11, during the first days of the electoral convention, but

not published in Augsburg until October 30 declared that despite Saxony's intercession, the reformation of religion was to continue in Augsburg.[37] And so it went until the Swedes came to south Germany.

Meanwhile, in the Italian theater, March 1629 had seen France force a
reluctant Savoy to ally with it, place a garrison in the Savoyan city of
Susa, and take possession of Casale, the key fortress of Montferrat,
where the Spaniards were compelled to raise their siege and withdraw.
Richelieu then called a halt to the French advance and turned to diplomacy. On April 8, four days after finally concluding peace with England,
he added Venice to the Franco-Savoyan alliance.

Ferdinand's primary concern in the contest with France now became
the recognition of imperial jurisdiction in the Italian fiefs of the Empire.
In April, as we have seen, he sent troops to occupy the Swiss passes
leading from Austria to Milan including the Valtelline to prepare for the
invasion he was planning.[38] During the summer and fall then of 1629,
the imperial military suffered minor but significant setbacks in the northwest and northeast. In April the Dutch had undertaken the siege of 's
Hertogenbusch. To the Spanish plea for help Wallenstein responded with
troops, but the city fell anyway on September 14, and his soldiers returned in October, followed into the Rhineland by the Dutch. In June
Wallenstein had sent a major force under Hans Georg von Arnim to
assist Polish troops against the Swedes. But by the end of September
active French mediation had brought about a Swedish-Polish armistice
highly favorable to the Swedes, who were being courted by Richelieu as a
force to be played off against Ferdinand in the Empire. Arnim, who lost
many of his soldiers, resigned shortly afterwards from Wallenstein's service and went over first to Brandenburg and then to Saxony.[39]

Throughout the second half of 1629 hope remained for a peaceful
solution to the Mantuan problem. The electors led by Maximilian urged
it in Vienna, and some evidence exists that Stralendorf supported them.[40]
Lamormaini continued to speak out openly against the war before Ferdinand and the imperial councilors. Pallotto and Agnelli-Soardi encouraged
him. So did Cardinal Pazmany, who went so far as to tell Lamormaini
and others that if he were the imperial confessor, he would not give the
emperor absolution unless he desisted from war in Italy.[41] But the Bishop
of Mantua complained that "the confessor, formerly all-powerful, no
longer has a voice that penetrates to the heart of His Majesty."[42] Pallotto
credited Lamormaini's efforts with more success, and Rome certainly
acknowledged them. According to the nuncio, Lamormaini's opponents
defused his arguments by pointing out to Ferdinand, as Olivares had,

that other theologians approved the war and that Ferdinand must in any event maintain his reputation in the Mantuan affair. Eggenberg and Collalto were most aggressive in favoring the war, asserting the need to forestall France and Venice. According to the Bishop of Mantua, Eggenberg went so far as to advise the Empress herself to stay out of Italian affairs, and he and Collalto delighted in talk of commemorating the Sack of Rome in the Eternal City. At one point Lamormaini hinted to Vitelleschi that he would resign if hostilities broke out in earnest, but the superior general instructed him to put aside any such thoughts.[43]

An envoy of Richelieu, Melchior de Sabran, appeared in Vienna in late July. His purpose was to sound out the intentions of the emperor and to work for the investiture of Nevers. The French had only intervened in Italy, he let it be known, to obtain justice for Nevers, a French vassal and ally whose right to the Mantuan succession was indisputable. Sabran galled the imperial court by claiming that Louis wanted to help the emperor carry out his oath to uphold justice, the implication being that Ferdinand was either unwilling or unable to do so in the face of Spain. The French had sent troops to Italy, Sabran explained, only after Spain had marched into Montferrat. To sanction the Spanish grab by asserting that Spain was only carrying out the imperial sequester was a dodge. According to Sabran, Louis was determined to secure justice and would not back down.

Ferdinand's chief demand was that Nevers accept the sequester, which was only to last until the case was adjudicated. In other words, the emperor wanted his jurisdiction in the Italian fiefs acknowledged. Spain and Savoy had both promised to abide by his decision, Ferdinand claimed during Sabran's audience with him. Nor did he attempt to interfere with the administration of justice in France.[44] Unfortunately, as both Ferdinand and Lamormaini later complained, Sabran's manner as much as his message only aggravated the differences at hand.[45] His mission proved a failure.

The conflict in Italy underwent another escalation in the fall of 1629. By early September an imperial army of thirty-six thousand with Collalto at its head began to approach Mantuan territory. At the same time, imperial troops were assembling in Alsace for a diversionary action into France should this be necessary. Many outrages and atrocities were reported committed by the imperial soldiers as they crossed Lombardy, and this deeply troubled Ferdinand. By December the imperials were laying siege to the great fortified city, Mantua itself, but they were forced to withdraw on Christmas Day 1629. This plus a minor defeat inflicted on the retiring troops made the war party in Vienna more resolute than ever to bring Nevers under control. In January plague broke out in the city of Mantua, and it soon spread throughout northern Italy, leading to the suffering so vividly described by Manzoni in *I Promessi Sposi*.[46]

Richelieu had not been inactive, despite severe opposition to his policy at home. His plan had been to turn the forces of Denmark, Sweden, and the German princes all against the emperor. His efforts to frustrate the peace negotiations between the emperor and Christian of Denmark had failed, but his influence, as we have seen, was largely responsible for the Swedish-Polish armistice of September 26, 1629, the goal of which for Richelieu was to free Gustav Adolph to advance into the Empire. Long and difficult French negotiations with the Swedish king were to follow. French emissaries visited the courts of Brandenburg and Saxony, but with little success. Developments were more promising in Bavaria. In October, after nearly a year of secret contacts encouraged by the papal nuncio in Paris, Giovanni Francesco Guidi di Bagno, Richelieu proposed to Maximilian the draft of a defensive alliance that was intended to draw Maximilian and the League away from the emperor. As a wedge Richelieu used Maximilian's fear of Wallenstein and his resentment of the emperor's action in Italy and the Netherlands. For the time being, his initiative was unsuccessful, but Paris and Munich kept up their covert contacts.[47]

Wallenstein quietly opposed the intervention in Italy. After abandoning his short-lived enthusiasm for a campaign against Venice, he discretely warned Vienna of the folly of the Italian war, and he stalled the dispatch of troops to the extent he dared as he moved from Mecklenburg to Halberstadt in July 1629, then to Bohemia for the winter, and eventually to southwest Germany in the spring of 1630.[48] In early September 1629, just as the army under Collalto was preparing to enter Mantuan territory, Lamormaini received a letter from Wallenstein attesting to his opposition to the war for legal and political reasons already known to us. The best solution, he felt, was to convince France that if Nevers submitted to the emperor and accepted the sequester, Ferdinand would surely acknowledge his claim to the two duchies. Thus the war would be prevented and the emperor spared embarrassment.[49]

Lamormaini was overjoyed to receive the general's communication precisely when the advocates of the war were pressing him hard. Wallenstein had asked Lamormaini to show the letter to only three persons, the emperor, Eggenberg, and Trautmannsdorf. The general obviously did not want his view to become widely known with the probable effect of embarrassing Eggenberg. But Lamormaini in his enthusiasm showed the letter to Pallotto and the Bishop of Mantua, and it soon caused a sensation at court. This angered Wallenstein. Even though he himself had presented a further development of his plan to the Bishop of Mantua through an emissary, he disavowed his letter to Lamormaini.[50] In reality, he maintained his opposition to the war at least until the French advanced further into Italy in March, when he seems to have become more sympathetic to imperial military action to the south.[51]

Toward the end of 1629 there did appear a greater inclination to peace on both sides. Contacts between Paris and Vienna were made through Munich.[52] At the same time, Lamormaini took up and carried further an initiative of Jean Suffren, the French Jesuit confessor of both Louis XIII and the queen mother, Marie de Medicis. Suffren had written in late September inquiring what might be done to prevent war between the two rulers. Both confessors acted with the consent of their penitents. Lamormaini affirmed this for himself, and it is difficult to believe that Suffren would have undertaken such a move without the approval of Richelieu, given the close scrutiny under which he found himself at the French court and his normal abstention from politics.[53]

The exchange between the two confessors disclosed profound differences not only over the political situation but also over the role of the Jesuits themselves. Lamormaini had long argued the need for unity among Catholic rulers: the emperor, the pope, the German Catholic princes. Now in his response to Suffren he proposed for the first time an alliance against the heretics that would include France, Spain, and the emperor.[54] Rome was eventually to take up the idea, but it always foundered on the rivalry between France and the Habsburg states. Lamormaini clung to it for years, embodying as it did his vision of the war as a crusade for religion. Neither in Paris nor in Madrid, nor even in Rome, was the war so much a religious enterprise as it was in Vienna. Lamormaini simply could not believe that the Most Christian King, with a cardinal as his chief minister, would pursue a policy that obstructed the advance of the Counterreformation in Germany. Lamormaini's views were shared by many Frenchmen, the so-called dévots including Marie de Medicis, Cardinal Pierre Bérulle, and others close to the throne. They were determined to oust Richelieu and revert to a pro-Habsburg foreign policy. As a result, the cardinal's situation was precarious during the whole period of the Mantuan crisis.[55] The extent to which Lamormaini was aware of this is uncertain; there is no evidence of further contacts of his with the French court. But his hopes for a reversal of French policy and French adherence to a grand Catholic alliance were shared by major figures in Paris.

Peace and understanding were necessary among Christian princes, Lamormaini emphasized to Suffren, and especially between the emperor and the Most Christian King, if heresy and infidelity were to be put down, religion restored in Europe, and the Kingdom of Christ established throughout the world. The emperor desired peace with France. His goal was "by just means and methods to restore the Catholic religion not only in his hereditary kingdoms and provinces (the whole world knows how and to what extent this has been carried out) but also in the empire to the degree the imperial constitution and public agreements permit at this time." Ferdinand, Lamormaini continued, wanted the King of France as his ally in the battle, and he would try with the help of God to obtain the participation of the King of Spain too.

Before criticizing the conduct of Nevers and France and proposing a solution to the Mantuan problem, Lamormaini made some allegations about the emperor's attitude toward Spain that would embarrass the Habsburg rulers if they ever became public. Eggenberg himself had told him, Lamormaini wrote, that the emperor was unhappy with the Spanish invasion of Montferrat. Had the imperial troops not been occupied with the heretics at the time, Ferdinand would have sent them to raise the siege of Casale and thus free Italy from the disturbances caused by Spain. But the emperor was also displeased with Nevers for failing to heed the decree of sequestration with which he had intended to keep out the Spaniards. Nor was Ferdinand happy with the French advance into Italy, which was undertaken without any attempt to communicate with him. Only months afterward did an obnoxious envoy, Sabran, show up in Vienna, and he did nothing more than mouth threats and show disrespect for the emperor. He cut the ground out from under the peace party in Vienna.

Ferdinand was ready to overlook the insulting conduct of Sabran if the king would disavow him, affirm his respect for the emperor, and declare it had never been his intention to infringe on the emperor's rights or jurisdiction. If Nevers then submitted to the emperor and apologized, and if Louis interceded on his behalf, Ferdinand would show how much he esteemed the intercession of the king and, Lamormaini guaranteed, render the decision the King of France desired.

Lamormaini's proposed solution was essentially what Wallenstein had suggested several months previously and what was to be agreed upon in the Treaty of Regensburg the next year. It went beyond the position the emperor assumed in a January letter to Maximilian, who was attempting to mediate between Vienna and Paris. To him Ferdinand expressed the willingness to allow the electors to participate in the decision on Mantua, but he left the form of this participation vague and gave no assurance of the final outcome.[56] One reason for Ferdinand's greater generosity when dealing with Paris through Lamormaini may have been that he could much more easily withdraw an offer communicated through him than through Maximilian. In addition, Lamormaini may have privately convinced Ferdinand to allow him to see what he could achieve on his own through his contact with Suffren, the imperial councilors not being informed at all about his activity.

As he informed Suffren, Lamormaini sent a copy of his letter to the Curia. About the same time, Urban notified Ferdinand that he was sending his brother, Cardinal Antonio Barberini, to north Italy to help the negotiations in progress there, and the emperor welcomed the initiative.[57] Vitelleschi expressed his and Barberini's satisfaction with Lamormaini's letter to Suffren, but he did not have much hope for the projected alliance of Catholic rulers.[58] Neither Ferdinand, nor Lamormaini, nor Vitelleschi, of course, knew of the Curia's encouragement of a Franco-Bavarian defensive alliance.

Suffren's response to Lamormaini was surprising, inasmuch as he had been the one to open the communication between them. He showed little restraint in his letter of January 9.[59] Jesuits, he felt, were gradually withdrawing from the ministries peculiar to the Society, such as preaching, teaching, and hearing confessions. They were becoming involved in activities that were in some sense contrary to the nature of the Society and about which they knew little and were easily deceived. An example of this, he thought, was Lamormaini's account of the conduct of Sabran in Vienna. Obviously, Lamormaini had neither met the emissary personally nor read the message he had brought but was dependent on the doctored reports of others. Never would a man such as Sabran act so boorishly. Moreover, he was merely carrying out his instructions. If Jesuits continued their political activities, people would begin to question their competence in matters for which they really were suited.

Lamormaini extolled the emperor's piety and zeal, Suffren continued, but Ferdinand's actions belied them since in the matter at hand he acted unjustly. With this the French Jesuit made the transition to an attack on imperial policy. He raised the point which Lamormaini knew to be the weak spot in the emperor's position. Nearly everyone admitted the right of Nevers to the succession in the two territories. Why then was there a need for a sequester at all? Vienna claimed this was to prevent an anticipated Spanish invasion. But the Spaniards marched into Montferrat anyway. Why did the emperor not take up arms against them, Suffren queried? Nevers had no place to turn for help but to France, with whom he had a long-standing and public alliance. Ferdinand then dispatched an army, mostly Protestants, to Italy, where they did untold damage to the country. "No wonder heresy, infidelity, ugliness triumph when iniquity prevails over justice," he wrote. France made a reasonable effort to come to an agreement through Sabran, but he got nowhere. Nor could the king disavow him. If the emperor wanted peace, he should look to himself and treat other rulers justly. Then "there will be hope that other princes stirred by his example will unite to seek to conquer iniquity throughout the world, to strive to advance piety. Otherwise let him expect a bitter war; although the outcome of such wars is usually uncertain, as St. Bernard says, if the cause of fighting is just, the result cannot be evil."

There is no record that Suffren's letter ever reached Lamormaini. In mid-March Vitelleschi remarked that perhaps Suffren thought it best not to answer since he was powerless to do anything.[60] Shortly afterwards, however, Vitelleschi learned that Lamormaini's letter had been read at table in several French Jesuit houses and even published in part. For this he reprimanded Suffren.[61] Eventually the letter came to the attention of Olivares, prompting him to undertake another effort to reduce Lamormaini's influence in Vienna. One cannot escape the suspicion that Richelieu managed Suffren's initiative to try to learn how far Ferdinand was ready to go in pursuit of a solution to the Mantuan dispute, and then leaked Lamormaini's letter in order to sow discord between Spain and the emperor.

Richelieu left Paris for the front on December 29, and he was soon leading a new French advance in Italy. The French seized the Savoyan fortress of Pinerolo in late March 1630; by June they had occupied much of Savoy, which had proven to be an untrustworthy ally. But the Habsburg powers were not inactive. By the middle of July imperial troops again were encamped before the fortress of Mantua. This time they reduced it within a few days and put the city to a vicious sack. "The Mantua of Isabella, the Mantua of Federigo Gonzaga disappeared forever."[62] Meanwhile, the Spaniards took possession of most of Montferrat. Thus the military position of the emperor in Italy improved vastly during the early weeks of the electoral convention in Regensburg.[63]

Throughout 1629 and the first half of 1630 the Catholic electors' fear of Wallenstein and their determination to be rid of him mounted. Perhaps if they had been aware of his opposition to the war in Mantua, their attitude would have been different. Wariness of the general was a chief reason for Maximilian's secret contacts with France. Complaints about the imperial army had been loud at the league conventions at Heidelberg in February–March 1629 and at Mergentheim in December 1629–January 1630, but the Catholic electors thought it best not to undertake any drastic initiative until the electoral convention, when they would be able to deal directly with the emperor.[64] Ironically, the Catholic electors wanted to force the reduction of the imperial army precisely when they needed it so much the more to enforce the Edict if no concessions were to be made on it.

FERDINADVS SECVNDVS DEI GRATIA ROMANORVM IMPE
RATOR, SEMPER AVGVSTVS, GERMANIÆ, HVNGARIÆ, BOHEMIÆ,
DALMATIÆ, CROATIÆ, SCLAVONIÆ, ETC. REX, ARCHIDVX AV-
STRIÆ, DVX BVRGVNDIÆ, STYRIÆ, CARINTHIÆ, CARNIOLÆ,
WIRTEMBERGÆ ET VTRIVSQ SILESIÆ, MARCHIO MORAVIÆ ET IN
VTRAQ LVSATIA, COMES HABSPVRGIÆ ET TYROLIS. &c.

De facie depinxit Francofurti ad Mœnum Martinus à Falckenbg   Et expreßit Iacob. ab Heyden. Men. Sep. Æ dↄ bↄ xix.

FERDINAND II

This portrait was drawn by Martin von Falckenberg in September 1619
just after Ferdinand's coronation as emperor. It points up his device
"To those fighting a just fight goes the crown" (Legitime certantibus
corona). From Georg Hirth, *Kulturgeschichtliches Bilderbuch aus drei
Jahrhunderten*, 6 vols. (Munich and Leipzig; Knorr und Hirth, 1882–90).

CHRIST SPEAKING TO FERDINAND

This illustration, taken from the *Annales Ferdinandei* (1726), represents the legend that at the time of the enemy's near seizure of Vienna and Ferdinand himself in 1619, Christ spoke to Ferdinand as he prayed before the crucifix, "Ferdinand, I will not desert you." Courtesy of The Newberry Library, Chicago

THE JESUIT OR UNIVERSITY CHURCH, VIENNA

The dedicatory inscription runs under the cornice. Photograph from the Bildarchiv der öst. Nationalbibliothek. Courtesy of the Austrian Press and Information Service

FERDINAND'S IMPERIAL CORONATION (1619)

The coin distributed to the crowds after the ceremony is represented
at the bottom center. Again it illustrates Ferdinand's motto. Taken from
Giulio Belli, *Laurea Austriaca* (1627). Courtesy of The Newberry
Library, Chicago

...andi II. Zum Römischen Käyser. 1619.

§ Ferdinandus hie gesalbet wirt
    Zum Römschen Keyser, und geziert
Mit Scepter, Schwert, Ring, Apfel, Cron,
    Maynts solchs mehrntheils verzichtet schon.

ANNOTATED PAGES FROM

The Virtues of Ferdinand II, Emperor of the Romans

This page and the manuscript page are taken from Lamormaini's

6   EERDINANDI   II.

ctus, aufus eft Dominicis diebus Græcij in Provinciæ
palatio ~~Lutheranas~~ conciones prælegere, audito-
il confluebat,   resq; , qui frequentes è Nobilitate ~~aderant~~, in ~~Hæroñ~~ *bus*
confirmare. Statim ac id Ferdinandus refcivit, fe-
verè prohibuit ; ac ne Decreto audacior aliquis illu-
deret, fui ipfius corporis cuftodes ~~armigeros~~ juffit
pro palatij foribus excubare, adituq́; venientes pro-
hibere. Memoriâ digniffima funt verba, quæ adjecit:
oppetiturù fe morte libentiùs, quám poft tot ferias
inhibitiones, fuis fubditis, fuo ip cófpeɑu, Acatho-
licum hoc quale ~~quæle~~ publicum exercitium per-
miffurum.   *9*

Agebatur in Silefia de pace cum Acatholicis Prin-
cipibus componenda. Fridlandiæ Dux, penes quem
belli adminiftrandi fumma poft Imperatorem pote-
ftas erat, eam urge~~bat dicebatur~~. Ferdinandus refti-
tuendæ tranquillitatis ac quietis cupidiffimus, pacem amabat, & verô etiam miffis legatis curabat.
Fuêre interea qui fuggererent, nec à Fridlando fin-
cerè rem agi, nec è bono Religionis eam pacem fu-
turam. Cupidiffimus propugnandæ Religionis Im-
Pacem amat,   perator illicò in genua fe dejecit, & Beatiffimâ Vir-
fed gratam   ginem eft obteftatus; fi pax illa ejus Filio ipfiq́; non
Deo   effet grata ; fi Catholicæ Fidei perniciofa : averteret
illam porrò, ac perturbaret, quibuscunq́; demùm
rationibus, modis ac medijs ; etiam, fi opus fit, diffi-
cilibus & cæteroqui parùm gratis.

Non facile eft referre, quo perfundebatur gau-
dio,

R.P.GUILIELMUS LAMORMAI
NI.S.J.Ferdinandi II,Imperatoris Confeſſarius
è Seminario Pragenſi Anno 1587 pri
mâ Philosophiæ Laureâ decoratus.
Obijt Viennæ Auſtriæ
A° ætatis ſuæ 89.

WILLIAM LAMORMAINI, S.J.

Portrait by S. Dworzak, from A. Hamy, *Galerie Illustrée de la Compagnie de Jésus* (1893). Courtesy of the Cudahy Library, Loyola University of Chicago

HANS ULRICH VON EGGENBERG (1568–1634)

From Khevenhiller, *Conterfet Kupfferstich* (1722). Courtesy of The Newberry Library, Chicago

THE EGGENBERG PALACE, GRAZ

This magnificent structure displays the self-consciousness of Ferdinand's
first minister. Courtesy of the Verkehrsverein der Stadt Graz

6. Lamormaini's Triumph: Regensburg, 1630

he Electoral Convention of Regensburg differed from Mühlhausen in that the emperor was personally in attendance to negotiate with the electors. The general purpose of the convention was twofold: to find the way to a just peace in the Empire and to determine the measures necessary in the meantime to defend it against internal and external enemies. The Edict was the most important issue at Regensburg even though it was not on the formal agenda. Would the emperor and the Catholic electors yield on it for the sake of internal peace and Protestant support against the enemies of the Empire, which now included the formidable King of Sweden? Encouraged by France and freed for the time being from his involvement in Poland, Gustav Adolph landed on the Baltic coast with an army of fourteen thousand during the second week of the convention. His initial purpose was to prevent the establishment of a Catholic Habsburg state that would be strong enough to control north Germany and the Baltic area, consequently check Sweden's ambitions there, and perhaps even challenge Sweden's independence and its Protestant religious settlement.[1]

Ferdinand came to Regensburg ready to make some compromises. He was prepared to discuss the complaints against the imperial military. However, the Catholic electors aimed at the dismissal of Wallenstein and a complete reorganization of the imperial army that would greatly reduce the emperor's influence. Since Mühlhausen Ferdinand had been intent on securing the imperial succession for young Ferdinand. The Catholic electors, however, had resolved at the League Convention of Heidelberg in the spring of 1629 that there would be no election of the King of the Romans until agreement had been found on the problems facing the Empire. Saxony and Brandenburg were opposed to any election before their grievances were remedied, especially those following from the Edict. Ferdinand foresaw the outcome, and he did not include the election on the agenda he proposed at the start of the convention. Ferdinand sought the electors' support in Italy, in the northwest against the Dutch, who had occupied imperial territory, and in the north against the Swedes. The Catholic electors showed understanding for the need for cooperation against Sweden, but they were as determined as ever not to become involved in Italy and the Netherlands.[2]

Having been called by Mainz for June 3, the convention opened officially after the normal delays on July 3. Ferdinand traveled by boat up
the Danube, arriving on June 19 with a large and magnificent entourage
that included the Empress Eleonora, the King of Hungary, the privy
council, and most of the aulic council. The four Catholic electors with
their parties followed within the week: Maximilian; Philip Christoph
von Sötern, the Archbishop-Elector of Trier; Ferdinand, Maximilian's
younger brother, the Archbishop-Elector of Cologne; and Anselm Casimir von Wambold, who had succeeded the deceased Greiffenklau as
Archbishop-Elector of Mainz.[3] Despite the efforts of the emperor and
Catholic electors to persuade them to come in person, Saxony and Brandenburg were content merely to send delegations as a protest against the
emperor's refusal to modify the Edict and relieve the oppressive burden
of the imperial troops. The chief official body for the conduct of business
was the council of electors, over which Mainz presided as Archchancellor
of the Empire. The electors themselves rarely attended, preferring to send
their deputies. Neither the emperor nor his delegates were present at the
sessions of the council of electors, and the council communicated officially with the emperor as a college. But as one would expect, considerable business was carried on through unofficial contacts and at private
conferences, the most important being the conference of the Catholic
electors or their deputies that met regularly.

The major European states all sent representatives to Regensburg to
look to their interests. Richelieu's emissaries, Charles Brûlart de Léon
and the legendary Capuchin, Father Joseph du Tremblay, arrived together
on July 30. The Spaniards sent Carlos Doria, Duke of Tursi, as an extraordinary ambassador to Regensburg, with instructions to maintain
close contact with Eggenberg.[4] The principal English representative was
Sir Robert Anstruther. His main concern was the Palatinate question,
and he came accompanied by Joachim von Rusdorf, minister of the
exiled Count Palatine. There was, in addition, a host of emissaries from
the Protestant and Catholic German states plus envoys from the major
Italian states such as the Republic of Venice and the Grand Duchy of
Tuscany.[5]

To represent the pope there came the new nuncio in Vienna, Ciriaco
Rocci. The previous fall Pallotto had been named a cardinal, and his new
status threatened to raise insoluble questions of protocol at Regensburg.
When the pope suggested he might be present as a legate, Ferdinand
responded that a legate belonged at a diet, not an electoral convention.
Rome then transferred Rocci to Vienna from his post as nuncio to the
Swiss in Lucerne. Due to the last-minute nature of the assignment, he
arrived in Regensburg only on August 13, after first consulting in Vienna

with Pallotto, who did not leave for Rome until late October.[6] Highest priority for Rocci was the attainment of peace in Italy through the investiture of Nevers. Rocci used his first audience with Ferdinand to encourage the peace negotiations that had already begun in Regensburg. He was directed to maintain close contact with Maximilian and to be guided by his views in all matters of interest to the electors. But just as Barberini had never informed Pallotto of the secret negotiations Rome was promoting toward a Franco-Bavarian alliance, neither did he mention them in his correspondence with Rocci. Nor did Barberini instruct Rocci to keep in close touch with Lamormaini as he had Pallotto two years before, and he warned the new nuncio "to proceed with caution and reserve" when dealing with the religious at court.[7] Earlier, the apostolic inquisitor in Cologne had recommended to the Curia that the papal representative in Regensburg ought to be a person "who would frequently be present at their [the German princes and councilors] conversations and discussions and regularly be found with them at their parties, where the Germans after being made happy by wine, are accustomed to reveal the secrets of their heart."[8] One wonders whether Rocci qualified in this respect.

The noted humanist and polemicist Kaspar Schoppe was present at the convention, having arrived from Mantua on July 22.[9] His reputation as a bitter enemy of the Jesuits dates from Regensburg. Schoppe had been born a Lutheran in Neumark in the Upper Palatinate in 1576. He early displayed precocious ability, publishing his first humanist commentaries when only nineteen. His conversion to Catholicism the following year in Prague was a great disappointment to the Protestants. From 1598 to 1607 he resided in Rome, where he made important contacts in the Curia. During these years he generally advocated tolerance and patience as the best means to win back the German Protestants. In 1607 he returned to Germany to represent the pope at the Diet of Regensburg, and he filled the next two decades with voluminous writing on a variety of subjects, plus some political activity, such as an unofficial mission to Madrid to help develop closer ties between the Catholic League and Philip III. As the Calvinist threat in Germany grew more serious, Schoppe assumed an increasingly anti-Protestant, or more precisely, anti-Calvinist attitude. He began to call for preventive military action and as a result had to retire to Milan in 1616 for his own safety. On the eve of the outbreak of the war, he was the most intransigent polemicist writing against the Calvinists. His *Trumpet Call to a Holy War*, published in 1619, summoned the emperor to an aggressive policy in defense of the Peace of Religion, which according to Schoppe the Calvinists aimed to overthrow.[10]

After a second sojourn in Rome from 1621 to 1626, where he became involved in a number of questions including the Galileo issue, Schoppe returned to Milan. By 1630 the religious and political situation had changed again, and with it Schoppe's posture. Now that the Calvinists had been defeated, he felt that tolerance and understanding would lead to reconciliation in Germany between the Catholics and the Lutherans. In 1630 Schoppe convinced the imperial commander in Italy that he should be sent to Regensburg to assist in the negotiations on the Mantuan question. He hoped to use the opportunity to present to Ferdinand his ideas for peace in Germany as well as to obtain a much-needed imperial pension. The pursuit of a modus vivendi with the Protestants was now what Schoppe favored. A flexible and humane implementation of the Edict was necessary to prevent the emperor's loss of Saxony and Brandenburg. Shortly before leaving Mantua, Schoppe composed a short work entitled "The Art of Serving Kings and Princes."[11] Its purpose was to encourage rulers to greater independence vis-à-vis their religious advisers, and it was clearly directed against Lamormaini.

In Regensburg Schoppe found an ally in Tursi, the Spanish ambassador, which is surprising because Schoppe openly opposed Spanish policy in Italy. But from the very start Spain shared Schoppe's reservations about the Edict. Tursi was instructed not to attempt to influence imperial policy directly but rather to point out as opportunity arose the consequences to be feared from a break with Saxony: it could lead to a united German Protestant front against Ferdinand.[12] Spain wanted peace in the Empire as the condition for assistance from the emperor and the League in Italy and the Netherlands. The Edict would only foment more conflict. Thus Lamormaini clashed once again with the Spaniards as well as with Schoppe, who was received by the emperor the day after his arrival in Regensburg.

According to Reinhard Ziegler, who continued to serve as confessor to the new elector of Mainz, there were thirty-odd Jesuits crowded as guests into the college in Regensburg during the convention. Contzen, confessor of Maximilian, and Georg Schröttel, confessor of Ferdinand of Cologne, stayed there.[13] Attached to the emperor's party besides Lamormaini were Fanini and Philippi, Ambrosio Peñalosa, a Spaniard, formerly professor of theology at the University of Vienna and now instructor in Spanish for the King of Hungary, and Johannes Weingartner, a young German priest from Prague who had recently been appointed a court preacher.[14]

Between the emperor's arrival and the start of the convention, Lamormaini made his quick trip to Augsburg, stopping along the way in Neuberg, Ingolstadt, and Dillingen, where he may have met with Laymann, who was later to be summoned to Regensburg. During the early days of the convention he spent some time with the three confessors, Contzen,

Ziegler, and Schröttel, at Amberg, only a day's distance from Regensburg. He was optimistic that despite the anticipated difficulties, the convention would produce great results for the progress of religion. His trust was in the Lord. "The Emperor is of a heart noble and confident in God," he wrote. "It is nearly incredible how many threats the non-Catholics keep making, how many rise up against the Emperor. But God has been the helper and protector of the Emperor up to now and will be, I hope, in the future."[15] Ziegler was not quite so optimistic. He felt the Catholics would have to make some concessions if there was to be peace.[16] Interestingly, Mainz was to prove relatively conciliatory toward the Protestants during the convention.

The first question the Catholic electors wanted taken up at Regensburg was the reform of the imperial military. By this they understood the removal of Wallenstein, the reduction of the troops under arms, and relief from the burden of supporting the army. Ferdinand at the start was determined to keep the general. He intended to grant the electors a few superficial reforms for the sake of their assistance against his enemies on the fringes of the Empire. He was unprepared for the onslaught of the Catholic electors who were the real protagonists on the Wallenstein issue. In the first meeting of the council of electors on July 8, they saw to it that military reform was placed first on the agenda.[17] On July 16 the electors voted to demand the dismissal of the general, the two Protestants going along reluctantly for the sake of electoral unity, even though they were aware of Wallenstein's opposition to the Edict. That same day the electors sent their demand to Ferdinand, along with the rest of their program for military reform.[18] After several exchanges with the emperor, the four Catholic electors went to Ferdinand in person on July 30 with the demands of the electoral college.[19]

On August 5 the privy council recommended that Ferdinand release Wallenstein. They recognized that the general had been neither insubordinate nor disloyal; yet they did reveal a wariness of the power he had accumulated. Above all, they stressed that the alternative was an open break with the Catholic electors, and this simply could not be allowed to happen. It would probably lead to a common front of all the electors against Vienna, and there was no telling where events might go from there, especially when the Empire faced yet another challenge from the Swedes. Conflict with the electors would almost certainly set back plans for the succession. After a week's further deliberation, Ferdinand informed the Catholic electors in an audience on August 13 that he was ready to release Wallenstein from his command. But the decision was not made public for nearly a month.[20]

Lamormaini advocated that Ferdinand yield to the electors and let

Wallenstein go. He had reason to be dissatisfied with the general, especially because of Wallenstein's lack of enthusiasm for the Edict, but he was also aware of Wallenstein's opposition to the war in Italy and his generosity to the Society. His principal reason for favoring the dismissal does not seem to have been different from that of the privy councilors: the need for unity with the Catholic electors, which Lamormaini of course saw as the basis for an aggressive program of Catholic restoration. His support for Wallenstein's release followed logically from his whole political position.[21]

An unclear, handwritten note of Ferdinand to Lamormaini, dated merely August, points up the importance of both Lamormaini and Contzen as go-betweens and shows that Eggenberg was also under attack by the electors. Ferdinand directed Lamormaini to try to create in Contzen a favorable impression of Eggenberg, whose fidelity he could guarantee after so many years of friendship. "For Friedland I do not vouch at all," he wrote, "and I hope in the Lord that after I have revealed my opinion to the Elector and to him [Contzen], if we have not been able to agree the first and second time, we will at last come to a good conclusion in common agreement."[22] Probably the purpose of this note was to inform Maximilian of Ferdinand's decision on Wallenstein prior to its announcement to all the electors as well as to strengthen support for Eggenberg. Eggenberg's failure to make any serious effort to save Wallenstein may have been dictated in part by the realization that if he did, the electors might go after him.[23] Perhaps, more importantly, he too sensed the political necessity of avoiding an open clash with the electors, much as he resented the need to defer to them.

The dismissal of Wallenstein did not resolve the struggle for control of the imperial military nor did it completely put to rest fears about Ferdinand's ultimate design for the government of the Empire. Who was to be the new commander of the imperial army and what was to be its relationship to the army of the League? The Catholic electors insisted at first that Maximilian be named commander of the imperial forces, under the emperor, with the same extensive powers Wallenstein had enjoyed, and that the League army remain independent. Vienna along with the Spaniards envisioned the merger of the two armies. This unified force would then be supported by all the states of the Empire and would be available to the emperor for use wherever he desired, in Italy, the Netherlands, or his own crown lands. This would in effect dissolve the League, Maximilian's power base, and facilitate imperial assistance to the Spaniards.[24]

Aware of their own lack of a suitable replacement for Wallenstein, the imperials were even willing to accept Maximilian as commander of this single army, provided severe restrictions were placed on his authority. In this context, the imperial councilors thought to raise the issue of the election of the King of the Romans.[25] If Ferdinand agreed to Maximilian as commander of the imperial army, then the Catholic electors might be ready to consent to the election of young Ferdinand, and the Protestants would probably go along lest they be isolated. Early September found Eggenberg broaching the issue with Catholic and Protestant electoral delegations.[26] The responses were slow in coming, and they were negative. There was not time to deliberate properly on the matter, Saxony wrote the emperor on October 13, especially since it had not been foreseen for the agenda. If the election, moreover, were to take place now, it would appear the electors had acted under pressure. Better to wait for more settled times. Brandenburg responded in much the same manner.[27] The Catholic electors cautiously held off their answer until late October, and then gave it orally.[28] But there was never any real chance they would change the position they had taken before the convention. Neither the Catholic nor the Protestant electors wanted the election at Regensburg, and Ferdinand did not really try to force the issue.

Meanwhile, Maximilian came forward on September 23 with an initiative that was meant to break the deadlock on the reorganization of the military. Perhaps it was provoked by a communication from Saxony informing Ferdinand that he intended to summon a conference of Protestant states to discuss their common grievances. This looked like the beginnings of an alliance of German Protestant states similar to the Union of prewar days.[29] Maximilian realized the need to avoid a break between the Catholic electors and the emperor. To the other Catholic electors he suggested he withdraw his candidacy for commander of the imperial army. He gave a number of reasons, including his understanding of the emperor's unwillingness to have him in the post and his desire to avoid the odium that would fall upon the commander as the one entrusted with enforcing the Edict. The electors, however, were not enthusiastic and did not act on his initiative.[30]

Maximilian's action may have been related as well to simultaneous negotiations on the Palatinate question. Here Maximilian found himself in disagreement even with the other Catholic electors. Ferdinand had agreed to a joint electoral statement asking that Frederick or his family receive back a portion of his lands provided he accepted the conditions drawn up at Mühlhausen. Ferdinand then asked the electors what lands should be returned and what measures should be taken to protect religion there in the unlikely event Frederick went along with the conditions. The Catholic electors were willing to restore some territory to Frederick, Mainz without restrictions on religion. Maximilian was not. Lamormaini wrote Ferdinand on September 18.[31]

The Most Serene Elector of Bavaria has seen to it that I was told humbly to insinuate the following to the Sacred Imperial Majesty when a good opportunity arose: although it was recommended in the name of all the electors that something be restored to Frederick, the Count Palatine, nevertheless this was and is not his opinion, which is completely contrary. He judges that no restitution would ever be in the interest of religion. Regarding this matter, secret information has been entrusted to me, which I have recommended be passed on to Your Majesty directly or through Prince Eggenberg. I do not know whether this has been done. This too is a matter of conscience and religion.

The "secret information" Lamormaini wanted to send Ferdinand may have been Maximilian's intention not to seek the command in the army. This, we can surmise, Maximilian thought would encourage Ferdinand to support his stand on the Palatinate. As it was, Frederick's continued insistence on complete restoration eliminated the possibility that pressure would build up for a compromise unacceptable to Maximilian.[32]

Maximilian's first efforts at a compromise on the organization of the military foundered on the other Catholic electors. A month later he suggested another arrangement. By this time the emperor and the French representatives had agreed to the Treaty of Regensburg, which much to the satisfaction of the electors was thought to end the war in Italy. Significantly, Maximilian made his new proposal on October 21 at the same conference of the Catholic electors at which he steadfastly refused to take the responsibility for initiating any discussion with the Protestants about a compromise on the enforcement of the Edict. According to Maximilian's proposal, which was accepted by the Catholic electors and the emperor, both armies were to remain as presently constituted until permanent peace was achieved. Regular conferences were to be held between imperial and League officials in order to coordinate policy on strategy, quarters, mutual assistance, and other problems. Later, Tilly was made commander of both armies, with responsibility to Maximilian for the League forces and to Ferdinand for the imperial army. Thus Maximilian's initiative helped preserve the basic bond between the emperor and the Catholic electors.[33]

The conflict over the Catholic military had repercussions among the Jesuits in Regensburg. As might have been expected, Lamormaini and Contzen were the two principals. One Jesuit wrote pessimistically to Vitelleschi, on the very day Maximilian launched his compromise, that he feared no solution would be found to the question of military leadership.[34] A week earlier, Contzen had complained to Vitelleschi about "some Jesuits," who were too closely identified with Austrian councilors.[35] Contzen was already expressing ideas that he would later write in an anonymous anti-Habsburg manuscript that became notorious as it circulated in German Catholic circles. The Spaniards exploited the Empire for their own ends, he asserted, and some imperial ministers—certainly Eggenberg was meant—consorted with them to line their own pockets. Maximilian had saved Ferdinand in his hour of need, and now the Habsburgs were trying to rob him of his army.[36] Six months later Contzen wrote Lamormaini criticizing his continued advocacy of the dissolution of the League. Lamormaini admitted that at one time, that is, at Regensburg, he had favored the unification of all the Catholic troops into one army, but he denied he still did, and he went on to encourage all Jesuits to work for Catholic unity.[37]

The friction between the two confessors reflected the continuing struggle between Maximilian and the League on one hand and Ferdinand, encouraged by the Spaniards, on the other over control of the military and the power that went with it. The conflict always remained, sometimes more, sometimes less close to the surface. Fundamental agreement between Habsburg and Wittelsbach on the goals of the war kept the disagreement from producing an open break.

The presence of two French representatives in Regensburg made it easier for electors and emperor to tackle that other source of tension between them, the war in Italy. According to their instructions, Brûlart de Léon and Father Joseph were to make contact with the electors and cooperate with them, but nothing was said about negotiations with the emperor. Yet two days after their arrival Father Joseph met privately with Ferdinand and Lamormaini. The Catholic electors then convinced Ferdinand to suggest to the two Frenchmen that negotiations be transferred from north Italy, where they were in progress, to Regensburg. After the imperial conquest of Mantua in July and the Spanish successes in Montferrat, the emperor was in a strong bargaining position. The electors urged him to extricate himself from the Italian morass and free troops to confront the oncoming Swedes. Ferdinand agreed to talks, and they began on August 11, two days before Ferdinand announced his decision on Wallenstein. For the imperials, Abbot Anton was the chief negotiator, assisted by Otto von Nostitz, a privy councilor, and Hermann von Questenberg, an aulic councilor and brother of the Abbot of Strahov.[38] Unofficially involved was Valeriano Magni, who found himself on the side opposite from his fellow Capuchin, Father Joseph.[39] Rocci reported on August 19 that the Swedish advance and fear of new uprisings in the crown lands inclined most of the ministers to peace, though it seems the number did not include Eggenberg. Ferdinand assured Rocci several times peace was near and declared that had it not been for the offensive Sabran, an agreement would have been reached long before.[40] Lamormaini himself was optimistic.[41]

Finally, on October 13, despite a last minute snag, the Treaty of Regensburg was concluded.[42] For the emperor it was an advantageous peace. As Wallenstein and Lamormaini had suggested, the agreement called for Nevers to submit to the emperor in proper form; Ferdinand then promised, at the request of the King of France and the pope, to invest him with Mantua and Montferrat within three months. Compensation was to be given the Duke of Guastalla and other claimants. Had the critical first article of the treaty been implemented, it would have frustrated Richelieu's efforts to form an anti-imperial alliance. This provision committed France not to offend the emperor directly or indirectly by giving assistance of any kind to his enemies inside or outside the Empire. Ferdinand promised the same for France. Complicated articles of the treaty called for the withdrawal, in carefully balanced stages, of imperial troops from Mantua and the Swiss passes and of French forces from all Italy including Savoy. The Spaniards, who were not party to the treaty, were expected to leave Casale to the Duke of Mantua. Other details were left to further negotiation.

Lamormaini had good reason to rejoice. Only at the very end of the convention did the news arrive in Regensburg that Richelieu would not ratify the treaty signed by his emissaries who had, however, exceeded their instructions.[43] Despite his precarious position at home due to the serious illness of the king and the growing influence of his enemies, including the queen mother, Richelieu would not accept the crucial article one and thus abandon the alliance system he was constructing against the emperor. Just then a French envoy was negotiating with Gustav Adolph regarding the terms on which France would support his invasion of the Empire. The cardinal also had difficulties with the terms the treaty laid down for Italy.[44]

The principal grievance of the Protestant electors as well as the numerous Protestant states whose emissaries flocked to Regensburg was the Edict of Restitution. For different reasons, Maximilian and Saxony did not want it on the agenda. Saxony feared being manipulated by a Catholic majority as he felt had happened at Mühlhausen. Maximilian was firmly committed to the Edict, and during the convention he opted clearly for a policy of solidarity with Ferdinand on it over a course that would have led him to make common cause with Saxony and Brandenburg. But as far as possible he wanted to avoid revealing to the Protestants his responsibility for the Edict.[45] Had Ferdinand and Maximilian been able to find it in themselves to compromise, they would have been able to retain the allegiance of many Protestant states, especially the two electorates, and probably to have repulsed the Swedish invasion, certainly to have prevented it from becoming the rout it became. But for them to yield would have been in their eyes to sell out the restoration of Catholicism in the Empire, their highest priority. The issue of the Edict reveals most clearly the ideological nature of the German war.[46]

Many talks and conferences at Regensburg had the Edict as their subject. Saxony continued to press the emperor and Catholic electors for its revocation or at least its suspension and for the cessation of the Counterreformation in Augsburg, Württemberg, and elsewhere. Other Protestant states brought their protests to Regensburg. And there was some sentiment among the Catholics for compromise. The resources of their states were simply exhausted, some Catholics argued, and the population could not be expected to make further sacrifices for the Edict. In mid-July intimations were made to the chief delegate from Brandenburg that perhaps special satisfaction would be given the two Protestant electors. A Bavarian privy councilor let the Saxon delegate, Nicholas von Miltitz, know at the start of the convention that the Catholic electors had not yet decided how far they would go on the Edict; he assured him Bavaria would work for flexibility.[47] Both Pallotto and Rocci reported with alarm that consideration was being given to relaxation of the Edict, especially with respect to the two Protestant electors.[48]

Early in August, the deputies of the Catholic electors met with the three confessors, Ziegler, Contzen, and Schrottel, to sound them out about the position to be taken toward Saxony. The three Jesuits agreed, upon being pressed by Mainz, that church lands could be left unchallenged in Protestant hands for a number of years "if we do not have the means to carry out the work." But the question was, had this point been reached? Virtually no one denied that in cases of necessity concessions might be made. But what constituted necessity? Who was to determine when it existed? Catholics like Lamormaini and Contzen, who believed that the Catholic princes could expect special divine aid in their efforts to restore Catholicism, would have great difficulty in admitting a case of necessity. This was especially true if they looked to the Most Christian King as the vehicle of divine help. Negotiations would soon end the Mantuan war, and this they saw as the first step toward cooperation with France. Contzen, who was privy to Maximilian's secret contacts with Richelieu, looked with greater confidence in that direction than did Lamormaini. Of the three electoral confessors, Ziegler showed the greatest readiness to permit concessions.[49] Two weeks later, at a conference of the Catholic electors, Cologne called attention to a theological opinion drawn up by an anonymous Dominican that in the words of the Bavarian vice chancellor, "goes further than our [Bavarian] theologians," in the direction of concessions.[50] To it we shall return.

According to his own account, Schoppe urged moderation on the Catholics at Regensburg. Whether he brought up the Edict or the war in Italy in his interview with Ferdinand on July 23 he does not tell us, but he did suggest the convocation of a national council or synod that would undertake the reform of the Catholic Church as a prelude to reconciliation with the Protestants. Ferdinand referred him to Lamormaini, with whom according to Schoppe he had been acquainted for some thirty years, and the two spent a whole day in conversation. Schoppe's forceful complaints about corruption in the imperial government bore fruit in strong admonitions of the confessor to Ferdinand that he take measures against the abuses in the administration of justice. Lamormaini even went so far as to suggest to Ferdinand that the failure to elect the King of the Romans was God's punishment for these abuses.[51] But Schoppe's idea of a national council did not get far with Lamormaini, who considered the time for it "most unfavorable."[52] Schoppe does not seem to have discussed the Edict during their talk, but he did lobby for flexibility on it at Regensburg in order to prevent the defection of Saxony and Brandenburg.[53]

There was, then, sentiment for concessions on the Edict among the Catholics at the start of the convention. Nevertheless, the electors backed the emperor in his rigid stance. Ferdinand ordered the continuation of the Counterreformation measures in Augsburg on July 11, with Lamormaini's express encouragement.[54] A Württemberg protest against the enforcement of the Edict was rejected on August 31.[55] Ferdinand notified Saxony on August 23 that he expected his support against the Swedes, who according to John George's ominous report had just seized Stettin, the residential city of Duke Bogeslaw of Pomerania at the mouth of the Oder. Regarding the Edict, Ferdinand repeated what he had written so often. He was only administering justice with the Edict, and there was no better way to peace than the observance of the law. He was carrying out his duty, and he trusted the Lord, the just God, would help him over any difficulties. Letters from Mainz and Maximilian to Saxony supported him.[56]

John George's announcement in early September that he intended to call a conference of Protestant states disturbed the Catholics. It was this that had brought home to Maximilian the need for a compromise on the military question. Ferdinand's response, in turn, alarmed Pallotto. The emperor declared that he was willing to discuss with the Protestants at Regensburg the manner of implementing the Edict. Significantly, he did not speak of modifying the Edict itself. Ferdinand pressed John George to come to Regensburg in person to facilitate the talks.[57] Among the

Catholic electors, Mainz took the lead in fostering a policy that encouraged negotiations with the Protestants and envisioned some compromise on the Edict itself, especially its suspension for forty years for Saxony and Brandenburg. Soon to emerge as a mediator between Catholics and Protestants was Landgrave George of Hesse-Darmstadt, John George's son-in-law. He saw to it that on October 1 Mainz was given a paper that was to become known as the "Hessian Points." It elaborated a current Protestant interpretation of the Religious Peace. Neither Protestant elector, however, supported the Hessian Points; both felt they went too far in their effort at conciliation. Whether the Catholics were aware of the failure of the two electors to back the Points is not clear. In any event, developments encouraged Mainz.[58]

Pressure thus built up among the Catholic electors for some form of compromise. Lamormaini requested special prayers from the whole Society.[59] Maximilian was the key figure among the electors, and he hesitated to follow the lead of Mainz. About this time there must have taken place a meeting reported by Schoppe. Maximilian and Tursi went to Lamormaini to try to convince him to move Ferdinand in the direction of compromise on the Edict. According to Schoppe, Lamormaini "closed his eyes and answered them: the Edict must stand firmly, whatever evil might finally come from it. It matters little that the emperor because of it lose not only Austria but all his kingdoms and provinces and whatever he has in the world, provided he save his soul, which he cannot do without the implementation of his Edict."[60] Maximilian thus knew Lamormaini's stand, which scarcely differed from Contzen's and was almost certainly that of Ferdinand himself. In retrospect, Maximilian was to affirm that it was the confessors at Regensburg, Lamormaini and Contzen above all, who had convinced the Catholic electors and the emperor that concessions were unacceptable to conscience and that God would give the Catholics complete victory if only they persevered in confidence. Therefore they rejected compromise on the Edict.[61]

At a critical meeting of the Catholic electors on October 21, Maximilian refused to take the responsibility for any initiative toward a compromise with the Protestants, thus acting against the advice of some of his own councilors.[62] For his part, he was willing to stand firm and continue the struggle. Should the other electors decide in favor of concessions, he had no choice but to go along with them, since he could not stand alone. But obviously he would do this only with great reluctance, and the ecclesiastical electors would have to take the responsibility for it. At this meeting Maximilian launched the compromise that successfully resolved the dispute with the emperor over military reorganization. Only eight days before, the Peace of Regensburg seemed to make possible the transfer of troops from Italy to meet the invading Gustav Adolph, and it eliminated another source of strife between emperor and Catholic electors. Maximilian and Ferdinand were closing ranks.[63]

On October 22, the deputies of the Catholic electors met with a group of imperial councilors that included Stralendorf, Trautmannsdorf, and Abbot Anton. Eggenberg was not present.[64] Though hampered by Maximilian's reluctance, Mainz's delegate speaking on behalf of the Catholic electors explained that the Edict was now the principal cause of a war the exhausted states could no longer support. Moderation of the Edict would probably make it possible to unite all the electors with the emperor against Sweden and thus open the way to peace. He therefore requested approval to begin in Regensburg talks with the Protestant delegates about its modification.

The next day the imperial councilors agreed to recommend to Ferdinand that he permit such talks provided any results be subject to his ratification. The Catholic electors could be trusted, they felt, "to proceed with care and caution, since it was their interests above all that were at stake." The councilors' suggestion that Ferdinand seek further information from the electors in writing "as a permanent record" indicated their desire to make clear to posterity who was responsible for concessions.[65]

Mainz then made contact directly with Eggenberg and the emperor himself during the next two or three days, and reported back to the Catholic electors on October 26 that Eggenberg favored the start of negotiations with the Protestants in Regensburg. Ferdinand approved the contacts with the Protestants but emphasized that he was not interested in a new Peace of Religion nor in a change of the Edict, which was merely a return to the Peace of Religion. The electors then decided it would be better at this point merely to assure Ferdinand they had no intention of departing from either the Peace of Religion or the Edict. They would carry on their discussions with the Protestants privately and not send a detailed report to the emperor. At this same conference, probably as a result of Eggenberg's prodding of Mainz, the electors determined to give him the clear answer that they did not think the time suitable for the election of the King of the Romans.[66] They could now hide behind the Protestant electors' negative response, which the emperor had already received.

Undoubtedly the emperor's attitude further restrained the electors. Following Maximilian's lead, they decided that any discussion at Regensburg should deal only with arrangements for further talks, not with substantive questions. Mainz accordingly suggested to Hesse-Darmstadt February 3 in Frankfurt as the time and place for Catholics and Protestants to gather to discuss the interpretation of the Peace of Religion. Ferdinand approved this.[67] A few days later, to dispel rumors about a suspension of the Edict, he instructed the imperial comissioners charged with its enforcement to proceed as usual with their task.[68] This was the situation when the convention came to a close on November 12.

What was the policy of the Curia at Regensburg? Here the distinction must be kept in mind between the policy of Rome as it really was, about which not even the nuncios were fully informed, and the policy as it was perceived in Vienna. Ferdinand and Lamormaini were certainly justified in thinking the Curia was behind them. The papal brief of May 5, 1629, seemed to indicate Urban's firm backing for the Edict, and nothing had intervened to change this impression. Pallotto tended to outdo himself to accommodate the emperor. He disclosed his own feelings to Rome when he urged the pope to press Ferdinand not to suspend the program for the restitution of church lands, and even to overthrow the Peace of Augsburg and thereby clear the way for the complete restoration of Catholicism in Germany. If the pope "did not obtain the satisfaction and glory of achieving such a great good, he would not lose that of having pursued it with all his energy, in the best manner, nor [would he lose] the merit with God of having completely satisfied the part of a holy and zealous pastor."[69] According to one account, Pallotto wrote Urban that Ferdinand was "a holy prince, a man according to the heart and will of God, as was King David, because of the candor of his conscience and the certainty of his confidence in God." His whole career showed a special providence God had for him that transcended human understanding.[70] Pallotto seems to have taken on the mind of Lamormaini.

If we judge from the correspondence, Rocci did not work as closely with Lamormaini as did Pallotto. But he presumed that after the conclusion of the Italian peace a major charge of his was to hinder concessions on the Edict, and on September 2 he reported that he had spoken about this with imperial ministers including Eggenberg.[71]

In reality, papal policy continued to be complex, ambivalent, and sometimes confused. The juridical position of the Church remained a primary concern of Urban. Rocci was directed at the start to avoid any action that might be construed as papal consent to the Peace of Augsburg. He was, however, to do what he could to call attention to Protestant violations of the Peace and to point out the need to remedy them. In the same sense, he was to give no positive approval to any concessions to the Protestants. Rome had heard from a reliable source (Maximilian?) that the electors were united in their opposition to concessions, so that, it was implied, there was nothing to worry about. If he could not prevent all concessions, Rocci was to do the best he could to soften the blow and secure adequate compensation for the Catholics.[72] Gradually it was to become clear, especially after the great reversal in the fortunes of war, that Rome was willing to allow Ferdinand to make the best arrangement he could for the Church. Urban would not attempt to contest effectively any such settlement through political action or ecclesiastical measures, but he would withhold formal consent.

Urban was far from ready to give his firm support to Ferdinand's program for Germany, reluctant as he was to contribute to the growth of Habsburg power. Papal policy toward the election of young Ferdinand was disingenuous. When it appeared an election might take place at Regensburg, Rocci took steps to leave the impression the Curia favored Ferdinand by delivering to the electors briefs formally recommending him. These had been sent him from Rome with the directive to use them if necessary. At the same time, following instructions, Rocci intimated to Maximilian and the other electors that the pope could hardly oppose the emperor's desire but that he really favored Maximilian as a candidate.[73] Urban continued to promote the secret negotiations between France and Maximilian toward an alliance that would create a Catholic balance to the power of Habsburg Austria and Spain. Negotiations were carried on secretly at Regensburg in late October and early November between Father Joseph and Maximilian's councilors. But only in May 1631 was the secret Franco-Bavarian Treaty of Fontainebleau concluded.[74] Its revelation would cause a stir soon enough.

Lamormaini was satisfied, to say the least, with the results of the electoral convention, and well he might have been. Vitelleschi remarked that neither Contzen nor Ziegler saw the situation in such a bright light but that he realized "how much better than the others you are able to keep everything in perspective."[75] The dismissal of Wallenstein removed a major source of division between the Catholic electors and Ferdinand. Strong tensions over the military remained, but there seemed to exist a basic will not to allow them to develop to the point where they could drive a real wedge between the emperor and the electors. Peace with France eliminated another source of conflict with the electors, and for Lamormaini seemed to presage future cooperation between the emperor and France. Even Richelieu's refusal to ratify the agreement did not dampen his spirits noticeably; he looked to a quick conclusion of a new settlement. Differences that might have arisen between Ferdinand and Maximilian over the Palatinate were set aside when Frederick turned his back on any realistic settlement. Above all, the Edict stood. Lamormaini's most enthusiastic letters were written to Vitelleschi immediately after the threat of concessions on it had been warded off.[76] Besides, in a series of events to be dealt with in the next chapter, Ferdinand had shown himself unusually generous in carrying out Lamormaini's plan for the dissemination of Jesuit colleges throughout Germany and especially in Lower

Saxony. Lamormaini came out ahead on every issue at Regensburg. His authority was at its zenith.

Regensburg was a defeat for a number of the imperial councilors and for Eggenberg in particular. They made known their frequently dissenting views. This is clear from later criticism they leveled against the theologians and remarks they made for Ferdinand's benefit to the effect they had pointed out the way to peace before "the unhappy trip to Regensburg."[77] But in the case of his colleagues if not with Eggenberg himself, the evidence points less to vigorous opposition than to passive discontent with the drift of events combined with a sense of helplessness to reverse or divert this trend. With Ferdinand's permission, Eggenberg absented himself from some conferences at Regensburg, but only the following February or March did he retire to Graz to sulk.[78] His bitterness showed through in April when he evaluated for Ferdinand new terms for an understanding with France. The "apostasy of the electors," he wrote, "nearly broke my heart." He had not failed to speak his mind at Regensburg, he added, and he still had much to say about events there.[79]

Eggenberg considered the convention a capitulation to the electors and a humiliation of the emperor, a view in which the Spaniards concurred. The unhappy course of events began with the dismissal of Wallenstein, in which Eggenberg acquiesced reluctantly. The attempt to secure the dissolution of the League army and its incorporation into the imperial forces, so desired by the Spaniards, failed. Eggenberg and Tursi opposed the Peace of Regensburg in vain. The election of the King of the Romans hardly merited serious discussion. Eggenberg advocated further talks with the Protestants about the Edict and seems to have favored some compromise. Tursi certainly did. Both had little to show for their efforts. Eggenberg was discouraged and hurt. Regensburg marked the lowpoint of his influence with Ferdinand.

There had been a fair amount of opposition to Lamormaini's and Contzen's policy on the Edict among the Catholic electors. Mainz favored some modification of the Edict and succeeded in leading Cologne and Trier in this direction. Even Maximilian, under pressure from some of his privy councilors, wavered for a time. Later, as we have seen, he contended that the confessors had persuaded the emperor and Catholic electors not to yield. The rulers had inclined toward compromise, and they acted against their own better political judgment in rejecting it.[80]

Yet it would be a serious mistake to attribute the failure to reach an accommodation with the Protestants solely to the Catholic militants such as Lamormaini, Contzen, and Laymann, as if they had prevented a few minor concessions that would have produced a rapprochement with the Protestants. This would be to see events through the spectacles of later anti-Jesuit polemicists like Schoppe. There existed a wide gap between the moderates on both sides. This is evident from a comparison of the Hessian Points, which represented a moderate Protestant statement unacceptable to Saxony and Brandenburg, with the "Catholic Response," which constituted the unofficial answer of some Catholic moderates, including Mainz, to the Hessian Points.[81] A Bavarian privy councilor, who before the convention emphasized the need for an understanding with the Protestants, remarked upon seeing the Hessian Points that the Protestants could not have asked for more if they had just won a major battle.[82]

Catholic moderates at Regensburg were not at all willing to go as far as necessary to satisfy the demand of Protestant moderates. The Hessian Points stipulated, for example, that Saxony and Brandenburg retain unchallenged for fifty years the ecclesiastical lands they held, after which the lands would revert to the status of 1621. The Catholics could then bring the matter to court with the understanding that both sides renounced any resort to force. To resolve disputes and review earlier decisions on religiously related issues the Protestants repeated a long-standing demand, the formation of a new judicial body composed equally of Catholics and Protestants. This was virtually to leave permanently to Saxony and Brandenburg the church lands they held. The Catholic Response consented to allow the two electors the possession of the lands for forty years, after which the status of 1621 would revive and be open to juridical challenge. But this was conditioned on Protestant acceptance of all the other points of the Catholic Response, including acquiescence in the emperor's decision on the Palatinate, an issue on which the Hessian Points were silent. Regarding the mechanism for the settlement of conflicts, the Catholic response insisted on the traditional courts, either the aulic council or the imperial cameral court in Speyer. More profound differences existed with respect to the possession of territorial and imperial church lands and the regulation of religion in the cities.[83]

There were two basic differences between Lamormaini and his adversaries in the Catholic camp, and they were increasingly recognized at the time. One was theological, the other political. For Lamormaini, Ferdinand possessed a mission from God to restore Catholicism in Germany. Divine providence would assist him, as it often had in the past, when humanly or rationally speaking the odds were against him. To be sure, there remained the remote possibility the Catholic forces might go down in defeat. But Ferdinand had to respond to the clear call of the Lord. If he was ruined in the event, this was God's will. To make concessions to the Protestants was to reject God's summons and fail in confidence in God. Lamormaini had no problem acknowledging theoretically that when necessity required it, Ferdinand could legitimately yield on many points, but precisely to admit this necessity was to fail in trust in God. Lamormaini wrote Cardinal Barberini shortly after the conclusion of the convention of Regensburg:[84] "Little remains; God promises us the victory; he is active for it. It is as easy for God to give us victory when we are weak as when we are strong. Let the giants, the sons of Enoch, or the Goliaths, not strike fear in us. With God's aid we will devour them. Let us stand firm, and he will fight for us. If we should do otherwise and permit heresy to live, and again ally with the heretics, that course will most certainly lead to ruin and to scandal."

Lamormaini wrote in the tradition of the holy war of the Old Testament, which with appropriate adaptation for Munich was shared by Contzen. The opposition began to attack this theology by simply denying the parallel with the Old Testament, as can be seen from the opinion submitted to Cologne by an anonymous Dominican professor of theology at the university there.[85] God did guarantee victory to his people in the Old Testament through a special revelation, he wrote. What the Catholic militants were doing was to claim, at least implicitly, a divine revelation in support of their stand. However, for this there was no proof. God had given the Catholics no promise of victory. Human prudence, not appeals to providence, should govern policy. The Dominican drew at length on a natural law argument of Thomas Aquinas to show that this prudence permitted concessions to the Protestants in the circumstances. The Catholics could certainly surrender ecclesiastical lands, even permanently, without violating their consciences. Such a policy would benefit the common good of Empire and Church by establishing peace and thus providing a stable situation in which the Church could grow. Nor was there anything in the Scriptures or in canon law that stood in the way. Thus the theological issue gradually emerged as one of human prudence versus revelation. Was the decision about the Edict to be made on the basis of human and rational considerations or must a special divine revelation or vocation for Ferdinand be taken into account?

Lamormaini's basic political difference with his opponents was his attitude toward France. Lamormaini would not admit that in the long run France would obstruct Ferdinand's efforts to restore Catholicism in Germany. Eventually, the Most Christian King would become at least neutral toward the emperor and at best join the coalition against heresy. Nor was this totally unrealistic. Richelieu's enemies seemed to be on the verge of securing his dismissal and the appointment of one of their own as chief minister as the Convention of Regensburg ended. Marie de Medicis was already passing out offices to her dévot friends on November 10, the famous "Day of Dupes." But after wavering, Louis XIII renewed his firm support of Richelieu. Michel de Marillac, Richelieu's chief rival for office, was arrested and imprisoned. Soon the king took measures to isolate the queen mother, and the next July 30 she fled to the Spanish Netherlands, never to return to France. Henceforth, Richelieu's power was much more secure. But the forces in France sympathetic to Lamormaini's design had come within a hair's breadth of acquiring power.[86]

Nor was the cardinal without opposition in the future. Until the birth of the future Louis XIV in 1638, Louis XIII remained childless after twenty-two years of married life. Heir to the throne until then was Louis's brother Gaston d'Orleans, a flighty figure who never got along with Richelieu and who was involved in several plots to bring him down.[87] Lamormaini's dream that French policy would change was not as visionary as Eggenberg and the Spaniards portrayed it. To them he became increasingly an incorrigible Francophile and a victim of delusion.

7. The Monastery Controversy

 major item of concern at Regensburg was the disposition of the ecclesiastical lands already recovered and to be recovered from the Protestants. Before the Edict of Restitution was promulgated, questions about the future of the lands had surfaced and provoked disagreements among Catholics. At issue was the assignment and control of all the categories of regained ecclesiastical property. We have already discussed the disposition of secular benefices, especially bishoprics, and some of the problems that arose in connection with them. But the most bitter and far-reaching dispute arose over monastic foundations, the former monasteries and convents chiefly but not exclusively of the Benedictine, Cistercian, and Premonstratensian Orders. Were they to be returned to the orders to which they had belonged or were at least some of them to be assigned to active orders, especially the Jesuits, for what many Catholics felt would be more effective use, in particular for the endowment of colleges and seminaries? Lurking in the background was the related issue, who had the final say over the disposition of the monasteries, pope or emperor? As in the case of the secular benefices, tactful diplomacy kept it from moving into the center of the picture.

The "monastery controversy," as it came to be called, lost much of its actuality when many of the lands in question reverted to the Protestants following the victories of Gustav Adolph. Nevertheless it generated a drawn-out polemic whose effects could still be felt in the early twentieth century. All the orders involved suffered, but the Jesuits in particular, despite the fact that their conduct left the least to be desired.[1] The monastery controversy stimulated a great deal of anti-Jesuit sentiment in some Catholic circles, and it provided considerable grist for the mill of the polemicist Schoppe.

Lamormaini considered Jesuit colleges the principal long-term instrument for the propagation and firm establishment of the Catholic faith in Germany. They were for him not only schools but bases from which missionaries and preachers would operate in a city or town and then move out to evangelize the countryside.[2] Their fundamental work, however, was the conversion of the youth and their preservation in the faith. Closely associated with the colleges were the seminaries where zealous and competent priests were to be educated. These institutions had proved themselves; as Lamormaini once wrote, "if there had been no schools of the Society founded by the prudent design of the emperors and archdukes in Vienna, Prague, Graz, Olomouc, and elsewhere in Germany, there would have remained scarcely a vestige of the Catholic religion."[3]

Ferdinand founded, as we have seen, at least six Jesuit colleges and partially endowed many more. Besides this, he founded two Jesuit novitiates and at least four seminaries to be conducted by the Jesuits for diocesan seminarians.[4] Nearly all of these gifts were mediated through Lamormaini, who arranged the financing of further Jesuit establishments from other sources. With his encouragement, for example, Count Michael Adolf von Althan, a distinguished imperial field marshal during the Turkish wars and a convert from Lutheranism, founded colleges at Krems in Lower Austria and at Iglau (Jihlava) and Znaim (Znojmo) in Moravia.[5] After Ferdinand's death Lamormaini reminded his heir that the "most suitable and effective way" to promote the faith in Hungary was through Jesuit colleges, whither talented Hungarian youths would flock "to imbibe in an agreeable and wholesome fashion the Catholic faith along with the sciences."[6]

Obviously, Lamormaini's enthusiasm for the Edict was due in part to the opportunity it presented to secure endowed revenues for the support of Jesuit foundations in the Empire. Shortly after the Mühlhausen Convention of 1627, he had let nuncio Carlo Carafa know that the pope could promote good relations with Ferdinand by approving the emperor's plan "to found seminaries and colleges, to introduce new religious, and [to do] similar things" with the revenues of recovered ecclesiastical property for which there was no titleholder to whom they might revert.[7] From his experience in Bohemia Lamormaini seems to have learned that papal support was important for the success of his project, especially since the emperor's authority was considerably less in the Empire than in the hereditary lands.

The scope of Lamormaini's plans can be gathered from the list of ninety prospective locations for Jesuit colleges in north Germany that he presented to Ferdinand as a New Year's gift in 1630.[8] His design called for the foundation of four new Jesuit provinces, the Westphalian, the Lower Saxon, the Upper Saxon, which practically coincided with Electoral Saxony, and the Brandenburg or Baltic Province, which would comprise Brandenburg. Vitelleschi thought the plan clearly exaggerated, and it cannot be taken at face value. But to dismiss it as mere fantasy would also be a mistake. The new provinces were to be erected "with the help of God and under the auspices of Emperor Ferdinand II," and what could the emperor not do with the Lord's aid? If good fortune were to continue to accompany the imperial armies, the plan was by no means fantastic, especially if we further assume that many colleges were intended at first to be missionary outposts as much as schools, with a contingent of about ten Jesuits each. As early as January 1628, Lamormaini had impressed upon Vitelleschi the need to prepare missionaries for the territory to be regained from the Protestants and had recommended the opening of a new novitiate in Prague.[9] Vitelleschi had then agreed to give thought to the formation of a new province of Saxony.[10] Lamormaini's vision showed his interest in north Germany and helped explain his unwillingness to compromise with Saxony and Brandenburg on the Edict.

Thus Lamormaini foresaw an extensive transfer to the Jesuits of recovered ecclesiastical lands, many of them formerly the property of the monastic orders. Understandably, the monastic orders were not enthusiastic. From his Roman vantage point Vitelleschi sometimes found Lamormaini too aggressive in his dealings with other orders, and he was cautionary. In September 1628 he directed Lamormaini to support Carmelite efforts to secure a house in Vienna, since their monastery there had been turned over to the Society at an earlier date. The confessor was to attend to the project "with no less diligence than if the matter were our own. Furthermore, I recommend to Your Reverence as earnestly as I possibly can that if you should hear that there is anywhere question of giving any monastery of whatever religious to the Society, you oppose such a design with all your energy since it creates for us here as well as there the strongest ill-feeling and is construed as the ill-desire to expel all the other orders from their houses."[11]

Lamormaini did not always act in the spirit of this directive. He was dealing with an unusual historical situation, the distribution of extensive ecclesiastical lands that had been held by the Protestants for decades. Many of the monasteries and convents in question had been undermanned and were no longer models of religious life and discipline at the time they fell into Protestant hands. Lamormaini was convinced that the good of the Church required the passage of some former monastic property to the Society, which had received a special mission for the reconversion of Germany. The two nuncios in Germany, Pallotto and Pier Luigi Carafa, most German bishops, and many Catholics supported him because they did consider the Jesuits more suitable for the missionary and educational tasks involved.[12]

Lamormaini could claim in good conscience that the monasteries he sought for the Society were no longer the property of the monks. This was the position of Laymann, one of the leading canonists of the day. He argued convincingly in his *Just Defense*, published at Dillingen in early 1631, that the ownership of monastic property reverted to the bishop or, in the case of houses exempt from episcopal jurisdiction, to the pope

once all the monks or nuns of a foundation died. This followed because
each monastery was an independent unit and not part of a larger organization. The bishop or pope could then dispose of the monastery as he
saw fit.[13] Thus the monastic orders differed from the centralized mendi-
cant orders, such as the Franciscans, Dominicans, or the Jesuits themselves, where the property would remain with the order. This was the
case, Laymann contended, even when the monastic order possessed an
abbot-general, as with the Cistercians, or when a number of monasteries
had united to form a congregation, as with the Bursfeld Congregation of
Benedictines that had come into existence in 1446 and included most of
the Benedictine monasteries of north Germany.[14]

Most contemporaries, however, seem to have distinguished between
monasteries that were members of a congregation and those that were
not. Lamormaini himself in a joint position paper with Philippi and
Fanini argued, unsuccessfully, that the Benedictine monastery of Berge
near Magdeburg should not be turned over to Archbishop Harrach of
Prague, who desired the revenues for his Counterreformation efforts, but
should be returned to the Benedictines precisely because it had belonged
to the Bursfeld Congregation.[15] Most of the revenues Lamormaini hoped
to obtain as endowments for Jesuit colleges came from former convents of nuns that had been virtually autonomous. Moreover, there was
no question of the nuns' undertaking pastoral work as there was with
the monks.

The monastic orders laid claim to all the recovered monasteries, whether
of men or women, that had lived under their rules, and they took measures to protect their interests. In August 1628 there arrived in Vienna
Father Georg Schönhainz, a Premonstratensian of the Abbey of Roth in
Swabia, whose assignment was to represent the monastic orders at court.
Talking with Lamormaini in late October, he discovered that the confessor aimed to secure for the Jesuits most of the recovered monasteries of
women plus a portion of the revenues from the recovered monasteries of
men. Unfortunately, in the course of their conversation, according to
Schönhainz, Lamormaini let fall the remark that only the Society of
Jesus had stood firm against the onslaughts of the heretics, whereas the
older orders had failed in the crisis. Thus Schönhainz became wary of
the Jesuits and of the bishops who seemed to favor them.[16] The abbots of
Weingarten and Ochsenhausen petitioned the emperor in the name of
their order for the return of all recovered Benedictine monasteries. They
received a favorable reply on January 17, along with the expressed expec-
tation that they would undertake what was necessary for the restoration
of the liturgy and monastic discipline. Representatives of the Cistercians

and Premonstratensians were guaranteed only that their side would be heard before any action was taken.[17]

Later in the winter agreement appeared to have been reached at a crucial interview that Lamormaini described in a letter to Barberini of March 10.[18] Different versions of what transpired were later to come from the principal participants, who were Lamormaini on the one hand and the representatives of the Benedictines and Cistercians, the Archabbot of Harsefeld and the Abbot of Kaisheim, on the other. Also present was Abbot Anton. At the end of their discussion, according to Lamormaini, the Society had declared in writing for the emperor that it neither desired nor would accept any male monastery of another order in Germany, even if it had been deserted and held by heretics for years. The two abbots, then, when they realized all Lamormaini had done for the recovery of church lands, offered "spontaneously" to turn over to the Jesuits all the recovered convents of nuns where the Benedictine Rule had been observed, the revenues to be used to support colleges and seminaries. The two abbots agreed, Lamormaini wrote, that the faith could not be restored and preserved without the Jesuits. The emperor and his councilors had approved this agreement, he continued, and he asked Barberini to dispose the pope to accept it too.

But there was another provision of the agreement as approved by the councilors that Lamormaini did not mention in the communication for Barberini, namely, that a sum was to be levied on recovered monasteries of men to help pay the costs of restitution, that is, war costs, and then perhaps to finance colleges or other projects to be designated by the emperor.[19] Lamormaini may have left this out because he thought Rome would object to this form of subsidy for the emperor. In any event, these were the two points to which, Lamormaini consistently asserted, the two abbots had consented: the transfer of monasteries of women and the levy on monasteries of men. Whether or not his zeal led him to read into statements of the abbots more than they intended we will never know for certain, but there can be little doubt that he believed what he affirmed.

Shortly after the appearance of the Edict, signs of divergent imperial policies toward the recovered monasteries began to appear. The Edict itself and the instructions for the imperial commissioners charged with its implementation strongly implied that monasteries were to be returned to the order that had previously held them.[20] This corresponded to what the abbots of Weingarten and Ochsenhausen had been assured in January. Similarly, an imperial letter of April 14 instructed Prince Paul Savelli, the imperial representative in Rome, to work for the return of monasteries to those orders "to whom they belonged and from their first foundation were dedicated and consecrated, and to no other."[21] No distinction was made between houses of men and women.

But in early May Ferdinand wrote the Jesuit provincial superiors in Germany stressing the necessity of establishing the Society in the areas regained from the Protestants and asking them to suggest where colleges might best be founded, what was needed for their support, and what ecclesiastical lands might best be set aside for their endowment.[22] The same day he requested the two generals Wallenstein and Tilly to recommend locations for colleges and to name former Benedictine and Cistercian monasteries of women that might be applied to their foundation. The imperial commissioners were directed on May 23 to sequester such monasteries provisionally.[23] The Jesuit provincial superiors, in turn, told local rectors to continue to inquire after church lands, monastic or secular, confiscated after 1555, "since on this depends the whole implementation of the Emperor's intention to erect colleges."[24] They were not, however, to consider male Benedictine or Cistercian monasteries. According to information from Vienna, an agreement had been reached that the two orders would reacquire monasteries of men but surrender those of women.

The ambivalence of imperial policy contributed to the ambiguities in the position of the Curia. Instructions prepared for Pier Luigi Carafa by the Propaganda in March 1629 called for the restitution of ecclesiastical lands above all to orders "which are given over to the active life and are better able to benefit the propagation of the faith," without any specific mention of the Jesuits. At the same time, they directed that special concern be had for the return of church lands to their former possessors, "even if they were less suitable for the propagation of the faith."[25] Barberini was in a difficult position; he could not be certain of imperial policy, Savelli's representation of the emperor's intention having contradicted Lamormaini's letter of March 10. Gradually the two nuncios, first Pallotto and then Pier Luigi Carafa, who themselves were influenced by Lamormaini, helped edge Rome and Vienna toward an unambiguous espousal of the confessor's position. But the Curia never completely embraced it.

That summer of 1629 Barberini was concerned to fend off an imperial invasion of Mantua. At roughly the same time he was reaching an accommodation with Vienna on the appointment to secular benefices, he informed Lamormaini and Pallotto that Rome would approve the transfer of some monasteries to the Society.[26] Pallotto, then, apparently with more enthusiasm than the Curia had shown, let the emperor know that the pope and cardinals did not feel it to be in the interest of the Church to restore all monastic lands to their former owners; it would be better to reserve some for colleges and seminaries of the Jesuits and other orders. He requested Ferdinand in the pope's name to turn over the lands in question to the bishops or, where none had jurisdiction, to leave them in the hands of the imperial commissioners until disposition was made. He made no distinction between monasteries of monks and nuns.[27]

But within the imperial chancery there was obvious confusion and even opposition to Lamormaini's plan. An imperial letter of October 25, 1629, reminded Savelli of the instructions he had been sent on April 14. All monasteries, even those of women, were to be restored to the original owners. They were not to be conferred *in commendam*, applied to bishoprics, burdened with pensions, or conceded to another order under pretext of the common good. Conscience required as much. Neither pope nor emperor had the authority to transfer the property because this would be to violate the intentions of the benefactors who had initially endowed the monasteries. Copies of this letter, which was based on a memorandum of Schönhainz, were sent to most of the German bishops.[28] Another communication to Savelli of December 11 reiterated this stand and warned against designs of the bishops as well as other orders. But instructions sent the imperial commissioners the following day repeated those of May 23, directing them to sequester recovered monasteries of women that were suitable for the endowment of Jesuit colleges.[29]

Finally, Pallotto himself, after being shown a copy of Schönhainz's memorandum, brought the ambiguous nature of imperial policy to the attention of Lamormaini, who turned out not to have been aware of the letters to Savelli. But instead of going directly to Ferdinand as Pallotto wanted, Lamormaini thought it better first to pray over the matter and to investigate the situation.[30] He described his version of events in a letter to a Roman correspondent in mid-January. The Schönhainz memorandum was an invention of the devil, "lest the Catholic Church be restored in Saxony." The aulic council, he felt, had probably accepted it because it argued against the imposition of pensions on monasteries and their conferral in commendam, practices the emperor abhorred. He had not yet raised the matter with Ferdinand, but he had learned in talks with several councilors that they were not happy with the stand taken in the letters to Savelli. He would be careful not to offend other orders, Lamormaini wrote, but it was necessary to refute the view that the pope could not redistribute ecclesiastical property when the general welfare called for it. The councilors also came in for severe criticism from him for presuming to treat a matter of conscience without consulting the theologians.[31]

Finally, in a strong letter to Ferdinand, which he gave the emperor about the same time he presented him with his design for the foundation of colleges in north Germany, Lamormaini challenged the instructions given Savelli. They were a source of scandal and error, contravening as they did the practice of many emperors and popes and departing from accepted Catholic teaching. Undoubtedly, they had been formulated without either Ferdinand or the councilors realizing their implications. A joint committee of councilors and theologians should be formed to review the matter with him and to suggest the future course of action. Lamormaini obviously felt he had the Curia on his side when he stated that if there was no change in policy, it was not unthinkable that a censure would be forthcoming from Rome, an eventuality that would certainly give Ferdinand's enemies a chance to gloat. Lamormaini closed with a plea to the emperor "not to allow political tribunals easily to make pronouncements on matters which pertain to conscience without consulting the theologians and the confessor."[32] As it turned out, Ferdinand disclaimed any knowledge of what had taken place—he had not even seen Schönhainz's memorandum—and he ordered the formation of the recommended committee.[33]

Pier Luigi Carafa now intervened on the side of the Jesuits. In the fall of 1629 the nuncio in Cologne had encouraged Lamormaini to influence Ferdinand so that church property would be restored to those "who are truly able to help religion at this time by the foundation of parishes, seminaries, colleges, and not to those who are not suited for this." Lamormaini responded by recommending that Carafa seek a papal brief to this effect. This Carafa did on December 7.[34] After intense discussion in Rome, the Congregation of the Palatinate, whose competence overlapped to a degree with the Propaganda, determined largely on the basis of information from Carafa and Palotto that the application of lands of extinct monasteries to the endowment of colleges was of great importance for the restoration of Catholicism in Germany. It recommended that the pope enjoin the German bishops to recover all the lands they could and retain the property themselves provisionally except in those instances where a religious order had explicit permission to reoccupy it. There was opposition to this at court, the congregation realized, but the emperor was ready to comply.[35]

Urban, then, issued an enthusiastic brief for Ferdinand on February 16, which, however, skirted the main issue of the monastery controversy. The pope declared that "colleges must be constructed, Gymnasia opened, seminaries planted" with the help of the recovered lands. The Lord had used the emperor's forces to "extract from the belly of the heretics the riches they had devoured." These riches were now to be used to help support the preparation of laborers to gather in the rich harvest expected from Germany. However, the brief hedged by referring generally to church lands and not explicitly to monasteries, perhaps because still the only official indication Rome had of imperial policy were the representations of Savelli.[36]

As early as January 1630 the opponents of the Jesuits took up the pen to champion their cause. An anonymous Jesuit sent Vitelleschi several pamphlets so that he could see the degree of opposition some members of other religious orders felt to the Society's plans for restitution.[37] These probably included the anonymous *Discussion of Monasteries Recovered from the Heretics*[38] and Schönhainz's anonymously published *Judgment of Two Theologians for the Emperor about the Transfer of the Recovered Monasteries in the Empire from the Ancient Orders to the Society of Jesus.*[39] The first, besides treating the canonical question of the right to transfer ecclesiastical property from one order to another, led the discussion into the dangerous area of religious rivalry. After admitting the monasteries had not been all they should have been in the recent past, it affirmed the greatness of the monastic tradition and the monastic contribution to the Church. Schönhainz's publication of two opinions that had been drawn up for private use, allegedly by Jesuits, was obviously meant to embarrass the Society because of several derogatory remarks about the monks found in them. But a Jesuit clearly was not the author of the opinion that Schönhainz found more offensive. It was most likely the work of Pier Luigi Carafa or Pallotto.[40]

As the war of polemics began in the months prior to the Electoral Convention of Regensburg, the program to establish colleges gathered speed. On May 11 Ferdinand approved plans submitted by the two imperial commissioners for the Lower Saxon Circle, Franz Wilhelm von Wartenberg, Bishop of Osnabrück, and Johannes von Hyen, an aulic councilor. They included the foundation of colleges in the cities of Minden, Verden, Hameln, Nordhausen, and Mühlhausen, the expansion of the college already begun in Stade, and the construction of a Jesuit novitiate in Goslar. The major source of revenue for these was to be former convents of women religious, some of which had not yet been recovered from the Protestants.[41]

Regensburg offered the perfect opportunity to deal with the problems connected with the Edict. To the imperial city on the Danube flocked Catholics with plans or interests in the distribution of the recovered lands as well as Protestants with their petitions and legal briefs against the implementation of the Edict. Lamormaini saw to it, for example, that Hermann Baving, the provincial superior of the Lower Rhenish Province, came to Regensburg, "because if he is here much can be accomplished for the Society's work on behalf of the Lower Saxon Circle, since the emperor, the imperial commissioners for those parts, and the general, Tilly, will all be present."[42]

Rocci, the new nuncio, outlined for Barberini the two positions on the monastery question.[43] Lamormaini and some others, he wrote, stressed the authority pope and emperor held jointly to dispose of ecclesiastical, not merely monastic lands, for the greater good of the Church in Germany, "when there are no ecclesiastics who truly have a right to them and can properly be said to have been despoiled, such as they believe to be those monasteries that do not live under a general superior but are completely independent." The Bishop of Augsburg, Rocci reported, strongly favored Lamormaini's position, and there were other bishops he failed to mention.[44] Rocci was probably misinformed when he stated that the whole aulic council and many privy councilors including Abbot Anton held that justice required the return to the monks of all monasteries, whether they had been previously united with other monasteries or not. But the opposition to Lamormaini on this issue was formidable. It included Stralendorf, the vice president of the aulic council, who as imperial vice chancellor was almost certainly the person responsible for the instructions to Savelli, as we shall see. Perhaps some councilors decided to defeat Lamormaini at least on this issue and thereby thwart his influence. Rocci's own inclination was to side with the confessor, even though he thought Lamormaini played down the rights of the pope to the benefit of the emperor. He asked for instructions.

While the convention was in progress, the two Benedictine abbots, Placidus Spiess of Ochsenhausen and Maurus Baldung of Weingarten, took their case to Rome personally. Their interviews with Pope Urban and members of the Curia seem to have brought promises to seek more information. They spoke with Vitelleschi on July 10, and he assured them he had forbidden any Jesuit to try to gain possession of any monastery for which there existed a clear owner. He would be grateful for information about any violation of his directive. Extremely intent on avoiding disputes with other orders, Vitelleschi brought the matter to the attention of the provincial superior in Munich, Walter Mundbrot.[45]

Neither Lamormaini nor Mundbrot had any difficulty denying they sought monasteries to which anyone had a clear title.[46] Possession of the monasteries in question, they felt, had reverted to the bishops or to the Holy See. They also relied on the offer they understood the abbots of Kaisheim and Harsefeld had made in their conversation with Lamormaini in the winter of 1628–29. But the two abbots now denied they had ever made any arrangement with Lamormaini. The Abbot of Kaisheim wrote Lamormaini on August 31 asking him to squelch the rumor circulating at Regensburg that he and his fellow abbot had agreed to surrender all claims to monasteries of women formerly belonging to their two orders.

He had no recollection they had done any such thing, and if they had, they had clearly overstepped their authority. The rumors had brought both of them into disrepute within their respective orders. Shortly afterwards, the Benedictine Archabbot of Harsefeld wrote Lamormaini in the same sense; and the following month he made a notarized statement denying any agreement with him.[47]

After an exchange of letters which remained mild in tone, Lamormaini responded that for the sake of charity he had written Ferdinand that the two abbots did not recall making any commitment and that they denied they had any power to do so.[48] Lamormaini obviously still believed otherwise, nor can there be any doubt that the two abbots were under great pressure from their confrères. Abbot Anton, who also had been present at the interview, maintained at Regensburg that he was not aware of any concession made by the two abbots. Later, back in Vienna, he modified this somewhat. Anyone should realize, he remarked, that the two abbots did not have the authority to enter such an agreement. The abbots had urged Lamormaini to work for restitution, he recalled, and they had indicated they would not be opposed to assisting the Jesuits here and there in their efforts to build colleges and seminaries. He regretted Lamormaini had taken this statement too broadly. But there certainly was no question of a juridical promise having been made.[49]

At Regensburg, the plans of Wartenberg and Hyen for Jesuit houses in the Lower Saxon Circle came up for discussion again. They now included a university in Goslar. Lamormaini was asked to prepare an opinion on them. He hinted at the scope of his own designs when he declared that no Catholic could doubt the need not only for the projected colleges, noviatiate, and university but also for others in the circle and other circles, "so that the youth, the seed-bed of the State and the Church, may be brought up in the Catholic faith and piety and that finally the continual propagation of heresy may come to an end."[50] But a special problem to be faced concerned the three or four Cistercian convents of women among the ecclesiastical properties destined for the support of the new institutions.

Lamormaini began his treatment of this sensitive issue, which constituted more than two-thirds of the paper, by pointing out the gratitude the Jesuits owed both the Benedictines and Cistercians for the many benefits they had received from them over the years. After recounting his version of the conversation with the abbots, he took note of the letters he had received from them. They clearly indicated the two orders did not support the arrangement he understood had been reached, he wrote, and the Society would not press the affair further either in Vienna or Rome. But this did not clear up the matter for the emperor's conscience.

Are there other means of endowing the colleges or not? Are those
orders rightly unwilling, are they able to be rightly unwilling [to
surrender the monasteries]? After the death of all the nuns who by
reason of the profession they made there possessed the rights to
these monasteries, is the right of disposing of them acquired by the
Cistercian Order or does it pass to the supreme rulers of church and
state? Is the necessity of educating the youth by teachers of the
Society of Jesus so great, that even if the order is unwilling, these
lands can be used to build colleges and Gymnasia?

Somewhat disingenuously, Lamormaini disclaimed any intent to answer these questions. But he went on to emphasize that in accord with its
peculiar institute, the Society was prepared to supply missionaries who
would work diligently and without remuneration for the conversion of
Lower Saxony. Tactfully avoiding any discussion of the relative rights of
pope and emperor, Lamormaini went on to affirm that under certain
circumstances the two together had transferred and could transfer ecclesiastical property from one order to another. Indeed, there were times
when this was required. Lamormaini then took the opportunity to admonish the emperor gently once again about the letters to Savelli, which
had not yet been disavowed. Certainly unknown to Lamormaini, another
letter had been sent to Savelli on April 25 reiterating the stand of his
opponents at court: that all monasteries must be restored to the orders
that had founded them.[51]

Finally, Lamormaini suggested four steps he judged Ferdinand could
take in good conscience. First, he could continue to operate on the basis
of the instructions given the imperial commissioners by which they had
been told to retain the monasteries of women in imperial sequester.
Second, it would help to write the Father General[52] of the Cistercians
telling him that both pope and emperor had plans for the restoration of
religion in Germany and indicating that for this the revenues of some
former Cistercian monasteries might be necessary. The emperor should
assure him that the more famous monasteries of men were to be returned
to the order. The Father General would accept this arrangement in a
proper spirit for the good of the Church, Lamormaini felt. In the same
spirit, he would concede to Ferdinand for a number of years a regular
levy on the regained monasteries of men. Third, the emperor could represent to the pope the need to apply revenues of some former monasteries
to the support of men and institutions required for the restoration of
religion in Germany and, specifically, he could request papal approval of
the transfers proposed by Wartenberg. The nuncio could be empowered
to handle negotiations. Finally, if the pope gave his approval, which

Lamormaini obviously expected, then Ferdinand could proceed with the plans for the new foundations.

Lamormaini won a clear victory over the opposition at court when Ferdinand acted on his recommendation. On October 16, the emperor wrote seeking papal approval for the proposals of Wartenberg and Hyen.[53] To his request he added that what he had communicated earlier to Rome on the matter was to be understood according to canon and imperial law. He had not intended to limit the freedom of either pope or emperor to act for the benefit of the common good. The letter stressed once again the importance of winning the youth of an area if it was to be effectively recatholicized. Most suited for this were the Jesuits, "who opened Gymnasia and along with the sweetmeats of letters fed them firmly and gently the solid nourishment of piety and who taught as much by their lives as by their preaching and writing."

But Lamormaini's triumph was not yet quite complete. Stralendorf as vice chancellor held up the dispatch of the letters to Rome and on grounds of conscience remonstrated with the emperor about his decision. Thus he revealed himself as one of Lamormaini's staunchest opponents on this issue and almost certainly as the councilor who was responsible for the instructions to Savelli. Ferdinand in a short, hand-written note to the vice chancellor on November 7 replied that he had taken his objections into consideration, but Stralendorf was to carry out the orders he had received, "as I trust to take the responsibility for my decision, and consequently I have no scruple but hope for reward for myself with God because of the help I have given [the advancement of religion]." Ferdinand then directed Stralendorf to date the letters to Rome back to the date of his original order, that is, October 16.[54]

Rome, however, seems never to have taken any action on this request and thereby avoided committing itself further on the monastery question. Rocci had now been instructed to remain neutral in the dispute, probably because the Curia did not want to become involved in the developing polemics, which Rome soon took measures to halt.[55] Opposition to Lamormaini's vision of the restoration of Catholicism in Germany remained strong in Rome and in Vienna. Only earlier in 1630 had a final settlement been reached regarding ecclesiastical property in Bohemia, and the dispute over the university in Prague was still far from resolution. After the Battle of Breitenfeld in September 1631 and the reversal of fortune it brought, the monastery issue for Lower Saxony became largely moot. Before long both the emperor and the League were petitioning Rome that all the revenues from recovered ecclesiastical lands be applied to the war effort.

During the Convention of Regensburg, the polemical pieces, some published, others circulated in manuscript, grew sharper, a fact to which Rocci called attention in his dispatch of October 22.[56] A vicious attack on Lamormaini and the Jesuits was the anonymously published *Defense of His Imperial Majesty and the Instructions of the Same for his Resident.*[57] Its intent was to defend the original instructions to Savelli against the opinions of the two allegedly Jesuit theologians, which Schönhainz had published anonymously. The author was probably Schoppe, but may have been Roman Hay, a Benedictine of Ochsenhausen, who alongside Schoppe was to play an increasingly active part in the controversy.[58] The first to answer for the Society was Adam Contzen, whose more aggressive *Calm Discussion* followed his mild and brief *Friendly Response*, both published anonymously.[59]

The chief Jesuit response was Laymann's *Just Defense*, which has correctly been called the masterpiece of the dispute.[60] Laymann arrived in Regensburg on October 30 to begin work, and his book, all five hundred pages of it, came off the press in a little over three months.[61] In the meantime Rome intervened to impose silence on both sides in the controversy.[62] Vitelleschi acknowledged the quality of Laymann's work and thanked him for it, but he also expressed his regret that the papal prohibition had not come early enough to prevent its publication.[63] His fears that it would only ignite further polemics were soon realized. In 1634 Schoppe and Hay published in one volume their respective rejoinders, the *Ecclesiastical Astrology* and the *Unextinguished Star*, both affirming the monastic orders to be the brightest stars in the ecclesiastical firmament.[64] Laymann responded in 1635 with the last work he published before his death that year, *A Censure of the Ecclesiastical Astrology and the Unextinguished Star*,[65] which was followed in 1636 by a much more widely circulated edition of Hay's *Unextinguished Star*.[66] Then came more Jesuit refutations, and so it continued.[67]

Several issues were intermingled in the increasingly acerbic polemic. First, there was the canonical question, did the pope and emperor possess the authority to transfer ecclesiastical property for the common good, and if so, under what conditions? Not all the writings on the side of the monks denied this authority to pope and emperor but accused the Jesuits of greatly exaggerating it in order to accumulate lands for themselves.[68] The Jesuits misused the appeal to the common good to justify the neglect of rights and the departure from the rule of law. This argument Lamormaini rejected as early as his letter of October 7 to the Abbot of Kaisheim. "I would prefer to die rather than cooperate in propagating it [the Society] in a manner that would involve an injustice or an action at which anyone could reasonably take offense," he wrote.[69]

Another point of dispute turned upon the conversation between Lamormaini and the two abbots in early 1629. What promises of concessions had been made, if any? Implicit in the charges of the Jesuits' opponents was the accusation that Lamormaini and the Society had either manipulated the abbots into making a concession they were obviously not empowered to make or had taken a chance remark and twisted it into a promise. The Jesuits pointed out they had never considered the statement of the abbots a formal promise. At the same time, however, they implied that the abbots had gone back on an arrangement they had made. The Jesuits also argued that the monks had obtained the original instructions for Savelli in an underhanded fashion. After all, Ferdinand himself denied any knowledge of them.

The polemic overflowed into broader issues. A charge was brought against Lamormaini and the Society that would become much more frequent after the disaster at Breitenfeld. They exercised excessive influence at the German Catholic courts, and they unduly mixed theology with politics, for example, by insisting on the obligation of Ferdinand and the Catholic princes to crush heresy. More in the forefront in the writings over the monastery question was the Jesuits' own claim to a providential role in the battle against heresy. Unfortunately, the dispute came to encompass the relative merits and value to the Church of the Jesuits and the monastic orders. Hay's contention that a degree of arrogance was found among the Jesuits was not completely without foundation.[70] Lamormaini could speak disparagingly of other orders. In his *Just Defense*, after noting that the comparison of orders was odious to him but that he had not started it, Laymann extolled the labors of the Society in Germany:[71] "Let the reader consider the books written as heresy raged in Germany by the religious of the ancient orders (whom that author [Schoppe or Hay] arms against our Society) and compare them with those produced with such great usefulness for the Catholic faith by Rev. Father Peter Canisius." He went on to mention nearly twenty Jesuit writers. No wonder Vitelleschi regretted the publication of the book.

The events at Regensburg were the occasion for Schoppe's emergence as one of the most vitriolic anti-Jesuit writers in the history of the order. A passion, sometimes pathological, animated his writings against the Society. For a long time, criticism of aspects of the Society, in particular its educational theory and practice, had not been unusual in his publications. Still, in a letter of July 13 from Augsburg to a friend in the Roman Curia, he favored the transfer of monastic lands to the Jesuits. Everything about the Society did not please him, he admitted, but under God the Jesuits had done the most for the Church in Germany.[72]

Shortly afterward, his attitude underwent a profound change, as is clear from his publication of the *Defense of His Imperial Majesty and the*

Instructions of the Same for His Resident. Some have attributed this to
personal reasons, especially to his conviction that the Jesuits had frustrated his efforts at Regensburg to secure a badly needed imperial pension
and, more generally, that they were responsible for his failure to regain
his earlier influence with Ferdinand. There is certainly truth in this. But
just as certainly a factor was his experience of Lamormaini's adamantine
stance on the Edict. Schoppe saw this was bound to end in disaster. His
assigning the blame for the catastrophe to Lamormaini and the Jesuits
helps explain the passion of his polemic. Lamormaini and Laymann were
the two individual Jesuits attacked most consistently in his *Case for
Treason against the Jesuits, the Sworn Enemies of the Holy Roman Empire*, sometimes called *The Scourge of the Jesuits*, his *Anatomy of the
Society of Jesus*, and the aforementioned *Ecclesiastical Astrology*.[73] Most
of the criticism took as its point of departure the monastery controversy
or the dispute over the Edict. Later, both Jansenist authors and the
philosophes of the Enlightenment were to draw extensively on these and
other writings of Schoppe in their campaigns against the Jesuits,[74] so that
Lamormaini and Laymann were to have a far-reaching echo in anti-Jesuit
literature.

The position and influence Lamormaini enjoyed with the emperor
sometimes caused friction with fellow Jesuits in Vienna and Prague. To
provincial superiors he seemed at times to assume that he was directing
the apostolic work of the province, and they complained to Vitelleschi.
In early 1628 Christoph Grenzinus, provincial superior of the newly-
formed Bohemian Province, contended that in the continuing dispute
over the university in Prague Lamormaini had put forth a new initiative
as that of the Society without consulting him. This was undoubtedly due
to haste or forgetfulness, Vitelleschi replied, and not to any desire to
bypass the provincial.[75] About the same time, when Lamormaini was
eager to gather missionaries for Lower Saxony, Christoph Dombrinus,
provincial superior of the Austrian Province, lamented that Lamormaini
made administration of the province difficult by recommending the disposition of valuable men to the emperor. Vitelleschi admitted to Dombrinus that he had granted Ferdinand the privilege of making use of
Jesuits as if he were superior general, "which I judged could in no way be
denied him because of his benefits to the Society and his desire of the
divine honor." But he promised to write Lamormaini not to recommend
the assignment of Jesuits without first clearing it with the provincial.[76]
This he did, but after Lamormaini complained about the obstacles to his
work and threatened in a veiled manner to resign his post as confessor,
Vitelleschi indicated indirectly that he considered him chiefly responsible

for the Society's work in Austria and encouraged him not to be dejected because of the complaints of others, Jesuit and non-Jesuit alike. "Yet I will take care that in the future you will find not only Father Provincial but others also, as much as it is possible for me to bring it about, more in agreement with you in their thinking and counsel," Vitelleschi wrote.[77] Misunderstandings with Lamormaini may have been one reason Dombrinus served an unusually short period as provincial.

A difficult situation was provoked by the appointment in early 1630 of a Belgian Jesuit, Florence de Montmorency, to make a formal visitation of the Austrian Province. As Vitelleschi remarked to the new provincial superior, Georg Forer, not much time had elapsed since the previous visitation, but the number of complaints about a decline of discipline seemed to call for another.[78] A matter disturbing Vitelleschi the previous year had been the apparent failure of Jesuits in Vienna to undertake the traditional activity of teaching catechism to the youth. There was danger, he thought, that the people were being brought to the faith more by imperial authority than their own free will.[79] Several months after the visitation started, Vitelleschi wrote Montmorency that he was glad to hear that he and the provincial were working well together, and he encouraged the visitor to make every effort he decently could to get along with Lamormaini because of the benefits the confessor could obtain for the Society in Austria and all Germany. Later Vitelleschi warned Montmorency that Lamormaini had his detractors in Vienna and consequently the visitor was to be slow to believe allegations about him. Nor was he to take any measures that might disturb the confessor without first consulting Vitelleschi.[80]

But Montmorency had called several matters to Lamormaini's attention, and the confessor complained to Vitelleschi from Regensburg of the annoyance the visitor was causing him.[81] One subject Montmorency apparently raised was the roughness of manner that seems to have characterized Lamormaini all his life and at which Jesuits as well as others sometimes took offense. More serious was the visitor's request for an account of the funds that passed through Lamormaini's hands as a result of his heavy involvement in the endowment of colleges and the construction of houses. Other Jesuits, including the new provincial superior, Forer, complained that Lamormaini went ahead with construction projects without consulting superiors.[82]

Vitelleschi discussed Lamormaini in a long letter of October 19 to Montmorency.[83] Gently he reprimanded the visitor for too easily giving credence to complaints about Lamormaini. Vitelleschi noted that he had often taken up Lamormaini's roughness of manner with him and that the confessor was intent on improvement. "But the inclination of nature and the press of business often conquer the will, and so it sometimes happens that he deals with others and perhaps with superiors more roughly and freely than would be proper." Lamormaini's outstanding qualities and virtues, especially his zeal for the divine glory, with which he accomplished so much for the Church and the Society, were such that "religious prudence seems to advise that superiors admonish him about these defects so affectionately and mildly that they by sharpness do not turn his spirit away from the much weightier and more useful services he performs for the public good." But he would bring these matters to Lamormaini's attention, he promised the visitor, especially the "impetuous manner with which he dealt with Your Reverence." Several months later, Vitelleschi informed Montmorency he did not think it expedient to require of Lamormaini an account of his income or expenses. Vitelleschi would look to that himself. In fact, the superior general had already permitted him to make use of the alms entrusted to him as he saw fit.[84] There is no evidence Vitelleschi ever demanded an account.

8. Last Chance for Compromise: Frankfurt, 1631

uring the closing days of the Convention of Regensburg, the Catholic electors, with imperial approval, had proposed a new conference to resolve the difficulties regarding the Religious Peace. They suggested the conference convene in Frankfurt on February 3, but there was little room for optimism. The starting point for discussion was to be the unofficial papers exchanged during the last weeks at Regensburg, and these had displayed the gap even between Catholic and Protestant moderates. Moreover, both Saxony and Brandenburg had refused to subscribe to the Hessian Points because they were too liberal. Saxony's decision to pursue his intention to call a conference of Protestant states then forced the postponement of the meeting at Frankfurt. Though shaken by the action of the Protestant Leipzig Conference, which ran from late February until early April, the Catholics still intended to participate in the Frankfurt Conference, which was rescheduled for August 3.

Gustav Adolph, fortified by French subsidies granted him by the Treaty of Bärwalde on January 23, continued his advance in the spring. Frankfurt on the Oder fell to him on April 13; by then, in addition to Pomerania, much of Mecklenburg and Brandenburg was under his effective control. Elector George William was forced to accept a provisional agreement with him on May 14, and this was given a more permanent basis on June 20.[1] Spain redoubled its efforts to direct imperial policy away from peace with France and toward the formation of a common front with the electors, Catholic and Protestant, that would confront the oncoming Swedes, deal with the French, and it was hoped, intervene against the Dutch in the Netherlands. Clearly this meant compromise on the Edict. At the imperial court the struggle over policy was increasingly between Lamormaini and Eggenberg. Ferdinand's ratification on June 19 of the Peace of Cherasco with France, ending the war in Italy, was a victory for the confessor and for Maximilian of Bavaria. It removed one source of tension between Ferdinand and the League, but others remained, especially as Maximilian edged closer to France. Then in mid-September the overwhelming victory of Gustav Adolph over Tilly at Breitenfeld turned the whole state of affairs upside down.

At Regensburg Ferdinand had approved the Frankfurt Conference on condition that it deal only with the implementation of the Edict, not its substance, which he always saw as merely reiterating the Peace of Religion. But Lamormaini was afraid the conference might jeopardize the Edict, and he attempted to marshal Roman energies behind his policy. On January 11 he wrote Barberini urging that Urban encourage the Catholic electors to stand firm.[2] Ferdinand himself had said, according to Lamormaini, that he was willing to risk all he possessed rather than yield on the Edict, provided the Catholic electors, especially Maximilian, supported him. With Ferdinand's consent, Lamormaini added, he had just let Contzen know this. The proposed negotiations, he felt, might easily lead to further concessions, as had happened in the time of Charles V. Suspension, not to mention revocation, of the Edict would undo the successes already achieved and cut off future possibilities. Lamormaini seemed particularly disturbed by the proposal of the "Catholic Response" that foresaw a suspension of the Edict for Saxony and Brandenburg. Joining him in efforts to convince Rome of the need to forestall adverse decisions at Frankfurt were the two bishops, Wartenberg and Knöringen, and Contzen.[3] Already in mid-November Rocci had alerted Rome to the conference proposed for Frankfurt, and an ad hoc congregation was deliberating over the proper reaction when Lamormaini's letter arrived. To the same congregation had been referred the urgent appeal for subsidies that the Catholic League had sent from Regensburg.[4]

Urban's response to the warnings and appeals from Germany was a series of briefs to the emperor, the empress, the King of Hungary, Eggenberg, Maximilian, the ecclesiastical electors, and the five prince-bishops expected to attend the Frankfurt Conference.[5] The pope exhorted them to withstand pressures to compromise the rights of the Church. In his brief to Ferdinand, after lauding the emperor's zeal, Urban warned that the Protestants were now trying to win through negotiations what they had been unable to obtain on the battlefield. "Your Majesty, who thinks the exchange even of earthly happiness for the propagation of the Catholic faith a good bargain, will certainly not be able to permit anything to be decreed that is contrary to the divine law or canonical authority. We indeed, to whom the Almighty has committed the care of religion, not only request and hope for this consolation from Your Majesty, we also demand it." The two nuncios were instructed to do all they could to prevent the meeting itself and if this were not possible, to see that no agreement was reached hostile to the interests of the Church. To this end, Rocci was to work closely with Lamormaini, who had every reason to believe the pope was supporting him. Urban stated a clear position. To be sure, he did not threaten ecclesiastical censures or a formal protest should Ferdinand or the Catholic states yield to the Protestants. But this in itself could be interpreted as a realistic recognition of the limits of papal power as much as a sign of less than complete commitment to the Catholic restoration. Lamormaini never called for or advocated such measures.[6]

Disappointing to the German Catholics and more indicative of papal priorities were the minimal subsidies promised the League. The pope first granted the League one-half of the revenues from the church lands in the Upper and Lower Palatinates. When Maximilian informed him there was virtually nothing to be had from them, Urban conceded for three years one-half the revenue of all church lands recovered by the League. But the yield of these was minimal, Maximilian complained, and many were still in the hands of the Protestants. In addition, the allocation of these revenues to the League and not to the emperor created a new sore point between the two and generated another grievance of the emperor against Rome.[7]

Rocci presented the papal brief to Ferdinand personally on March 11. Ferdinand took the opportunity to tell him he could assure the pope "that to the extent this was possible, he would not consent to anything prejudicial to religion," for which he had already endangered his states and his own life several times.[8]

Indeed, Ferdinand had chosen as his chief delegate to Frankfurt Count Johann Caspar von Stadion. He was a former president of the war council, presently Grand Master of the Teutonic Knights, and at least a nominal privy councilor, who seems to have shared Lamormaini's rigid position on the Edict. The instruction sent Stadion on January 29 took a hard line.[9] Work on it had begun shortly after the return from Regensburg and a first draft had been submitted before the end of the year.[10] This draft clearly showed the Emperor's unwillingness to compromise on the Edict, along with a readiness to discuss the procedures for its enforcement. At a privy council session devoted to the instruction, at which both Ferdinand and Eggenberg were present, no serious objections were made to it.[11] A notation at the end of the version sent to Stadion indicated that at the emperor's command it had been shown to Lamormaini and Lucas Fanini, and both of them had endorsed it.[12] Shortly afterward Eggenberg returned to Graz complaining that the emperor no longer heeded him. Ferdinand's approval of this instruction may well have been the straw that broke the camel's back.[13]

The instruction began by noting Ferdinand's efforts for peace at Regensburg. He wanted nothing more than to end the war with its suffering. He had shown his intent to cooperate with the contacts between the Catholic electors and a number of states subscribing to the Confession of

Augsburg. But it was to be clear to all that as the highest judicial instance in the Empire he reserved to himself the right to ratify any decision reached. He would never approve measures contrary to the Peace of Religion or the Edict. Consequently, his representatives were to endeavor to prevent agreement on any such proposals, since the emperor would then have to bear the full odium of rejecting them. They were expected to keep Vienna informed on all that transpired at Frankfurt.

On February 15 Ferdinand sent copies of the instruction to Maximilian and to Mainz with a request for their opinions. An accompanying letter stressed the need for Catholic unity in the face of dangers threatening from Sweden, France, the Netherlands, and even the Turks. At the Frankfurt Conference efforts should be made to secure more assistance from Rome as well as papal pressure on Catholic states, that is, France, not to aid the enemy.[14] But by this time, it was evident that the Protestant meeting at Leipzig would compel the postponement of the Frankfurt Conference for some time. The final instruction, dated July 8, differed only in a few minor details from the one prepared in January.[15]

In the Saxon city of Leipzig there convened on February 20 princes and delegates from more than forty Protestant states.[16] Their purpose was to formulate a common policy in the face of the Edict of Restitution and the coming Frankfurt Conference, the advance of the Swedes, and the conduct of the imperial military: their marches across Protestant territory, forced contributions, and recruitment of troops. Saxony, the host state that had first called for the conference, subsequently hesitated and needed prodding from Brandenburg to complete the project. Though the success of the conference was limited, the very fact that it took place at all—it was the first convention of Protestant states in ten years—plus the statements it issued were enough to alarm the Catholics. The Protestants at Leipzig agreed on a protest against the Edict, the main source of their discontent. In letters to the emperor and the four Catholic electors they demanded not only that its enforcement cease but that all church lands restored by virtue of it be returned.[17] The cases of Augsburg and Württemberg came in for special mention. The Leipzig Protestants affirmed their intent to support the Frankfurt Conference, but they had little success in drawing up a common negotiating position. Most Protestant states, including the two electors, still thought that the Hessian Points went too far in the direction of accommodation.

The Protestants at Leipzig took another fateful step. In light of the emperor's failure to protect them, as his office required, from the continued depredations and harassment of the imperial soldiery, they declared they would no longer supply payments, troops, or quarters for his army. Then they announced their intention to form their own army in self-defense.[18] For the emperor, who was counting on their support against the Swedes, this resolution of the Protestants was a serious blow. Implied was the threat to resist any further attempt to carry out the Edict. Beyond this John George refused to go. He had consistently opposed as destructive of imperial unity alliances among German states, Catholic or Protestant. Now he would not enter the alliance, similar to the long defunct Protestant Union, proposed by some states, nor would he guarantee aid to any states other than his Saxon cousins. Agents of both Sweden and France were present at Leipzig, but no agreement was reached on policy regarding foreign alliances. Saxony showed much more reluctance to align with either power than did Brandenburg, which, to be sure, was in a more difficult position.[19] Nor was an effective plan drawn up to implement the decision to arm forty thousand soldiers. As it was, only the continued reassurance of his spiritual councilors persuaded John George to cooperate with the Calvinist states to the degree he did.

The meeting at Leipzig stimulated a rising awareness in Vienna of impending danger but little movement toward compromise. Shortly after the opening of the conference, Seifried Christoph von Breuner, Governor of Lower Austria from 1626 to 1640 and a privy councilor, presented his views about the expanding war with Sweden. His memorandum showed he was not far from Lamormaini's position.[20]

Although Breuner feared the Protestant states at Leipzig would ally with Gustav Adolph and receive increasing English and Dutch support, he tended to discount a threat from France, especially if the war in Italy was ended as he hoped. The emperor and the Catholic states had to cooperate and make mutual sacrifices, unless they were content to accept Protestant dictation. Breuner advocated a bold military policy in the hope of rapid victory. This was for him the only viable option. Specifically, he called for the vigorous prosecution of the siege of Magdeburg undertaken by Tilly. The previous August under the leadership of the former administrator, Christian William, the strategic city had been one of the first German states to ally with Gustav Adolph, and it was now anxiously awaiting relief from him.[21] The reduction of Magdeburg would intimidate Saxony, and it would enable Tilly to hinder Protestant military recruitment in the Lower Saxon Circle and to implement the Edict in the area. Paramount was the need for funds. The Austrian lands, especially Anterior Austria and the Tyrol, and the Catholic princes of the Bavarian Circle, particularly those who did not belong to the Catholic League, such as the Archbishop of Salzburg, had to do their share. Breuner, who was noted for his financial expertise, even suggested that loans be solicited from imperial ministers and officers. The monasteries had to make a greater contribution. After all, "the major cause of the present war is the ecclesiastical lands." But one could not impose such heavy burdens for long. If God did not grant the Catholics a major victory within the year, he wrote "we will have to accept the best conditions we can get, unless the good God chooses to provide us with other resources we cannot at this time foresee with our human reason."

Ferdinand asked a committee of councilors to evaluate the situation once again after news arrived of the pressure Gustav Adolph was putting on Brandenburg and especially of the Treaty of Bärwalde he had concluded with France on January 23. This agreement revealed a clear French commitment to the Swedish king. Richelieu promised him generous subsidies for five years for his campaign against the emperor. One article of the treaty obliged Gustav Adolph to observe neutrality toward the German Catholic states that did the same toward him. Whether this provision was known in Vienna or not cannot be said; it indicated Richelieu's intention to split the Catholic states from Ferdinand and to direct the full impact of the Swedish invasion against him.[22]

The councilors, whose names are not given, emphasized the seriousness of the situation in their report of March 17 and made recommendations that did not, however, constitute concessions to the Protestants.[23] "Your Imperial Majesty's hereditary kingdoms and lands along with the Catholic states are in greater danger than they have ever been and could come to ruin this year," they wrote. All the emperor's enemies were joining against him. Trouble could be expected soon from the Dutch and the English as well as from the Turks, whom the others were trying to incite. In addition to an alliance of the Leipzig Protestants with Sweden, the committee feared a general uprising in the Lower Saxon Circle. The war was devastating the Empire. Resources were drying up; the people were exhausted. In response to the situation, the committee called first for the formation of the Habsburg alliance that Spain was now promoting anew, to include the emperor, the King of Spain, the Infanta in the Netherlands, and Archduke Leopold.[24] Second, the army was to be built up as Tilly had pleaded at Regensburg. Third, close cooperation should be sought with the Catholic states and to this end a mission sent to Bavaria. Besides soliciting suggestions about the acquisition of new resources and means to a peaceful settlement with the Protestants, the emissaries should point out that the Franco-Swedish Treaty showed that France had no intention of peace with the emperor.

But when the privy council discussed the report, they thought it better to await the outcome of the Leipzig Conference before taking decisive measures. Instead of a delegation, then, Ferdinand sent a letter to Maximilian and Mainz that followed the recommendation of the report but lacked its sense of urgency.[25]

The opposition to Lamormaini within the privy council increased after the results of the Leipzig Conference reached Vienna. This was revealed by an incomplete draft of a position paper that, significantly, may never have been presented to Ferdinand.[26] The authors referred to themselves as the emperor's "most loyal" councilors, and they constituted a group within the privy council. They identified explicitly with Eggenberg, who was absent, and they were suspicious of the Catholic states. As far back as early 1628, after the Electoral Convention of Mühlhausen, they reminded Ferdinand, they had recommended the pursuit of a peaceful settlement in the Empire and had called attention to the dangers of a religious war. This statement implied lack of enthusiasm for the Edict and certainly unhappiness over the refusal to modify it at Regensburg.

These councilors now urged the emperor to take advantage of his response to the Leipzig resolution to open peace negotiations with the Protestants. This was the only way to escape greater evils. The sharp language at Leipzig made the danger evident. What was to be feared at Frankfurt was a separate agreement between the Catholic and Protestant states. This action would give the Catholic states the credit for taking the initiative for peace and burden the emperor with the odium of having opposed it to the end. Moreover, the councilors saw that the emperor would have no realistic choice but to go along with such an agreement, even though the instructions for Stadion claimed he would not do so. The authors also pointed out correctly that Richelieu intended to entice the Catholic states into a neutrality agreement with the Swedes. Ferdinand, for his part, they argued, should begin negotiations with Saxony and Brandenburg. An emissary should be sent to each, and lest the Catholic states become suspicious, they should receive a copy of the instructions. The restoration of the Dukes of Mecklenburg would prove to be a sticky point, so it would be advisable to secure Wallenstein's consent to yield on this ahead of time. When the councilors came to discuss Stadion's instructions for Frankfurt, they proceeded cautiously. The instructions, they felt, were too "limited" and would only be a hindrance to future talks. The theologians ought to be consulted once again to determine what concessions might be made "without compromising conscience."

Who were these "most loyal" councilors? The evidence points most convincingly to three, Stralendorf, Trautmannsdorf, and Abbot Anton, who had now become Bishop of Vienna. Along with Eggenberg, they represented Ferdinand's leading privy councilors. Back in January 1628 they had collaborated on position papers that insisted on the need to conciliate Saxony and Brandenburg and had tactfully recommended a cautious policy in pursuit of the goals set by the Catholic electors at Mühlhausen.[27] Generally, all three could be classified as moderates on the religious issue. More recently, Stralendorf had opposed Lamormaini's ideas about the disposition of monastic lands. This was obviously a different issue, but common to Stralendorf's position on both was hostility to Lamormaini's program and influence. Bishop Anton was not a supporter of Lamormaini's plans for monastic lands either. He was close to Eggenberg, who was endeavoring to secure a cardinal's hat for him, and he had only recently received high marks from Jacques Bruneau, a veteran Belgian diplomat in Spanish service.[28] Possibly two further members of the group were the privy councilors Johann Baptista Verda von Werdenberg and Cardinal Dietrichstein. Werdenberg, who had been appointed the first chancellor of the newly formed Austrian chancery in 1620, owed his advancement to Eggenberg.[29] Dietrichstein, who was soon to emerge as an advocate of a moderate policy, was considered a friend by the Spaniards.[30] But neither of these two seems to have belonged to the inner circle the way Stralendorf, Trautmannsdorf, and Bishop Anton did.

Ferdinand did dispatch emissaries to Saxony and Brandenburg, the aulic councilor Hans Hegenmüller and the Silesian nobleman Karl Hannibal von Dohna, respectively, both of whom were employed frequently on diplomatic missions.[31] But their instructions made it clear there would be no compromise on the substance of the Edict, which aimed at the restoration of true justice, the only basis for genuine peace.[32] Ferdinand did confirm his intention to send a delegation to Frankfurt, where he hoped any abuses in the enforcement of the Edict would be corrected. Such negotiations were the way to understanding. His emissaries were to complain to the electors that the states at Leipzig had abandoned him in his hour of need and were to deny that they had any right to raise an army without his approval. Their duty was to support him against Sweden. A subsequent imperial letter to all the signatories of the Leipzig resolution forbade them to arm and threatened to take action if they persisted.[33] Secret instructions for Hegenmüller directed him to sound out John George tactfully about his mediating an armistice with Sweden; however, this was to be done in a way not to prejudice Tilly's siege of Magdeburg, which was on the point of success. Hegenmüller and Tilly were to keep in touch with each other.

The tone of Saxony's response was noticeably milder than the Leipzig resolution, and the imperial councilors found this encouraging.[34] Caught between Gustav Adolph and Ferdinand, John George was "perplexed," as Hegenmüller related. He felt obliged, the elector wrote, to do his duty by contesting Ferdinand's right to interpret the Religious Peace. But he devoted more space to his complaint about the prohibition to arm, claiming that the Protestants were only acting in self-defense. After agreeing to undertake negotiations toward an armistice with Sweden, he closed with a strong expression of his desire for peace that did give some reason for optimism. Completely unsuccessful was Dohna's mission to George William, who was compelled to turn over several important garrisons to Gustav Adolph by the agreement of May 14.

In his next communication to Saxony, Ferdinand said nothing about concessions, and he encouraged John George to use his contacts with Sweden not to secure an armistice but to obtain Gustav Adolph's withdrawal from the Empire.[35] By this time heartening news had reached Vienna. Tilly had succeeded in reducing the obstinate Magdeburg, which fell to him on May 20. The city was destroyed and nearly twenty thousand people perished in a fire that broke out shortly after the imperial troops entered. Gustav Adolph had been unable to save his ally.[36]

While Hegenmüller was at Torgau in Saxony with John George, representatives of the Catholic League were meeting in the Swabian town of Dinkelsbühl to determine their policy vis-à-vis the Leipzig Conference and the advance of the Swedes.[37] The imperial delegate, the young aulic councilor Ferdinand Kurz von Senftenau, was at first skeptical about the League's willingness to stand by the emperor.[38] But he need not have been so. The results of the convention strengthened Ferdinand in his rigid policy. The League states maintained a firm stance on the Edict, while agreeing that negotiations in Frankfurt about its implementation were desirable. Ferdinand subsequently expressed his satisfaction to Mainz and Bavaria that the Catholic states were willing to go to the limit with him for Empire and religion.[39] At Dinkelsbühl they manifested a surprising readiness to promise contributions to the war effort. At the same time, they followed Maximilian's counsel not to launch a preventive attack against Saxony because they were not prepared for it nor did they want to create the myth that the Protestants had been forced to act in self-defense. After his triumph at Magdeburg, Tilly nevertheless continued to push for decisive military action before the Protestants had the chance to consolidate their forces.[40]

By mid-June the emperor, the Catholic states, and Saxony had all agreed on August 3 as the starting date for the Frankfurt Conference. The emperor and the Catholic states seemed to be in accord on the Edict. This was the case even though it was not until July 28 that Maximilian and Mainz explicitly informed the emperor of their approval of the imperial instruction for the Frankfurt Conference that had been sent them in mid-February.[41] But there remained serious points of friction between the emperor and the League. Contzen discussed several of these in a long letter to Lamormaini of June 8.[42] One was still the military. Contzen championed the need for the independence of the League army, concentrating his shafts on the ineptitude and corruption of the imperial forces, especially the officers. Had it not been for the League troops, the Swedes would long ago have been in Prague. Contzen denied there was any substance to the suspicion in Vienna that Maximilian and the League intended to negotiate a separate agreement with the Protestants. He then went on to complain about vicious rumors he had heard were circulating about Maximilian in Vienna. If difficulties existed, they ought to be brought out into the open. "I ask Your Reverence to let me know under what stone the scorpion lies."

One of the rumors certainly centered around Maximilian's relationship with France. In fact, one might conjecture that Contzen's letter was prompted in part by Munich's desire to find out how much was known in Vienna about this relationship. Early in 1631 a Spanish spy had broken into the apartments of Bagno, the departing nuncio in Paris, and made off with papers pointing to the secret negotiations taking place between Maximilian and Richelieu with the encouragement of the Curia. The discovery seemed to confirm what the Spaniards had long sensed. On May 8 Maximilian did sign the Treaty of Fontainebleau with France. It prohibited either party from attacking the other directly or indirectly and committed them to clearly spelled out defensive assistance in the event of an attack by a third party. Important for Maximilian was France's recognition of his and his heirs' title to the Palatinate. The treaty was to last eight years, and a special provision pledged both parties to secrecy.

Maximilian had been careful explicitly to safeguard his obligations to the emperor, and he certainly saw the treaty serving the interests of the Empire, in that as he understood it, it committed France to support him in the event of a Swedish attack. Contzen even more than Lamormaini looked for French assistance for the Catholic cause in Germany, and he thought the treaty to be a step in this direction. But most councilors in Vienna were bound to see Maximilian's contacts with France as playing into Richelieu's design to neutralize Bavaria and through it the League. To many at the imperial court, it looked like betrayal. At the beginning of August, Maximilian sent an emissary to Vienna who admitted the existence of a written agreement with France which had been approved by the pope—a fact, incidentally, never conceded by Rome—and who attempted to explain Maximilian's action. Ferdinand put up a good front and seemed convinced, but the affair awakened new mistrust between the two courts. The Spanish party in Vienna used it as an argument for a more conciliatory attitude toward Saxony.[43]

The Spaniards had long seen in Lamormaini a major obstacle to their policy. His persistent advocacy of peace with France and his championship of the Edict most angered them. So they endeavored to neutralize his influence at court. This explains in part the appearance in Vienna in February 1631 of a Spanish Capuchin, Don Diego de Quiroga.[44] He came as the confessor of the Infanta, Maria Anna, who became Queen of Hungary when she married the future Ferdinand III on February 20, 1631, in Vienna.

Preparations had begun in 1628 for the marriage of Ferdinand with Maria Anna, who would herself become a strong pro-Spanish force at court. Khevenhiller returned from Vienna to Madrid in April of that year after making preliminary arrangements for the wedding. One of the tasks entrusted to him by the emperor was to convince Philip IV that Maria Anna should bring a Jesuit with her as confessor. Already it was suspected in Vienna that she leaned toward a Franciscan or Capuchin because they traditionally served as confessors to the Spanish royal family. The Lord had chosen the Jesuits in a special way to work for the conversion of the Protestants in Germany, Khevenhiller informed Philip for Ferdinand. They enjoyed a high reputation there among Catholics and non-Catholics alike for their promotion of the faith. Thus the members of the Austrian ruling family, emperor, empress, King of Hungary, the archdukes, all made their confessions to Jesuits. For the new Queen of Hungary to appear without a Jesuit confessor would raise eyebrows and even cause scandal, Khevenhiller told Madrid. When it seemed Maria Anna would not yield, Ferdinand successfully sought Vitelleschi's permission to send to Madrid the Spanish Jesuit, Ambrosio Peñalosa, who had taught theology at the University of Vienna, tutored the young King of Hungary in Spanish, and become well known at the Spanish embassy. He was Ferdinand's choice for the Queen's confessor. His journey to Madrid was meant to impress on the Infanta and King Philip the importance Ferdinand attached to the matter.

But Maria Anna, backed by the Spanish government, remained firm in her determination to bring her Capuchin confessor with her, and Ferdinand finally gave up his design. Apart from the personal preference of the Infanta, a main reason the Spanish council of state supported Quiroga for the post seems to have been the belief that he would be more acceptable to the Protestants than a Jesuit.[45] Almost as soon as he arrived, Quiroga assumed a position of political importance and at times, especially in later negotiations with Wallenstein, he was more important than the official ambassadors. Soon he became a serious rival of Lamormaini. Peñalosa was named court preacher to the Queen of Hungary so that he might return to Germany without losing face.[46]

But even with Quiroga the Spaniards were unable to prevent the renegotiation of Regensburg that led to a settlement between the emperor and France over Italy. France was still working out the Treaty of Bärwalde with Sweden in January 1631, when Brûlart de Léon turned up in Vienna to resume negotiations. In the meantime talks dealing with the arrangements for Italy continued on the scene there, with the young Giulio Mazarini assisting as a papal mediator.[47] Vienna, of course, wanted the ratification of the whole Treaty of Regensburg as it stood, and in mid-March Rocci assured Lamormaini the Curia was doing all in its power to obtain this, adding, however, that Rome had little leverage in Paris.[48] In mid-April a courier arrived in Vienna with terms worked out in Cherasco in Italy and approved conditionally by the imperial negotiators on April 6. The new terms made some changes for Italy in the provisions of Regensburg. But they made no mention of the matter dealt with in the first article of the Treaty of Regensburg, a French commitment not to assist the emperor's enemies.[49]

The conflict over ratification now pitted Lamormaini and Rocci against the Spanish party, for whom, according to the nuncio, Quiroga was active.[50] The privy council was split. The majority favored acceptance of the terms, chiefly for two reasons: the need to remain on good terms with the Catholic electors, who insisted on the peace, and the necessity to free troops to face the advancing Gustav Adolph. Ferdinand was unable to make a decision, and he determined to consult Eggenberg.[51]

The opinion of "the oracle of Graz," as he was dubbed by Rocci,[52] arrived by special courier on April 21. Eggenberg opposed the agreement and he besought the emperor to adhere to the terms of Regensburg "vigorously, persistently, heroically, imperially."[53] Ferdinand should not withdraw the last of his troops from Italy until the terms of Regensburg were met. Under these terms Eggenberg obviously included the crucial article one, although he did not explicitly mention it; he was already aware of the Treaty of Bärwalde. With regard to Italy, he feared there were insufficient guarantees that the towns of Susa and Avigliana, which were to be returned by France to Savoy, and fortified places in the Valtelline, which were to be handed back by the emperor to the Protestant Swiss Grisons, would not soon end up in French control and thus give France the ready entrance to Italy it desired. Above all, he was disappointed, almost disgusted with the majority position in the privy council. It was another capitulation to the electors. Recently, he wrote, he had discussed the matter with Lamormaini, "to whom I have entrusted my soul for many years," and with other Jesuits. All of them had agreed that the Treaty of Regensburg was just in every sense and that "nothing more could be demanded from you, whatever God might send according to his holy and divine will." He evidently wanted to disarm any argument of Lamormaini that the emperor was obliged to bend over still further to satisfy the electors and the French in the interests of peace among Catholics and the program of Catholic restoration.

Ferdinand sided with Eggenberg and the Spaniards, and he ordered the reopening of negotiations. Scarcely back from Dinkelsbühl, Ferdinand Kurz von Senftenau was sent off to Paris in early June to try to convince the French to ratify the Regensburg agreement as it stood and to inquire about "rumors" of a treaty between Louis XIII and Gustav Adolph which had given the Protestants at Leipzig such encouragement. The emperor, his emissary was to assure Louis, wanted to work with the King of France for peace in Europe and the advancement of the Catholic religion.[54] Meanwhile, some changes were made in the Cherasco agreement for Italy that seemed to meet Eggenberg's objections, and Ferdinand ratified it on June 19, to the joy of the electors and Rome and the chagrin of Spain. The Mantuan War was over.[55]

On his return from Paris, Kurz von Senftenau reported that Louis conceded that he aided Sweden and justified it, rather dubiously, by pointing to Ferdinand's interference in Italy.[56] This seemed to make it clear Richelieu would not renounce his intention to aid the emperor's enemies. French subscription to article one of the Regensburg Treaty was out of the question. Kurz von Senftenau did receive assurances that France would abide by the settlement for Italy and would be accommodating in the recently intensified dispute over the three bishoprics on the western border of the Empire: Metz, Toul, and Verdun. These had been ceded to France by the Treaty of Cateau-Cambrésis in 1559, but whether they were still imperial fiefs and therefore in some way subject to the emperor was unclear. Related to this question was the status of two minor fortresses, Vic and Moyenvic, feudal dependencies of Metz that lay in Lorraine. The emperor, with the encouragement of the Duke of Lorraine, had garrisoned them in the spring of 1630 as a strategic move against the French.[57] But Kurz von Senftenau was skeptical about French assurances, as well he might have been. In October France received back the fortress of Pinerolo as a result of a secret treaty Richelieu had made with Savoy; thus Richelieu obtained the desired French opening into Italy.[58]

Throughout the spring of 1631, the Spaniards increasingly emphasized the need for a common imperial and electoral front against the Swedes and eventually the French. The need for Protestant support of the emperor was clear to them and with it the necessity of compromise on the Edict. The alternative to reconciliation with Saxony, which could easily lead to understanding with Brandenburg, was a religious war that in the long run could end in disaster for all Christendom. In June, Philip IV wrote directly to Ferdinand, encouraging him "to find a more opportune outlet for his piety and holy zeal," of which those jealous of his greatness, that is, Maximilian, took advantage in order to stir up trouble in the Empire and weaken his position.[59] The Spaniards realized Ferdinand's need of Maximilian and the League, but for them the villain was still the Bavarian elector, whose bridge to the French had now been revealed. Maximilian was a tool of the French, and Lamormaini was in collusion with him.[60]

Thus Spain made determined efforts to win over Lamormaini or if this was impossible, as it seemed to be, to moderate or even end completely his influence at court. Philip directed Guastalla, who now served as a Spanish ambassador in Vienna, to gain the favor of the confessor "at any price," even that of a cardinal's hat.[61] In May Spain took the matter to Vitelleschi in Rome. A Spanish state secretary in Naples was instructed to see that a complaint was brought to Vitelleschi about Lamormaini's activities, prejudicial as they were to both the Catholic religion and the House of Austria.[62] If the superior general did not remedy the situation, then the king himself would have to take measures to have Lamormaini removed from his post. The hope was that Vitelleschi would quietly bring about the resignation or transfer of Lamormaini. The Spanish cardinal Gasparo Borja y Velasco, resident in Rome, paid a visit to Vitelleschi to lament bitterly that Lamormaini, a Spanish subject by birth, always opposed the position of the Spanish king. Something had to be done. But the only specific charge he made was the far-fetched one that Lamormaini was responsible for the failure to elect the King of the Romans at Regensburg.[63] Perhaps Borja meant by this that had it not been for Lamormaini, Ferdinand would have made concessions on the Edict that would have secured the votes of Saxony and Brandenburg in the election. But the cardinal made no mention of the Edict, perhaps because Spain did not want its opposition to it known in Rome or figured this would make little impression on Vitelleschi.[64] Nor was anything said about the other principal reason Spain wanted him removed, Lamormaini's promotion of imperial understanding with France. This charge would not have helped much in Rome either.

But the Spanish strategy backfired. Vitelleschi immediately notified Lamormaini of Borja's grievances. He also wrote directly to the emperor, informing him of the Spanish attempt to have him recall Lamormaini and asking him to vouch for Lamormaini's loyalty to the King of Spain.[65] To Ferdinand the Spanish maneuver amounted to interference in his government. Both he and the King of Hungary testified to Lamormaini's innocence, and Cardinal Borja was forced to acknowledge it.[66] But Vitelleschi thought it would still be wise to obtain for Olivares a letter from Eggenberg clearing Lamormaini of any suspicion. This he wrote Lamormaini on September 27, but in a postscript he hastily withdrew the suggestion, adding that he would explain why in his next communication.[67]

Eggenberg himself was responsible for the Spanish campaign to oust Lamormaini, as Vitelleschi informed Lamormaini three weeks later.[68] He did not mention his source, and he asked Lamormaini to keep his involvement in the matter completely secret. His letter enumerated complaints made against the confessor. Lamormaini was charged with opposing Habsburg interests in Italy, but as Vitelleschi noted, this was not new, and he allegedly communicated secrets of imperial policy to Maximilian, to whom he was partial. The chief accusation was the sweeping one that he was unduly involved in political affairs, "and since he [Eggenberg] often differs with you, you with your diligent zeal draw the other councilors to your position with the result at times that this difference of views between the two of you on matters of great moment renders the Emperor himself uncertain and perplexed."

During his months in Graz—he did not return to court until late June and then only when Ferdinand summoned him with a handwritten note[69] —Eggenberg must have decided to take strong measures to remove Lamormaini from proximity to the emperor. His threats to resign, as Vitelleschi noted, were evidently intended to force Lamormaini's departure. But Lamormaini should not think of resigning, since this would disconcert the emperor and hinder the common good. Vitelleschi's recommendation was that Lamormaini say or write nothing that might be construed as hostile to Spain, "as much as the nature of your office will permit." But this was not much help, since Lamormaini's whole design defied Spanish policy. For Lamormaini to adhere to his conception and not offend Spain was an impossibility. Unfortunately, we do not have his response to Vitelleschi nor his reaction to the revelation about Eggenberg.

Madrid mounted a new effort in September to obtain support for its policies at the imperial court.[70] The list of those the ambassadors were to work on gives an indication of the individuals whom in addition to Eggenberg and Dietrichstein Spain considered important in Vienna: Stralendorf, Trautmannsdorf, the Bishop of Vienna, and Werdenberg. Also singled out for attention were Maximilian von Dietrichstein, young nephew and heir of the cardinal, who served as the steward of Empress Eleonora, and Count Christoph Simon von Thun-Hohenstein, who was very close to the young King of Hungary, having overseen his education, and was later to become his high chamberlain and a privy councilor, if a somewhat inactive one.[71] Frankness if necessary was to be used with the Empress Eleonora, who should be reminded that after Ferdinand's death her welfare would depend not on France or the pope but on Spain and the King of Hungary. "I feel certain," King Philip wrote, "that the confessor of the

Emperor will be more difficult to win over, although he is the most important because of the temperament of His Imperial Majesty and the ease
with which he allows himself to be guided by him," that is, Lamormaini.[72]

The Spaniards were also now planning another assault on Vitelleschi
through Cardinal Borja. They blamed the superior general for communicating their grievances to the emperor, thereby making Philip appear a
meddler in imperial affairs. Vitelleschi's curtailment of Lamormaini's
activities was not to be seen as provoked by Spanish action. But unless
he did something, Spain threatened retaliation against Jesuits in Spain
and elsewhere.[73]

Catholic military successes in the late spring and early summer raised
spirits and instilled new confidence in Vienna, as Rocci reported.[74] As we
have seen, on May 20 the prize, Magdeburg, fell to Tilly, though after the
disastrous fire he was left with little but a shell. Once peace was concluded with France, imperial troops returning from Italy were able to
disperse easily the Protestant militia assembling in Württemberg and to
force the submission of the duke. But Gustav Adolph was also active. He
continued to augment his army with new recruits, English, Scottish, but
predominantly German. His new treaty of June 20 with George William
gave him access to fortresses in Brandenburg and broad license to recruit
there. His troops and those raised by the two dukes with his encouragement were maneuvering the remaining Catholic troops out of Mecklenburg. In July Gustav Adolph made Johann Friedrich, the Administrator
of Bremen, his ally, and he was working on an agreement with Landgrave
William of Hesse-Cassel. Tilly, who had been ordered by Maximilian to
withdraw his troops from Hesse-Cassel lest he provoke the landgrave,
kept pressing both Maximilian and the emperor for permission to undertake a preventive attack against Saxony. Maximilian hesitated. Finally,
on July 23 Ferdinand directed the general to make one more effort to
negotiate with John George. Should this fail, the emperor authorized him
to use his own discretion about an attack.[75]

Rome continued to exhort the emperor to firmness but offered little in
the way of positive assistance. On May 7 Ferdinand directed Savelli to
seek an extraordinary audience with Urban to plead for funds. The German Catholics were in great danger, and should they succumb, Savelli
was to make clear to the pope, the Italians would be the next to experience the oncoming Protestant armies. Ferdinand wanted the pope to
grant him one-half the income of all church lands recovered by the imperial armies. This was a concession similar to one made to the League,
an imperial minister remarked pointedly to Rocci. The emperor also requested Urban to send him a regular monthly subsidy, as other popes had
done in the past, and if necessary for this, to dip into the papal treasure

chest preserved for emergencies in Castel San Angelo.[76] Disconcerting to Vienna, apart from Rome's unclarified role in the Franco-Bavarian nego-tiations, was Urban's attention to a matter of papal and Barberini family interest at a time when the fate of German Catholicism seemed to hang in the balance. In April the prefect of Rome had died, and Urban subse-quently bestowed this office on his nephew Taddeo. Urban's intention was to upgrade the office to the preeminence it had enjoyed in the Middle Ages, and a chief concern of the dispatches from Rome was to win the support of the emperor for this so that, for example, on certain cere-monial occasions the prefect would precede the imperial ambassador.[77]

Urban did issue an effusive brief for Ferdinand after the conquest of Magdeburg. "On such a great benefit of heaven we congratulate Your Majesty, whom the Almighty seems to have chosen to destroy heresy, the nurse of perpetual seditions, in the Roman Empire, the protector of the Roman Church."[78] The victory was surely an augury of greater things to come. Urban urged Ferdinand to remain steadfast in his intent not to permit "that any harm be inflicted on the Catholic Religion in any delib-eration about the affairs of Germany." Another brief two weeks later brought the same message.[79] But from Vienna Rocci reported that some imperial ministers let him know they expected more from Rome than pious exhortations.[80]

The Frankfurt Conference was doomed from the start. Regensburg had demonstrated the distance between even the moderate Catholics and Protestants, and neither side had shown any significant inclination to compromise since then. The imperial delegates arrived on August 4, Stadion being accompanied by Dr. Konrad Hildbrandt, an aulic coun-cilor. The two were joined in mid-September by Hermann von Questen-berg.[81] Besides the imperial delegates, who were not expected to be direct participants in the deliberations, thirteen Catholic states were repre-sented in Frankfurt, ten of them ecclesiastical territories.[82] Bavaria was most important. The Catholic delegates first met on August 11 to begin drawing up a common position. In their weekly reports to Vienna, the imperial delegates never showed anything but satisfaction with the stance of the Catholic representatives.[83] The Saxon delegation did not arrive until August 19 and then with instructions not to take part in any talks until the delegates of Brandenburg were present. By then it had become apparent to many representatives that there was little chance for compro-mise. Passing through Frankfurt in late August on his way back from a visit to Würzburg for the election of a new bishop, Pier Luigi Carafa went out of his way to encourage the Catholic delegates to firmness.[84]

By September 4 the Catholics were aware of the substantials of the Saxon instruction, which went well beyond the Hessian Points and the

Protestant position at Leipzig. It called for a suspension of the Edict, the continued exclusive exercise of the Confession of Augsburg in cities where it then was the case, and, above all, the establishment of the year 1620 as normative for the settlement of all disputes regarding ecclesiastical lands or rights. This would have given the Protestants title to all the church lands that had come into their hands from the Peace of Augsburg until the start of the war and would have required the Catholics to return all the property they had recovered in the previous ten years. It amounted to a new religious peace. Thus some Catholic delegates favored postponement of the conference even before its formal opening. The Brandenburg delegation finally turned up on September 12. They were more opposed to the Hessian Points than Saxony.[85] After the long delay, which had angered the Catholics, the conference formally opened on September 15 with the reading of the unyielding imperial proposition.[86] The Protestants then kept the Catholics waiting over a week for a response, but no Catholics departed lest they be accused of breaking up the conference. After the Catholics denied an unofficial Saxon request for a suspension of the Edict during negotiations, the Protestant answer came on September 24. It exhibited no intention of making concessions. So the two parties remained deadlocked when the news of Gustav Adolph's victory at Breitenfeld began to arrive.[87]

Tilly, feeling himself as threatened by Saxony on the flank as by Gustav Adolph from the front, had on August 29 formally enjoined John George to cease recruiting troops and to transfer those under arms to imperial service. He repeated the injunction on September 3, and when no answer was forthcoming, he crossed the border into Saxony, his goal Leipzig. The invasion led to John George's request to Gustav Adolph for aid and on September 11 the alliance of the two, something the Catholics had consistently tried to prevent. Leipzig fell to Tilly on September 15, but two days later the combined Swedish and Saxon armies, their approximately forty-two thousand troops having a clear numerical superiority, dealt Tilly a severe defeat at Breitenfeld outside Leipzig.[88]

Reports of the victory encouraged the Protestants at Frankfurt, though it was a while before they realized the scope of the triumph. Negotiations continued, but with no success. On September 30 the imperial delegates reported that the Catholics were not wavering, news that satisfied them as well as Ferdinand.[89] The Bishop of Würzburg told the Catholic delegates on October 13 that Gustav Adolph had seized his fortress at Königshofen and was expected to advance along the Main. The next day the Catholics left Frankfurt, not wishing to fall with all their papers into the hands of the Swedish king. The triumph of Gustav Adolph had reversed the whole course of the war. German history had reached a turning point.

9. The Nadir, 1631–1632

ustav Adolph's defeat of Tilly at Breitenfeld rang a critical hour in German history. The victory of the Swedish king ended the advance of the Counterreformation and, as Ranke asserted, probably saved Protestantism in Germany.[1] But the cost was high: large-scale intervention of a foreign power in the Empire and an ominous expansion of the war. Gustav Adolph and John George quickly followed up their triumph. Within a few days John George retook Leipzig; then he advanced into Bohemia and on November 15 seized Prague. The Swedish king moved to the west. The Bishopric of Würzburg fell to him in mid-October. On November 19 he invaded the Archbishopric of Mainz, and he marched into the city of Mainz on December 23, in time to celebrate Christmas, after first gaining control of Frankfurt. Then the precipitous military activity quieted down for the winter while Gustav Adolph consolidated his position. Thus the Catholics had a chance to regroup their forces.

Breitenfeld created a crisis for Ferdinand at least comparable to that following the Bohemian rebellion. His empire was caving in. Tilly's rout, his first serious defeat since the start of the conflict, was a severe blow to morale. The mantle of invincibility had passed to Gustav Adolph. The Catholic armies were in disarray. But amid all this adversity, Ferdinand was extremely reluctant to yield any ground on the religious issues. Concern for his conscience and his reputation kept him from accepting, much less initiating, concessions. Had God not saved him in apparently desperate situations before? Sensitive to the need for eventual concessions but aware of Ferdinand's mentality, his leading privy councilors including Eggenberg were cautious in advocating them, especially when there was any question of specifics. To be sure, during the year following Breitenfeld and especially after a Catholic-Protestant conference proposed for Mühlhausen in December failed to convene, there was little immediate pressure to make a decision on a specific compromise. Even the moderates were unwilling to yield the points that would have been necessary to pacify Gustav Adolph and the Protestants at the peak of their power. The establishment of a military and political balance was a prerequisite for a satisfactory peace. Thus no concrete decision was required of the emperor for the time being. For this Ferdinand was undoubtedly grateful and his councilors probably were too.

The months between Breitenfeld and the Battle of Lützen, where Gustav Adolph was killed in action, were the most difficult of Lamormaini's
career as confessor. The renewed ascendancy of the Spaniards and Wallenstein, now implacably hostile, boded ill for him. Many who had hesitated to criticize him in the past or had done so only obliquely now
joined openly in the assault. Public opinion turned against Lamormaini
and Jesuit colleagues identified with the hard line on the Edict. Cardinal
Pazmany remarked in December that the whole kingdom appeared to
want Lamormaini removed from his position.[2] Lamormaini's influence
at court if not personally with Ferdinand diminished drastically; Rocci
reported in February that he was reduced merely to hearing the emper-
or's confession.[3] Fellow Jesuits found fault with him, and in April Vitelleschi, under pressure, joined in the criticism. On top of all this, illness
confined him to bed during much of the late winter and spring of 1632.
But he stuck to the Edict and to his vision of the Catholic restoration.

Tension increased notably between Munich and Vienna after Tilly's
defeat, but their common religious goals and realization of mutual dependence always kept them from a break. Vienna's suspicions were kin-
dled anew as Maximilian openly professed the need for French mediation
with Sweden on the German Catholics' behalf and then apparently inclined himself toward neutrality. While Vienna feared a secret arrangement by Maximilian with France and Sweden, Munich was afraid of a
deal between Ferdinand and Saxony at the expense of Maximilian and
his conception of Catholic interests, which was precisely what the Spaniards and soon Wallenstein advocated. Also, Maximilian wrote Saxony
asserting he had not approved of Tilly's invasion. His action greatly
vexed Vienna. The claim was literally true, but as Ferdinand pointed out
to him, Maxmilian had not responded to a query about a major decision
that could not be postponed.[4] Moderate heads prevailed in Vienna, and
for the sake of harmony the question was dropped but not forgotten.

A committee of councilors including Eggenberg first met to discuss the
new situation on October 6.[5] They did not think it likely that in the
circumstances Saxony would withdraw from the position he had taken at
the Leipzig conference. This comprised the demand for the suspension of
the Edict and the return of the lands recovered by virtue of it; implicitly it
would fix March 6, 1629, as the normative date for the possession of
most ecclesiastical lands and privileges. Sweden would encourage John
George to seek more now, the councilors thought, so there was little
chance he would be attracted by terms Ferdinand could offer consistent
with his conscience and reputation. Perhaps they were not yet aware that

at Frankfurt Saxony had already raised his demands substantially by proposing 1620 as the normative year. The councilors did suggest, however, that indirect contacts be established with Saxony through Wallenstein and through Hesse-Darmstadt, who undertook to organize another Catholic-Protestant meeting when it had become evident that the Frankfurt Conference would fail. Eggenberg himself authorized Wallenstein to make contact with Saxony through Hans Georg von Arnim, his former general now in Saxon service.[6]

The arrival in Vienna of a Bavarian emissary was the occasion for another look at the picture. The elector's concern was to plan for a military buildup and for negotiations with Saxony. But Maximilian was reluctant to propose concrete concessions. This the committee of councilors interpreted in their report as an attempt to sidestep responsibility.[7] They obviously hoped for an initiative from the Catholic states that would push Ferdinand toward accommodation, at least with Saxony, but Maximilian was as unready to take the lead in this direction as Ferdinand was.[8] They implicitly criticized Ferdinand himself and gave vent to their lingering bitterness over Regensburg when they pointed out that they had then made clear the difficulty of continuing the war. Now it would be much harder to secure acceptable terms. In a slap at Lamormaini, they added that in the past whenever Ferdinand submitted terms to the theologians for evaluation, they always found serious shortcomings and so hindered a settlement even in purely political matters. But despite their pessimism about the chances for success, they affirmed the need for negotiations with Saxony.

Ferdinand's councilors strongly urged him to participate in the conference promoted by Hesse-Darmstadt, now scheduled for mid-December in Mühlhausen, but they failed to suggest a concrete position to be taken on the Edict, recommending that this be decided in concert with the Catholic electors.[9] The emperor and Maximilian then agreed that the Catholic states would first send delegates to Ingolstadt to develop a common negotiating position and work on plans for closer military cooperation.[10] Two drafts of a letter to the Catholic electors revealed conflicting views in Vienna. The first stated specifically that it might be wise to discuss concessions on the Edict, which was responsible for driving the Protestant states into alliance with Sweden. The revision eliminated this suggestion; it called only for a general discussion of the means to peace and emphasized the need for cooperation between the two "chief pillars" of the Catholic religion in Germany, the emperor and the Catholic states. According to both drafts, neither of the two was to blame for the defeat at Breitenfeld. The responsibility for it "was to be left in Christian patience to the hidden judgment of God, which was always at work and which undoubtedly had been provoked to inflict such a punishment by serious sins of all types committed by the undisciplined soldiery."[11]

As the date for the conference at Mühlhausen drew near, the imperial councilors sought to bypass Lamormaini and perhaps other political ecclesiastics too. On November 13 they secretly inquired of six theologians whether the emperor might approve concessions that corresponded roughly to the Protestant demands at Leipzig and would implicitly establish 1629 as the normative year for at least the temporary possession of ecclesiastical lands and privileges. Among those consulted were Peñalosa and Ottaviano da Ravenna, a Franciscan conventual and professor of theology at the University of Vienna.[12] The questions put to them presupposed that the Catholic states urged the concessions in order "to avert the complete ruin of the Empire and of religion in the same Empire." In other words, they foresaw the Catholic states, not the emperor, taking the initiative. If they did do this, might the emperor in good conscience consent to (1) the suspension of the Edict, (2) the return to the Protestants of ecclesiastical lands recovered by virtue of the Edict including the (arch)-bishoprics of Magdeburg, Osnabrück, Minden, and Verden, (3) the return in Augsburg to the status before the recent Counterreformation measures there. A fourth prospective concession was a special guarantee to Saxony and Brandenburg that they might retain for an undetermined period the church lands they held. Such a guarantee had not been mentioned by the Protestants at Leipzig but had been foreseen by the Catholic Response at Regensburg and for a definite period of forty years.[13]

The following week the theologians were summoned to give their opinions orally before Dietrichstein, the Bishop of Vienna, Stralendorf, and other councilors. Afterward Stralendorf asked them to put their positions in writing; they all seemed to have taken a stance similar to that of Ottaviano da Ravenna, whose paper alone survives. Generally speaking, he accepted the principle of the lesser evil, meaning that a lesser evil might be tolerated in order to avoid a greater one; he left the evaluation of the concrete situation to the judgment of the political councilors. Thus he agreed that if in the opinion of the councilors the Empire and the Catholic religion were in imminent danger of ruin and there was no alternative means to save the situation, the emperor could suspend and even revoke the Edict. But Ferdinand was restricted in his competence regarding the other concessions. He could grant them only on condition the pope approved, since they all involved the surrender of ecclesiastical property now held by the church. Canon law vested in the pope the ultimate disposition of all church property; only he could alienate it. Moreover, Ottaviano argued, the four (arch)bishoprics mentioned had been regained by postulation and election, not by virtue of the Edict, and presumably would not fall under any general policy on the Edict. Under the circumstances, Ottaviano felt the pope should and would grant the required dispensation; indeed, in the case of extreme necessity the emperor might presume papal consent. In his closing remarks, however, Ottaviano returned to cast doubts on the councilors' assessment of the situation in a manner similar to what one would have expected from Lamormaini. Was it really as perilous as they painted it? Was the only alternative the spiritual ruin of many souls, the suppression of Catholic worship, the attendant disgrace of the Roman Empire? One must hope in God, he concluded.[14]

The theologians' insistence on papal approval of concessions put Rocci in a difficult position. To the nuncio's urgent request for instructions, Barberini wrote on December 13 that under no conditions would Pope Urban accept the projected concessions. Ottaviano had judged wrongly. The pope was determined not to surrender the juridical position of the Church. But Urban did not want to make a big issue of the matter. If he could do so credibly, Rocci was to act as if he knew nothing of the projected concessions. If not, then he should make clear the pope's disapproval but undertake no further efforts to hinder developments. The last thing Urban wanted was a direct request for a dispensation, since he would have to deny it. Otherwise he was willing to leave the emperor free to make the best possible arrangement for the Church. With this Urban would not actively interfere.[15] But Ferdinand was not yet ready to exercise such independence; he would arrive at this stage only at the time of the Peace of Prague. Nor was Lamormaini likely to urge him to do so, since it would militate against the long-range design he still nourished for the restoration in the Empire.

By mid-December, however, it was evident that Sweden had no intention of permitting the conference at Mühlhausen. Gustav Adolph had not yet reduced the Catholics to the point where he thought they would agree to satisfactory terms.[16] Thus the need for papal consent lost its urgency and dropped from mind in Vienna, to the relief of Rome. What the councilors would not forget was the theologians' acceptance of the principle of the lesser evil, their leaving to the councilors the determination of the existence of a state of necessity, and their conditional approval of the four concessions and especially the return to the status of 1629. Thus the consultation of these theologians was to have permanent importance.

Ferdinand chose Hermann von Questenberg, who had participated in the Frankfurt Conference, for his delegate to the meeting of the Catholic states at Ingolstadt, which was to take place despite the cancellation of Mühlhausen. Questenberg's task was to get a clear statement from the

Catholic states indicating how far they felt the Catholics might move in the direction of concessions. At the same time he was to let them know that Ferdinand was ready alongside them "to persevere through good and evil to the end of this war, that we therefore look for nothing else than the same from them, that they stand by us courageously with the unchanging loyalty that is their duty."[17] Ferdinand, Questenberg was to make clear, was confident they would make no separate neutrality agreement. The suspicion behind this directive was justified, because Hercule de Charnacé, a distinguished French diplomat, had begun talks in Munich on December 3.[18] In addition, Questenberg had to report on the military measures planned by the Catholic states and had to explain to the irritated Bavarians Ferdinand's failure to transfer troops from Bohemia to the west.

Questenberg arrived in the Bavarian fortress town on December 21 and found only a handful of delegates. The Bavarians turned up on December 27, after the negotiations with Charnacé had produced a tentative neutrality agreement between Bavaria and Sweden. About two weeks previously, troops of Archduke Leopold in Alsace had intercepted communications of Charnacé revealing his presence and the nature of his business in Munich. Copies were sent from Vienna to Questenberg for his information and directly to Maximilian with the request for an explanation.[19] In his talks with the delegates Questenberg noted the perplexity of the Bavarians. They had grown despondent, thinking that measures they might take toward concessions would offend God and that measures to continue the war were simply beyond their strength. Most of the delegates seemed to share this spirit, with the exception of the Bishop of Augsburg's representative, who expressed Knöringen's intent to offer up all for the cause. At one point three delegates including the Bavarian Johannes Peringer approached Questenberg privately to let him know they felt the only way out of the situation was through French mediation. Bavaria had already begun negotiations with France, they later added, and the Bishop of Würzburg was planning a trip to France on behalf of himself and Cologne. Would Ferdinand approve this?

In remarks that Ferdinand later endorsed, Questenberg responded that the alliance between France and Sweden rendered negotiations with the former tantamount to negotiations with the enemy. Moreover, the French policy of weakening the Empire had not changed for over a century. And even if France did sincerely intend to help the German Catholics, given the present military superiority of the Protestants, there was little chance it could provide effective aid. In any event, Questenberg pointed out, it was necessary to discuss possible terms of accommodation with the Protestants and alternative military plans. But neither side was willing to descend to particulars when it came to concessions to the Protestants, so the meeting at Ingolstadt ended without any concrete results.[20]

The imperial government had its own plans to counter the Swedish advance. Many in Vienna, chiefly among them Eggenberg, now looked to Wallenstein's return to military command and his conduct of negotiations with Saxony. As early as the winter of 1630–31, Ferdinand had begun to regret the dismissal of the general and to turn to him for advice. Wallenstein renewed his contacts with Arnim in November 1630; starting in May 1631, he was in touch with Count Matthias Thurn, the leader of the Bohemian exiles, and later through Thurn, with Gustav Adolph himself. The exact nature of these contacts remains unclear. Most likely they merely allowed the principals to probe each other's position, though they do seem to have given rise to hope among the exiles that Wallenstein was sympathetic to them.[21]

In mid-October Eggenberg and Gerhard von Questenberg, a war councilor, brother of Hermann and Casper, and a Wallenstein partisan, had conveyed to Wallenstein the council's request that he attempt through negotiations with Arnim to prepare the way for peace with Saxony. The same two took the lead in recommending Wallenstein's return to command. From his retirement in Friedland the general turned down Ferdinand's first approach, but on November 17 he indicated readiness to talk terms with Eggenberg. Before doing so, however, he met with Arnim near Prague, which the Saxon general had recently taken. Their subject was the need for peace in Germany, but as is the case with many of Wallenstein's negotiations, the specific topics, let alone agreements, if any, are not known.[22]

Wallenstein and Eggenberg finally met at Znaim in Moravia on December 10. Wallenstein agreed to return to the army command, but he limited his stint to three months, just enough to reorganize the army and bring it up to strength but not to lead it into the next campaign. The emperor and the King of Spain made heavy financial commitments to the army, and Maximilian promised to make his contribution. In an effort to satisfy the young King of Hungary, who was eager to demonstrate his military ability, Spain had proposed that he be entrusted with the formal command of the army and Wallenstein, who would be effectively in charge, be given a lesser title. But there was little likelihood Wallenstein would accept this, and the idea was quickly dropped at Znaim. Wallenstein was also assured that measures would be taken to restrict Lamormaini's influence at court. Neither Lamormaini nor other political ecclesiastics would be allowed to interfere with Wallenstein's activity through their "varying and ill-founded principles," according to the instruction prepared for Eggenberg by Gerhard von Questenberg, probably under Eggenberg's own direction.[23]

Wallenstein had long considered the Edict, which he blamed first of all on Lamormaini, a disaster for the emperor and for Germany. As a condition for his acceptance of the army command he set the eventual revocation of the Edict and the return to the status at the time of its issuance.[24] Undoubtedly he knew this was roughly what the Protestants at Leipzig had required. Eggenberg agreed to this, it can be assumed, since it scarcely differed from what the six theologians had approved conditionally only three weeks before. These are the terms then that Wallenstein seems to have suggested in further talks with Arnim the next month.[25] Whether the emperor explicitly approved them or not cannot be determined; most likely he did not. The previous fall Wallenstein had with his encouragement carried on a secret correspondence with Christian of Denmark in the hope of enlisting him against Gustav Adolph. But Ferdinand had vetoed Wallenstein's suggestion that as an enticement Christian be promised several north German bishoprics to which his family had earlier held title. Only the pope could assign these properties.[26] Eggenberg probably counted on being able to convince Ferdinand to accede to the terms when the time for a decision came. For the time being, there was no need to take a position on the Edict because the Mühlhausen Conference had been canceled, and nearly all in Vienna agreed there could be no serious negotiations with the Protestants until a balance of forces had been achieved. In the meantime, Eggenberg would continue to work at Lamormaini's removal from court.

On December 24 Charnacé left Munich for Mainz, where he would present Gustav Adolph with a tentative neutrality agreement to which Maximilian had consented, even though the Bavarian elector knew it would be misunderstood and turned against him in Vienna. The Swedes already occupied several states of the Catholic League, including Mainz and Würzburg. Bavaria lay defenseless in their path. Tilly's army was a shambles, and Ferdinand could spare no troops. Under these circumstances, Maximilian agreed to observe neutrality toward Gustav Adolph, provided the king promised to permit the exercise of the Catholic religion in conquered Catholic states, to respect the borders of the member states of the Catholic League, and to restore their rightful rulers to the states of the League he had overrun. These were favorable, indeed unrealistically favorable, terms for Maximilian; one wonders whether he really expected Gustav Adolph to accept them. Maximilian realized they would lead to the concentration of the Swedish attack on the Habsburg lands, but he reasoned they would also preserve religion in the Empire and enable the

League to recoup its forces quickly and come to Ferdinand's aid. Maximilian even made a genuine if unsuccessful effort to include the emperor in the agreement. In the event that Gustav Adolph refused the terms, Charnacé guaranteed that France would break with Sweden and enter the war on the side of the Catholics. This would mean the achievement of a goal many Catholics, among them Maximilian and Lamormaini, had long pursued. One can even conjecture that Maximilian's real purpose was to put pressure on France to come to the aid of the German Catholics. His mistake lay not so much in the belief that Gustav Adolph would accept the terms but in the trust that France would abandon Sweden if he did not.[27]

In mid-January Maximilian's high chancellor, Joachim von Donnersberg, came to Vienna to defend his action to a government that under Wallenstein's growing influence was increasingly less inclined to show him understanding. The promotion of Habsburg-French harmony was also his purpose, because Swedish success had shown more clearly than ever the need for Catholic unity. But a committee of councilors composed of Trautmannsdorf, Stralendorf, the Bishop of Vienna, and Hermann von Questenberg rejected Donnersberg's arguments in defense of Maximilian's neutrality negotiations.[28] Public opinion in Vienna also strongly condemned him.[29] In the meantime, Gustav Adolph turned down the terms of neutrality and offered much more stringent ones in their place. These Maximilian was determined not to accept, since they required that he sacrifice some League states and compromise the practice of Catholicism in the Swedish-occupied lands. By mid-February it was obvious that despite Charnacé's promises, France would not break with Gustav Adolph. This forced Maximilian to turn still more completely to Vienna. Towards the end of March Donnersberg returned to Munich, the differences with the emperor having been papered over. But Maximilian's ordeal was only beginning.[30]

Spanish influence rose dramatically in Vienna in the aftermath of Breitenfeld. To many Spain appeared as the rock of salvation in the moment of crisis. On October 20, 1631, Ferdinand had renewed the secret Oñate Treaty, more at his own initiative than Spain's, thus clearly reaffirming in his moment of trial the bonds between the two branches of the House of Habsburg.[31] Madrid realized Ferdinand badly needed its help, and it intended to exploit the situation to attain those elusive goals of Spanish policy, an alliance with the emperor and German states that would commit them to Spanish goals in the Netherlands and to war with France.[32] But there were limits to what Spain could achieve. The position paper drawn up by the aforementioned four councilors, without the participation of Eggenberg, showed they did not accept the Spanish stand that

France had to be kept out of German affairs at any cost. Under certain circumstances they were ready to accept Maximilian's recommendation that France serve as a mediator at a peace conference.[33]

Ferdinand concluded a treaty of alliance with Spain signed in Vienna on February 14 by two of Philip IV's representatives there, Jacques Bruneau and the Marquis of Cadereyta, who was now a second ambassador alongside Guastalla. But it was ambiguous and admitted of an interpretation that explained Lamormaini's satisfaction with it.[34] Spanish influence can be detected in the deemphasis of the confessional element indicated by the alliance's purpose, the defense of the Empire rather than the faith, and the invitation to Protestant states such as England, Denmark, and the Protestant electors to join. But a principal goal the treaty envisioned was an end to the enmity between the House of Habsburg and France, on the unrealistic basis, to be sure, of the Treaty of Regensburg and the return of Pinerolo to Savoy; it quickly came to be considered by at least some in Vienna as the foundation for the long-desired grand Catholic alliance against the heretics and even the Turks. This was the conception of Cardinal Pazmany, whom the emperor sent to Rome in late February to secure the pope's adherence.[35]

What the Spaniards found most difficult to swallow was the dispatch to Paris in early March of Baron Peter von Schwarzenberg, who was to invite Louis XIII to join the alliance. Schwarzenberg carried with him an instruction corrected by the emperor himself requesting the French king to send an agent to Vienna, should he be interested in negotiations.[36] Meanwhile, Philip IV refused to ratify the alliance because it did not stipulate imperial intervention in the Netherlands or eventual war with France. He also recalled the Marquis of Cadereyta who had had the misfortune to sign the treaty shortly before his instructions of January 30 arrived. Despite the loss of its fortress in Maastricht to the Dutch, Spain did, however, send an army down from the Netherlands to operate along the Mosel and in the Palatinate on the left bank of the Rhine thereby assisting in the defense against the Swedes.[37] This did not, of course, please the French, who, as we shall see, had moved toward the Rhine themselves.

During the fall of 1631 the Spanish government had renewed its campaign to force Vitelleschi to restrict the activity of Lamormaini. Olivares summoned to Madrid seven prominent Spanish Jesuits for a meeting in mid-November. There he explained to them the king's grievances and threatened severe measures if they were not remedied. Instead of acknowledging the benefits they had received from the Spanish crown, Olivares contended, the Jesuits colluded in plots against the king. This was especially true of Lamormaini, who counseled against the best interests of the Empire, Spain, and even the Catholic religion itself. Vitelleschi himself favored France, Olivares charged, in order to win the good will of the pope, and he went on to suggest that the support of the King of Spain might be more valuable, since there were twenty-four provinces of the Society in his dominions. Vitelleschi was also blamed for attempting to stir up dissension within the House of Habsburg by the manner in which he had notified the emperor of the previous Spanish dissatisfaction with Lamormaini.

Olivares left it up to the fathers to determine the action necessary to improve the situation. But should they fail to act, he promised measures that would greatly increase royal influence over the Society in Spain and that were reminiscent of actions taken under Philip II that nearly provoked a schism in the Society.[38] The government would demand the appointment of a general commissioner with extensive power over the Society in Spain, and it would strongly recommend that every second superior general be required to make a visitation of the houses in Spain. All Spanish ministers of state would be prohibited from going to confession to Jesuits on the grounds that the Jesuits used the sacrament to exercise undue influence. Louis de la Palma, one of the Jesuits present at the interview, warned Vitelleschi that the government meant business and urged him to act to forestall harm to the Society.[39]

Vitelleschi calmly defended himself in a long letter of February 7, 1632, to the provincial superiors of the Jesuits in Spain. He was not aware of any Jesuit who at present was deficient in his obligation to the King of Spain, to whom the Society assuredly was heavily indebted. He had tried to correct previous failures, he wrote, and had required an explanation of his actions from Lamormaini. If he had exaggerated the king's intent in his handling of the royal complaint, he was sorry. He had meant only the best, as the Spanish cardinals in Rome would testify. In the future, he would see to it that all Jesuits satisfied their duties to the crown of Spain.[40]

Vitelleschi now urged Lamormaini to write to Spain himself in his defense.[41] But even before Vitelleschi's letter arrived, Lamormaini, at the suggestion of the Marquis of Cadereyta, had undertaken to write the King of Spain to exonerate himself from three charges, none of them directly touching the Edict.[42] The charge that at Regensburg he had opposed young Ferdinand's election to King of the Romans he rightly dismissed as ridiculous. To the accusation that he consistently obstructed the policy of the Spanish king he replied, perhaps somewhat disingenuously, that the Spanish ambassador never informed him of Spanish intentions. How then could he hinder their execution? Lamormaini did admit his opposition to Spanish designs in Italy, but, he added, many friends of

Spain in Vienna and Madrid shared his view, as the emperor himself had told him. The third charge was to Lamormaini's mind the most damaging, namely, that he aided and abetted the enemies of the House of Habsburg. He readily confessed his indebtedness to the House, in whose lands he had lived virtually his whole life. For forty-three years he had been a member of the Society of Jesus, more than two-thirds of whose members labored in Habsburg dominions, he wrote, and whose progress was closely tied to that of the House. One who wished to prove disloyalty to the Habsburgs on his part would first have to demonstrate he, Lamormaini, had lost his senses. The House of Habsburg was "the strongest defender and propagator" of the Catholic Church. "But I come to the end and here supplicate Your Majesty with humility and complete submission of my soul and body, that you do not lend your ears to such false accusations but instead, with Austrian mercy and kindness, preserve me and the whole Society in your royal grace and protection against all detractors and calumniators."

Probably because it did not point to any change in the confessor's policy, the letter did not content Olivares, who, nevertheless, does not seem to have followed through on the threats against the Spanish Jesuits.[43] Vitelleschi expressed his satisfaction with the letter to Philip IV, but he was on the point of sending Lamormaini the strongest criticism he ever sent him.[44] Complaints had been coming into Rome about Lamormaini, as Vitelleschi wrote him, "from nearly all the provinces of Germany."[45] The superior of the professed house in Vienna, where Lamormaini resided, informed Vitelleschi that many in the city blamed the Jesuits for the war and the calamities it brought them.[46] Peñalosa confirmed this when he wrote that even the religious laid the present state of affairs at the foot of the Society and especially of Lamormaini.[47] Though Lamormaini was a good religious, Peñalosa went on, sounding a little like Eggenberg, the confessor tended to trust excessively in his own moral judgment. Often he, Peñalosa, had suggested to him that he seek more contact with the Spaniards at court, but Lamormaini maintained he saw no need for this. In a revealing remark Peñalosa let Vitelleschi know that he did not think Jesuits should criticize the confessor in front of non-Jesuits, who then used this against him. Some Jesuits had become increasingly unhappy with Vitelleschi's handling of the confessor. In fact, when war and attendant plague in Italy forced the postponement of the triennial congregation of procurators, which brought delegates from each Jesuit province to Rome, Vitelleschi had to deny the rumor that the real reason for the action was the fear that the congregation would degenerate into a forum for criticizing Lamormaini and himself.[48]

In a manner typical of his procedure, Vitelleschi in his letter of April 3

laid before Lamormaini the charges leveled against him without neces-
sarily identifying himself with them.[49] There was no mention of specific
issues or of pressure from the Spanish Jesuits. Lamormaini's excessive
frankness angered Spanish officials, Vitelleschi wrote. But the main grievance seemed to echo Eggenberg's accusation of undue intrusion into
political affairs. Lamormaini allegedly not only gave his views to Ferdinand and the proper ministers; he also went about at court canvassing
support and aggressively attacking those in disagreement with him. Many
considered him reluctant to go along with ideas originating with others
and, instead, eager to find reasons to undercut them. This cavalier manner of dealing with the recommendations of others, Vitelleschi thought,
was perhaps the main reason for the hostility to him and to the Society.

Another charge taken up by Vitelleschi was that when Ferdinand asked
him to query other Jesuits on an issue, Lamormaini attempted to pressure them to accept his view and when he failed, he tried to prevent them
from communicating their opinion to the emperor. This, the superior
general reminded Lamormaini, clearly violated the instruction "On the
Confessors of Princes." Vitelleschi again brought to Lamormaini's attention the accusation that he was a source of government leaks, and he
remarked that many were scandalized by the file cabinet in his room that
displayed to every casual visitor the extent of his political correspondence. The least he could do was move or cover the cabinet, so as to put a
stop to the suspicions and rumors it fed. Even Ferdinand himself, Vitelleschi noted, was not happy with the extent of his correspondence.

Lamormaini had been sick in bed for about six weeks when this letter
reached him, and he remained ill for much of the spring.[50] According to
what must have been an exaggerated account, "the whole city of Vienna,
even all Austria and the Empire itself gnashed their teeth at Father William, as the author of the wars and tragedies they were enduring, and so
they wanted him torn apart (*discerptum*)." He was even accused of keeping a woman at court, a charge the accuser was forced to recant publicly.[51]
Attacks on the Society were appearing in print. That summer Schoppe's
*The Case for Treason against the Jesuits, the Sworn Enemies of the Holy
Roman Empire* came off the press. And Wallenstein's influence was
growing ominously.

But if Lamormaini was lying low during the first half of 1632, he was
not inactive nor had he lost his influence with Ferdinand. This is clear
from a handwritten note of the emperor to him, dated January 21: "I
hope in my God," he wrote, "and I await the confusion of his enemies
and of all the political councilors."[52] The message would not have pleased
Eggenberg, nor would Lamormaini's reminder to the emperor that he
alone could be counted on to give Ferdinand completely disinterested

counsel. The opinions of all the other councilors were colored to a greater or less extent by their own desire for advancement and wealth.[53]

Wallenstein's original commission lapsed at the end of March. After a preliminary talk with Bishop Anton, he met with Eggenberg on April 13 at Göllersdorf near Vienna, where they reached an understanding about the terms of his continued service.[54] According to their agreement, which appears to have been unwritten, the general was promised regular sums for the army from Spain and from the hereditary lands, these to be supplemented by revenues from confiscated lands. The Silesian principality of Grossglogau along with a sum of four hundred thousand gulden was made over to him, personally, but the full compensation for his services and for the loss of Mecklenburg was left to the future. His authority to negotiate with Saxony and through it with the other German Protestant states was renewed. Wallenstein's attitude about the terms for Saxony was clear from a remark he made to an agent of Rocci who brought him a papal brief congratulating him on his return to imperial service. He was not happy with the Edict of Restitution; he would rather war with Turks than heretics.[55] The strength of Wallenstein's position resulted not so much from any agreements or promises but from the political situation itself. The emperor needed him, and Wallenstein well knew this.

The general at this time was almost certainly given new assurances against a repetition of his dismissal and against the interference of ecclesiastics in political affairs. Lamormaini had sought to improve relations with him. In a New Year's greeting, Lamormaini wished him "the wisdom of Joshua, the sword of Gideon, the bravery and piety of Judas Maccabaeus, the spirit and trust in God of David, both a man of war and one according to the heart of God, the religion, the zeal, the standard (*Labarum*) of Constantine the Great."[56] He admitted frankly that the previous summer, before the great reversal of fortune, he had opposed the general's recall, out of consideration for the Catholic electors, he implied. Now the situation was different. "What prudent man would justly hold this as a crime against me?" But Wallenstein turned a deaf ear to this and to Lamormaini's subsequent Easter greeting.[57] His feelings were expressed in a story, perhaps apocryphal, then making the rounds. Shortly beforehand construction on the new Jesuit church in Vienna had been slowed by the collapse of two towers. To this Wallenstein allegedly commented it was unfortunate the towers had not been filled with Jesuits, with Lamormaini at the top.[58]

Vienna's relations with Rome grew more tense during the last months of 1631 and the first half of 1632. This was the case even though on November 20, 1631, Barberini had directed Alessandro Bichi, the new nuncio in Paris, to cease encouraging the efforts to separate Bavaria from the emperor and to remonstrate with Richelieu about his support of Sweden. Rome realized the preservation of the Catholic religion now depended on the emperor and Maximilian's standing together.[59] Vienna continued to seek funds from Rome as well as clear papal commitment to the Habsburgs in the German conflict. The emperor simply could not understand why Urban would not come out more clearly against the French, in view of Richelieu's refusal to withdraw his support from the heretic Gustav Adolph. In December Urban did approve a monthly subsidy of five thousand scudi each for the emperor and the League, but Ferdinand considered the sum paltry, as it was indeed compared with the funds Urban spent on family projects, and he resented sharing the money with the League.[60]

New efforts were made to pry funds loose from Rome. In February Cardinal Pazmany was dispatched thither with a twofold purpose, to obtain financial assistance and to convince the pope to take a leading part in the alliance of which the Imperial-Spanish treaty of February 14 was the basis and which was now presented as directed against the heretics and eventually the Turks. Pazmany impressed upon the pope that the war in Germany was a religious one, its principal cause being the Edict of Restitution, "which," he told Urban, "Your Holiness praised so highly."[61] Ferdinand was fighting for the Church, and the pope had the duty to aid him in all possible ways, especially by pressuring France to stop helping the heretics. Now was the time for Urban to demonstrate the leadership earlier popes had shown in times of crisis.

Pazmany's journey to Rome was a disillusioning experience. He made his grand entrance into the Eternal City on March 28, three weeks after the famous consistory of cardinals at which the Spanish Cardinal Borja vigorously protested papal policy in Germany and so created a memorable scene.[62] Such methods were not the way to win over Urban. Pazmany's audiences with the pope and his sessions with Roman officials soon showed him that Urban would not participate in the alliance because of his fear of France. Indeed, the alliance would have committed Urban to the imperial position on the Treaty of Regensburg and the French evacuation of Pinerolo. The most he could do, Urban told Pazmany, was to continue urging France to desist from aiding the Protestants. And, in truth, the thought of a French schism did haunt the pope.[63] A further reason Urban later gave Pazmany for not joining the alliance was that its goal to defend the Empire included the maintenance of the Peace of Religion with its recognition of Protestant rights. Urban would probably provide the emperor with more funds, Pazmany reported, but he would not open up the treasure in Castel San Angelo as Vienna hoped.[64]

What most jolted Vienna, however, was a statement Urban made in the course of an audience with the cardinal. When Pazmany in his efforts to make clear the religious character of the war asserted that the pope had praised the Edict, Urban interrupted him to deny that he had ever done so; in fact, he had been displeased by it, as the documents would show, "unless perhaps (which he said was accustomed to happen often), the secretaries had written something more [than they should have]." To Vienna this was betrayal. Perhaps, Urban went on infuriatingly, the losses suffered by the German Catholic princes were a divine punishment for the failure to return the recovered church lands to their rightful ecclesiastical owners.[65] There was, as we have seen, some basis in fact for Urban's denial that he had approved the Edict, but Ferdinand could hardly have interpreted otherwise the effusive missives from Rome encouraging his zeal and often communicated to him through supporters of the Edict like Lamormaini and Pallotto. As the emperor wrote Pazmany, Vienna could not be expected to know that papal secretaries did not correctly interpret the mind of the pope. Copies of a number of Roman communications to the emperor including the brief of May 5, 1629, were sent to Pazmany in Rome to prove the extent of papal support for the Edict and to demonstrate Rome's approval of the emperor's disposition of church lands.[66]

Despite the anger in Vienna, Ferdinand had no intention of acting in pique. He needed papal aid. Pazmany was directed to continue his efforts, and when he returned in July he did not come back emptyhanded. His mission undoubtedly confirmed Rome in a decision taken at Bavarian suggestion prior to his arrival, namely, to dispatch extraordinary nuncios to the three capitals, Madrid, Paris, and Vienna, with the goal of reconciling the respective rulers and eventually bringing them together in an alliance.[67] When Girolamo Grimaldi, the extraordinary nuncio for Vienna, arrived in late June, he brought with him eighty thousand talers for the emperor and fifty thousand for the League. Several times in the years before the Peace of Prague in 1635 similar modest sums flowed north in addition to the regular monthly subsidy.[68]

The cornerstone of papal policy thus became the active promotion of reconciliation among the Catholic states, especially the Habsburg states and France, and the formation of a Catholic alliance. This corresponded to the long-standing design of Lamormaini, who could take encouragement from the French response to Schwarzenberg's mission. Louis expressed a desire for peace and even indicated a readiness to assist Ferdinand against Sweden should Gustav Adolph reject reasonable terms. The catch was in the conditions the French laid down. They expected Ferdinand to recognize their possession of Pinerolo, to accept the French interpretation of the arrangement made for the Valtelline in the Franco-Spanish Treaty of Monzon in 1626, and to acquiesce in the presence of French garrisons in the fortresses of Moyenvic and Metz. The emperor was to try to convince Spain to go along with these conditions and should he fail, to remain neutral in any conflict that might ensue between France and Spain.[69] This would, of course, split the two Habsburg powers and so achieve a long-standing French objective.

How seriously Richelieu took the Schwarzenberg mission is difficult to determine. He may have sought to keep in touch with Vienna merely because he had to show some interest in Rome's plan for the reconciliation of the three crowns. More likely his response to Schwarzenberg was conditioned by the new Franco-Swedish relationship that the unexpected success of Gustav Adolph had created. The French had not anticipated he would stand on the Rhine by December 1631, and they did not want to see him expand his position there. Made partly with an eye on the Swedish king were several French treaties. Two were concluded with Trier, one in December 1631 and the other the following April. They guaranteed the elector French protection and provided for French garrisons in the two Rhine fortresses, Ehrenbreitstein (opposite Coblenz) and Philippsburg. Two other treaties were imposed in January and June 1632 on Duke Charles of Lorraine, who had aided the king's domestic enemies. They granted France broad rights in his territory and then committed the duke to remain always attached to French interests.[70] Richelieu seems to have kept in contact with Vienna to provide himself with an emergency exit through which he might pass and still obtain at least some of his goals in the event the anti-Habsburg coalition he was building collapsed or proved unmanageable, as the triumphs of Gustav Adolph showed it might.

Through the nuncios, who now handled many of the communications between Vienna and Paris, Ferdinand urged Louis to send a man to Vienna for negotiations. But Louis declined, claiming that he could send no representative until the emperor gave a definite answer to his proposals. The dispatch of an emissary would arouse the suspicion of his allies, a risk he could not take without greater hope of success. Ferdinand followed the recommendation of his privy council when in response he explained the reasons for his adherence to the Treaty of Regensburg and requested a clearer statement of the French position.[71] But it took another turn of events to bring a French negotiator to Vienna in February of 1633.

For many in Vienna the hope of an acceptable imperial understanding with France was an illusion, the product of wishful thinking. But Grimaldi worked at it. The extraordinary nuncio spent much of his time defending the pope's refusal to break with France; he simply could not do so and maintain his claim to be "universal father" of all Catholics.[72] Among the imperial ministers he found Trautmannsdorf and Werdenberg open to the possibility of rapprochement with France.[73] On the other side were Eggenberg and the Bishop of Vienna, who remained at court as the principal minister when Eggenberg returned to Graz for a visit in mid-September.[74] Grimaldi was especially critical of certain religious at court, whom he felt exacerbated the situation by their adamant rejection of any reconciliation with France. He meant the Capuchin agent of Cardinal Harrach in Vienna, Basilio d'Aire, whom he characterized as "completely Austrian," and even more so Quiroga, who in one meeting, according to Grimaldi, defended all the actions of the Spanish crown since the days of Peter of Aragon, who died in 1381.[75] Lamormaini's name rarely appeared in the dispatches of the nuncios during the spring and summer of 1632; this probably reflected his diminished status at court. Grimaldi did report that Lamormaini paid him a visit shortly after his arrival to assure him of his assistance. But this time there was no papal brief for the confessor.[76]

Spring and summer saw hard times continue for the Catholic forces. For the League, only the troops of Maximilian and his brother, Ferdinand of Cologne, remained in the field. The Swedes crossed the River Lech into Bavaria near Rain on April 15. Tilly was wounded in the action and died two weeks later. The Bavarians held Ingolstadt and the line along the Danube to Regensburg and Passau, but Gustav Adolph bypassed Ingolstadt and marched to the west through Bavaria, deliberately ravaging the country. On May 17 he entered Munich, where he held court until June 7, Maximilian having moved his court and government to Braunau in Upper Austria and Salzburg respectively. Earlier, Swedish troops had occupied Augsburg, and they now controlled much of south central Germany.

Wallenstein in the meantime broke camp from Znaim on April 23 with the intention of gaining the advantage in Bohemia. On May 25 he retook Prague. This movement forced Gustav Adolph to march eastwards lest an advance by Wallenstein into poorly defended Saxony make negotiations more attractive to the elector and possibly cut the king's supply lines to the north. Wallenstein's forces joined with Maximilian's in the Upper Palatinate in early July, and soon Gustav Adolph's troops were encamped not far from them near Nuremberg. There the two armies remained most of the summer, while Maximilian grew impatient with the general's refusal to press his numerical advantage and thus secure the major victory the Catholics hoped would redress the balance between the two sides. Wallenstein preferred to wait until shortage of supplies compelled Gustav Adolph to come out of his defensive positions and attack.

In early September he did so, but he was thrown back with heavy losses, thus losing his reputation for invincibility. But again, much to the chagrin of Maximilian, Wallenstein did not follow up the victory.[77]

Pessimism continued to reign among the Catholics. A peasant rebellion flared in Upper Austria in September and October, stirred by hopes fixed on Gustav Adolph.[78] From Rome Vitelleschi directed an impassioned letter to Lamormaini, the only one in which he ever addressed him in the familiar form. He besought Lamormaini to work to end the differences between the pope and Spain as the only way to save Germany, Belgium, and perhaps even Italy itself.[79] In a long position paper, Stralendorf lamented that if the Catholics did not obtain a major victory before the onset of winter, the situation would indeed be desperate.[80] The resources of the Bohemian lands were exhausted. Spain was hard pressed in the Netherlands, and it was only from that quarter that there was hope for human aid. The pope, it seemed, had deserted the emperor; he and many Italian princes still smarted from Ferdinand's intervention in Italy. Stralendorf even thought he could detect a note of *Schadenfreude* in a recent conversation with Grimaldi. Ferdinand ought to seek peace on the best terms he could get in order to avoid a total collapse. Wallenstein was the man to handle the negotiations.

But this raised familiar problems of conscience. Knowing Ferdinand's mind well, Stralendorf took them into consideration and proposed the safest course. Ferdinand ought to take no positive initiative with regard to the religious issues, so that it would be clear that he accepted only what necessity imposed on him. Thus there would be no danger of his alienating the Lord, his sole support. This procedure, of course, took from the emperor the opportunity to exercise effective leadership toward a settlement and left the initiative on the Catholic side to the electors, from whom little could be expected, or, Stralendorf may have thought, left it to the councilors who would deal directly with the Protestants.

Gustav Adolph did sound out Wallenstein about negotiations, and the general forwarded the Swedish suggestions to Vienna. They included the revocation of the Edict, the return to the Protestants of most of the ecclesiastical lands recovered in the war, freedom of religion for Lutherans in the Catholic states, and a major redistribution of territories within the Empire. Wallenstein himself would hardly have expected Ferdinand to take them seriously. The emperor did ask for his opinion, at the same time noting that the terms were extremely hard. He had little confidence that negotiations at this time would lead anywhere, Ferdinand wrote, and in any event, talks with Saxony and Brandenburg were decidedly preferable.[81]

Then an event took place that raised the spirits of the Catholics. The armies had maneuvered about until once again in mid-November, after Wallenstein had moved into Saxony, they found themselves opposite each other near Lützen, not far from Leipzig. On November 16 Gustav Adolph attacked. The battle itself was a standoff, with heavy losses on both sides, but in the heat of the fight Gustav Adolph fell, and the Swedes were robbed of their charismatic leader.[82] Ferdinand saw the king's death as a response to his prayer, especially since with confidence in God, he had rejected a plan to assassinate Gustav Adolph.[83] In thanksgiving Ferdinand now ordered the construction of a monastery for the Spanish Benedictines near the Schottentor in Vienna. When the military prefect of the city objected that this would create a dangerously weak spot in the city's defenses, the emperor responded that the assistance of the Blessed Virgin Mary, to whom the monastery would be dedicated, would more than offset this.[84]

For Lamormaini the event was another instance of the Lord's miraculous care for Ferdinand, and according to Grimaldi, he claimed to have convinced Ferdinand of this. Lamormaini, Grimaldi reported, now foresaw a continuation of the war until the military situation improved notably, followed by an invitation to France and other Catholic states to conclude a settlement on terms the emperor had thus far considered detrimental to his reputation.[85] In other words, Ferdinand first needed to achieve a superiority over the Swedes and German Protestants. Then, from a position of strength, he would be ready to make some surprising concessions to the French for the sake of an enduring settlement. One can only think of the terms suggested by France in reply to Schwarzenberg's mission. This scenario remained an option for imperial policy until the Peace of Prague. Its weakness lay in the belief that France would be willing to live peacefully with a revived imperial power in Germany. Meanwhile, Lamormaini was again concerned with the financing of colleges in the territory to be regained from the Protestants.[86]

10. Recovery, 1633–1634

ienna considered Lützen a major triumph because of the death of Gustav Adolph. Most of the policymakers realized that otherwise it had been a draw at best. Only with the victory at Nördlingen in September 1634 would the military advantage swing back to the emperor and Catholic states. A small committee of councilors including Stralendorf recommended in early December that the emperor press forward with peace negotations while at the same time exploiting the momentum gained by Lützen. Reasonable conditions could not yet be hoped for. Total victory, however, was out of the question. The enemy was far superior in resources as a result of the territory held in Germany and connections with France, Holland, Denmark, and England. The suggestion that Ferdinand send an emissary to Paris now that the Franco-Swedish alliance had lapsed with the death of Gustav Adolph may well have come from Justus Gebhardt. He now began to turn up with greater frequency on conciliar committees and in privy council sessions and may have served as the ears if not the voice of Lamormaini in these bodies.[1] The privy council meeting four days later rejected this recommendation, preferring to await the anticipated arrival of a new French resident. Both the committee and the privy council agreed the emperor should secure the views of the Catholic electors, Wallenstein, and Eggenberg, who was absent from the meetings, before making any decisions.[2]

At the request of Ferdinand, Cardinal Pazmany submitted an opinion on December 8. His paper showed that he favored a compromise peace with the Protestants.[3] Pazmany pointed out the impossibility of defeating the enemy militarily and called attention to the exhaustion of the hereditary lands and the troubles facing Spain in the New World and the Old.

> If there were hope either of completely subduing the Empire or radically extirpating heresy, it would be impious and execrable to raise the question of a settlement. But given the present state of affairs and considering the situation in France, Belgium, Italy, and the Indies as well as the exhaustion of the [Catholic] princes and [hereditary] provinces, it [subjection of the Empire and complete uprooting of heresy] seems morally impossible (divine miracles, reserved to the supreme heavenly council, do not enter into the

deliberation), whereby the resources of the Empire could be totally destroyed.

The remark in parentheses was obviously made with Lamormaini in mind. Pazmany did not discuss specific terms of peace in his paper, but according to a later conversation with Lamormaini reported by Grimaldi in mid-March, he was willing to accept any settlement that would preserve Catholicism intact in the Habsburg lands, where his primary interest obviously lay. Thus he was prepared to go well beyond what the six theologians had approved the previous year.[4]

Pazmany's failure to mention the likelihood of assistance from either Paris or Rome, much less of a Catholic alliance, was perhaps the result of his frustrating sojourn in Rome the previous year. Another consideration Pazmany raised was to be of growing concern to the Catholic electors, namely, the deteriorating health of the emperor and the increasing possibility that Ferdinand would die before the election of the King of the Romans. Uncertainty over the imperial succession would only encourage more foreign interference and chaos. Pazmany's remark that some military leaders seemed intent on prolonging the war for their own benefit echoed a conclusion already drawn by others in Vienna from Wallenstein's reluctance to commit his troops to battle and to follow up his victories. It indicated that the cardinal was among those advocates of compromise who were not sympathetic to Wallenstein.

New consultations were held in later January after Ferdinand accepted a Danish offer to mediate in the Empire. Stralendorf prepared a long report with the assistance of Bishop Anton and Trautmannsdorf.[5] The arguments were similar to those of early December advocating negotiations and prosecution of the war effort. The councilors lamented the discrepancy between the immense benefits the Protestants garnered from their one victory at Breitenfeld and the little the Catholics had to show for all their success on the battlefield. This they attributed to the greater popular support of the Protestants. As far back as early 1628, in the aftermath of Mühlhausen, they reminded Ferdinand, they had advocated a policy of caution.

They then turned to the religious issue, with an eye on Lamormaini it would seem. They were vague about specific concessions, though they assumed some would have to be made. "But it has already been sufficiently deliberated what can be conceded in this matter by reason of necessity in order to avoid greater evil to religion," they wrote in an apparent allusion to the opinion of the six theologians. But it is not clear whether their reference was to the general principle of the lesser evil elaborated by the theologians or to their sanction of 1629 as normative year for at least the temporary possession of most church lands. If the former was the case, then they could be understood to have approved implicitly the position that not only Pazmany, as we have already seen, but also Dietrichstein and Bishop Anton himself assumed by mid-March, namely, that nearly any settlement was acceptable in the Empire provided the status of Catholicism in the Habsburg lands was safeguarded.[6] The principal concern of the three prelates was for the emperor's own territories.

"Then for one thing," the paper went on, "it is more beneficial to preserve religion in some fashion after the example of Ferdinand I than in the end to risk absolutely everything." Thus the writers appealed to the moderation shown by Ferdinand when he signed the Peace of Augsburg and the positive results this had brought. Between 1555 and the "accursed" Bohemian war, Catholicism had made great progress in Germany. The present war and especially the last few years had reduced the Church to its worst state since the Reformation. Protestant preachers were active in areas occupied by the enemy where they had never been known to set foot before. Many souls had been lost as a consequence. The three councilors remarked pointedly that God's support of a just cause was revealed as much by his granting useful counsel as military victories, "since it is the nature of a rational creature to overcome by prudence and counsel rather than by force."

But toward the end of their paper, in a manner reminiscent of Lamormaini, the three noted God's providential care for Ferdinand. It had been shown again in the death of Gustav Adolph. There were limits to the concessions the emperor might make, but these limits were not elaborated. "Therefore also such a great helper [God] is not at all to be offended by yielding to conditions of the sort that might be opposed to his holy name or divine glory. Rather much more is everything else that the divine omnipotence might decree to be suffered and born in patience, because he is the one who puts to death and raises up again, who in the midst of the greatest danger can easily send His Imperial Majesty the best fortune." The councilors recommended the emperor cooperate with the peace initiatives of Denmark and Hesse-Darmstadt, and Bishop Anton and Hermann von Questenberg were soon deputed to represent Ferdinand at talks with the Landgrave of Hesse-Darmstadt scheduled for Leitmeritz in Bohemia in March.

Lamormaini, as we have noted, read more significance into the victory at Lützen than did the councilors. He assured Ferdinand, according to Grimaldi, that if he maintained his confidence in God and did not misuse the "miracles" God worked for him, he would have the honor of rooting out heresy in Germany, "since in ancient times heresy had never lasted longer than one hundred years." Ferdinand had promised to consult with him before making any agreement with the Protestants, Lamormaini told Grimaldi. But the nuncio doubted "that his opinion will be enough against the mind of the others."[7] Eggenberg voiced nearly the same sentiment to the Bavarian Donnersberg when he remarked that some ecclesiastics still opposed peace but that Ferdinand scarcely took them seriously.[8] In his talks with Lamormaini Ferdinand appealed to the views of Bishop Anton, Pazmany, and Dietrichstein, Pazmany having been summoned to Vienna precisely to help the emperor resolve his problems of conscience associated with the religious issue.[9] But it was too early to count out the confessor who persistently looked with hope toward France.

The news of Gustav Adolph's death was not completely unwelcome in Paris. Since his triumphant march through Germany, he had proved quite inaccessible to Richelieu's control. The cardinal's efforts to secure neutrality for Bavaria and the Catholic League had ended in failure. Now that the king had left the scene, Richelieu hoped to refashion an anti-Habsburg alliance he could dominate. He planned continued support for Sweden, but he wanted to see the leadership of the Protestant cause in Germany pass to Saxony and Brandenburg. For Richelieu it was also important to win over some German Catholic states, especially Bavaria, at least to neutrality with his coalition, partly because this would lessen the religious nature of the war and along with it Catholic criticism of him at home. The Marquis de Feuquière was the principal diplomat sent to Germany in early 1633 to implement this policy. He was to deal with Axel Oxenstierna, the Swedish chancellor who was now Sweden's effective policymaker, and the two electors, John George and George William.

Feuquière's efforts showed few positive results. Saxony had no intention of allying with another foreigner, and Brandenburg, though more receptive, would not yet do so without Saxony. John George was more interested in the imminent negotiations with the emperor. Oxenstierna turned out to be much stronger than either Paris or Vienna anticipated. There was to be no Swedish collapse. On April 19 at Heilbronn in Swabia, Feuquière and Oxenstierna renewed the Franco-Swedish alliance on virtually the same terms as at Bärwalde. Several days later, Oxenstierna concluded an alliance with the newly formed Heilbronn Confederation of Upper German Protestant states that made him director of their combined forces and kept Sweden in firm control. Feuquière's weak attempt to obtain recognition of neutrality for the states of the Catholic League was frustrated, and Saxony, which had hoped to secure influence with the Upper German states, was nearly isolated. The following September 9 at Frankfurt, France allied directly with the Heilbronn Confederation but without attaining any major concession on neutrality for the Catholic states, so that Richelieu did not ratify the agreement until June 1634. Wallenstein's successes in the east, meanwhile, pushed Brandenburg into the Franco-Swedish alliance on October 28, 1633. Richelieu kept working to gain influence among the south and west German states, Catholic as well as Protestant. Lorraine was largely under French control by early 1633, and much of the electorate of Trier, where French and Spanish troops had clashed, was occupied by its French protectors.[10] His efforts would bear more fruit the following year.

Meanwhile, Richelieu with the help of the nuncios maintained his contacts with Vienna. Nicolas de Charbonnière, who arrived in Vienna as a permanent resident in early February 1633, brought with him a treaty outline to be presented to the emperor by Grimaldi. It raised the price of a French understanding with Ferdinand from what had been quoted to Schwarzenberg the year before. Ferdinand was expected to accept French possession of Pinerolo and, more or less, the French position on the arrangement in the Valtelline. The emperor would have to recognize French claims not only in Metz but in the other two disputed bishoprics, Toul and Verdun, as well as the growing French hold on Lorraine, including Moyenvic. On the other hand, France would agree to withdraw from some areas it had occupied in Trier. A completely new French demand was the convocation of a German peace congress at which France would serve as mediator and full-fledged participant. This would obviously make possible all sorts of mischief, particularly as long as the succession question remained unresolved. Any pact with France would again require a promise not to aid Spain in the event of a Franco-Spanish conflict.[11]

Only at the end of March did imperial councilors take up Charbonnière's proposal. After reviewing the course of Franco-Imperial relations since the unratified alliance with Spain of February 1632, they found little basis in the French offer for an understanding with France or a general European peace. Charbonnière, however, remained in Vienna, and Ferdinand did assure the nuncios of his willingness to participate in the peace congress of the Catholic powers that the papacy was now promoting to resolve the problems of Europe.[12]

Spanish policy underwent no significant change after the death of Gustav Adolph. The loss of the fortress of Maastricht shortly before Lützen made the Spaniards more determined than ever to secure German support in the Netherlands. This was a major task assigned the Marquis of Castañeda, who left Madrid in October 1632 to replace Cadereyta and the now deceased Duke of Guastalla as ambassador in Vienna. Castañeda was to pursue the efforts to organize a league of Habsburg and German states against the Swedes, the Dutch, and the French. A new Spanish plan foresaw the march of an army of twenty-four thousand under the command of the Governor of Milan, the Duke of Feria, through the Valtelline into the Tyrol, then along the western border of the Empire, to relieve the Spanish forces in the Netherlands. Another purpose of the expedition was to escort to Brussels the Cardinal Infant, Don Fernando, the newly-appointed Governor of the Netherlands. Part of the army was to remain in the Spanish-occupied Palatinate to operate against the French or the Swedes as necessity arose. In January the veteran diplomat the Count of Oñate left Madrid as an extraordinary ambassador to Vienna with the special commission to win Wallenstein over to this plan.[13]

Madrid continued to rely on Quiroga to play a key role in Vienna. Eggenberg's health was manifestly failing. Quiroga was to attempt to bind closer to Spain the Bishop of Vienna, whom the Spaniards saw as his successor, since "it is feared that Trautmannsdorf cannot be won over."[14] Quiroga was also to use his influence with Wallenstein, "his friend," for Spanish purposes, and to try to reconcile the differences between Count Thun, who wanted a major military role for his master, the King of Hungary, and Eggenberg, who shared Wallenstein's opposition to this.[15]

Vienna's primary interest in the early spring of 1633 was the negotiations with the Protestants. The two moderates, Bishop Anton and Hermann von Questenberg, held their talks with Hesse-Darmstadt at Leitmeritz from March 23 to 25. They do not seem to have received specific instructions beyond what was found in the January paper of Stralendorf, Trautmannsdorf, and Bishop Anton, probably because the discussions were only meant to be exploratory. Ferdinand expected the two to remain in contact with Wallenstein. The general, for his part, was not inclined to cooperate with the moderate party in Vienna because he felt they moved too slowly and because he wanted to handle matters himself.[16]

The discussions at Leitmeritz produced no results apart from the agreement to continue negotiations at Breslau in May with the help of Danish mediation. The failure was due to what even the moderates in Vienna considered the exorbitant demands of the Protestants. They included the revocation of the Edict and the determination of 1612 as the normative date for the permanent possession of ecclesiastical lands and for the free exercise of religion. This meant not only the surrender of all the lands recovered by the Catholics during the war but something Ferdinand would never grant, the widespread free exercise of religion in Upper and Lower Austria and in the Bohemian lands.[17] By such a concession the emperor would give up for himself the right granted all imperial princes by the Peace of Augsburg to determine the religion to be practiced in their lands. Hesse-Darmstadt proposed explicitly that Maximilian retain the electoral title until his death, when it would return to Frederick's heirs. All the Palatinate lands would revert to them immediately except the Upper Palatinate, which Bavaria would keep permanently. Some imperial fiefs would have to be ceded to Sweden as compensation for its exertions in Germany. Hesse-Darmstadt came back to a long-standing Protestant demand when he called for a new body composed equally of Catholics and Protestants to decide issues touching religion in the Empire; such decisions were no longer to be made by majority vote in the diet, either in the council of electors or the council of princes. Moreover, he wanted equal representation of Catholics and Protestants on the two imperial courts, the imperial aulic council in Vienna and the imperial cameral court in Speyer.[18] After Bishop Anton and Questenberg returned, Rocci reported that as far as Vienna was concerned, the Protestant position meant that peace was a long way off.[19] But negotiations were to continue through Wallenstein and, later than planned, at Breslau.

During the course of 1632 Lamormaini had attempted, unsuccessfully, to rebuild his bridges to Wallenstein. At the start of the new year Vitelleschi urged him to continue his efforts, since the support of the general would be most helpful for the planting of the faith in the lands to be recovered from the Protestants. He also sent to Lamormaini, with instruction to deliver it or not as he saw fit, a letter congratulating Wallenstein on his victory at Lützen and acclaiming him the instrument of divine providence for the restoration of the faith in the north.[20] But Lamormaini thought it better not to pass the letter on to Wallenstein.[21] Long pressed on the matter by Contzen in Munich, Vitelleschi took up Wallenstein's astrological practices with Lamormaini. According to his informant, who was left unnamed, Wallenstein consulted the stars about his every action. This was said to be a tool of the devil, Vitelleschi wrote, and it explained Wallenstein's failure to exploit his military advantage. Vitelleschi suggested Lamormaini raise the issue with the emperor, but Lamormaini responded that he was powerless to do anything in the matter.[22] Lamormaini's position was a difficult one. The obvious tension between him and Eggenberg made Grimaldi reluctant to urge recognition of the Prefect of Rome through Lamormaini, since it might hurt rather than help the papal cause.[23] At the triennial congregation or meeting of the Jesuits' Austrian Province held in April, there were a number of voices raised against the confessor, but Vitelleschi came to his defense.[24]

Wallenstein himself was engaged in negotiations in the late spring and summer of 1633, but it is difficult to discover their precise character and purpose. On May 17 he began to move with his army into Silesia, but shortly afterward he and Arnim concluded an armistice that was renewed regularly except for a few brief periods until October 2. The lack of action in the east allowed the enemy to concentrate its efforts to the west, especially in Bavaria. This provoked Maximilian, who could not understand Wallenstein's failure to take the offensive and was suspicious of his secret negotiations. In their first talks on June 6, Wallenstein and Arnim seem to have tentatively agreed on the return in the Empire, exclusive of the Habsburg lands, to the ecclesiastical and political status of 1618, including the surrender of the Palatinate by Maximilian. But they made no commitments. This would serve as the basis for a union of the imperial and Saxon armies, who would then proceed against all who opposed the settlement, German or foreign. Wallenstein quickly learned, however, that neither the emperor nor leading councilors in Vienna were ready to go this far. He then let Arnim know this with the result that the Saxon general grew more uncertain of the degree to which Wallenstein spoke for the emperor.[25]

Indecision and perplexity characterized Ferdinand when in June and July first Wallenstein's negotiations and then the talks planned for Breslau seemed to require him to take a position. A struggle was in progress for Ferdinand's mind. Vigorous action on the part of Lamormaini and the two nuncios almost certainly influenced him, and perhaps others, in the rejection of the terms suggested by Wallenstein. At the least they confirmed him in it. Rocci, before asking for instructions about how far he ought to go in opposing concessions—he himself clearly thought positive action required—reminded Lamormaini of his duty as confessor "to warn His Majesty not to agree out of human considerations to a peace so prejudicial to the Catholic religion." Neither the confessor nor the emperor had reason to doubt that Rocci, and presumably the pope, strongly opposed concessions to the Protestants. Lamormaini assured Rocci he had already spoken "freely enough" with both Eggenberg and Ferdinand, and "he had found them sufficiently constant on the point of not prejudicing the Catholic religion." Ferdinand would not permit Wallenstein to draw up an agreement with Saxony before he, Ferdinand, went over it carefully and made necessary adjustments. The emperor, Rocci wrote, would never agree to 1618 as normative for Habsburg lands, a proposal that had now been brought into the discussion by Protestants in contact with Wallenstein and that hardly differed from the 1612 date put forth at Leitmeritz. But Ferdinand and, more so, Eggenberg were inclined to accept the status of 1618 for the Empire. Eggenberg reminded Rocci that the emperor had his own theologians, who according to Eggenberg had accepted the principle of the lesser evil and left its application up to the political councilors. Rome had never approved the Treaty of Passau but had tolerated it, Eggenberg pointed out to the nuncio, at the same time rejecting out of hand Rocci's suggestion that Ferdinand seek more actively an understanding with France.[26]

The following week Rocci took his case personally to the emperor, and on July 2 he reported that peace was not so close as some imagined.[27] But the situation remained fluid. Ferdinand assured Wallenstein on July 9 that he would follow his recommendations for a settlement, and a few days later Gerhard von Questenberg was optimistic about one.[28]

Preparations were now under way for the negotiations in Breslau. The imperial delegation had Trautmannsdorf at its head, assisted by Hermann von Questenberg and Justus Gebhardt. The three were to cooperate with Wallenstein, but his enthusiasm diminished when he learned the composition of the imperial negotiating team.[29] He probably was unhappy that the Bishop of Vienna had excused himself, according to Rocci on the grounds that it was not proper for a bishop to treat with heretics about the surrender of church lands,[30] and he probably knew that Gebhardt was close to Lamormaini. He must not have been pleased by the appointment of Trautmannsdorf either, who tried to avoid the assignment, precisely because of the difficulty he found in working with Wallenstein.[31] A couple of months earlier, Trautmannsdorf had told Grimaldi that he and many others were disgusted with the "impertinences" of the general, and he indicated his support for the King of Hungary when he added that they hoped to convince the emperor and Eggenberg to place the young king at the head of the army. Under him many nobles would fight who refused to do so under the absolute command of Wallenstein. According to Trautmannsdorf, Grimaldi reported, "if the Emperor were convinced and we were [all] in agreement to remove Wallenstein from command, it would be enough to write the principal captains, since he is no less hated in the army than he is feared by all."[32] So it was to turn out. Nor was Trautmannsdorf ready to accept a return to the status of 1618 in the Empire, apart from the Habsburg lands, as the basis for a settlement with the Protestants.[33]

The three delegates to Breslau did not depart until August 28, heading first for Wallenstein's camp.[34] Just a few days after they left, the nuncios brought Ferdinand a brief that had been sent in response to their request for instructions.[35] Without the rhetorical flourishes of earlier briefs, Urban encouraged Ferdinand to remain steadfast. Perhaps the Curia now kept a more careful eye on its secretaries. Adhering to his policy hitherto, the pope made clear that he was opposed to concessions and thus protected the Church juridically; but he made no further effort to pressure the emperor to reject a peace. Ferdinand, it seems, was being torn apart by the conflict at court. Rocci reported he was showing "melancholy and much perplexity of soul." He speculated this was the result of excessive dependence on Wallenstein, but one might attribute it as much to his anxiety over the related problem of the peace settlement.[36]

The long delay in the departure of the three delegates for Breslau augured the failure of the conference. It never did convene. But the instructions are important because they elaborated an imperial negotiating position.[37] For Vienna the purpose of the negotiations was to find an agreement between the Catholic and Protestant states, by which were meant Saxony, Brandenburg, and the signatories of the Leipzig resolution, that would serve as the basis for an alliance to expel the foreigners from the Empire and bring the other German states into line. A difficult task was assigned the delegates when they were directed to coordinate their efforts with both Wallenstein and the envoys expected from Bavaria and Mainz. The instructions pictured Ferdinand as the judge who would pass on any arrangement reached by the Catholics and Protestants. But he clearly did not want to act one way or the other without the Catholic electors. Religious concessions were to be made only with their approval; both emperor and Catholic electors were responsible for the Edict and both would have to share the responsibility for yielding on it. If the electors for their part did decide to accept concessions, the emperor had no choice but to go along, lest he be stigmatized as the obstacle to peace. As it turned out, neither Maximilian nor Mainz responded to the emperor's request for delegates or even an opinion for the conference. This was due more to the unwillingness to commit themselves until absolutely necessary than to the difficulties of communication.[38] Neither Ferdinand nor the Catholic states wanted to take the responsibility for either prolonging the war or making religious concessions.

The instructions bore a clear resemblance to what the six theologians had approved in the fall of 1631. They authorized the delegates to agree to the suspension of the Edict until some form of imperial assembly was held, which might or might not be a diet, but for which a date was to be set lest there be an indefinite delay. The year 1629 might be granted as the norm for the possession of church lands, not the free exercise of religion, in the sense that all lands recovered by virtue of the Edict might be returned. But the instructions noted that this did not apply to properties regained by the ordinary legal procedure and not by virtue of the Edict, whether before or after 1629. Mentioned as belonging to this category were Magdeburg, Bremen, and Halberstadt, all claimed for Archduke Leopold William. No concessions were to be made on these without consulting Vienna. This was a far cry from the 1612 norm called for by Hesse-Darmstadt or the 1618 one (not applicable to the Habsburg lands) acceptable to Wallenstein and, it seems, Eggenberg and the three prelates, Bishop Anton, Dietrichstein, and Pazmany. Significant was the readiness now to grant Denmark several north German bishoprics occupied by the Protestants in order to win his favor as mediator. Regarding the bishoprics held by Saxony and Brandenburg, the delegates might renew the Mühlhausen guarantee of 1620 that promised no effort would be made to reacquire them by force until the case was heard in the courts. If this did not satisfy the two Protestant electors, the delegates might go along with whatever the Catholic states approved or point to the projected imperial assembly; otherwise they were to guarantee no claims.

Where church lands had to be surrendered, every attempt was to be made to preserve freedom of religion for the Catholics. Obviously, the imperial courts would be crucial in the future, and for this reason Hesse-Darmstadt had made several proposals concerning them at Leitmeritz. But the instructions indicated no willingness even to discuss changes in judicial procedure. Any concessions on the Palatinate were subject to Bavarian approval, and only a partial restoration of Frederick's lands to his heirs seems to have been envisioned. Highly unrealistic was the insistence that there was to be no compensation for Sweden, which was to be kept out of the negotiations. Nor were there to be any further limitations on the emperor's rights to require contributions for defense or to wage war. Ferdinand was ready to grant an amnesty only to those who had broken with him since 1631 and had not gone beyond the position stated in the Leipzig resolution of that year.

The instructions reflected well the state of mind in Vienna, especially the indecision on the religious issue and the intent to avoid responsibility. One can imagine Ferdinand breathing a sigh of relief when he realized the conference would not take place. The delegates were still in Prague on November 26 awaiting the arrival of the Danish mediators.[39] A rumor of the plague was partly responsible for the failure of the conference, but the chief reason was the opposition of the Swedes and the French to negotiations they knew were directed against their interests. The Swedes refused the necessary passes to the Danish participants.[40]

After it became clear to him that nothing could be expected from the conference at Breslau, Wallenstein resumed negotiations with Arnim. Ferdinand expressed his delight to learn that the two were on the verge of an agreement, but the negotiations then suddenly collapsed on September 25, according to the general because Arnim brought in new conditions at the last moment.[41] After taking to the battlefield long enough to win an engagement at Steinau that gave him control of Silesia, Wallenstein chose to reopen negotiations instead of pursuing his advantage. Ferdinand authorized contacts with Saxony and Brandenburg, but he indicated he wanted a report on the religious settlement Wallenstein envisioned before the general entered into any negotiations with Sweden or its allies.[42] Wallenstein then offered Arnim a return to the status of 1618 in the Empire, a position that went beyond that of the court as expressed in the instructions for Breslau.[43] Trautmannsdorf, whom Wallenstein notified of the proposed agreement, considered it unacceptable.[44]

By now Arnim as well as Saxony and Brandenburg doubted whether Wallenstein really represented the emperor. On November 13 Wallenstein informed Ferdinand that the talks had broken down once again. About the same time Duke Franz Julius of Saxony-Lauenburg, who had been assisting in the negotiations, let the emperor know that Arnim and the two electors wanted to deal directly with the delegates of the emperor and Denmark.[45] Wallenstein had played out his role as a negotiator, at the same time alienating those in Vienna who felt he had been too ready to make concessions and who resented his independence. This clearly included Lamormaini. Still, contacts with Saxony and Brandenburg continued through him and Franz Julius.

In the fall of 1633 the opposition to Wallenstein was mounting. Until then Madrid had always supported him, blaming Lamormaini for his first dismissal and in October reprimanding Castañeda for paying attention to Lamormaini's complaints about him.[46] But Spain was moving toward a break with the general over the Spanish plan to station an army in the west of the Empire. Wallenstein opposed this, since the Spanish presence was certain to disturb his delicate negotiations with the Protestants and provoke the French. It would also bring into the Empire a military force independent of him. Ferdinand at first sided with Wallenstein. But the Spaniards then modified their plan. The troops would not remain permanently in the Empire, and they would be employed to raise the Swedish siege of the critical fortress of Breisach on the Upper Rhine, whose loss would open south Germany to an eventual French invasion. Maximilian, usually so wary of Spain, was enthusiastic, and Ferdinand finally consented to the project. But Wallenstein remained adamant in his opposition, and his long refusal and then reluctant concession of troops bordered on open insubordination to the emperor's express orders. Oñate, the extraordinary Spanish ambassador, acting on his own initiative later ratified by Madrid, now turned against the general and actively sought his dismissal.[47]

The gap between Maximilian and Wallenstein had widened in the course of 1633 as a result of old rivalries and especially differences over the conduct of the war. Maximilian threw his forces into the successful effort to save Breisach, even though he knew this exposed Regensburg in the east, from which the Swedish ally, the condottiere Bernard of Weimar, could either invade Upper Austria and even march on Vienna or move into Bavaria. Maximilian warned Wallenstein and the emperor, who ordered the general to send troops. Bernard did seize Regensburg on November 14, and he then began a foray of pillage into Bavaria. Wallenstein remained deaf to Ferdinand's orders and Maximilian's cries for help. Finally, he started out in the direction of Regensburg. Then he turned back. Maximilian soon learned of his retreat and on December 18 ordered the emissary he had just sent to Vienna, his vice chancellor Bartholomew Richel, to start to work actively for the removal of Wallenstein from his command. He was to seek out others likely to be of similar mind, including Lamormaini, Oñate, and Heinrich Schlick, president of the war council.[48] Just four days earlier in Vienna Eggenberg had told Richel that his retreat was "the most harmful, the most dangerous, the most unconsidered thing" Wallenstein had ever done. If the general did not obey, Ferdinand would have to act so "that all should see that His Majesty was master and the Duke [of Friedland] a servant." People considered him a friend of Wallenstein, Eggenberg went on, and so he was, but his religion and his country came first. Ferdinand would not allow his House and that of Bavaria to be destroyed because of Wallenstein.[49] Thus Wallenstein was losing one of his most powerful supporters.

Wallenstein's position was growing shaky. He decided to quarter troops in hard-pressed Bohemia and Upper Austria after he had promised to find a place for them in enemy territory that winter. This caused great consternation in Vienna. It increased when Wallenstein resisted an imperial command to engage Bernard of Weimar and calmly followed his own plan for the soldiers for the winter. A sharp disagreement with Eggenberg over the size of the contribution to be levied on Styria widened the breach with him. Those in Vienna who saw the whole year 1633 as a failure that had produced neither a substantial victory nor successful negotiations felt it was time for the King of Hungary to take over the army. Among these were Trautmannsdorf, the aforementioned Schlick, and young Ferdinand himself.[50] As it was, events bore out the assertion of Wallenstein's enemies that under the King of Hungary the situation would improve.

Wallenstein's health was ruined. Rumors now circulated about him, his alleged contact with the Bohemian exiles, France, and Sweden, his slavery to astrology, his ultimate intentions. Some had a basis in fact, others were wildly exaggerated; all of them fed on the personal antagonism many felt toward him, often as a result of Wallenstein's own past conduct. One could make a good military argument for many of Wallenstein's moves, such as his reluctance to send troops to Maximilian or to pursue Bernard of Weimar, though he had undoubtedly misunderstood the importance of Regensburg. But given the atmosphere, Wallenstein's disobedience was certain to be emphasized. By the end of December, Ferdinand had reached a decision to dismiss him.[51] His chief reason was the belief that Wallenstein had become too powerful and was a threat to his rule. But as often happened, Ferdinand was not in a hurry to act on his decision.

Meanwhile, Wallenstein was aware that Vienna was preparing to move against him. He remained in touch with the two Protestant electors and renewed his contact with Sweden and France. Many of his senior officers were summoned to his winter headquarters at Pilsen, where they found the general scarcely able to rise from bed. On January 13, after their discussion of the military situation, the officers signed a pledge of loyalty to Wallenstein. News of this reached Vienna at about the same time as an alarming report from one of Wallenstein's generals, Ottavio Piccolomini, alleging Wallenstein intended to overthrow the emperor and the House of Habsburg and reorder the map of Europe. Thus the meeting at Pilsen was bound to be interpreted in the worst possible sense. It pointed to treachery. This called for action.

Ferdinand now followed a procedure suggested by Gundacker von Liechtenstein, long an inactive privy councilor who had reemerged as an important figure at court in the course of 1633.[52] Three privy councilors were chosen to go over all the available information on Wallenstein and then decide whether he was guilty and what measures were to be taken. Two of them, Eggenberg and Bishop Anton, had long been associated with the general, and there can be little doubt they gave their verdict with a heavy heart. The third was Trautmannsdorf. They agreed on January 24 that Wallenstein had to be removed from office. Orders were to be issued to this effect releasing the soldiers from their obedience to him. General Gallas was to take over the army until a new commander was named. The second part of the verdict called for the general to be arrested and brought under guard to Vienna, where he would be given a hearing. If this was not possible, and the three certainly thought that it probably was not because he would resist such treatment, then Wallenstein and his leading fellow conspirators were to be killed as men justly convicted. Implementation was entrusted to the three generals, Matthias Gallas, Piccolomini, and Johann von Aldringen. The decision was kept a tight secret until the generals were ready to carry it out. Vienna feared trouble in the army, unduly as it turned out.

At Ferdinand's initiative, that very evening of the twenty-fourth Lamormaini was asked by Bishop Anton for his opinion and so given, it seems, a certain right of veto over the decision. He gave his clear approval. Then he sought the prayers of the Vienna Jesuits and through Vitelleschi in

Rome those of Jesuits around the world for the favorable outcome of the event.[53]

The three generals assured themselves of the army's support and prepared the way for decisive action. Only on February 20 was the order of dismissal published in cities considered friendly. Wallenstein, sensing trouble, fled Pilsen on February 21 with a few supporters and a small force, hoping to reach Arnim or Bernard of Weimar. They stopped at Eger in western Bohemia. There three subordinate officers loyal to the emperor, after judging it impossible to bring Wallenstein back alive and taking precautions to prevent rebellion, killed three associates of the general and then, as he lay in bed, the general himself. So Wallenstein met his end.[54]

Lamormaini certainly advocated the dismissal of Wallenstein in the winter of 1633–34. But his basic reason was different from what it had been in 1630. Then the preservation of Catholic unity had required the general's removal from office. His failure to share Lamormaini's religious goals was also a factor. Both these considerations undoubtedly influenced Lamormaini now. Maximilian had to be placated for the sake of Catholic unity. Wallenstein was offering unacceptable concessions to the Protestants. But the chief reason was Lamormaini's belief, shared with many others, that Wallenstein had become too powerful and was a threat to the emperor's authority and even to his crown. Beyond this, Lamormaini's letter to Vitelleschi of March 3–4, 1634, shows that he and many others were convinced that Wallenstein was linked in a conspiracy to seize power in the Habsburg lands and depose the emperor.[55] Once one is aware of Lamormaini's conviction that Wallenstein was a present danger to Ferdinand's throne, that he was actively engaged in conspiracy, and that he would resist dismissal and attempt to turn the army against Ferdinand, it is easier to understand how the confessor could indeed consent to the execution of Wallenstein if he could not be taken alive. He felt certain of Wallenstein's guilt.

Lamormaini could not help interpreting the elimination of the threat from Wallenstein as another instance of the Lord's providential care for Ferdinand. As usual, this was expressed in Vitelleschi's letters. "The more intently I look," the superior general wrote, "the more clearly I see that the merciful God was moved by our prayers, and that at the same time I had applied another one thousand Masses weekly for the safety of the emperor and the happiness of the Empire, such marvelous deeds were done by the arm of the Most High."[56] Philip IV likewise interpreted the outcome as a revelation of God's special care for Ferdinand and the whole House of Habsburg.[57] Ferdinand himself saw the frustration of the alleged conspiracy as a response to a vow he had taken, and he proceeded to endow the novitiate of St. Anna in Vienna so generously that Lamormaini had to restrain his munificence.[58] Rocci reported that "Father Lamormaini has returned to a better state of favor with His Majesty." Eggenberg, on the contrary, looked to be in bad health, probably as a result of "sickness of spirit" caused by recent events.[59] But a week later Rocci revised his opinion about Eggenberg. The chief minister appeared to be in good health and to enjoy the favor of the emperor, despite his many enemies.[60] Among them were those who had long urged that the military command be entrusted to the King of Hungary. They were about to have their way.

During the months of the Wallenstein crisis, from November to March, contacts were kept open with Saxony through Wallenstein himself for a time and through Duke Franz Julius, who traveled between Vienna, Dresden, and Berlin and even journeyed to Denmark to affirm the continued interest of Vienna in the king's mediation.[61] After Wallenstein's death, the King of Hungary was given formal charge of the peace negotiations as well as command of the imperial army. The memorial drawn up for him in the emperor's name directed him to take advantage of Saxony's willingness to negotiate.[62] Talks began between the imperials and the Saxons on June 15, 1634, in Leitmeritz.[63] The imperial delegates were the same as those for Breslau, Trautmannsdorf, Hermann von Questenberg, and Gebhardt, and they took with them the same instruction. Thus began the negotiations that led directly to the Peace of Prague.

The initial Saxon position was similar to the proposals of Hesse-Darmstadt at Leitmeritz in March 1633. The issues were soon divided into private matters (*privata*), which concerned the special arrangements between Saxony and the emperor, and public matters (*publica*), which looked to the general settlement in the Empire. In his effort to split Saxony from the Swedes and the other German Protestants, Ferdinand was more inclined to be generous in the first category, but he was not ready to concede the initial Saxon demands. These included permanent retention of the two (arch)bishoprics, Magdeburg and Halberstadt, and of the two Lusatias, which John George still held in lieu of payment of his expenses for the Bohemian campaign of 1620. Regarding public matters, Saxony considered the two most important points to be adequate compensation for Sweden—the imperial instruction refused discussion of any compensation—and the determination of a normative year for the permanent possession of ecclesiastical lands and privileges. Saxony proposed 1612 and stated explicitly that this was to apply to the free exercise of religion and to be valid for Upper and Lower Austria, the Bohemian lands, and even Hungary, which lay outside the Empire. As we have seen, the imperial instruction foresaw 1629 as the normative year, and this with notable exceptions, conditioned upon the acceptance of the Catholic states, and valid only until the convocation of some form of imperial assembly that would make a final settlement. Saxony was willing to leave the Palatinate electoral title to Maximilian until he died, but the lands would have to be restored at the time of the settlement. John George expected Ferdinand to issue a general amnesty, whereas Ferdinand was ready to grant one only to those who had parted with him since 1631.[64]

Negotiations continued at Leitmeritz until July 17, when the invasion of Bohemia by the Swedish general Baner forced their transfer to the Saxon town of Pirna.[65] But before this the imperial delegates took it upon themselves to make some concessions not authorized in their instructions, explaining to the emperor that they felt the alternative was the collapse of the talks and continued war. Vienna made no objections, though of course all the terms were subject to imperial ratification. The delegates agreed to the surrender of several counties of Magdeburg that had not originally belonged to the archbishopric and therefore were not strictly ecclesiastical property. They then proposed March 6, 1629, the date of the Edict, as the norm for the possession of all ecclesiastical lands, to be valid for Saxony and Brandenburg for forty years and for the other states of the Augsburg Confession for fifteen years. This dropped the distinction between lands recovered by virtue of the Edict and those regained by ordinary legal process, thereby eliminating the many exceptions held out in the imperial instructions.[66]

After the move to Pirna and before another break in the talks in early August to permit the Saxon delegates to consult with Dresden, the two parties came closer on the normative date. Saxony proposed 1620, to be valid for himself permanently and for the other Lutheran states for one hundred years. The counterproposal of the imperial delegates was November 12, 1627, to be valid for the shorter durations proposed earlier.[67] Trautmannsdorf had recommended this date to the emperor in October 1633. He thought that in addition to providing for Catholic possession of most of the (arch)bishoprics and the protection of Bavaria in the Palatinate, this date was likely to win the support of Saxony and Brandenburg because it returned to the point where all the electors had cooperated, that is, to the date of their joint request, at the end of the Mühlhausen Convention, that the emperor render a decision on the grievances about the observance of the Religious Peace.[68] Eventually this would become the date accepted in the Peace of Prague. However, events on the battlefield affected the talks shortly after they resumed on August 28.[69]

The fall of Wallenstein had no serious effect on Spanish policy. Spain continued to urge a settlement with the Protestants that would permit

Ferdinand and the German princes, Catholic and Protestant, to aid Spain
against the Dutch and the French, the latter becoming increasingly active
militarily as well as diplomatically. For the Spaniards the enemy in Vienna was still Lamormaini and the nuncios with their vision of Habsburg-
Bourbon rapprochement.[70] Spanish efforts to form an alliance met with
continual failure due to the unwillingness of Maximilian and the League
to commit themselves to war against the Dutch or the French. But the
removal of Wallenstein fostered closer cooperation among the Spanish,
imperial, and League armies, which the Spanish ambassadors were wise
enough to accept without the formalization of an alliance. This led, first,
to the recapture of Regensburg by the imperials on July 26. Later in the
summer another Spanish army marched through the Alps under the leadership of the Cardinal Infant, Don Fernando, whom illness had prevented
from coming north with the army the previous year as planned. The con-
junction of the two armies, that of the King of Hungary and Don Fernando, was to lead to one of the decisive battles of the Thirty Years War.[71]

The papacy continued doggedly to promote reconciliation of the three
crowns but with little success. Richelieu kept up his encouragement of
the Protestant states against the emperor. The Spanish appearance in the
Empire with Feria's army had provoked the French, as Wallenstein foresaw. Under the guise of protecting Alsace against both the Swedes and
the Spaniards, Richelieu began to move into parts of it. Then in September 1633 he completely occupied Lorraine, whose Duke Charles had
long been a thorn in the side of the cardinal because of his assistance to
dissident elements in France, including Gaston d'Orleans.[72] In October
Ferdinand appointed Sebastian Lustrier, a canon of Olomouc, as imperial
resident in Paris, where he arrived only the next February. As Lustrier
told Grimaldi, his instructions were very limited and he was not fully
informed about the emperor's position on major issues.[73] Nevertheless,
in November 1633 Ferdinand and Eggenberg expressed through the nuncios a readiness to yield on the issues of Pinerolo and Moyenvic, the
fortresses in Savoy and Lorraine, provided France guaranteed Spain a
clear route from Italy to the Netherlands. For a short time there appeared
hope of progress, but it fell through due to the counterdemands of Richelieu, the renewal of confidence in Vienna after the resolution of the
Wallenstein crisis, and Spanish pressure.[74]

Grimaldi was growing discouraged at the prospects for the peace he
had been sent to promote as extraordinary nuncio. The ministers in
Vienna remained skeptical, he reported, when he assured them the pope
was doing all he could to prevent the French from aiding heretics. Once
he asked whether they really expected the pope to resort to ecclesiastical
censures against Richelieu or Louis XIII, and not one of them thought

this would be a wise course. They were well aware of the "unhappy" effects of Clement VII's excommunication of Henry VIII of England. Eggenberg was always polite, he added, but he held rigidly to the Spanish position.[75] Shortly before Christmas 1633, Grimaldi informed Ferdinand that the pope could no longer afford to maintain two nuncios in Vienna and that he was being recalled. Actually, he left Vienna on his own account, without Rome's permission. He departed for the south convinced the Austrians' mistrust would never permit them to negotiate seriously with the French.[76]

Rocci remained in Vienna for nearly another year. His successor, Malatesta Baglione, was named on April 1, but he did not turn up in Vienna until November 25. His instructions represented no policy change. He was directed to establish contact with Lamormaini, "always well-affected" toward the Holy See.[77] Vitelleschi, praising Baglione's attachment to the Society, recommended him warmly to the confessor.[78] But Rocci felt that the positive outlook for an agreement with Saxony now prevented the imperial councilors from serious dealings with France. This was the case, he thought, even though Bishop Anton told him the Austrians were ready to negotiate despite the French renewal of their alliance with the Dutch on April 15, 1634, which committed them to subsidize heavily the war against Spain.[79]

Then came the military victory the Catholics had been awaiting. In early September the combined forces of the King of Hungary and the Cardinal Infant overwhelmed the Swedes outside Nördlingen in Swabia. This tilted the military balance in favor of the Catholics once again. It restored imperial control over most of Upper Germany east of the Rhine, including Württemberg. The victory would surely affect the talks in Pirna. At the same time it confirmed Richelieu in his decision, made in midsummer after the start of the Imperial-Spanish offensive, that France would have to enter the war openly. This was the only way he could hope to obtain his anti-Habsburg objectives; there was now no chance Vienna would consider peace with France on the terms under discussion. Richelieu continued to extend French control over the west bank of the Rhine, where in October French troops replaced the Swedes in a number of Alsatian cities including Schlettstadt and Colmar after taking over from them the fortress of Phillipsburg in August. A new alliance between France and the Heilbronn Confederation on November 1, 1634, made France the dominant partner. In December a French army even marched across the Rhine to defend Heidelberg against the Catholic forces, a move that enraged Munich as well as Vienna. But the cardinal delayed formal entrance into the struggle until he could extract from his Swedish and German allies the highest possible price.[80]

Lamormaini saw Nördlingen as another manifestation of the Lord's care for Ferdinand. It was "a miraculous victory," which gave solid reason for not making a peace with Saxony prejudicial to religion.[81] Vitelleschi wrote similarly that the victory was a great stimulus to hope, "so that I do not doubt that it is the bright and glorious beginning of help from on high, the end of so many evils and calamities under which the emperor lay overwhelmed almost to the point of hopelessness."[82]

The scene was now set for a final confrontation in Vienna. On the one side was Lamormaini, who continued to oppose concessions to the Protestants and to promote rapprochement with France as the basis for at least French withdrawal of support from the Protestants. He stood nearly alone, with some support from the nuncios, but he retained a strong hold on the emperor. Against him were aligned Pazmany, the court Capuchins, and the leading privy councilors, Stralendorf, Trautmannsdorf, Bishop Anton, and Dietrichstein. All of them felt the time had come for a compromise peace with Saxony and the more conservative Protestant states, followed by a campaign to drive the foreigners from the Empire and deal with the recalcitrant German states. One of the principal actors, however, was to be absent from the final scene. Eggenberg died on October 18 in Laibach, where he was taking the baths, having left Vienna for the last time in late June. Despite rumors to the contrary, he died on the best of terms with Ferdinand, though not with the King of Hungary, whose appointment to the command of the imperial army he had long opposed. His last year had been a difficult one, with the painful Wallenstein affair, a loss of favor with the Spaniards for remaining loyal to the general as long as he did, and continually failing health.[83] No single councilor would emerge to take his place.

11. The End of a Program: Prague, 1635

O n December 7, 1634, the imperial negotiating team of Trautmannsdorf, Hermann von Questenberg, and Gebhardt returned to Wiener Neustadt, not far from Vienna, where a plague scare had compelled the court to move. With them they brought the Pirna Points, the draft of a treaty with Saxony that had been worked out in the weeks following Nördlingen. The imperial representatives were expected to return on January 13 to the Bohemian town of Aussig with the emperor's ratification for the final conclusion of the agreement.[1] But matters were not to be so simple. Lamormaini was now to make his last stand.

The Pirna Points represented a compromise between the emperor and John George, in which Ferdinand secured the better part. But they constituted a virtual revocation of the Edict and thus the surrender of Lamormaini's militant program for a Catholic restoration in Germany. The agreement accepted in principle the historical development of the eighty years since the Peace of Augsburg that the Edict had attempted to reverse. November 12, 1627, was to serve as the normative date for the possession of disputed ecclesiastical lands, rights, and privileges, including the right to free exercise of religion. What was valid on that date was to be valid for the next forty years. Thus, strictly speaking, Ferdinand was not permanently surrendering Catholic claims. During this period a body composed equally of Catholic and Protestant representatives was to work out a definitive settlement. Thus the long-standing Protestant demand for such a body to decide the religious issues in the Empire was honored to a degree. Should their efforts fail, allowance was first made for an extension of the time period. If agreement still was not forthcoming, both sides reserved the right to go to the imperial courts, for which, however, the discussion of any changes in structure was postponed indefinitely. Meanwhile, both sides renounced any resort to force. Thus the emperor gave up his claim to issue or enforce a final decision. The situation of 1627 could easily become permanent.[2]

Concretely, this settlement meant the restoration and/or preservation for the Catholics of the imperial church lands in the south and west, many of which including Mainz were still occupied by the enemy. It also seemed to provide—there was some vagueness here—for the return to the Catholics of the most important (arch)bishoprics in Lower Saxony that had been held by the Protestants for decades prior to the war and were now in hostile hands. The exception was Magdeburg, which was assigned to John George's son, August, for life. According to the normative year, the Protestants would enjoy religious freedom in these territories, such as Halberstadt, which was to go to Leopold William.[3] To the northeast, the terms recognized the status quo, a concession the negotiators had been willing to make to Saxony and Brandenburg from the start. Perhaps of greatest significance for the emperor was the recognition of his right of reformation in the Austrian and Bohemian lands. John George gave up his demands for the free exercise of religion for Protestants there. This had been non-negotiable for the emperor from the start. The only exception was the city of Breslau and several Silesian principalities, where free exercise of religion for Protestants was recognized. With respect to territorial church lands, the compromise allowed many Protestant states, especially in north Germany and in the Franconian and Swabian Circles, to retain ecclesiastical lands they had acquired since 1555.

Special concessions were made to John George. He and George William of Brandenburg were to retain unchallenged the church lands they had acquired since 1555 for fifty years instead of forty. Besides the allotment of Magdeburg to his son for life, Saxony was to keep permanently the four counties detached from the archbishopric. Ferdinand also made over to him as an imperial fief the two Lusatias, which John George still held in lieu of the payment owed him for his part in the suppression of the Bohemian rebellion. Here the Catholics were to enjoy freedom of religion. The solution of the delicate Palatinate question was left to future arbitration, though the Saxon negotiators intimated John George's intention to yield on it, provided the Catholics accepted the rest of the agreement. The imperial councilors took for granted in their subsequent deliberations that at the least Maximilian would retain the Upper Palatinate permanently and the electoral title for his lifetime.[4]

The Pirna Points aimed to settle the internal problems of the Empire and to prepare the way to end the foreign presence in Germany, peacefully it was hoped but by force if necessary. The terms foresaw the other German princes and states ratifying the agreement and allying with the two principals. But Ferdinand offered full amnesty and restitution to their territories only to those secular princes and states that had taken up arms against him after the landing of Gustav Adolph in 1630. To implement the peace against recalcitrants, a unified imperial army was to be formed, in which Saxony would have a major command. Furthermore, apart from family agreements approved by the emperor, all alliances among imperial states were to be prohibited in the future. This meant the end of the Catholic League as well as the Heilbronn Confederation. The leading foreign powers were also invited to associate themselves with the agreement, but a chief cause for the eventual failure of the Peace of Prague was the neglect to provide compensation for Sweden as Saxony had originally insisted. It was unrealistic to think the Swedes would quietly pack up and return home after five years of war in Germany. The victory at Nördlingen was not that complete.

Ferdinand himself received an abstract of the Points on December 11.[5] Copies were dispatched with a request for their opinions to the three Catholic electors, Maximilian, Mainz, and Cologne. Trier was not consulted because it was felt that by his alliance with France in 1632 and a subsequent neutrality agreement with Sweden he had broken with the other Catholic princes to pursue his own policy.[6] A change introduced into the original draft of the covering letter to Maximilian was significant.[7] In the final copy Ferdinand informed the elector, who had been kept abreast of the negotiations all along, that this was the best his negotiators could do; he requested Maximilian, should he find the terms unacceptable, to suggest where the resources might be found to continue the war. But a long passage intended to impress upon Maximilian the need for peace was deleted, a change that pointed up a division between Ferdinand and the councilors who had drawn up the draft. According to Rocci, nearly all the emperor's advisors favored the peace, but Lamormaini opposed it. He was "the cause that the emperor showed little inclination to accept it."[8] Already it was apparent that more time than had been planned would be required to reach a decision on the peace.

Papal policy generally supported Lamormaini, but unenthusiastically, "with prudence," as Barberini had instructed Rocci in October.[9] The situation was complicated by the fact that there were now three papal representatives in Vienna, the departing Rocci, his replacement, Baglione, and a Capuchin with long experience in political affairs, Alessandro d'Ales, who had come to Vienna the previous April as the personal agent of Francesco Barberini.[10] Sometimes Urban seemed more concerned about imperial support for his project to revive the office of Prefect of Rome than about the war in Germany, and this attitude did not increase his popularity in Vienna. A fundamental of papal policy remained the refusal to approve formally any concession to the Protestants. In the summer of 1634 Cologne and Mainz had jointly dispatched Ziegler as an emissary to Rome, where he inquired whether they could yield ecclesiastical lands to the Protestants. This direct question was precisely what the pope wanted to avoid, and in the circumstances his firm negative response was not surprising.[11] However, he had no intention of supporting the German militants with either a greater financial commitment or with positive political or ecclesiastical pressure, such as the threat of a formal protest against concessions or excommunication for the offenders. He seems, in the last resort, to have been willing to allow the emperor to make the best political arrangement he could for the Church. At the same time, papal diplomacy continued its efforts to reconcile the three Catholic powers. The principal assignment of Alessandro d'Ales was to promote the negotiations between Vienna and Paris. But Rome was growing less hopeful.[12]

Spain continued to urge peace with Saxony and an imperial break with France. Both Spanish ambassadors and Quiroga lobbied actively in Vienna. After the renewed French commitment to the Dutch in April 1634, Madrid felt that only the bribery of imperial ministers could explain the emperor's failure to act in the manner it wanted.[13] This sentiment could only grow as French diplomatic and military activity increased, itself partly the reaction to the expanding Spanish presence in the Empire in the form of Feria's army in 1633 and the Cardinal Infant's the following year. By the summer of 1634, as we have seen, Richelieu was convinced France would have to enter the war openly. He concluded a new treaty with the Heilbronn Confederation on November 1, 1634, and he sent French troops across the Rhine to the relief of Heidelberg in December. At the same time, he arranged treaties with a number of the German Protestant princes of southwest Germany who had lost much of their territory after Nördlingen, such as the Duke of Württemberg, the Landgrave of Hesse-Kassel, the Margrave of Baden-Durlach. By the end of the year the French controlled the left bank of the Rhine from Basel to Coblenz, and on the right bank they held the fortresses of Ehrenbreitstein and Philippsburg.[14] Under these circumstances, the Spaniards could only gnash their teeth at Lamormaini's persistent advocacy of rapprochement with France and rejection of peace with Saxony. They suspected him, incorrectly, of secret contacts with Richelieu.[15] According to Baglione, imperial ministers openly asserted that Lamormaini could not have been a less suitable choice for the emperor's confessor if he had been appointed by the King of France himself.[16]

The wheels of government in Vienna now moved even more slowly than usual. The emperor was forced to request Saxony for a postponement of the return of his delegates.[17] Finally, on January 20, a lengthy position paper prepared under Stralendorf's direction and representing the views of the privy council was read before the emperor at a session of the council.[18] The case for peace was presented convincingly.

The greater good of both Empire and Church required concessions for the sake of peace, the paper argued. The enemy still possessed the advantage politically and militarily, especially in view of the increasing French intervention and activity along the Rhine. They were far superior in financial and material resources. The states of the Catholic League were either occupied or devastated, and little could be expected from the war-torn lands recovered after Nördlingen. Of the Habsburg territories only the Austrian lands could still contribute, and they were reaching their limits; the two Lusatias and most of Silesia were in enemy hands, and Bohemia and Moravia were ruined. Experience showed that foreign aid always made it possible for the Protestants to recover after a defeat, whereas one more disaster like Breitenfeld would mean collapse for the Catholics and much more severe terms. Nor was significant foreign assistance to be expected, the paper continued. The aid received from the pope and friendly Italian states amounted to little, and the Spaniards though still anxious to help were themselves on the point of exhaustion. The enemy presently controlled the Lower Saxon and Westphalian Circles, and they enjoyed the support of the imperial and Hansa cities. This assured them money, the "sinews of war," as well as effective lines of supply. France guaranteed them control of the Rhine. In addition, they could count on Dutch aid and according to reports, both the English and the Danes were preparing to send contingents of troops. In Constantinople at the moment, the paper went on, French and Swedish envoys were attempting to mediate a peace between the Persians and Turks that would free the latter for an offensive in Europe. Nor could one overlook the popular support the enemy enjoyed in the Empire. Discipline and firm organization had still not been reintroduced into the imperial army, according to the paper, and if the government could not pay the troops regularly, misconduct of the soldiers and even rebellion could be anticipated.

To conquer Germany simply was not possible, the paper went on, intimating what the council felt was the only alternative to accepting the Pirna Points. Not even the Romans had succeeded in doing this. A few more victories would accomplish little, "since the German spirit would never allow itself to be subdued by force of arms." But supposing complete victory were possible, the Catholic courts, by which the paper certainly meant Paris and Rome, would never stand for the increase of power that would thereby accrue to the emperor. Neither French words nor deeds indicated any sign of willingness to come to an agreement with Ferdinand. In fact, Richelieu clearly intended to intervene in the struggle for the succession should Ferdinand die before his son was elected King of the Romans. Ferdinand's early death could lead to an interregnum in which the two Protestant states, Saxony and the Palatinate, would attempt to exercise their functions as imperial vicars. That would mean the end of the Habsburgs on the imperial throne, which in turn would be a disaster for Catholicism, since the House of Habsburg was clearly "the fulcrum of the Catholic religion" in Germany.

To be sure, the paper granted, some concessions were to be made to the Protestants, but they were more than offset by the advantages to be won: the exclusion of Protestantism from the Habsburg lands, the restoration of the exiled ecclesiastical princes, especially along the Rhine, the reacquisition of imperial church lands in Lower Saxony, and the retention of the Palatinate by Maximilian, thus guaranteeing the five-to-two Catholic majority in the electoral college. Charles V had made even greater concessions for the sake of peace, Ferdinand was reminded.[19] He was urged to consider those who favored peace. There were the "well-affected" cardinals and ministers in Rome, the estates and loyal subjects in the Habsburg lands as well as the Empire, the King of Spain along with his ministers. In Vienna itself there were religious of different orders as well as "High Cardinals," undoubtedly a reference to Pazmany and Dietrichstein. The emperor's generals and the war council, who ought to be most familiar with the military situation, the imperial council, the treasury council, all the emperor's loyal servants were in favor of the peace. The paper closed with a vivid description of the sufferings of the common people that simply could not be permitted to continue. Families had lost their substance to pillaging troops. Women and girls had been raped, and thousands of orphans created. Schools were closed, and there was no one to look to the education of the youth. Churches lay in ashes. Such conditions could not help stirring in the heart of every patriot an overwhelming desire for peace.

Indeed, a rational analysis of the situation seemed to point to the acceptance of the Pirna agreement. But the paper made several points betraying a fear that the decision would not be based on such an analysis. They were directed to the arguments of Lamormaini. "Human reason" must dictate the decision, it was affirmed. Policy could not be based on an alleged divine revelation. If we were certain of ultimate victory, it was asserted, then we should continue to fight despite the cost. But in fact, the outcome was known to God alone. The emperor's advocacy of justice, the glory of God, and the Catholic religion did not guarantee him victory. There were many examples in Scripture where God had ordered a holy war but then had punished the Israelites with defeat for the misconduct and idolatry of the soldiers. In the Christian era, justice on the side of the Christians did not preclude the loss to the Church of the Eastern Empire, not to mention extensive areas of Asia and Africa. The good did not always emerge victorious in this world.

So the paper ended. But it did not provoke the final decision. The electors had not yet been heard from. Also, since the return of the delegates from Pirna Ferdinand had indicated he intended to convoke a conference of theologians to evaluate the terms. The day the paper was read in council, he requested Cardinal Dietrichstein to chair the projected conference and to select for it theologians "who were not only learned and conscientious but also loyal and honestly inclined to see Our good and that of Our House."[20] Not until February 5 were the theologians able to convene in Vienna. Once again the return of the imperial delegation to meet with the Saxons had to be put off. Altogether, twenty-four theologians took part, including members of eight different religious orders and one diocesan priest.[21] They were to discuss the peace among themselves but to give no common opinion. Instead, each individual or each group from a religious order was to submit its own view in writing at the conclusion of the sessions. On the eve of the deliberations, Alessandro d'Ales, who was not a participant, reported that the emperor tended strongly toward peace, but that Lamormaini told him that he could not accept the terms in good conscience. For this reason, Ferdinand was "very sad," especially since Maximilian of Bavaria had let it be known unofficially that he was ready to accept the terms if nothing better could be obtained. Rumors in Vienna accused Lamormaini, Father Alessandro wrote, of maintaining his opposition in the hope that Rome would reward him with a cardinal's hat.[22]

A crisis of confidence held Ferdinand in its grip. He now had to make a decision, perhaps the most important one of his life. Three times he formulated the questions to be put to the theologians. Finally, they were reduced to two. The theologians were not asked to judge whether the present situation constituted a state of sufficient necessity to justify the projected concessions. They were simply asked whether there were any provisions in the treaty touching religion that were intrinsically evil and hence could not be permitted under any circumstances without mortal sin. Secondly, if the conditions of the peace were acceptable, what was the most appropriate language in which to formulate them? For the sake of his conscience and his reputation, Ferdinand wanted it clearly expressed in the terms that his religious concessions were essentially the passive tolerance of evil extorted from him by necessity. A third question, evidently loaded against Lamormaini's position, was dropped: if the emperor could agree to the peace with a good conscience, was he bound to do so? Or could he rather, in the hope of miraculous divine aid, expose the Catholic states, the Empire itself, the Habsburg territories, and his Most August House to evident danger, or was this to tempt God?[23] The theologians were given as the basis for their discussions a copy of the ecclesiastical terms of the peace, the position paper of the privy council of January 20, and other papers favoring the peace. In addition, the imperial negotiators Questenberg and Gebhardt were to be on hand to respond to questions. The conference lasted until February 16, and in the days following, the written opinions were delivered to Dietrichstein.

All the theologians including Lamormaini were in agreement that there was nothing in the terms intrinsically evil and therefore prohibited under all circumstances. Consequently, a number of them felt it would be enough merely to assert the principle that in case of necessity the proposed concessions might be made to the Protestants and to leave its application up to the imperial councilors. This was what the latter wanted. But Lamormaini insisted it would be insufficient as a guide for the conscience of the emperor, for which he was responsible. To the consternation of Dietrichstein, he succeeded in obtaining from Ferdinand more detailed information than the councilors, for security reasons, had wanted to make available to the theologians, and Lamormaini convinced most of them to render a decision on the concrete situation.[24] Differences then arose in the appraisal of the actual state of affairs: did a state of necessity really exist? would ratification lead to the avoidance of a greater evil or the acquisition of a greater good as the advocates of the treaty maintained? Nevertheless, thirteen of the sixteen written opinions submitted stated clearly that if better conditions could not be obtained, the emperor could without scruple accept the terms as they stood.

Among the participants, two principal factions are discernible. One comprised the three Capuchins, and the other Lamormaini and four of the seven other Jesuits who took part. Quiroga headed the Capuchins. With him stood Magni, who was back in Vienna for a short time after nearly three years at the court of King Ladislaus of Poland, and Basilio d'Aire, who had replaced Magni as adviser to Harrach and correspondent for the Congregation of the Propagation of the Faith.[25] Quiroga and Basilio both declared in their papers that the emperor could not only accept the terms of the peace but that he was bound to do so under pain of mortal sin.[26] Barberini's agent, Alessandro d'Ales, later complained of his treatment at the Capuchin convent in Vienna where he had been dubbed "*il papalino.*"[27]

The militant ideology was a central feature in the argument of Lamormaini's group, though assurance of victory seems to have lost ground to a new element, Stoic insistence on fidelity to duty, come what might. Lamormaini himself did not write up an opinion, but he spoke considerably more than any other participant during the conference. Early in the course of it, his letter to Dietrichstein was read to the assembled group.[28] He implored the theologians to set aside human respect and outside pressures and to answer only that for which they could take responsibility before God at the Last Judgment. This was what Ferdinand wanted. The future of the Empire and of religion in all Northern Europe was at stake. He warned his colleagues lest they become like the Sorbonne theologians who were always ready to approve anything that was considered necessary to preserve France. What would they have responded if Pilate had asked them whether he could put Christ to death because it was necessary for one man to die for the people?

Though he did not say so with complete clarity, Lamormaini obviously thought that no state of necessity sufficient to justify the proposed concessions existed, and he implied—to the embarrassment of the other theologians, according to Basilio who kept the minutes—that the information supplied by the ministers was unreliable. His friend Gebhardt agreed when he asserted that Saxony intended to retain the ecclesiastical lands permanently and accepted the limitation of forty or fifty years only to make the step easier for the Catholics, but Questenberg, the other imperial representative, dissented.[29] Now was the time for "heroic action," Lamormaini asserted in a long, final address to the assembled group. He still envisioned an agreement with France, as the proceedings show.[30]

> Given equally unfavorable conditions, ought one not rather attempt peace with the Frenchman, who is at least Catholic, than with those whose firm purpose is to destroy Catholics and Catholicism? This, he said, could be considered according to the principle so often cited in the conference, the lesser of two evils is to be chosen. For the Saxon seeks our possessions and our souls, the Frenchman at least not the souls. About this, nevertheless, he said, I make no judgment, I only discourse.

Ludwig Crasius, professor of theology at the Jesuit academy at Olomouc, claimed that Lamormaini endorsed his paper, which insisted that the emperor could not accept the terms of peace without sin.[31] The terms, Crasius wrote, shamefully compromised both the Church and the House of Austria. In the event the emperor was unable to secure a more favorable agreement, "we should have recourse to God through the private prayers of religious and the public ones of the whole Catholic community, nor should we doubt that God, who up to this point has rescued our most pious Emperor from so many dangers, in this extremity will also show us the way either to continue the war or to obtain a better peace." Crasius reminded Ferdinand that St. Thomas of Canterbury had not hesitated to sacrifice his life for the rights of the Church.

Other Jesuit participants, whether they stood with Lamormaini or not, showed that they were influenced to a greater or less degree by the idea that God would come to the aid of the emperor in a special manner. Blase Slaninus, for example, rector of the academy at Olomouc, admitted that if the situation was truly as the councilors described it, then the emperor could as a last resort ratify the terms, but he questioned the accuracy of the information provided the conference and alluded to Lamormaini's idea of an alliance of the Catholic powers against the heretics. Nor did he see why even if he could licitly yield to the Protestants, Ferdinand still could not continue the war anyway. For according to the belief of all peoples and nations, he possessed a pledge of divine protection and was thought to have been singularly called by God to the government of the Empire for the purpose of suppressing heresy in the north of Europe.[32] The Spaniard Peñalosa, close to the Queen of Hungary and thus to Quiroga, surveyed the situation from a different standpoint. He had little difficulty in approving Ferdinand's ratification of the terms under the circumstances, and he argued that God's special care for the emperor would show itself in the guidance he gave him toward making the right decision.[33]

Several participants who favored acceptance of the terms made a special point of contesting elements of the myth. Quiroga and Basilio, both familiar with the thinking at court, dealt with it. The former asserted the emperor was not excused from the obligation to accept the terms "by a fiducial faith in God, even though this was based on long experience of benefits by which Divine Providence had preserved, defended, and protected His Imperial Majesty." Ferdinand had more than satisfied his obligations as Defender of the Church.[34] Basilio, along with the lone Augustinian at the conference, Ignacio a Santa Maria, a Portuguese, emphasized that it would be presumption and temerity to rely on divine assistance to bring victory in the absence of a clear divine revelation such as Gideon had received according to the Book of Judges. Human reason had to be the norm.[35]

A point touched upon by most of the theologians was whether positive papal consent was required prior to any concessions to the Protestants. The question had been raised back in 1631, but circumstances had made it easy subsequently to overlook the response of the theologians. But this consideration was never as important in Vienna as it was to the Catholic electors. In October Mainz and Cologne had communicated to Vienna Urban's negative response to their inquiry in Rome, and Cologne was to raise the question once again.[36] Lamormaini brought it up in the theologians' conference; however, he never made it central to his argument, as did his colleague in Munich, Contzen, whose sensitivity on the point was much greater. Lamormaini was too attached to the imperial tradition to do this, and perhaps he was sufficiently aware of the papacy's real position to realize that for him to insist on the need for positive papal approval of any concessions would have brought his penitent into an insurmountable conflict of conscience. At the conference, most of the theologians agreed that under normal circumstances consultation with the pope—

generally considered under the title "Supreme Master of Ecclesiastical Possessions" (*Dispensator Supremus bonorum ecclesiasticorum*)—would be a requisite, but if this were not possible, then the emperor could presume papal permission. Several added that the pope was bound in conscience to give his consent to any reasonable solution. Only the two Capuchins, Valeriano and Basilio, realized that Urban preferred not to be put on the spot and for this reason encouraged the emperor to move ahead without consulting him.[37] What might have happened had the pope seriously attempted to pressure the emperor to reject the peace, as German militants like Franz Wilhelm von Wartenberg were urging him to do, is hard to say.[38] In any event, he did not do so; this would have been to reverse his policy.

By the time the theologians' conference closed, the opinions of the three Catholic electors had arrived. Father Alessandro expected these would carry more weight than the views of the theologians.[39] But the opinions of the electors did not bring the expected clarity. Contrary to all past experience, they split. Mainz and Maximilian, after encouraging Ferdinand to secure all possible improvements in the terms, agreed to accept the Pirna Points if the alternative was continued war. Both had agonized over their decision. Mainz asserted in his defense the two maxims: no man was bound to the impossible and the lesser of two evils was to be chosen. His people, who had borne the burden of the Swedish occupation, simply could not support the war any longer. His suspicions of French intentions—he spoke of French attempts to dismember the Empire—confirmed him in his position during the next two months.[40]

The main factor in Maximilian's refusal to make any concessions had been a belief analogous to Ferdinand's that to yield would be betraying his responsibility as a Catholic elector and endangering the Wittelsbach reputation as a pillar of the faith in Germany. Moreover, Contzen impressed upon him that he could not cooperate in the surrender of church lands without papal sanction. Previously, under pressure from moderate privy councilors, the prince had often wavered, but only now did he break with militant policy. Essentially his justification was the same argument put forth in the paper of the imperial councilors. For the sake of the greater good, the Catholics could make concessions to the Protestants. In addition, the French defense of Heidelberg had infuriated him, and he feared more than ever the results of an interregnum in the Empire. Important too was the stand taken by Mainz, of which Maximilian was informed before he made his final decision. If an ecclesiastical elector took the initiative, then he was safe in conscience and reputation. A new personal relationship drew the Houses of Habsburg and Wittelsbach closer together during these months. Maximilian's wife, Elizabeth of

Lorraine, having died on January 4, he wed the emperor's daughter, Maria Anna, in Vienna on July 15. It was a marriage that evidently had a political aspect.[41]

Cologne, however, Maximilian's brother, sharply rejected the Pirna agreement.[42] Necessity did not justify such a peace. Perhaps because he had benefited from French protection during the Swedish invasion, he did not feel the French movements along the Rhine were to be taken seriously. According to Cologne, the long-term concession of the free exercise of religion in many areas and the surrender of ecclesiastical lands amounted to a new religious peace. Without the approval of the German Catholic states and the pope, the emperor was not empowered to conclude such an agreement. Especially shameful was the renunciation of Magdeburg and the concession of free exercise of religion to the Protestants in Halberstadt. The recent victories God had granted the Catholics, the elector affirmed, gave solid grounds for new confidence. Where would the Church be if Constantine and Charlemagne had shown such timidity? In early March Wartenberg came to Vienna as Cologne's representative, but after failing to win over Maximilian in talks held with him en route, he seems to have kept a low profile at the imperial court.[43]

The division among the electors disturbed Ferdinand. The opinions of Mainz and Maximilian were well received, but Ferdinand went out of his way to assure Cologne on February 21 that the terms were only tentative and that negotiations were still in progress.[44] The elector was asked to be more specific in the points he felt ought to be changed. That Cologne's arguments were taken seriously is shown by the draft of a detailed answer to his charges.[45] The emperor had no intention of concluding anything involving the electors without their approval, it read, but communications were of the utmost difficulty because of the military situation along the Rhine. Most of the theologians summoned to present their views had agreed that the terms could be accepted for the greater good and for the avoidance of the imminent dangers threatening Church and Empire. What would the princes answer to God if because of "scruples of this sort" they let Church and Empire go under? The projected treaty had its weaknesses, the author conceded, but no human work was perfect. The same could be said of the Peace of Augsburg. It too had yielded on a number of points to the Protestants, but as a result, the Catholic religion had made great progress in the second half of the previous century.

Once the opinions of the electors had arrived and the results of the theologians' conference were available, Ferdinand, now back in Vienna, summoned eight "intimate" (*intimi*) councilors to draw up a final position paper on the peace. The group comprised Lamormaini, the two cardinals, Pazmany and Dietrichstein, Bishop Anton, Stralendorf, Trautmannsdorf, Werdenberg, and Heinrich von Schlick. They met from February 27 to March 10. Ferdinand was perplexed in conscience, as Crasius observed to a correspondent in Munich.[46] From the one side he was told that there were neither soldiers nor funds with which to continue the war, from the other that the war could still be brought to a successful conclusion. Before committing the matter to the eight, Ferdinand impressed upon them its importance; it touched on the salvation of his own soul. He charged them to advise only that for which he and they could take the responsibility before the judgment seat of God.[47]

Again Lamormaini was alone in his opposition to the Pirna Points. His recommendation of special imperial missions to both Paris and Rome indicated that he still hoped for an alliance of the Catholic powers. A week before the councilors convened, a courier arrived from the nuncio in Paris with word that France was prepared to send a delegate to the peace conference proposed by the pope, provided Spain and the emperor would do the same. This encouraged the papal representatives in Vienna as well as Lamormaini, even though the same courier brought news of a French military buildup and war preparations. Baglione reported that the confessor was "most inclined" toward peace with France, and he added that the Spaniards were upset by the new development. Lamormaini and Quiroga had had a sharp exchange.[48] Lamormaini, after suggesting that the young Prince Liechtenstein, son of the privy councilor, be sent to Paris, stated that even if this proved fruitless, the sight of an imperial emissary in Paris might lead Saxony to yield to major revisions in the terms and at the same time give the Turks second thoughts about French enticements. The proposed envoy to Rome would keep the pope informed about the negotiations, once again request him to dip into the treasure stored in Castel San Angelo, and offer imperial mediation to put an end to the persistent friction between Rome and the Spanish crown.

But the papers finally submitted by the "intimates" did not see matters this way. For them "this opportunity to obtain once again and to extend a just peace was to be seized upon effectively and not let go." Twice before the emperor had allowed the chance to make an advantageous peace slip by, once when he possessed a clear advantage in the Empire, probably an allusion to the Electoral Convention of Regensburg in 1630, and again after Gustav Adolph was killed at Lützen; for the second squandered opportunity they held Wallenstein to blame.[49] The same mistake was not to be made again. The councilors showed no confidence in alleged French willingness to negotiate, and they called attention to French efforts to divide the Empire for over eight hundred years. If Ferdinand rejected Saxony, John George would turn to France himself. Just then French emissaries were bombarding him with offers of an alliance.[50] That would mean the end for the Habsburg succession. At the moment, a special mission to Paris would be inconsistent with the emperor's reputation, since it would give the impression he was begging for aid. The regular imperial resident was capable of keeping the pope informed of developments, the councilors felt. Nor was there any likelihood a special emissary would be able to coax more money out of Urban or contribute meaningfully to an understanding between Rome and Madrid.

The heart of the position papers argued the pros and cons of the terms as had the opinion of January 20, and with the same result. But there were several additions or new emphases aimed at dealing with the conscience of the emperor. Eighteen theologians, it affirmed, had voted that the emperor could accept the peace in good conscience. The people were crying for peace, and "the voice of the people is the voice of God." The councilors were intent on showing that the conclusion of peace with Saxony did not betray pusillanimity on the part of Ferdinand. True, it was written in 2 Paralipomenon (Chronicles) 25 that if one placed his trust in the strength of his army alone, God would send him to defeat at the hands of his enemy.[51] But Christ himself in Luke 14 advised the king not to proceed to war without first calculating his own strength and that of his enemy. Without a doubt the emperor's cause was just, but God's judgments were inscrutable. Sometimes misfortune struck those fighting in holy causes, as was clear in the case of St. Louis of France, who was defeated in his first expedition to liberate the Holy Land and died of the plague during the second. One had no assurance that God would grant the emperor victory. Again they insisted policy could not be based on anticipated miracles but had to be determined rationally. And if misfortune struck once again as it had at Breitenfeld, that would be the end for Ferdinand in Germany and in the Habsburg lands.

Thus the council came out clearly in favor of the peace with Saxony. But partly as a result of the prodding of the electors and theologians, they urged Ferdinand to extort as many further concessions as he could. Lamormaini's influence was evident in the effort to retain as much of the Edict as possible. In the discussions he called for the explicit exclusion of the Calvinists and the clear recognition of the emperor's right to make a final decision on the ecclesiastical issues after the lapse of the forty-year period. Both of these points were worked into the councilors' report in a modified form. Should Saxony reject an explicit acknowledgment of the emperor's authority to render a final decision, the councilors suggested Ferdinand propose a plan that committed the emperor to abide by the "unanimous" counsel of a group of delegates drawn equally from Protestant and Catholic states; should they fail to agree, the delegates would return the decision to him. If Saxony turned this down, the imperial negotiators should seek further instructions. The emperor should also attempt to substitute the term *Adherents of the Augsburg Confession* for *Protestants*, thus implicitly excluding the Calvinists from the settlement.

The councilors drew up a scale of demands for the imperial negotiators. At first an attempt was to be made to restrict the full application of the normative date to Saxony alone. To this end all the concessions intended for his private satisfaction were to be granted. The hope was to split John George from the other Protestant states. The normative date would be conceded the other German states only until the foreigners had been expelled and an imperial diet or convention determined the status of the church lands for the future. If this proved unacceptable to John George, the imperial negotiators might then agree to concede the normative date for forty years to the two Saxon Circles, including Brandenburg, and the Westphalian Circle. This still allowed for the implementation of the Edict in the four Upper German Circles, the Franconian, the Swabian, the Upper Rhenish, and the Rhenish Palatine. The next step would be to yield the normative date for the Upper Circles but for a more limited period of time. Only in the last resort should the negotiators agree to 1627 as normative for the whole Empire and for the full forty years, and even then they should endeavor to make exceptions that would allow the greatest possible implementation of the Edict in the Upper Circles. Also emphasized was the need to guarantee the Palatinate electoral title and lands to Maximilian. But the councilors were willing to leave this issue open to further negotiations, should this be necessary to win over Saxony. Maximilian had indicated his readiness to accede to this provided he retained the title and lands in the interim. The paper foresaw the return of his patrimonial holdings to Ludwig Philip, Frederick's brother, if he accepted the peace, which was considered unlikely.

At the privy council sessions of March 5 and 10, Ferdinand finally accepted these position papers as the basis for the instruction for the imperial negotiators to be sent to Prague, whither the negotiations had been transferred. But he made important comments and qualifications that showed his concern for conscience and reputation. The negotiators were to work diligently to secure the modifications advocated by the council, especially those touching the Edict. Gebhardt, in whose hand the remarks of Ferdinand were noted, wrote: "The Emperor makes this formal statement: I place my trust in you (meaning us delegates), that you keep your oath and your duty in mind and that you zealously take into consideration all [your instructions]." Both the temporary nature of the concessions and Ferdinand's power of ultimate decision were to be made clear, lest he be burdened with "an odium with all the Catholics." In particular, he wanted his delegates to maintain the Catholic position in Württemberg and to broaden his power to exclude from amnesty.[52] The text of the instruction, dated March 12,[53] read: "Our delegates should make every effort to secure the limitations and modifications herein urged, since they concern the glory of God and his Church, so that we cannot be accused of yielding excessively on points touching the Church's and the Catholic [states'?] interests or of not taking their rights sufficiently into consideration."

This instruction marked Ferdinand's break with the myth so long represented by Lamormaini, that the emperor's mission to restore Catholicism in Germany assured him special divine aid and forbade him to make concessions to the Protestants that went beyond the Peace of Religion. What might have happened had John George refused any essential moderation of the Pirna Points is hard to say. As it was, he was to prove more flexible than the imperial ministers dreamed.

By March 14 the imperial delegation was on its way to Prague. Ferdinand Kurz von Senftenau replaced Questenberg, who had asked to be relieved of yet another diplomatic mission.[54] The negotiations dragged on for two months largely because of the difficult communications. Gebhardt implicitly criticized Trautmannsdorf when he wrote the court secretary, Johann Söldner, that he did not share the minister's confidence in the good faith of the Saxon representatives and felt the imperials could obtain better terms than it appeared they were going to get.[55] In mid-March Bavarian troops intercepted a letter of the magistrates of Nuremberg showing how earnestly they desired peace. This encouraged Maximilian to propose that the imperial cities be excluded from the normative year, so that to participate in the peace they would have to accept the status of 1555, that is, the Edict. But Vienna was not enthusiastic about this, being particularly concerned to bring Nuremberg with its wealth, prestige, and central geographical position into the peace.[56]

In the end, John George acceded to virtually all Ferdinand's new demands. He did insist that the normative date apply formally to the whole Empire. But the implicit exclusion of the Calvinists, which Saxony welcomed, and the recognition of a broad imperial right to exclude from amnesty enabled Ferdinand to secure many of his goals in the four Upper Circles by negotiating their admittance to the peace with individual princes and states. This was especially the case with Württemberg, then almost completely occupied by the imperials. Here acceptance of the current status of ecclesiastical lands was made a condition of Württemberg's participation in the peace and the duke's restoration.[57] The normative date was to be valid for only four imperial cities in the Upper Circles: Nuremberg, Frankfurt, Strasbourg, and Ulm. All others had to accept the Edict if they wanted to share in the peace. Augsburg was the subject of a special arrangement that provided for some modification of the imperial measures ordered in 1629.[58] Saxony also agreed that the status of lands for which a valid judicial decision had been issued, at the request of both parties, either before or after 1627, would be determined by that decision. This provision safeguarded the validity of past court decisions. According to an agreement reached between the two parties but not mentioned in the treaty text, it was understood that the terms meant the return of the Lower Saxon bishoprics Minden, Bremen, and Verden to the Catholics.[59]

Two further points were of great importance. Saxony acquiesced in Maximilian's permanent retention of the Palatinate electoral dignity and the lands on the right bank of the Rhine. References to a possible extension of the forty-year period were eliminated, and John George recognized the emperor's final jurisdiction over ecclesiastical matters after the lapse of forty years if no satisfactory solution was found by then, though the emperor was required first to hear the views of a body composed equally of Catholics and Protestants and sworn to fairness. These changes were obviously intended to prevent the status of 1627 from automatically becoming permanent.

Finally, on May 30, the imperial and Saxon delegates signed the Peace of Prague, eleven days after Richelieu formally issued a declaration of war on Spain in Brussels. But even with the concessions wrung from Saxony, the peace represented the final renunciation of Lamormaini's plans for the restoration of Catholicism in Germany.[60] Several days later the news of the peace unleashed spontaneous popular rejoicing in the streets of Vienna, where Bishop Anton ordered that it be announced from the pulpits.[61]

Ferdinand notified the pope on June 2 of the conclusion of the Peace of Prague—there was no question of requesting approval for it—and soon afterward he sent to his resident in Rome, now Sciopione Gonzaga, Prince of Bozolo, a long justification of the Peace that was later published as a broadsheet. Urban's reaction turned out to be much more positive than Bozolo anticipated. As the resident neared the end of his presentation, the pope interrupted to object that he was hearing only the advantages of the peace, not its disadvantages. Urban was decidedly happy with the terms, and he acknowledged they were much more beneficial for religion than he had realized. Subsequently, the terms were studied by a curial committee; on the basis of a position paper drawn up by the German humanist and convert Lucas Holstein, a brief was sent to Ferdinand on July 22. This was phrased in such a way that it recognized the emperor's efforts for the Church and praised his zeal while avoiding anything that could be interpreted as papal approval of the concessions to the Protestants. Thus Urban maintained the juridical position of Rome. He also continued to work for peace among the Catholic powers, despite the setback that the French declaration of war on Spain administered to his policy. Having secured agreement in principle from Austria, France, and Spain for a peace congress to be held in Cologne, in August he named a cardinal legate, Mario Ginetti, to represent him there. But the congress never really was to get off the ground.[62]

The Peace of Prague did not bring a final settlement to Germany despite the initial enthusiasm in Vienna. It greatly reduced the level of conflict among the German states and the emperor, but it did not lead to the effective gathering of forces and consolidation of authority that the two principals hoped would make possible the expulsion of the foreigners.[63] Most German states including all the electorates affiliated with the Imperial-Saxon alliance, but some remained outside, the most important being Hesse-Kassel, which soon allied with France. Bernard of Weimar placed his largely German army at the service of France in exchange for a promise of a principality in Habsburg Alsace. Some Protestant states, unhappy with the restrictions on amnesty, accepted the agreement only halfheartedly and never intended to throw themselves into a united effort behind the emperor. Such was the case with Brunswick-Lüneburg and Mecklenburg, both of whom feared to provoke Sweden, as well as with Württemberg.

The prohibition of alliances spelled the dissolution of the Catholic League and the Heilbronn Confederation. This was a goal Vienna had long envisioned and seemed to strengthen the emperor's position. But the anticipated military reform and creation of a unified army never took place.[64] Saxony and then Maximilian were given major and relatively independent commands, so that in practice there were three armies, the imperial, the Bavarian, and the Saxon. To be sure, the emperor did achieve a long-time aspiration when his son was elected King of the Romans at the Electoral Convention of Regensburg on December 22, 1636. Thus he provided for the succession just in time, since he himself died less than two months later. But the Empire was far from sufficiently united to deal with the two major powers to the north and west. For a brief time it appeared that imperial negotiations with Sweden might remove it from the war; but these failed and the Franco-Swedish alliance survived the strain, especially after the Swedish victory over a combined Imperial-Saxon army at Wittstock in October 1636.

The open involvement of France in the war shattered the hopes for the Peace of Prague. While the appearance of Catholic France on the side of the Dutch, the Swedes, and the dissident German Protestants served to lessen significantly the ideological character of the war, it greatly ex-

panded the conflict. Prior to his declaration of war against Spain, Richelieu had allied with the Dutch to drive Spain from the Netherlands. The
next year imperial troops came to the aid of the Spaniards there, thus
realizing a long-standing goal of Spanish policy. In the late summer of
1636 the imperials assisted by the Bavarians launched an unsuccessful
invasion of France from Breisach. Between these two actions Ferdinand
issued a formal declaration of war against France. For this he had the
support of Maximilian, who was angry at the constant French encroach-
ments in the west and their interference in imperial affairs; Maximilian
was ready, for the time being, to enlist Spanish help against France.
Ferdinand seems still to have hesitated about declaring war on France
and to have taken the measure only at the urging of his son, the King of
Hungary,[65] who was closer to Spain than his father. In the winter of 1637,
Ferdinand sent two delegates to the papal peace conference planned for
Cologne, but their instructions showed that he had little hope for an
understanding with France. As it was, irreconcilable differences between
France and the Habsburg powers were a major reason why the conference never convened.[66] Meanwhile, Richelieu supported Hesse-Kassel
and Bernard of Weimar in the Empire. He mediated another Swedish-
Polish armistice in 1635 that freed Sweden from concern about attack
from the east; after a shaky period in the relationship, he renewed the
alliance with Sweden in 1638. Thus the Dutch war and the German war
merged with the Habsburg-Bourbon war for hegemony in Europe that
was now to be fought largely on German soil.[67]

But though the settlement at Prague did not bring peace to the Empire,
it was of major significance for German history. It stripped the German
war of much of its ideological nature. Lamormaini himself referred to it
in 1638 as half-abrogating the Edict.[68] The Peace of Prague was the first
official step beyond the Peace of Augsburg and a milestone on the way
toward religious toleration in Germany. Inasmuch as it ended the most
aggressive phase of the Counterreformation in the Empire, it was both a
return to the moderate policy of Ferdinand I in 1555 and an anticipation
of the Peace of Westphalia. Many German Protestants found themselves
on the side of the emperor once again. The Peace of Prague was the
graveyard of the militant ideology that arose in the wake of the White
Mountain and played a decisive role in the middle period of the Thirty
Years War. The anti-Protestant crusading spirit that had departed from
Spain and Rome to move north was now put to rest in Germany as well.
The belief that Ferdinand had been specially selected by God and promised assistance to lead the Church to complete triumph in the Empire was
no longer to be an effective factor in the formulation of policy. This does
not mean that the emperor would overlook the welfare of the Church in

the future. Neither Ferdinand II nor Ferdinand III did this. But the principle had been established, or perhaps reestablished, that religious concessions could be of greater benefit to Church and Empire than conflict and war. When rational analysis showed this to be the case, they could be made without fear of betraying an alleged divine mission or failing to trust in the Lord. The moderates had gained the upper hand in Vienna, and they were not to relinquish it.[69]

Two specific movements toward the secularization of imperial politics can be discerned as resulting from the Peace of Prague. One was precisely the demise of the aforementioned crusading spirit. The era of the "holy war" among Christians was ending. The second concerned the role of the papacy in German affairs. Prague confirmed the direction which had been taken at Augsburg in 1555 but which subsequently became uncertain. A major decision regarding religion in the Empire was reached without the participation or consent of the papacy. As much as anything, this was due to papal policy itself. Urban's refusal to soften his juridical stand and to sanction any concessions greatly restricted his ability to affect the course of political events. The Peace of Prague revealed the declining influence of the papacy in German and European politics. In this it also foreshadowed the Peace of Westphalia.

The Peace of Prague, particularly in the compromise on the Edict, signaled a notable retreat from a policy of aggressive assertion of imperial authority in Germany, not from a policy aimed at the eventual creation of an absolute hereditary monarchy. This Ferdinand had never intended, and he resented the accusations that he looked to the establishment of an absolute state in the Empire.[70] Perhaps Wallenstein at one time envisioned an absolute monarchy for Germany; Ferdinand did not. The armies he sent into the Empire had as their chief task the fulfillment of his obligation to defend the faith. The development of Ferdinand's power in the Empire was largely the outgrowth of his activist religious policy. A dominant position in the Empire was seen as a prerequisite for the restoration of Catholicism. Ferdinand's energetic imperial policy with its constitutional implications was at the service of his religious program, for which Lamormaini was largely responsible. The important instances when he was thought to have stretched the imperial constitution, even though with much justification he considered his actions legal, were closely connected with the advancement of Catholicism and were usually supported by the Catholic electors. This was the case with the transfer of the electoral title to Maximilian and the promulgation of the Edict. Even the bestowal of Mecklenburg on Wallenstein was associated with the promotion of religion, in that it was intended to strengthen the imperial position in the north of Germany.

Especially after the defeat at Breitenfeld but even well before then, leading councilors pointed out to Ferdinand the impossibility of dominating Germany and the need to make concessions in the Empire for the sake of consolidating his position in the Habsburg territories. This was true of Stralendorf, Trautmannsdorf, Bishop Anton, and the two cardinals, Dietrichstein and Pazmany, not of Eggenberg, whose advocacy of concessions in the Empire was dictated more by the desire to throw effective imperial support to Spain. Once it became clear to Ferdinand, as it did in 1635, that it was not possible to obtain the goals of the militants and he was no longer obliged to pursue them, his imperial activism waned; its raison d'être no longer existed. In a codicil to his testament of August 8, 1635, Ferdinand reaffirmed his intention, first asserted in 1621, to hand on his Habsburg lands to his heir as an indivisible hereditary monarchy.[71] The Peace of Prague pointed toward the increasing priority the Habsburgs were in the future to give their own territories over the Empire.[72] In this again it presaged Westphalia.

Lamormaini remained an important and respected figure in Vienna until his death in 1648, but after the Peace of Prague his political influence diminished drastically. He accompanied Ferdinand to the Electoral Convention of Regensburg in the fall of 1636, but in contrast to 1630, he played only a marginal part.[73] However, the personal bond between Lamormaini and Ferdinand remained strong. While staying over in Straubing in Bavaria the night of January 25 on the return trip from Regensburg, where Ferdinand had suffered a stroke, the emperor asked Lamormaini to dispense him from his usual hour of morning prayer; otherwise he would have to rise at four.[74] When they arrived back in Vienna, the end was obviously near for the emperor. After spending most of the previous day with Lamormaini, Ferdinand died the morning of February 15, 1637, attended by his confessor and long-time friend.[75] Almost immediately, Lamormaini began work on his biography of Ferdinand, the final part of which was published the next year as *The Virtues of Ferdinand II, Emperor of the Romans.*[76]

Lamormaini continued with many activities in Vienna. He heard confessions regularly in the Jesuit church, supervised the construction of buildings including the novitiate of St. Anna, promoted the foundation of colleges, and urged Catholic claims to church lands in the Empire, especially in Württemberg.[77] From 1639 to 1643, he served again as rector of the college in Vienna, and after the provincial superior died suddenly in 1643, he held this office for nearly a year despite his advanced age.

Ferdinand III was generous to the Jesuits, but he did not lavish the Society with gifts as his father did. Under the new emperor ecclesiastics no longer enjoyed the influence on political affairs they had under his predecessor, a change attributed to Trautmannsdorf and Thun, two of the most important councilors under the new regime.[78] Dietrichstein preceded Ferdinand to the grave (1636), and Pazmany (1637), Stralen-dorf (1637), and Bishop Anton (1639) soon followed, so that Traut-mannsdorf was the one figure to serve as a leading privy councilor under both emperors.

After the death of Heinrich Philippi in 1636, Ferdinand III took as his confessor the Jesuit Johann Gans, a native of Würzburg, who was his court preacher. Gans was inclined to involve himself much less in politi-cal affairs than Lamormaini, and he tended to share the views of Quiroga, who remained a major figure in Vienna as confessor to the empress until his death in 1648. When asked for his opinion about the amnesty Ferdi-nand intended to propose at the Diet of Regensburg in 1641, Gans referred to the majority opinion of the theologians' council of 1635 regarding the Peace of Prague and pointed out that the same arguments justified the measure the emperor was then considering. He explicitly rejected the Edict of Restitution, asserting that it was the principal source of all the trouble in the Empire. With the unwitting help of a few zealous and well-meaning but politically inept advisers, the emperor's enemies had promoted it in the hope of dividing and weakening the Empire.[79] This view approached the position suggested in Khevenhiller's *Annals of Ferdinand II*, that Richelieu was the ultimate source of the Edict.[80] Thus the centerpiece of Lamormaini's program for the restoration of Catholi-cism in Germany was evaluated by his successor before Lamormaini died on February 28, 1648, the year the Peace of Westphalia finally ended the long war.

Notes

Abbreviations to the Notes

ACPF	Rome, Archivio Congregazione de Propaganda Fide
ACPF, 1st.	Istruzioni
ACPF, SR	Scritture originali riferite nelle Congregazioni Generali
ARSJ	Rome, Archivum Romanum Societatis Jesu
ARSJ, Aust.	Provincia Austriae
ARSJ, Boh.	Provincia Bohemiae
ARSJ, Germ.	Assistentia Germaniae
ARSJ, GS	Provincia Germaniae Superioris
ASV	Rome, Archivio Segreto Vaticano
ASV, EP	Segreteria dei Brevi, Epistolae ad Principes
ASV, Misc.	Segreteria di Stato, Miscellenea
ASV, NC	Segreteria di Stato, Nunziatura Colonia
ASV, NG	Segreteria di Stato, Nunziatura Germania
BA	*Briefe und Akten zur Geschichte des Dreissigjährigen Krieges*, New Series, Part 2, vols. 1–5
BAGW	Hermann Hallwich, ed., *Briefe und Akten zur Geschichte Wallensteins, 1630–1634*, vols. 1–4
BH	Munich, Bayerisches Hauptstaatsarchiv
BH, Jesuitica	Allgemeines Staatsarchiv, Jesuitica
BH, Kriegs.	Allgemeines Staatsarchiv, Akten zur Geschichte des Dreissigjährigen Krieges
BH, KSchw	Geheimes Staatsarchiv, Kasten Schwarz
BL	Rome, Vatican Library, Fondo Barberini Latini
CS	Florence, Biblioteca Mediceo-Laurenziana, Codici Scioppiani
DA	Brno, Státní Archiv, Dietrichstein Archiv
Duhr	Bernhard Duhr, *Geschichte der Jesuiten in den Ländern deutscher Zunge*, vols. 1 and 2:1, 2:2
HHStA	Vienna, Österreichisches Staatsarchiv, Abteilung Haus-, Hof- und Staatsarchiv, Reichskanzlei
HHStA, Friedens.	Friedensakten
HHStA, GC	Grosse Correspondenz
HHStA, Kriegs.	Kriegsakten
HHStA, Mainz	Mainzer Erzkanzleiarchiv, Reichtagsakten
HHStA, Religion.	Religionsakten
HHStA, RHR	Reichshofratsprotokolle
HHStA, RTA	Reichstagsakten
HHStA, Staaten.	Staatenabteilungen

HHStA, Traut.	Trautmannsdorffisches Familienarchiv
Kiewning	Heinrich Kiewning, ed., *Nuntiaturberichte aus Deutschland: Nuntiatur des Pallotto, 1628–30*, vols. 1–2
Repgen	Konrad Repgen, *Die römische Kurie und der westfälische Friede*, vols. 1:1 and 1:2
Virtutes	Wilhelm Lamormaini, *Ferdinand II Romanorum Imperatoris Virtutes*
"Vita Lamormaini"	Eustachius Sthaäl, "Speculum Christiani hominis et Jesuitae . . . ," ARSJ, Vitae 139

Chapter 1

1. *Ferdinandi II Romanorum Imperatoris Virtutes*, opposite p. 5. Lamormaini's personal copy of this first edition is in the Österreichische Nationalbibliothek, Vienna, Handschriftensammlung 7378. A blank page for the author's notations has been inserted between each printed page. References to this book will be to this copy, and references to Lamormaini's annotations will be clearly distinguished from those to the printed text.

For the editions and translations of the *Virtutes*, see Coreth, *Pietas Austriaca*, p. 13, n. 19. It also was published in German translation at the end of Khevenhiller, *Annales Ferdinandei*, 12:2381–468. For a positive evaluation of its literary qualities, see Richard Müller, "Wiens höfisches und bürgerliches Leben im Zeitalter der spanischen Habsburger. Unter Einbeziehung der gleichzeitigen Literatur," *Geschichte der Stadt Wien*, edited by Anton Mayer, 6:314.

2. Sturmberger, *Aufstand in Böhmen*, pp. 10–19, 34–61; Ritter, *Deutsche Geschichte*, 3:3–31, 52–54; Hantsch, *Geschichte Österreichs*, pp. 338–41.

3. For the early history of the Catholic League, see Franziska Neuer-Landfried, *Die Katholische Liga. Gründung, Neugründung und Organisation eines Sonderbundes 1608–1620*, Münchner Historische Studien, Abt. Bayerische Geschichte, 9 (Kallmunz, 1969).

4. A *Deputationstag* brought together a committee of the imperial diet (*Reichstag*) to conduct business that could not be handled at a session of the whole diet; see Zeeden, "Glaubenskämpfe," p. 149.

The diet or representative body of the Empire was composed of three councils, the council of electors or electoral college, the council of princes, and the council of cities. The electoral college, whose number had been fixed at seven by the Golden Bull of 1356, enjoyed the privilege of electing the emperor. It comprised the Archbishops of Mainz, Trier, and Cologne, the Duke of Saxony, the Margrave of Brandenburg, the Count Palatine of the Rhine, and the King of Bohemia. The last named could vote only in imperial elections, not in other business that came before the college.

5. Albrecht, "Das konfessionelle Zeitalter," pp. 378–87; Ritter, *Deutsche Geschichte*, 3:191–92.

6. Part of the Oñate Treaty, dated Prague, Jun. 6, 1617, has been published in

Dumont, *Corps universel diplomatique*, 5:2:298–300. The secret provisions, dated Prague, Mar. 20, 1617, have not been published; see Bittner, *Verzeichnis der österreichischen Staatsverträge*, pp. 37–38. On the Oñate Treaty, see Hantsch, *Geschichte Österreichs*, pp. 329–30, 395; Khevenhiller, *Annales Ferdinandei*, 10:158–66; Chudoba, *Spain and the Empire*, pp. 189–227 passim.

7. Parker, *Dutch Revolt*, pp. 263–66.

8. Ritter, *Deutsche Geschichte*, 3:244–45; O'Connell, *Richelieu*, pp. 83–87. For the legal status of the strategic Valtelline, see ibid., pp. 77–80.

9. Albrecht, *Auswärtige Politik*, pp. 55–61, 77–78, 159–60.

10. Ritter, *Deutsche Geschichte*, 3:240–53; Mecenseffy, *Protestantismus in Österreich*, pp. 160–61; Zeeden, "Glaubenskämpfe," p. 152.

11. On the Counterreformation in Inner Austria under Archduke Carl, see Loserth, *Geschichte der Gegenreformation in Innerösterreich unter Erzherzog Karl*, pp. ix-xxxiv; Mecenseffy, *Protestantismus in Österreich*, pp. 71–82. For the beginnings of the Jesuits in Graz, see Duhr, 1:163–69.

12. Hantsch, *Geschichte Österreichs*, p. 295.

13. Dudik, "Korrespondenz Kaiser Ferdinands," pp. 223–24.

14. On Viller, see Duhr, 1:698–99; on Becan, ibid., 2:1:452–54 and 2:2:219–25.

15. *Virtutes*, p. 94.

16. The six were at Laibach (Ljubljana) in Carniola, Klagenfurt in Carinthia, Gorizia (Görz) in Friuli, Kuttenberg (Kutná Hora) and Leitmeritz (Litoměřice) in Bohemia, and Glogau in Silesia. See *Virtutes*, pp. 92–93, and Lamormaini to Vitelleschi, Feb. 28, 1637, ARSJ, Vitae 161, ff. 41–44. A seventh, at Linz in Upper Austria, is attributed to Ferdinand in the letter to Vitelleschi, but in the later *Virtutes* Archduke Matthias is credited with the original foundation of the college.

17. The codicil is published in Turba, *Grundlagen der Pragmatischen Sanktion*, pp. 351–55.

18. Duhr, 2:2:691–97.

19. "Vita Lamormaini," ARSJ, Vitae 139, ff. 66, 121. The author gives this quote as approximate. Of great importance for Lamormaini's biography is this manuscript of 122 folios whose full title reads "Speculum Christiani hominis et Jesuitae, sive Vita et Virtutes P. Gulielmi Germaei Lamormaini, Societatis Jesu Presbyteri, Ferdinandi II Romanorum Imperatoris Confessarii. . . ." A copy was sent to Rome in 1649, the year after Lamormaini's death, by the author, Eustachius Sthaäl, a fellow Jesuit who by his own testimony lived in the same community with Lamormaini for twenty-four years; see Sthaäl to Florence Montmorency (acting superior general of the Society of Jesus in Rome), Oct. 10, 1649, ARSJ, Vitae 139, and the preface to the manuscript. Sthaäl had access to Lamormaini's private papers including his spiritual notes, which have since been lost, and he incorporated many excerpts from them into the manuscript. He intended that this material be used for a later biography of Lamormaini or for the writing of the history of the Society. Another copy of the manuscript is in the archives of the Benedictine monastery of Pannonhalma near Györ in Hungary,

no. 37 (118 G30). Sthaäl is obviously partial to Lamormaini, and the manuscript must be used with care.

20. This has been published in Dudik, "Korrespondenz Kaiser Ferdinands." See esp. pp. 232, 249. On Lamormaini's relationship to Leopold and his part in preserving harmony between the two brothers, see Posch, "Zur Tätigkeit und Beurteilung Lamormainis," pp. 376–77.

21. *Virtutes*, pp. 6 (annotations), 30, 54. Lamormaini noted that he left out deliberately the names of the Jesuits who favored the marriage. On the prospective marriage, see Pastor, *Geschichte der Päpste*, 12:535, 537–42, 547.

22. Lamormaini's memorandum, dated April 1620, is in ARSJ, Boh. 94, ff. 65–66v. Becan's position has long been known; see Duhr, 2:2:220–22, and Lecler, *Toleration and the Reformation*, 1:299–300.

23. Kollmann, *Acta sacrae congregationis de Propaganda Fide*, 1:1: no. 4b.

24. "Vita Lamormaini," f. 37.

25. Vitelleschi to Joannes Argenti (Visitor of the Austrian Province), Aug. 13, 1622, ARSJ, Aust. 3I, ff. 294–95; Duhr, 2:2:696–97. A visitor was an official appointed by Rome to inspect and report on the state of a particular Jesuit province.

26. Duhr, 2:1:546–47 and 2:2:713.

27. Ibid., 2:1:541–52; Kink, *Geschichte der Universität zu Wien*, 1:1:323, 331–33, 338–40, 345–50, 353–66.

28. "Vita Lamormaini," ff. 45v–46.

29. Vitelleschi to Argenti, Mar. 2 and 9, 1624, ARSJ, Aust. 3I, ff. 489, 493; Vitelleschi to Lamormaini, Mar. 2 and Apr. 6, 1624, ibid., ff. 489–90, 499.

30. On Vitelleschi, see Ludwig Koch, *Jesuiten Lexikon* (Paderborn, 1934), col. 1822–23.

31. "De Confessariis Principum," *Institutum Societatis Jesu*, pp. 281–84; Vitelleschi to Lamormaini, Apr. 6, 1624, ARSJ, Aust. 3I, f. 499.

32. See, for example, Bireley, *Maximilian von Bayern*, pp. 49–50.

33. *Institutum Societatis Jesu*, p. 332.

34. See Hans-Dieter Hertrampf, "Hoé von Hoénegg: Sächsischer Oberhofprediger 1613–1645," *Beiträge zur Kirchengeschichte Deutschlands* 7 (1969): 129–48.

35. *Virtutes*, p. 68.

36. Ibid., pp. 17–18, 21–26, 57, 59–61, 71–72, 81, 103; *Status Particularis regiminis S. C. Majestatis Ferdinandi II* (Leiden, 1637), pp. 34–35. This was one of a series of short books written by anonymous authors and published by the Elzevir Press that dealt with the court and government of different countries. See also Felix Stieve, "Ferdinand II," pp. 660–62.

37. Opel, *Der niedersächsisch-dänische Krieg*, 2:152–53. Opel cites a Leuker report of December 1625.

38. On Ferdinand's absolutism, see Sturmberger, *Kaiser Ferdinand II*, esp. pp. 45–46.

39. The testament is published in Turba, *Grundlagen der Pragmatischen Sanktion*, pp. 335–51; Sturmberger, *Ferdinand II*, pp. 43–44.

40. Hurter, *Geschichte Ferdinands II*, 8:312–14.

41. Turba, *Grundlagen der Pragmatischen Sanktion*, pp. 351–55; see Sturmberger, *Ferdinand II*, pp. 40–42.

42. Dated Aug. 19, 1625, Carafa, *Commentaria*, pp. 130–43, documentary appendix. For the Counterreformation in Inner Austria under Ferdinand, see especially Loserth, *Geschichte der Gegenreformation in Innerösterreich unter Ferdinand II*, 1:v–lxxvii and 2:ix–xlix.

43. *Virtutes*, p. 5.

44. This was adapted from 2 Tim. 2:5; see Franzl, *Ferdinand II*, pp. 7, 363.

45. Georg Stobäus von Palmburg, Bishop of Lavant, to Archduke Carl, Aug. 1, 1604, cited in J. Stepischnegg, "Georg III Stobäus von Palmburg," p. 105.

46. *Virtutes*, p. 48; for the background, see Loserth, *Geschichte der Gegenreformation in Innerösterreich unter Ferdinand II*, 1:xliv–lx.

47. Pp. 9–11; Sturmberger, *Aufstand in Böhmen*, pp. 44–46; Tomek, *Kirchengeschichte Österreichs*, p. 518, n. 700. This crucifix was preserved as a Habsburg family treasure and was given to members of the House for veneration at the time of their death. According to the legend that grew out of this event, Protestant members of the estates threatened Ferdinand's person when in the nick of time a troop of imperial cavalry came to the rescue.

48. See, for example, Contzen, *Politicorum Libri Decem*, Dedication (toward the end).

49. *Virtutes*, pp. 29–30; see also pp. 5, 14.

50. Ibid., p. 75; Stieve, "Ferdinand II," p. 661; see also Hantsch, *Geschichte Österreichs*, pp. 297, 336, and Sturmberger, *Ferdinand II*, p. 10.

51. Hantsch, *Geschichte Österreichs*, pp. 340–44; Schwarz, *Imperial Privy Council*, pp. 30–32; on Dietrichstein, see ibid., 221–24.

52. Schwarz, *Imperial Privy Council*, p. 32; Hantsch, *Geschichte Österreichs*, p. 309.

53. Hantsch, *Geschichte Österreichs*, p. 330; see also Khevenhiller, *Annales Ferdinandei*, 10:447–48, 718. Leopold became the ruler of all the Anterior Austrian lands in 1630, following another agreement with Ferdinand.

54. On the imperial privy council under Ferdinand, see Schwarz, *Imperial Privy Council*, esp. pp. 114–16, 121–23, 130, and the succinct biographical sketches of each councilor in the Supplement. See also Fellner and Kretschmayr, *Die österreichische Zentralverwaltung*, pp. 38–67. Lamormaini in *Virtutes*, pp. 75–77, illustrates Ferdinand's procedure in reaching a decision, and the *Status Particularis*, pp. 72–88, describes the government and its operation.

Those present at the committee or conciliar meeting at which a paper was discussed are frequently but by no means always listed on the paper itself in the archives. But individual votes are not recorded, so that one cannot tell who supported or rejected the recommendations. There are, however, some minutes of meetings in the archives which do permit this, and of course it can sometimes be learned from other sources. I use the terms position paper, paper, and report interchangeably.

55. Philip IV to the Duke of Guastalla, Spanish ambassador in Vienna, Sept.

15, 1631, Günter, *Habsburgerliga*, no. 55 (pp. 294–96); Gerhard Marauschek, "Leben und Zeit," in *Giovanni Pietro de Pomis*, ed. Kurt Woisetschläger, pp. 23–24, 47.

56. On Eggenberg, see Schwarz, *Imperial Privy Council*, pp. 226–28, and Heydendorff, *Die Fürsten zu Eggenberg*.

57. Apr. 20, 1631, published in Zwiedineck-Südenhorst, *Eggenberg*, pp. 192–97.

58. On the imperial aulic council, see Gschliesser, *Der Reichshofrat*, esp. pp. 7–15, 65–67; see also Schwarz, *Imperial Privy Council*, pp. 16–24, and Fellner and Kretschmayr, *Die österreichische Zentralverwaltung*, pp. 143–59, 229–31. For a 1636 list of the members of the council, see the *Status Particularis*, pp. 103–5.

59. Chancellor of the Empire *ex officio* was the Archbishop of Mainz. On the imperial chancery and its relationship to the new Austrian chancery, see Schwarz, *Imperial Privy Council*, pp. 19–24, 42, and Lothar Gross, *Geschichte der Reichshofkanzlei*, esp. pp. 40–43, 143.

60. Schwarz, *Imperial Privy Council*, pp. 360–62; Gross, *Geschichte der Reichshofkanzlei*, pp. 326–34.

61. On Ferdinand's finances, see Hurter, *Geschichte Ferdinands II*, 8:234–308 passim. Gundacker von Liechtenstein, who served as a treasury official from 1613 to 1619 and then as president of the treasury council until 1623, continually advocated financial reform but without success; see Mitis, "Gundacker von Liechtensteins Anteil an der kaiserlichen Zentralverwaltung," pp. 46–50, 57, 70–73.

62. Schwarz, *Imperial Privy Council*, pp. 386–87; Hopf, *Anton Wolfradt*, 3 vols. These are extremely slim volumes.

63. See Eggenberg to Francesco Cardinal Barberini (Rome), Dec. 10, 1630, and Feb. 3, 1632, BL 6902, ff. 50–51, 59; and Günter, *Habsburgerliga*, p. 47.

64. Koch, *Geschichte des deutschen Reiches unter Ferdinand III*, p. 14.

65. Schwarz, *Imperial Privy Council*, pp. 372–74; Gschliesser, *Der Reichshofrat*, pp. 183–84.

66. Lamormaini to Sigismund Frederick von Trautmannsdorf, Feb. 14, 1631, HHStA, Traut. 157.

67. "Vita Lamormaini," f. 43v.

68. Ibid., ff. 44, 54v, 72v.

69. Ibid., ff. 43v, 44v.

70. Ibid., f. 41v; *Virtutes*, p. 5 (annotation); Vitelleschi to Lamormaini, May 29, 1624, ARSJ, Aust. 3I, ff. 507–8.

71. "Vita Lamormaini," f. 43v.

72. Lamormaini to Barberini, Aug. 3, 1624, BL 7054, f. 54. Important for the vow is the account in Cordara, *Historiae Societatis Jesu Pars Sexta*, 2:487. Cordara wrote in the mid-eighteenth century, although this volume was not published until 1859. He had access to materials gathered by Vincent Giuniggi, S.J. (1601–53), secretary to Vitelleschi, with a view to writing a history of the Society. They have since been lost. See Carlos Sommervogel, *Bibliothèque de la*

Compagnie de Jésus, 2 (Brussels and Paris, 1891): 1416; 3 (Brussels and Paris, 1892): 1941. For the vow, see also Vitelleschi to Lamormaini, May 29, 1624, ARSJ, Aust. 3I, ff. 507–8, and *Virtutes,* p. 4, plus annotation, where the dating is confusing.

On the position of Francesco Barberini in the Roman Curia and especially his relationship to the secretaries of state under Urban VIII, see Kraus, *Das päpstliche Staatssekretariat unter Urban VIII,* pp. 9–20.

Chapter 2

1. In 1512 ten imperial circles (*Reichskreise*) had been formed. By the early seventeenth century the principal institution of the circle was an assembly (*Kreistag*), analogous to the imperial diet, representing the states of the circle. Its chief tasks were to keep order in the circle and to raise troops and funds for the defense of the Empire, though it sometimes assumed other functions. The imperial circles were only of significance where there was no dominant territorial prince and political fragmentation was considerable, as in Lower Saxony, Swabia, Franconia, the Rhineland.

2. Albrecht, *Auswärtige Politik,* pp. 123–25, 128–32, 144–45; Ritter, *Deutsche Geschichte,* 3:258–348 passim; Pagès, *Thirty Years War,* pp. 83, 94–99, 104.

3. Goetz, "Wallenstein und Kurfürst Maximilian," esp. pp. 111–117; Ritter, *Deutsche Geschichte,* 3:295–306, 326–28.

4. The term *politici* did not always carry a negative connotation even in the mouths of the militants. Often it merely designated the political councilors as opposed to the theological advisers, the *theologi.* Insofar as it did bear the negative connotation, the term derived from the French *politiques* of the sixteenth century. See, among others, Federico Chabod, *Giovanni Botero* (Rome, 1934), p. 37.

5. Opel, *Der niedersächsisch-dänische Krieg,* 1:80–82, 87; Tupetz, "Der Streit um die geistlichen Güter," pp. 341–43.

6. Published in Mareš, "Die maritime Politik der Habsburger," pp. 576–78; see also Gindely, "Die maritimen Pläne der Habsburger," pp. 2–3, and Messow, "Die Hansestädte und die habsburgische Ostseepolitik," pp. 11–14.

7. Catholics and Protestants disputed whether 1552, the date of the preliminary Treaty of Passau, or 1555, the date of the Peace of Augsburg, was the norm laid down by Augsburg. The Catholics argued for the former. Their position was stronger in 1552 than in 1555, by which time the consequences of the defeat of Charles V had worked themselves out more completely. The dispute is not of significance for this study, which will normally use 1552.

8. A critical edition of the Religious Peace can be found in Brandi, *Der Augsburger Religionsfriede,* pp. 32–52; see also Holborn, *A History of Modern Germany: The Reformation,* pp. 243–45.

9. Heckel, "*Autonomia* und *Pacis Compositio,*" pp. 142–44, 208–11;

Dickmann, "Das Problem der Gleichberechtigung der Konfessionen," pp.
286–88; Urban, *Restitutionsedikt*, pp. 245–46.

10. Urban, *Restitutionsedikt*, pp. 245–55; Zeeden, "Glaubenskämpfe," p.
146.

11. Zeeden, "Glaubenskämpfe," pp. 140–50.

12. Ritter, *Deutsche Geschichte*, 3:192–94, 239, 258–59; Repgen,
1:1:165–68. For Catholic efforts to regain lost church lands before the outbreak
of the war, see Ritter, "Ursprung des Restitutionsedikts," pp. 138–58.

13. On Ziegler, see Duhr, 2:2:272–73.

14. Presented in Munich, Sept. 17, 1625, BH, KSchw 769, ff. 147–50v; see BA,
2:368, n. 1.

15. Instructions for Ziegler's mission to Munich and Vienna, Sept. 6, 1625,
HHStA, Mainz 120; see BA, 2:368, n. 1. On the background, see Klopp, *Der
dreissigjährige Krieg*, 2:451–54, 585.

16. Carafa to Barberini, Jan. 21, 1626, BL 6949, ff. 6–8; Klopp, *Der dreissigjährige Krieg*, 2:466; Opel, *Der niedersächsisch-dänische Krieg*, 2:180–82.

17. Message of Maximilian given Ziegler for Mainz, Sept. 21, 1625, BH,
KSchw 769, ff. 171–81; Ziegler to Mainz, Sept. 22 and 23, 1625, HHStA, Mainz
120; Ziegler to Mainz, Oct. 6, 1625, BA, 2:no. 117; imperial response to
Ziegler's proposition, Oct. 12, 1625, HHStA, Mainz 120; see also BA, 2:371, n.
3 and 399, n. 2, and Opel, *Der niedersächsisch-dänische Krieg*, 2:275.

18. Duhr, 2:2:698.

19. Carafa to Barberini, Nov. 26, 1625, BL 6948, ff. 196–99v, and Jan. 14,
1626, BL 6942, ff. 6–9v; Carafa, *Commentaria*, pp. 206–24; Khevenhiller,
Annales Ferdinandei, 10:693–703; see also Uhlirz, *Geschichte Österreichs und
seiner Nachbarländer*, pp. 210–26.

20. Lamormaini to Vitelleschi (Extract), Dec. 2, 1625, BL 7054, f. 66.

21. Winter, *Barock, Absolutismus, und Aufklärung*, pp. 59–61; Albert Hübl,
"Die Schulen," *Geschichte der Stadt Wien*, ed. Anton Mayer, 5:427–29. For a
general appreciation of the importance of Pazmany see Kornis, *Le Cardinal
Pázmány*, and E. Amann, "Pazmany, Pierre," *Dictionnaire de théologie
catholique*, 12:1 (Paris, 1933): 97–100.

22. For Lamormaini's efforts on behalf of the Church in Hungary and especially the foundation of colleges, see the "Vita Lamormaini," ff. 54–55, and a
petition he prepared for Ferdinand III, dated Mar. 31, 1637, less than six weeks
after his father's death, and entitled "De Collegiis in Ungaria stabiliendis et
erigendis." The latter summarizes much of his previous activity as well as his
plans for the future; it is now in the archives of the Benedictine monastery of
Pannonhalma, no. 116 (119 A2).

23. The sources disagree on Pazmany's stance at the diet; see above, n. 19.
Carafa's dispatch of Nov. 26 lists him among those who at first opposed the
coronation, but his *Commentaria* and Khevenhiller indicate Pazmany advocated
election and coronation from the start. My inclination is to accept the latter view,
especially since Pazmany consistently adopted a more pragmatic position on
toleration than did Lamormaini.

24. Pazmany to Ferdinand II, Apr. 7, 1625, *Epistolae Collectae*, 1:no. 291; Pazmany to Cardinal Ludovico Ludovisi (Prefect of the Propaganda), Jun. 7, 1627, ACPF, SR 67, ff. 27–27v; Pazmany to the Propaganda, Jul. 7, 1627, ibid., ff. 28–29v.

25. Sturmberger, *Ferdinand II*, pp. 24–31; Mecenseffy, *Protestantismus in Österreich*, pp. 53–56, 129–33.

26. Vitelleschi to Lamormaini, Apr. 26, 1625, ARSJ, Aust. 3II, f. 617; Wiedemann, *Reformation und Gegenreformation im Lande unter der Enns*, pp. 595–97; Tomek, *Kirchengeschichte Österreichs*, p. 524.

27. Hantsch, *Geschichte Österreichs*, pp. 344–47; Mecenseffy, *Protestantismus in Österreich*, pp. 160–68; Sturmberger, *Adam Graf Herberstorff*, pp. 199–308 passim.

28. Petry, "Politische Geschichte unter den Habsburgern," pp. 60, 74–77. According to Hurter, *Geschichte Ferdinands II*, 8:622–23, Lamormaini explicitly approved the settlement for Silesia.

29. Richter, "Die böhmischen Länder von 1471–1740," pp. 283–90.

30. Carafa to the Propaganda, Sept. 25, 1624, Kollmann, *Acta sacrae congregationis de Propaganda Fide*, 2:no. 165 (esp. pp. 256–68).

31. Richter, "Die böhmischen Länder von 1471–1740," p. 286; Ritter, *Deutsche Geschichte*, 3:254–55; Gindely, *Gegenreformation in Böhmen*, pp. 202–5.

32. On Magni's activity in Bohemia, see Abgottspon, *Magni*. The best introduction to his thought is Edouard d'Alencon, "Magni, Valerien," *Dictionnaire de théologie catholique*, 9:2 (Paris, 1927): 1553–65. Also important is Winter, *Barock, Absolutismus, und Aufklärung*, pp. 41–46.

33. Kroess, *Geschichte der böhmischen Provinz der Gesellschaft Jesu*, 2:1:105–6; see also Spiegel, "Die Prager Universitätsunion," pp. 6–12.

34. Kroess, *Geschichte der böhmischen Provinz*, 2:1:107–16; Spiegel, "Die Prager Universitätsunion," pp. 13–14, 17–20.

35. On the new archbishop, see Schwarz, *Imperial Privy Council*, pp. 239–40; on his father, see ibid., 242–44, and Mann, *Wallenstein*, p. 384. Wallenstein was the son-in-law of the privy councilor and brother-in-law of the archbishop.

36. Vitelleschi to Lamormaini, Aug. 31, 1624, ARSJ, Aust. 3II, ff. 534–35; Kroess, *Geschichte der böhmischen Provinz*, 2:1:111–12, 116–22; Spiegel, "Die Prager Universitätsunion," pp. 20–22.

37. Kroess, *Geschichte der böhmischen Provinz*, 2:1:121–31; Spiegel, "Die Prager Universitätsunion," pp. 22–24.

38. Lamormaini to Eggenberg, undated but before Oct. 14, 1624, Kollmann, *Acta congregationis de Propaganda Fide*, 2:no. 182; Kroess, *Geschichte der böhmischen Provinz*, 2:1:131–34.

39. Oct. 5, 1624, ARSJ, Aust. 23, ff. 28–28v; see Kroess, *Geschichte der böhmischen Provinz*, 2:1:132.

40. Vitelleschi to Lamormaini, Oct. 26, 1624, ARSJ, Aust. 3II, f. 554; the agreement is published in Kollmann, *Acta congregationis de Propaganda Fide*, 2:no. 202. See also Kroess, *Geschichte der böhmischen Provinz*, 2:1:133–34.

41. Gregory XV created this papal congregation on Jun. 22, 1622. Its purpose was to foster and oversee missionary activity in non-Catholic lands, which included Protestant areas of Europe as well as territories overseas. For the foundation of the Propaganda, see Tüchle, *Acta SC de Propaganda Fide*, pp. 1–4.

42. Kollmann, *Acta congregationis de Propaganda Fide*, 2:295–97, 318–20; Spiegel, "Die Prager Universitätsunion," pp. 15–16.

43. Kroess, *Geschichte der böhmischen Provinz*, 2:1:134–36; see the minutes of the meetings of the Propaganda congregation, Aug. 25 and Oct. 29, 1625, Tüchle, *Acta SC de Propaganda Fide*, pp. 101, 107. The pope participated personally in the deliberations.

44. Lamormaini to the emperor, Jan. 5, 1626, HHStA, Staaten., Romana, Varia, 6.

45. Magni to the Propaganda, Jan. 22, 1628, ACPF, SR 69, ff. 258–61.

46. See, for example, the minutes of the Nov. 12, 1630, meeting of a committee of the Propaganda, Tüchle, *Acta SC de Propaganda Fide*, p. 302.

47. Kroess, *Geschichte der böhmischen Provinz*, 2:1:136–44; Spiegel, "Die Prager Universitätsunion," pp. 62–63, 67, 89–90; Abgottspon, *Magni*, p. 49.

48. Kroess, *Geschichte der böhmischen Provinz*, 2:1:193–98. A copy of the plan of Lamormaini and Philippi is in ARSJ, Aust. 23, ff. 1–21, and it is summarized in Kroess, ibid., 2:1:198–205. A marginal note in Lamormaini's hand indicates that the first four chapters were read and approved by the faculty of theology of the University of Vienna, and it goes on to name them. These four chapters dealt with the emperor's obligations to reform religion in Bohemia, the personnel and procedures of the reformation commission, the long-range means of establishing the faith in Bohemia, and the emperor's obligation to return ecclesiastical property to the church. The last three chapters treated the financing of the planned reform and the circumstances under which some Protestants might be tolerated.

49. My sources for Magni's conception of the reform of religion in Bohemia are an undated "Discorso" of his in ACPF, SR 214, ff. 166–75v, and a long report on the negotiations at the imperial court sent to Rome by Harrach, ibid., ff. 193–243v. These were discussed in the May 21, 1627, meeting of the Propaganda Congregation; see the minutes in Tüchle, *Acta SC de Propaganda Fide*, p. 153; see also Abgottspon, *Magni*, pp. 32–35.

50. Magni to the Propaganda, Jan. 22, 1628, ACPF, SR 69, ff. 258–61.

51. "Vita Lamormaini," f. 55.

52. See, for example, Adam Contzen, *Politicorum Libri Decem*, p. 98.

53. Handschrift no. 1159, 1, pp. 216–18, 228–34, Universitätsbibliothek, Graz. The library contains several manuscripts of notes taken by students of Lamormaini's lectures; the manuscript cited is dated 1608. For an excellent discussion of the medieval tradition of toleration and its evolution during the period of the Reformation, see Lecler, *Toleration and the Reformation*, esp. 1:71–89, 282–304 and 2:481–82, 499–501.

54. Abgottspon, *Magni*, p. 52.

55. Ibid., pp. 39–42.

56. See his memorandum on the reform of the church in Bohemia, Kollmann, *Acta congregationis de Propaganda Fide*, 1:1:no. 4b (esp. pp. 33–34) and n. 36.

57. Becan's opinion, dated Jun. 5(?), 1623, is in HHStA, Traut. 171, at the start. A notation in Lamormaini's hand indicates that he had shown this opinion to Eggenberg in December 1625, who asked him to draft a letter seeking papal permission. I have found no record of the draft. This matter is related to the more specific question of the transfer of the lands of the Charles University to the Jesuits. Carafa originally undertook to secure papal approval for this, and he even gave the Jesuits permission to take the lands over provisionally. But he withdrew this later when he reversed his position on the university question. See Kroess, *Geschichte der böhmischen Provinz*, 2:1:134.

58. Minutes of a discussion within the Propaganda Congregation, Jul. 7, 1628, ACPF, SR 69, f. 75. Magni was the source of this report.

59. Printed in Carafa, *Commentaria*, pp. 85–94 (documentary appendix).

60. Harrach's report, ACPF, SR 214, ff. 201–5; minutes of the Propaganda Congregation, Nov. 13, 1627, Tüchle, *Acta SC de Propaganda Fide*, p. 172; Abgottspon, *Magni*, pp. 41–43.

61. Abgottspon, *Magni*, pp. 43–46; Richter, "Die böhmischen Länder von 1471–1740," pp. 365–66.

62. Hallwich, *Fünf Bücher*, 1:272.

63. BL 6949, ff. 118–24; see Duhr, 2:2:709–10.

64. For the admonitions sent Magni for his hostility to the Jesuits, see the minutes of the Propaganda Congregation, Sept. 7 and Oct. 9, 1629, Tüchle, *Acta SC de Propaganda Fide*, pp. 253, 255.

65. Re, *La Curia Romana*, pp. 367–68.

66. Carafa to Barberini, Nov. 11, 1626, Mar. 24, Jun. 9, Jul. 7, 1627, BL 6949, f. 110 ff., BL 6950, ff. 20–21, 50, 59v, 63.

67. Pastor, *Geschichte der Päpste*, 13:281–90.

68. Albrecht, "Finanzierung des Dreissigjährigen Krieges," esp. pp. 386–412; see Seppelt, *Geschichte der Päpste*, pp. 275–302, for the best appraisal of Urban's papacy.

69. Vitelleschi to Lamormaini, Jul. 6 and Aug. 24, 1624, ARSJ, Aust. 3II, ff. 518–20, 531.

Chapter 3

1. Vitelleschi to Lamormaini, Mar. 13, 1627, ARSJ, Aust. 3II, f. 809; see also the "Vita Lamormaini," ff. 45v–46, which, however, recounts events of 1624–25.

2. Ritter, *Deutsche Geschichte*, 3:346–47, 358–60, 365–67.

3. Vitelleschi to Lamormaini, Oct. 9 and 23, 1627, ARSJ, Aust. 3II, ff. 900–901, 908–9; Khevenhiller, *Annales Ferdinandei*, 11:304–6; Wiedemann, *Reformation und Gegenreformation im Lande unter der Enns*, pp. 597–666, esp.

597–600, 613–24, 647–62; Mecenseffy, *Protestantismus in Österreich*, pp. 168–69; Tomek, *Kirchengeschichte Österreichs*, pp. 524–26.

4. Mecenseffy, *Protestantismus in Österreich*, pp. 170–71; Sturmberger, *Ferdinand II*, pp. 18–20, 24; Loserth, *Geschichte der Gegenreformation in Innerösterreich unter Ferdinand II*, 1:xxxvi, 2:xlviii–xlix.

5. Mecenseffy, *Protestantismus in Österreich*, pp. 166–69, 176; for a clear reference to Lamormaini's hand in the measures for Upper Austria, see Cordara, *Historiae Societatis Jesu Pars Sexta*, 2:184; for a recent discussion of the parts played by Maximilian and Ferdinand in the Upper Austrian Counterreformation, see Sturmberger, *Adam Graf Herberstorff*, pp. 199–308 passim.

6. Mecenseffy, *Protestantismus in Österreich*, p. 173.

7. Richter, "Die böhmischen Länder von 1471–1740," pp. 287–89; Petry, "Politische Geschichte unter den Habsburgern," pp. 78–80.

8. Wedgwood, *Thirty Years War*, pp. 224–25; for a description of the trip from Vienna to Prague, see Lamormaini to Dietrichstein, Oct. 20, 1627, DA, Karton 435.

9. Goetz, "Wallenstein und Kurfürst Maximilian," esp. pp. 111–17; Ritter, *Deutsche Geschichte*, 3:295–306, 326–28.

10. Mann, *Wallenstein*, pp. 441–50; Ritter, *Deutsche Geschichte*, 3:355–56.

11. Ritter, *Deutsche Geschichte*, 3:357–58.

12. Instructions for the Bavarian delegates to the League Convention at Würzburg, Feb. 15–16, 1627, BA, 3:no. 349 (pp. 447–58); ibid., pp. 465–66; Ritter, *Deutsche Geschichte*, 3:356.

13. Vitelleschi to Lamormaini, Jun. 3, 1628, ARSJ, Aust. 3II, f. 1012; Kroess, *Geschichte der böhmischen Provinz*, 2:1:94, 218–24, 318, 342; Cordara, *Historiae Societatis Jesu Pars Sexta*, 2:187–88.

14. Cited in BA, 3:511. Goetz dates this note sometime in 1627, and he surmises its recipient was the Bavarian privy councilor Wilhelm Jocher. For Magni's contacts with Esaias Leuker, the Bavarian agent in Vienna, see Mann, *Wallenstein*, p. 533.

15. Vitelleschi to Lamormaini, Dec. 27, 1625, ARSJ, Aust. 3II, ff. 672–73; Mann, *Wallenstein*, p. 636; Ritter, *Deutsche Geschichte*, 3:299.

16. Vitelleschi to Lamormaini, Sept. 26, 1626, ARSJ, Aust. 3II, f. 746; Vitelleschi to Contzen, Sept. 26 and Oct. 10, 1626, ARSJ, GS 5, ff. 450v, 453.

17. Dec. 5, 1626, cited in the "Vita Lamormaini," f. 64; notes of Leuker, Dec. 2, 1626, BA, 3:no. 294; Duhr, 2:2:716. A statement in the "Vita Lamormaini," f. 43, indicates that at one time Ferdinand and some councilors seriously considered proposing him for the cardinalate, nor did Lamormaini deny the existence of the rumors to this effect.

18. Minutes of the negotiations of the delegates of the League in Vienna, May 10–Jun. 7, 1627, BA, 3:no. 389; Duhr, 2:2:706–7; Gindely, *Waldstein während seines ersten Generalats*, 1:256–59.

19. Mainz to Maximilian, Aug. 30, 1627, BA, 3:no. 442, and n. 2.

20. Albrecht, "Das konfessionelle Zeitalter," pp. 387–93; Bireley, *Maximilian von Bayern*, pp. 66–69.

21. Hurter, *Geschichte Ferdinands II*, 9:534, makes use of Lamormaini's paper which I have been unable to locate. There is reference in Vitelleschi to Lamormaini, Apr. 24, 1627, ARSJ, Aust. 3II, ff. 327–28, to a paper of Lamormaini on the means to maintain Catholicism in the Palatinate even if a part of it were restored to Frederick. A joint memorandum of Becan and Lamormaini on the Palatinate question is in HHStA, Staaten, Spanien, Varia 4, ff. 529–31, 532. For the background and date, see Albrecht, *Auswärtige Politik*, p. 109, and Khevenhiller (Madrid) to Ferdinand II, Nov. 23, 1623, BA, 1:no. 153, and n. 1.

22. Hurter, *Geschichte Ferdinands II*, 9:532–37.

23. From the Diary of Preysing, Sept. 12, 1626, published in Aretin, *Bayerns auswärtige Verhältnisse*, pp. 211–12; see also P. L. Carafa to Barberini, Jul. 22, 1625, ASV, NC 7, ff. 237–37v. Carafa served as nuncio from 1624 to 1635; he was not related to Carlo Carafa in Vienna. See M. Raffaeli Cammarota, "Carafa, Pier Luigi," *Dizionario Biografico degli Italiani*, 19 (Rome, 1976): 596–99.

24. Sept. 26, 1626, HHStA, Staaten., Romana, Hofkorrespondenz 9.

25. Feb. 6, 1627, ibid.

26. Carafa to Barberini, BL 6950, ff. 13–16v.

27. Undated, BA, 2:no. 272. The councilors are not identified, but the paper clearly represents the majority opinion of the privy council.

28. Carafa to Barberini, Mar. 10, 1627, BL 6950, f. 17. Here it seems appropriate to recall the limitations of the nuntiature reports as historical sources. Often the nuncios had difficulty finding out precisely what was taking place at court; sometimes they were deliberately kept in the dark or misled. See the important article by Lutz, "Glaubwürdigkeit und Gehalt von Nuntiaturberichten."

29. Günter, *Restitutionsedikt*, pp. 8–12; Bireley, *Maximilian von Bayern*, p. 76.

30. Hurter, *Geschichte Ferdinands II*, 10:26–27.

31. Jul. 25, 1627, ACPF, SR 67, ff. 144–45 (Latin trans., ff. 143–43v); Stralendorf stated in his response of Aug. 17, HHStA, Kriegs. 76, ff. 146–46v, that he had received the emperor's letter only on Aug. 11. His response was sent from Kolmb, a place I have been unable to locate but which may have been a spot where he was vacationing prior to his departure for Mühlhausen.

32. Stralendorf to the emperor, Mühlhausen, Sept. 17 and n.p., Sept. 27 (?) (incomplete draft), HHStA, RTA 97b, ff. 162–62v and Kriegs. 77, 89–90.

33. Emperor to Stralendorf, ibid., ff. 206–7v.

34. The word *all* is not used in this instruction but the sense is clearly all the lands taken since 1552. See below, n. 37.

35. Stralendorf to the emperor, Oct. 12, 1627, HHStA, RTA 97b, ff. 199–200.

36. Stralendorf to the emperor, Oct. 4, 1627, HHStA, Kriegs. 77, ff. 39–40, 41v.

37. Private minutes kept by Mainz, BA, 3:no. 470 (p. 737). The word *all* is used in the emperor's message as communicated to Mainz. Goetz, ibid., incorrectly states that Stralendorf only arrived in Mühlhausen on Oct. 22.

38. Bireley, *Maximilian von Bayern*, pp. 76–78, 82–83.

39. Ibid., pp. 78–82, 124.

40. Ritter, "Ursprung des Restitutionsedikts," p. 164.

41. See, for example, Duhr, 2:1:464.

42. Vitelleschi to Contzen, Oct. 9, 1627, ARSJ, GS 6, f. 23.

43. Anton Brück, "Das Erzstift Mainz und das Tridentinum," *Das Weltkonzil von Trient: Sein Werden und Wirken*, ed. Georg Schreiber (Freiburg, 1951), 2:238.

44. BL 6747, ff. 315–16v. This is a copy sent to Rome with Carafa's dispatch from Liège, Nov. 19, 1627, ibid., f. 311. That Ziegler was the author is clear from Carafa's dispatch of Nov. 26, ibid., f. 314.

45. Stralendorf to the emperor, Nov. 2, 1627, HHStA, RTA 97b, ff. 228–33.

46. In the original, "so weit und viel darinnen submittirt." Electors to the emperor, Nov. 4, 1627, BA, 3:no. 470 (pp. 738–40); see Ritter, "Ursprung des Restitutionsedikts," p. 169.

47. BA, 3:697, n. 1.

48. Bireley, *Maximilian von Bayern*, pp. 86–87; Ritter, *Deutsche Geschichte*, 3:372.

49. Carafa to Barberini, Nov. 3, 1627, BL 6218, ff. 253–57.

50. Bireley, *Maximilian von Bayern*, pp. 85–86.

51. Ibid., pp. 87–88.

52. The most important paper was read before the emperor, the King of Hungary, and Eggenberg on Jan. 21–22, 1628. It is in HHStA, Kriegs. 79, ff. 58–91, and it is discussed by Ritter, *Deutsche Geschichte*, 3:376, Opel, *Der niedersächsisch-dänische Krieg*, 3:449–56, and (?) Hurter, *Geschichte Ferdinands II*, 9:544–45, but they all miss, in my opinion, the note of caution. A second section of this paper is in ibid., ff. 93–97v. Another paper that I would date from early 1628 and attribute to Stralendorf is in HHStA, RTA 97b, ff. 424–29. See also Stralendorf to the emperor, Kolmb, Dec. 19, 1627, HHStA, Kriegs. 78, ff. 122–23. The two sections of the first paper are in Stralendorf's hand. In their much later position paper of Jan. 28, 1633, BAGW, 3:no. 1801, these three councilors seem to indicate they were responsible for these papers; see below, pp. 157–58, 190–91.

53. Emperor to the privy council and president of the aulic council, Jan. 15, 1628, HHStA, RTA 98, ff. 1–1v.

54. Carafa to Barberini, Dec. 8, 15, 22, 29, 1627, BL 6218, ff. 287–91, BL 6944, ff. 17–20, 21–25, 29–34.

55. Carafa to Barberini, Dec. 22, 1627, BL 6944, ff. 26–27.

56. Dec. 21, 1627, BL 6944, ff. 28–28v.

57. Vitelleschi to Lamormaini, Jan. 15, 29, and Feb. 12, 1628, ARSJ, Aust. 3II, ff. 954, 962, 976, and ARSJ, Congregationes 60, ff. 188–98.

58. BL 6951, ff. 24–29. That Carafa knew of the Catholic plans for a general restitution by Dec. 20 seems clear from Preysing's account of an interview with him on that date. According to Preysing, Carafa encouraged the Catholic electors in their design. See the Diary of Preysing, Aretin, *Bayerns auswärtige Verhältnisse*, p. 284.

59. Carafa to Barberini, Feb. 16, 1628, BL 6951, ff. 36–38.

60. Feb. 16, 1628, BL 6951, ff. 30–35v. For the background, see Heinrich Kretschmayr, *Geschichte von Venedig*, vol. 3, *Der Niedergang* (Stuttgart, 1934; reprint, Aalen, 1964), pp. 428–29.

Chapter 4

1. Albrecht, "Das konfessionelle Zeitalter," p. 387. Maximilian's attitude toward the Palatinate lands on the left bank of the Rhine was ambivalent. He does not seem to have positively coveted them for himself; but he was extremely reluctant to permit the restoration of Frederick to any part of them, and he was unhappy with the continued Spanish occupation. See Bireley, *Maximilian von Bayern*, p. 110, and n. 8.

2. Maximilian's response to Trautmannsdorf's proposal, Feb. 21, 1628, BA, 4:no. 30; Bireley, *Maximilian von Bayern*, pp. 90–91.

3. Carafa to Barberini, Feb. 9, 1628, BL 6951, ff. 24–29; Vitelleschi to Lamormaini, Feb. 12 and 19, 1628, ARSJ, Aust. 3II, ff. 973–74, 976.

4. P. L. Carafa to Barberini, Jan. 14, 1628, ASV, NC 10, f. 3.

5. Mar. 25, 1628, BL 2198, f. 40v.

6. Kiewning, 1:96, n. 2.

7. Carlo Carafa to Barberini, Feb. 9, 1628, BL 6951, ff. 24–28; Bireley, *Maximilian von Bayern*, p. 90.

8. Tupetz, "Der Streit um die geistlichen Güter," p. 434; Bireley, *Maximilian von Bayern*, pp. 104–5; Ritter, *Deutsche Geschichte*, 3:422–23; Vitelleschi to Lamormaini, Jun. 17, 1628, ARSJ, Aust. 3II, f. 1016.

9. Ritter, *Deutsche Geschichte*, 3:422–23.

10. Gebauer, *Kurbrandenburg*, p. 32; Günter, *Restitutionsedikt*, pp. 28–36.

11. Report of the aulic council with annotations of the discussion of the privy council, Jul. 7, 1628, HHStA, Religion. 33, ff. 4–5v; emperor to Mainz, Jul. 7, 1628, ibid., ff. 6–7; emperor to the Bishop of Lavant, Jul. 7, 1628, ibid., ff. 8–9v.

12. Lamormaini to Barberini, Dec. 21, 1627, BL 6944, ff. 28–29.

13. Mann, *Wallenstein*, pp. 510–16, 597–98; Ritter, *Deutsche Geschichte*, 3:381–82. Khevenhiller, *Annales Ferdinandei*, 11:61–71, prints and discusses the position papers of those at court for and against the bestowal of Mecklenburg on Wallenstein. He is also the source of the remark about the ecclesiastics. See, in addition, 11:683–700, 713.

14. Mann, *Wallenstein*, pp. 499–505, 516–18, 540–42; Ritter, *Deutsche Geschichte*, 3:376–82; Giovanni Battista Pallotto (new nuncio in Vienna) to Barberini, May 26, 1628, Kiewning 1:no. 17.

15. Mann, *Wallenstein*, pp. 523–42; Ritter, *Deutsche Geschichte*, 3:383–84, 394–95; instruction for Donnersberg's mission to Vienna, Jun. 22, 1628, BA, 4:no. 100.

16. Vitelleschi to Contzen, Jun. 24, 1628, ARSJ, GS 6, f. 9.

17. Vitelleschi to Lamormaini, Jul. 29, 1628, ARSJ, Aust. 4I, ff. 2–3; see also Vitelleschi to Contzen, Jul. 29, 1628, ARSJ, GS 6, f. 97.

18. Aug. 12 and Sept. 2, 1628, ARSJ, GS 6, ff. 102, 107.

19. Vitelleschi to Contzen, Oct. 28, 1628, ARSJ, GS 6, f. 123; Ritter, *Deutsche Geschichte*, 3:394–95.

20. Quazza, *Guerra di Mantova*, 1:7.

21. Ibid., p. 18; Posch, "Zur Tätigkeit Lamormainis," p. 383.

22. D. P. O'Connell, *Richelieu*, pp. 184–87; Ritter, *Deutsche Geschichte*, 3:397–99; Khevenhiller, *Annales Ferdinandei*, 11:31–33.

23. Quazza, *Guerra di Mantova*, 1:29, 44–47, 55, 91–92, 106, 108, 132–33, 141–46; Ritter, *Deutsche Geschichte*, 3:399; O'Connell, *Richelieu*, 186–89.

24. Quazza, *Guerra di Mantova*, 1:78, 124–25, 216, 2:358–59; O'Connell, *Richelieu*, 184–85.

25. The brief for Lamormaini, dated April 15, 1628, is in BL 2198, ff. 47v–48.

26. Vitelleschi to Lamormaini, Apr. 25 and 29, May 13, 1628, ARSJ, Aust. 3II, ff. 997–98, 1004–5, 1008.

27. Repgen, 1:1:172; Georg Lutz, "Carafa, Carlo," *Dizionario Biografico degli Italiani*, 19 (Rome, 1976), col. 512.

28. Pallotto to Barberini, May 26 and 28, 1628, Kiewning, 1:no. 17 (p. 56); ASV, NG 116, ff. 5–6 (Kiewning, 1:no. 21); Barberini to Pallotto, Jun. 10, 1628, ASV, NG 116, ff. 7–9 (Kiewning, 1:no. 29).

29. ARSJ, Aust. 23, f. 40.

30. Lamormaini to Barberini, Jul. 15, 1628, ibid., f. 44.

31. Jul. 14, 1628, ibid., ff. 42–43v.

32. Pallotto to Barberini, Aug. 19, 1628, Kiewning 1:no. 77. Lamormaini's list was sent as an enclosure with this, p. 196.

33. For Lamormaini's encouragement of Ferdinand's promotion of the Immaculate Conception as a dogma of the faith, see Wiedemann, *Reformation und Gegenreformation im Lande unter der Enns*, pp. 624–28. The Immaculate Conception was defined as a Catholic dogma in 1854.

34. Albrecht, "Finanzierung des Dreissigjährigen Krieges," p. 388. The precise nature of the concession of revenues from the two Palatinates is not clear; for references to it as well as some dissatisfaction with it, see Vitelleschi to Lamormaini, Jun. 17 and Jul. 1, 1628, ARSJ, Aust. 3II, ff. 1016, 1022–23; see also Stiegele, "Beiträge zu einer Biographie Lamormainis," p. 852.

35. Pallotto to Barberini, Dec. 9, 1628, Kiewning, 1:no. 153. Vienna formally requested Magdeburg for Leopold William on Sept. 23; Francesco Barberini assured Vienna of papal approval on Oct. 15. But problems with the juridical form of the papal approval and with the choice of an administrator for Leopold William, who was a minor, held up further action; see ibid., pp. 243–44, 268, 296–97, 306, 316, 330, 336.

36. Barberini to Pallotto, Aug. 26 and Sept. 9, 1628, Kiewning, 1:no. 82 and no. 93.

37. Lamormaini to Pallotto, undated, Kiewning, 1:no. 52 (p. 136), enclosure with Pallotto to Barberini, Jul. 22, 1628, ibid., (pp. 135–36); Pallotto to Barbe-

rini, Jul. 29, 1628, ibid., 1:no. 54; Lamormaini to Franz Christoph von Khevenhiller (imperial ambassador in Madrid), Jan. 3, 1629, ASV, NG 118, ff. 31v–33v, enclosure with Pallotto to Barberini, Jan. 6, 1629, Kiewning, 2:no. 6. There are major discrepancies between the version of Lamormaini's letter to Khevenhiller in the Vatican Archives on the one hand and, on the other, translations of it in German in Khevenhiller's *Annales Ferdinandei*, 11:595–600 and in Italian in Gualdo Priorato, *Historia delle Guerre*, pp. 244–45. Most of the material elaborated in the next paragraph of the text is missing in the Vatican version, which is not the copy sent from Vienna but a further copy. The discrepancies are probably due not to Lamormaini's failure to send an accurate copy to Rome but to the intent of the Vatican copyist to leave out delicate material. Gualdo Priorato's book first appeared in 1641 in Bologna, and subsequent editions followed in rapid succession. The author served as imperial historian in Vienna from 1664 until his death in 1678. See Coreth, *Österreichische Geschichtsschreibung*, pp. 72, 84.

38. Pallotto to Barberini, Jul. 22, 1628, Kiewning, 1:no. 52; Quazza, *Guerra di Mantova*, 1:199, 206.

39. Pallotto to Barberini, Aug. 19, 1628, Kiewning, 1:no. 76.

40. Pallotto to Barberini, Jul. 19, 22, 29, and Aug. 5, 1628, Kiewning, 1:nos. 51, 52, 54, 61; Carafa to Barberini, Jul. 22, 1628, BL 6952, ff. 89–94.

41. Lamormaini to Pallotto, Jul. 26, 1628, Kiewning, 1:no. 54 (p. 143), enclosure with Pallotto to Barberini, Jul. 29, 1628, Kiewning, ibid., (pp. 139–43); Quazza, *Guerra di Mantova*, 1:144, 152; Ritter, *Deutsche Geschichte*, 3:400–401.

42. Pallotto to Barberini, Feb. 10 and Apr. 14, 1629, Kiewning, 2:nos. 37, 87; Quazza, *Guerra di Mantova*, 1:259, 263–67, 278, 302, 322, 361; Ritter, *Deutsche Geschichte*, 3:401–6.

43. Lamormaini to Khevenhiller, Jan. 3, 1629, see above, n. 37. I have not been able to locate Khevenhiller's letter, which was dated either Nov. 7 or Nov. 17.

44. Barberini to Pallotto, Jan. 27, 1629, Kiewning, 2:no. 22.

45. Vitelleschi to Lamormaini, Mar. 3, 1629, ARSJ, Aust. 4I, ff. 70–71. What version of the letter Vitelleschi, Barberini, and Urban saw is not clear.

46. Olivares to Khevenhiller, undated, Gualdo Priorato, *Historia delle Guerre*, pp. 245–47; Khevenhiller, *Annales Ferdinandei*, 11:600–604, where it is dated Jun. 27, 1629. Both of these are translations from a presumably Spanish original.

47. Khevenhiller, *Annales Ferdinandei*, 11:604.

48. Sept. 7, 1628, HHStA, Religion. 33, ff. 12–13v, 30–31v (BA, 4:no. 134).

49. Position paper of the aulic council, Sept. 15, 1628, discussed in the privy council the next day, HHStA, Religion. 33, ff. 17–29v.

50. Carafa to Barberini, Sept. 23, 1628, BL 6952, ff. 132–135v.

51. Günter, *Restitutionsedikt*, pp. 43–44.

52. The draft is in BH, KSchw 69, ff. 110–28.

53. See Ritter, *Deutsche Geschichte*, 1:501–8.

54. BH, KSchw 69, ff. 63–65.

55. Pallotto to Barberini, Dec. 16, 1628, Kiewning, 1:no. 156.

56. BH, KSchw 69, ff. 69–70 (BA, 4:no. 159).

57. There was a great deal of confusion about the legal status of these and many other church lands. When precisely had they been secularized, when the bishop was forced to leave, for example, or when he died, perhaps years later? At the time of secularization had the bishopric been mediatized or not; that is, was it an imperial or territorial church land?

A document dated Mar. 20, 1629, HHStA, Religion. 33, ff. 121–24, shows that Stralendorf put chancery officials to work to determine the precise juridical status of these three bishoprics. This was not an easy task. Even consultation of Conrad Eubel, *Hierarchia Catholica Medii et Recentioris Aevi*, 3:242, 247, 261, leaves some doubt about the date of secularization, though it seems to indicate that Naumburg was secularized before 1552, Merseburg and Meissen afterward.

58. Bireley, "Origins of the *Pacis Compositio*," pp. 107–8, 114–15; on Laymann, see also Duhr, 2:2:411–12, and P. Bernard, "Laymann, Paul," *Dictionnaire de théologie catholique*, 9:1 (Paris, 1926):86–87.

The first edition of the *Pacis Compositio* appeared at Dillingen early in 1629, and a second, slightly expanded edition appeared that same year. The following year a German translation was published at Dillingen, partly to offset the errors in an unauthorized translation that appeared at Frankfurt early in 1630. See Duhr, 2:2:388, and n. 3.

59. Gschliesser, *Der Reichshofrat*, pp. 221–22.

60. P. 61; Bireley, "Origins of the *Pacis Compositio*," pp. 119–20. In HHStA, Religion. 33, ff. 129–35v, there is a document entitled "Pronunciata Circa Pacificationem Religionis." It is undated but is found among the documents of late 1628. In my opinion, it is clearly a summary of Laymann's *Pacis Compositio*. I disagree with the position of Helmut Urban that for the Catholics, especially in Vienna, the Edict was a *conscious "Unrechtsakt."* See Urban, *Restitutionsedikt*, pp. 214–15, and "Druck und Drucke," pp. 648–50. For a strong statement supporting the legality of the Edict, see Schwarz, *Imperial Privy Council*, p. 94.

For a discussion of Laymann's interpretation of the Peace of Augsburg, see Heckel, "*Autonomia* und *Pacis Compositio*," esp. pp. 229–43. For a much briefer discussion, see Bireley, "Origins of the *Pacis Compositio*," pp. 110–12, and see below in chap. 5.

61. Minutes and position paper of the aulic council, Jan. 14, 1629, HHStA, RHR XVII (1629) and Religion. 34^i, ff. 9–19; Bireley, *Maximilian von Bayern*, pp. 96–97.

62. Notes in Gebhardt's hand, undated but filed with material from Jan. to Mar. 1628, RTA 98^{iv}, ff. 9–20. On Gebhardt, see Gschliesser, *Der Reichshofrat*, pp. 219–21; on his conversion, see Lamormaini to Dietrichstein, Oct. 20, 1627, DA, Karton 435. The author of the "Vita Lamormaini" suggested that a copy of the manuscript be presented to Gebhardt; see Eustachius Sthaäl to Florence de Montmorency, Oct. 10, 1649, ARSJ, Vitae 139, f. 2.

63. *Pacis Compositio*, bk. vi, art. 34, no. 26 (p. 150). All references are to the first edition.

64. Position papers of the aulic council, Jan. 14 and Feb. 15, 1629, HHStA,

Religion. 34^i, ff. 9–19 and RTA 98^{iv}, ff. 63–70; minutes of the aulic council, Feb. 15, 1629, HHStA, RHR XVII (1629); position paper of the aulic council, Feb. 27–Mar. 1, 1629, HHStA, Religion. 34^i, ff. 25–33v.

65. HHStA, Religion. 34^i, f. 36v; see emperor to Maximilian, Mar. 27, 1629, BA 4:no. 255.

66. See n. 65, and the minutes of the aulic council meeting of Mar. 9, HHStA, RHR XVII (1629).

67. Bireley, "Origins of the *Pacis Compositio*," pp. 109, 119; the text of the Edict is in Londorp, *Acta Publica*, 3:1048–54. For the history of the printing of the Edict, see Urban, "Druck und Drucke."

68. Mar. 28, 1629, BL 7054, f. 72.

69. Feb. 28, 1629, DA, Karton 435.

70. Vitelleschi to Lamormaini, Apr. 21 and 28, ARSJ, Aust. 4I, ff. 95–96, 98–99.

71. Collalto to the emperor, Dec. 14, 1628, BA, 4:no. 191; on Collalto, see Schwarz, *Imperial Privy Council*, pp. 215–17.

72. Quazza, *Guerra di Mantova*, 1:313. Heydendorff, *Die Fürsten zu Eggenberg*, pp. 104–5, is much more cautious than Zwiedineck-Südenhorst, *Eggenberg*, pp. 90–91, in evaluating Eggenberg's position on the Edict in 1628–29. For the latter, Eggenberg clearly opposed it.

73. Mann, *Wallenstein*, pp. 573–600, esp. 576–77; Nolden, "Die Reichspolitik Kaiser Ferdinands II in der Publizistik," p. 150, n. 47.

74. Ritter, *Deutsche Geschichte*, 3:353, 386–93, 410–14, 417–19; Mann, *Wallenstein*, pp. 521–22, 559–72, 609–19; Messow, *Die Hansestädte und die Habsburgische Ostseepolitik*, pp. 79–82.

75. Mann, *Wallenstein*, pp. 635–39; see also Gindely, *Waldstein während seines ersten Generalats*, 2:184–86, 203. I am not as convinced as Mann that prior to its publication Wallenstein's position on the Edict was clearly known in Vienna. Urban, "Druck und Drucke," p. 642, finds it strange that there were two printings of the Edict at Rostock in Mecklenburg despite Wallenstein's opposition to the Edict.

76. Wallenstein to Lamormaini, May 27, 1629, ARSJ, Aust. 21, f. 44.

77. Mann, *Wallenstein*, pp. 646–50, 656–57; Ritter, *Deutsche Geschichte*, 3:405–06.

78. Urban VIII to the emperor, Mar. 25., 1628, BL 2198, f. 40v.

79. Minutes of the Propaganda Congregation, Oct. 24, 1628, Tüchle, *Acta SC de Propaganda Fide*, p. 206. Pallotto received Bandini's letter on Dec. 1 (not Oct. 1, as in Kiewning, 1:346, n. 4) and answered on Dec. 23, 1628, ACPF, SR 70, f. 97. See also, Barberini to Pallotto, Feb. 10, 1629, Kiewning, 2:no. 35.

80. Kiewning, 2:no. 41; see the Minutes of the Propaganda Congregation, Feb. 13, 1629, Tüchle, *Acta SC de Propaganda Fide*, p. 222.

81. Pallotto to Barberini, Mar. 3, 1629, Kiewning, 2:no. 59.

82. Pier Luigi Carafa to Barberini, Apr. 6, 1629, BL 6748, ff. 59–60.

83. "Commonitorium S. Congregationi propagandae fide de reformatione Ecclesiarum Inferioris Saxoniae," undated, BL 6886, ff. 74–80. The writer was

clearly familiar with the situation in Lower Saxony. One might speculate that Carafa himself was the author, but the tone points to a German.

On the mission of Cardinal Cajetan to the Diet of Augsburg, see Erwin Iserloh, "Die Protestantische Reformation," *Handbuch der Kirchengeschichte*, edited by Hubert Jedin, 4 (Freiburg, 1967): 53–74.

84. Pallotto to Barberini, Apr. 7, 1629, Kiewning, 2:no. 85.

85. Francesco Crivelli (Bavarian resident in Rome) to Aurelio Gigli (Bavarian aulic councilor), Apr. 28, 1629, BA, 4:no. 281.

86. Apr. 28, 1629, Kiewning, 2:no. 97.

87. Pallotto to Barberini, Jun. 9 and 16, 1629, Kiewning, 2:nos. 120, 126; P. L. Carafa to Barberini, Jul. 6 and Aug. 24, 1629, ASV, NC 11, f. 216, with enclosure, ff. 217 and 286. The minutes of the Propaganda Congregation for Jun. 22, 1629, Tüchle, *Acta SC de Propaganda Fide*, pp. 245–46, seem to indicate that Rome had not yet made up its mind on the matter.

88. Pallotto to Barberini, Aug. 18, 1629, Kiewning, 2:no. 160.

89. See, for example, the instruction of the Propaganda for Pallotto, Mar. 31, 1629, Kiewning, 2:no. 79 (pp. 129–30), and the remarks of Repgen, 1:1:176–81.

90. See the long discussion in Repgen, 1:1:162–89, esp. 183–89.

91. Kiewning, 2:no. 102. For a different interpretation of this brief, see Repgen, 1:1:183–86. Our differences are considerably reduced if it is kept in mind that Repgen is concerned with the papal understanding of the brief and my concern is the interpretation it was bound to receive in Vienna.

92. May 5, 1629, BL 6253, ff. 192–92v.

93. May 26, 1629, Kiewning, 2:no. 115.

Chapter 5

1. Khevenhiller, *Annales Ferdinandei*, 11:427–30; Hurter, *Geschichte Ferdinands II*, 10:34.

2. Ritter, *Deutsche Geschichte*, 3:437.

3. Bireley, *Maximilian von Bayern*, pp. 104–5. The term *Lower Saxon* was not always used with precision in contemporary documents when applied to ecclesiastical territories. It sometimes designated territories in the Westphalian Circle, for example. See ibid., p. 104, n. 48.

4. According to the minutes of the Propaganda Congregation, Jan. 20, 1629, and Feb. 1, 1630, Tüchle, *Acta SC de Propaganda Fide*, pp. 218, 270, it was ready in principle to approve the arrangement proposed by Wallenstein for Mecklenburg. Cf. Mann, *Wallenstein*, p. 636.

5. Khevenhiller, *Annales Ferdinandei*, 11:430–35; see also, Gebauer, *Kurbrandenburg*, p. 17. All the bishoprics mentioned in this paragraph except Schwerin were on this list.

6. The best overview of the lands claimed by the Catholics and of those actually recovered is in the map and commentary by G. Teitz, *Atlas zur Kirchengeschichte*,

edited by Hubert Jedin, Kenneth Scott Latourette, and Jochen Martin (Freiburg, 1970), pp. 63, 91. According to Teitz, by the fall of 1631 two archbishoprics, five bishoprics, two imperial abbeys, and about 150 monasteries, convents, and churches had actually been regained by the Catholics. See also Ritter, *Deutsche Geschichte*, 3:428–32, and Repgen, 1:1:158. Tupetz, "Der Streit um die geistlichen Güter," publishes in an appendix an accurate (?) list of all the lands claimed by the Catholics.

7. "Vita Lamormaini," f. 67v; on Forer, see P. Bernard, "Forer, Laurentius," *Dictionnaire de théologie catholique*, 6:1 (Paris, 1915): 539–40.

8. *Pacis Compositio*, bk. iv, art. 25, nos. 17–18 (pp. 106–7); bk. vi, art. 31, nos. 4–6 (pp. 136–38); bk. viii, art. 54, no. 1 (pp. 270–71).

9. Ibid., bk. v, art. 32, nos. 10, 13 (pp. 141–42); bk. vi, art. 42, nos. 100–101 (pp. 192–93).

10. Emperor to Mainz, Apr. 3, 1629, BH, KSchw 777, f. 103; Maximilian to Mainz, Apr. 20, 1629, ibid., f. 119 (BA, 4:no. 272).

11. Maximilian to the emperor, Apr. 26 and Jun. 25, 1629, HHStA, Religion. 34[ii], ff. 21, 161.

12. Saxony to the emperor, Apr. 6 and 28, 1629, BH, KSchw 777, ff. 114–17, and HHStA, Religion. 34[ii], ff. 25–43; Bireley, *Maximilian von Bayern*, pp. 122–23.

13. Khevenhiller, *Annales Ferdinandei*, 11:458–65. Though no precise date is given, this paper obviously discusses the Saxon response to the Edict.

14. Undated, HHStA, Traut. 102, ff. 18–18v, 27. Internal evidence shows that this was composed in mid-June, 1629. On Fanini, see Duhr, 2:2:226, on Sumerckher, ibid., 2:1:320, n. 2.

15. Emperor to Saxony, Jun. 26, 1629, HHStA, Religion. 34[ii], ff. 163–84; Pallotto to Barberini, Jun. 16 and 30, 1629, Kiewning, 1:no. 124, no. 134; Bireley, *Maximilian von Bayern*, pp. 123–24.

16. Emperor to Maximilian, Jul. 30, 1629, HHStA, Religion. 35[ii], ff. 42–43; BA, 5:17–18, n. 1.

17. Position paper, Jul. 28, 1629, HHStA, RTA 98[iii], ff. 33–37.

18. Maximilian to the emperor, Sept. 13, 1629, BH, KSchw 71, ff. 122–23.

19. Pallotto to Barberini, Mar. 30, 1630, BL 6962, ff. 128–37v.

20. Mann, *Wallenstein*, pp. 601–7, 631, 637–39.

21. Bireley, *Maximilian von Bayern*, pp. 125–27.

22. Emperor to Maximilian, Aug. 23, 1629, with enclosures, BH, KSchw 71, ff. 83–93.

23. Bireley, *Maximilian von Bayern*, pp. 127–30.

24. Forst, *Politische Correspondenz des Grafen Franz Wilhelm von Wartenberg*, no. 8 (Appendix).

25. Bireley, *Maximilian von Bayern*, pp. 123–24.

26. Heinz-Joachim Schulze, "Johann Friedrich," *Neue Deutsche Biographie*, 10 (Berlin, 1974): 481.

27. Instruction for the imperial commissioners in the Upper and Lower Saxon Circles, Mar. 27, 1629, HHStA, Religion. 34[i], ff. 96–100.

28. Presentation of the representatives of the Franconian Circle, HHStA, Religion. 35^{ii}, ff. 89–92v.

29. Report of the aulic council, Aug. 6–7, approved by the privy council, Aug. 14, 1629, HHStA, Religion. 35^{ii}, ff. 54–61v; response to the Franconian representatives, Aug. 14, 1629, ibid., ff. 95–98v. That there was some uncertainty in Vienna over this policy is clear from two letters of the emperor to Franz Wilhelm von Wartenberg, Bishop of Osnabrück, Aug. 14 and 23, ibid., ff. 93–94v and 138–40v. Wartenberg was also an imperial commissioner for the restitution of church lands for the Westphalian Circle.

30. "Vita Lamormaini," ff. 52–53; Duhr, 2:1:190.

31. Saxony to the emperor, May 11 and Aug. 22, 1629, HHStA, Religion. 32, ff. 40–41, 45.

32. Stetten, *Geschichte der Stadt Augspurg*, 2:2–11; Ritter, *Deutsche Geschichte*, 3:431.

33. *Pacis Compositio*, Preface; Heckel, "*Autonomia* und *Pacis Compositio*," pp. 229–32.

34. Paper of Gebhardt and vote, Dec. 14, 1628, HHStA, Religion. 33, ff. 318–30; Stetten, *Geschichte der Stadt Augspurg*, 2:11, 13–15, 24–27. A long report on the matter by Gebhardt and dated only Dec. 1628–Jan. 1629 is found in HHStA, Religion. 33, ff. 241–91v.

35. Maximilian to the emperor, May 1, 1629, HHStA, Religion. 34^{i}, ff. 43–46; see Bireley, *Maximilian von Bayern*, pp. 102–3.

36. "Vita Lamormaini," f. 52v; Stetten, *Geschichte der Stadt Augspurg*, 2:97–98.

37. HHStA, Religion. 32, f. 103; report of the committee of councilors, Jul. 10, 1630, HHStA, Kriegs. 88, ff. 26–27 (Lamormaini's opinion is noted on f. 27.); Stetten, *Geschichte der Stadt Augspurg*, 2:41–53, 57–58, 97–98.

38. Ritter, *Deutsche Geschichte*, 3:404–6; Quazza, *Guerra di Mantova*, 1:322, 341, 361–62.

39. Ritter, *Deutsche Geschichte*, 3:417–18, 437–40; Burckhardt, *Richelieu: His Rise to Power*, pp. 306–7.

40. Albrecht, *Auswärtige Politik*, pp. 288–89; see Quazza, *Guerra di Mantova*, 1:349, 378.

41. Pallotto to Barberini, Sept. 15, 1629, Kiewning, 2:no. 176.

42. Bishop of Mantua to Ercole Marliani (Mantuan councilor), Aug. 8, 1629, cited in Quazza, *Guerra di Mantova*, 1:395.

43. Vitelleschi to Lamormaini, Jun. 30, Jul. 14, Aug. 4, 1629, ARSJ, Aust. 4I, ff. 125–26, 129–30, 138–39; Quazza, *Guerra di Mantova*, 1:378, 387–89, 522.

44. Instruction for Sabran, Jun. 15, 1629, Avenel, *Lettres, instructions diplomatiques et papier d'état de Richelieu*, 3:343–49; imperial response for Sabran, Aug. 1, 1629, HHStA, Staaten., Frankreich, Noten 1628–35; Khevenhiller, *Annales Ferdinandei*, 11:622–38.

45. See Ciriaco Rocci (nuncio in Vienna) to Barberini, Aug. 19, 1630, Repgen, 1:2:no. 18.

46. Quazza, *Guerra di Mantova*, 1:421, 525–27, 2:37–38, 103–7, 119; Ritter, *Deutsche Geschichte*, 3:440, 447.

47. Albrecht, *Auswärtige Politik*, pp. 212–30 passim; Ritter, *Deutsche Geschichte*, 3:408–11, 440–41.

48. Mann, *Wallenstein*, pp. 646–51, 654–57; Ritter, *Deutsche Geschichte*, 3:405–7, 418–19.

49. Aug. 28, 1629, published in Gindely, *Waldstein während seines ersten Generalats*, 2:210–11; Mann, *Wallenstein*, pp. 650–51.

50. Wallenstein to Collalto, Oct. 13 and Nov. 29, 1629, Chlumecky, *Regesten*, 1:no. cclxiv, cclxxi; Pallotto to Barberini, Nov. 10, 1629, Kiewning, 2:no. 206; Count of Castro (extraordinary Spanish ambassador in Vienna) to Philip IV, Nov. 7, 1629, Günter, *Habsburgerliga*, no. 17.

51. Quazza, *Guerra di Mantova*, 1:449–50, 522, 2:18, 56–57, 66; Mann, *Wallenstein*, p. 691.

52. Albrecht, *Auswärtige Politik*, pp. 288–91.

53. See Vitelleschi to Lamormaini, Oct. 18, 1631, ARSJ, Aust. 4I, ff. 532–34; on Suffren, see Fouqueray, "Le Père Jean Suffren à la cour de Marie de Medicis et de Louis XIII." On the exchange of letters, see Pra, "Philippe IV d'Espagne et la Compagnie de Jésus."

54. Lamormaini to Suffren (copy), Nov. 24, 1629, BL 2172, ff. 117–24, and another copy, ARSJ, Franciae 32, ff. 579–80. The September letter of Suffren is lost. The Vatican copy of Lamormaini's differs somewhat from the copy in the Jesuit archives; a German translation in Klopp, *Der dreissigjährige Krieg*, 3:1:294–98, corresponds more closely to the latter. Carelessness on the part of the copyist might explain the discrepancies, but this seems unlikely. A postscript found only in the copy in the Jesuit archives deplored the fighting among Europeans and urged the application of their energies to bringing the faith to infidels. Otherwise they would destroy themselves.

55. For the domestic opposition to Richelieu in 1628–29, see Treasure, *Cardinal Richelieu and the Development of Absolutism*, pp. 107–15, and Burckhardt, *Richelieu*, pp. 313–20, 334–44.

56. Emperor to Maximilian, Jan. 29, 1630, BA, 5:no. 104, with notes; Albrecht, *Auswärtige Politik*, pp. 290–92.

57. BA, 5:280, n. 2.

58. Vitelleschi to Lamormaini, Jan. 19, 1630, ARSJ, Aust. 4I, f. 206.

59. (Copy), BL 2172, ff. 125–31v, and ARSJ, Franciae 33I, ff. 22–23. Again, there are discrepancies between the two copies.

60. Mar. 16, 1630, ARSJ, Aust. 4I, f. 243.

61. Vitelleschi to Suffren, Mar. 25, 1630, ARSJ, Franciae 5, 1, f. 312; see also Vitelleschi to Lamormaini, Oct. 18, 1631, Aust. 4I, ff. 532–34.

62. Quazza, *Guerra di Mantova*, 2:181.

63. Quazza, *Guerra di Mantova*, 2:62, 124, 143, 334; Ritter, *Deutsche Geschichte*, 3:450, 458–59.

64. Albrecht, *Auswärtige Politik*, pp. 222, 267; Mann, *Wallenstein*, pp. 680–81; Gindely, *Waldstein während seines ersten Generalats*, 2:146–50, 154–55, 163, 227–33.

Chapter 6

1. On the difficult problem of Gustav Adolph's initial war aims, see Roberts, *Gustavus Adolphus*, pp. 373–75, 417–25, and Goetze, *Die Politik des Oxenstierna*, pp. 2, 60–64, 72, 203–6, 214–21, 245–46, 252.

2. Ritter, *Deutsche Geschichte*, 3:449–51, 460–64; Albrecht, *Auswärtige Politik*, pp. 263, 266–67, 278–79.

3. On Anselm Casimir, see Anton Brück, "Anselm Casimir," *Neue Deutsche Biographie*, 1 (Berlin, 1953): 310–11.

4. Philip IV to Tursi, July 15, 1630, Günter, *Habsburgerliga*, no. 32.

5. BA, 5:414–15; Repgen, 1:1:191–92; Albrecht, *Auswärtige Politik*, pp. 264–66; Bireley, *Maximilian von Bayern*, pp. 130, 133.

6. Repgen, 1:1:194–96.

7. Barberini to Rocci, Aug. 10 and 17, 1630, Repgen, 1:2: nos. 16 and 17; see ibid., 1:1:201–22, and Albrecht, "Kurialen Anweisungen," pp. 283–84; Rocci to Barberini, Aug. 19, 1630, Repgen, 1:2:no. 18.

8. Memorandum sent to the Congregation of the Palatinate in Rome, ASV, Misc., Armarium 8, vol. 89, ff. 464–66. The author is designated only as *"Inquisitor Coloniensis."* On his identity, see below, n. 85.

The short-lived Congregation of the Palatinate was originally set up to deal with the restoration of Catholicism in the Palatinate after the Catholics conquered it in 1623. Its competence extended for a time to other parts of Germany, especially Lower Saxony, before the Propaganda absorbed it. See Tüchle, *Acta SC de Propaganda Fide*, p. 6, and Weech, "Mitteilungen aus dem Vatikanischen Archiv."

9. For this and the following two paragraphs, see d'Addio, *Il Pensiero Politico di Scioppio*, esp. pp. 1–37, 66, 106–21, 128, 145–49, 154–77, 191–95, 216–19. The Laurentian Library in Florence possesses considerable manuscript material of Schoppe. Especially important for this study are Codici Scioppiani nos. 220, 223, and 243. No. 220 contains correspondence of Schoppe for the period 1626–33. No. 223, entitled "De Vita Sua," contains autobiographical material for the period 1630–36. No. 243 is an autobiographical piece of 478 pages called "Philoteca" and edited in 1643. For an analysis of its contents, see G. Gabrieli, "La 'Philoteca Scioppiana' in un manoscritto Laurenziano," *Atti della Reale Accademia d'Italia*, Classe di Scienze Morali e Storiche, Series 7, 1 (Rome, 1940): 228–39. On these sources, see d'Addio, ibid., who publishes copious extracts in an appendix and cites them extensively in the notes.

10. *Classicum belli sacri; sive Heldus redivivus.*

11. The full title of this manuscript was "Ars servandi animas Regum ac Principum. Accessit Lucerna scrutandae Principum conscientiae seu secretum examen." Schoppe exhorted rulers not to be the *"succubi"* of their confessors. See d'Addio, *Il Pensiero Politico di Scioppio*, pp. 195–97.

12. Philip IV to Tursi, Jul. 23, 1630, Günter, *Habsburgerliga*, no. 34.

13. Ziegler to Theodor Busaeus (German assistant to Vitelleschi in Rome), Jul. 15, 1630, ARSJ, Boh. 94, f. 275.

14. On Peñalosa, see Duhr, 2:2:236, on Weingartner, Duhr, 2:2:235, and below, chap. 10, n. 55.

15. Lamormaini to Busaeus, Jul. 22, 1630, ARSJ, Boh. 94, f. 276.

16. Ziegler to Busaeus, Jul. 29, 1630, ARSJ, Boh. 94, f. 279.

17. Minutes, BA, 5:440–41; see also the minutes for the meeting of Jul. 10. (In BA 5, all the documentation for the Convention of Regensburg is comprised under no. 170, which runs for 315 pages. For this reason, I indicate the page rather than the document number.)

18. Minutes, BA, 5:454–455, and n. 2; see Gebauer, *Kurbrandenburg*, pp. 96–97.

19. Minutes of the audience of the Catholic electors with the emperor, BA, 5:471–72, and n. 3.

20. Mann, *Wallenstein*, pp. 679, 706–15; Ritter, *Deutsche Geschichte*, 3:455–56. The crucial paper of the privy council of August 5 is printed in Gindely, *Waldstein während seines ersten Generalats*, 2:280–87. Privy councilors were asked to submit individual papers earlier, but these have not survived.

21. There is little direct evidence that Lamormaini urged the removal of Wallenstein, but all the indirect evidence points toward this conclusion, which historians have generally accepted. Contzen, for example, in his highly critical letter to Lamormaini of Jun. 8, 1631, would certainly have accused him of supporting Wallenstein if there had been any substance to the charge; see below, n. 37. There is no evidence that either the Curia or Vitelleschi tried to influence Lamormaini on the Wallenstein issue at this time.

22. Published in Dudik, "Korrespondenz Kaiser Ferdinands," p. 273. Further evidence that the electors were discontent with Eggenberg can be found in the Sept. 16 report of the Tuscan representative at Regensburg, Niccolò Sacchetti, cited in BA, 5:704. The reasons Sacchetti gives are vague and deal only with Eggenberg's general mode of government.

23. Zwiedineck-Südenhorst, *Eggenberg*, p. 91, writes that at the decisive moment Eggenberg apparently did not exert all his power to retain the general.

24. Bireley, *Maximilian von Bayern*, p. 116; Albrecht, *Auswärtige Politik*, pp. 272–74.

25. Minutes of the conference of the imperial councilors and their position paper, Aug. 15–16, 1630, BA, 5:507–8, 510–13.

26. BA, 5:513.

27. See Saxony and Brandenburg to Mainz, Oct. 7, 1630, BA, 5:691–93, with notes.

28. Minutes of the conference of the deputies of the Catholic electors, Oct. 26, 1630, BA, 5:652–54.

29. This Sept. 3 letter of Saxony to the emperor was discussed at the Sept. 16 conference of the deputies of the Catholic electors; see the minutes, BA, 5:580–85, and 678.

30. Bireley, *Maximilian von Bayern*, pp. 116–17.

31. Published in Dudik, "Korrespondenz Kaiser Ferdinands," pp. 337–38.

32. Bireley, *Maximilian von Bayern*, pp. 115–16.

33. Ibid., pp. 117, 135; Ritter, *Deutsche Geschichte*, 3:455, 457–58.
34. Philippe Alegambe to Vitelleschi, ARSJ, Boh. 94, f. 285.
35. Vitelleschi to Contzen, Nov. 9, 1630, ARSJ, GS 6, f. 302.
36. Contzen's manuscript was entitled "Ad XII Argumenta seu Rationes quibus Romanorum Imperator Motus, quominus Electori Bavariae Supremum Exercitus Caesarei Directorium sive Regimen Censuerit Deferendum, a Fidelissimo Consiliario Austriaco Propositas Responsio Fidelissimi Consiliarii Caesareani ex Officio Demissione Oblata Sacrae Caesareae Majestati." A copy is in BH, Jesuitica 704, ff. 15–22. For a discussion of this manuscript and Contzen's conversation, see Bireley, *Maximilian von Bayern*, pp. 118–20.
37. Contzen to Lamormaini, Jun. 8, 1631, BH, Jesuitica 704, ff. 23–24; Lamormaini sent his response to Casper Hell, rector of the Jesuit college in Neuburg, Jun. 25, 1631, BH, Kriegs. 212, ff. 36–37. Annotations on this letter in Contzen's hand outlined points for Hell in his reply, which if ever sent has not survived.
38. Albrecht, *Auswärtige Politik*, pp. 270, 285, 292; Quazza, *Guerra di Mantova*, 2:188–95; O'Connell, *Richelieu*, p. 209.
Albrecht has shown that the two French emissaries did not influence the electors in the matter of Wallenstein or the election of the King of the Romans; see *Auswärtige Politik*, pp. 267–71, 274–81. The electors made their decisions independently of French influence, though of course they eminently suited French policy.
Hermann von Questenberg served in the aulic council from 1626 to 1637, and he was the secretary in the imperial chancery responsible for Latin correspondence for many years. See Gross, *Geschichte der Reichshofkanzlei*, pp. 418–20. On Nostitz, see Schwarz, *Imperial Privy Council*, pp. 315–16.
39. Magni to Pallotto, Oct. 12, 1630, Repgen, 1:2:no. 21; Quazza, *Guerra di Mantova*, 2:61–62, 196.
40. Rocci to Barberini, Aug. 19, 1630, Repgen, 1:2:no. 18.
41. Vitelleschi to Lamormaini, Oct. 12 and 25, 1630, ARSJ, Aust. 4I, ff. 344, 346–48. The latter is a response to Lamormaini's of Sept. 25 and 30.
42. The text of the Treaty of Regensburg is in Dumont, *Corps universel diplomatique*, 5:2:615–18. See also Quazza, *Guerra di Mantova*, 2:202, n. 2, and Albrecht, *Auswärtige Politik*, pp. 293–95.
43. Rocci to Barberini, Nov. 11, 1630, Repgen, 1:2:no. 25.
44. Klopp, *Der dreissigjährige Krieg*, 3:2:16–19; Burckhardt, *Richelieu*, pp. 370–77; Albrecht, *Auswärtige Politik*, p. 293. For a discussion especially of the legal aspects of Richelieu's refusal to ratify the treaty and the stimulus it gave to the development of international law, see O'Connell, "A *Cause Célèbre* in the History of Treaty-Making." Father Joseph later claimed that he and Brûlart de Léon had made it clear to the imperial negotiators that in some points they were going beyond their instructions. See Hugo Grotius to Axel Oxenstierna, Mar. 15, 1635, *Hugonis Grotii Epistolae Quotquot reperiri potuerunt* (Amsterdam, 1687), p. 135, cited in O'Connell, ibid., p. 89, n. 1.
45. Bireley, *Maximilian von Bayern*, p. 133.
46. Tupetz, "Der Streit um die geistlichen Güter," p. 315.

47. Gebauer, *Kurbrandenburg*, p. 105; Bireley, *Maximilian von Bayern*, p. 133.

48. Pallotto (Vienna) to Barberini, Aug. 2, 1630, Repgen, 1:2: no. 15; Rocci to Barberini, Sept. 2, 1630, BL 6967, ff. 39–48.

49. Minutes, Aug. 3, 1630, BA, 5:473–75. For Contzen's general position and especially his attitude toward France, see Bireley, *Maximilian von Bayern*, pp. 113, 131, 138, 155–56, 168–70.

50. Minutes, Aug. 19, 1630, BA, 5:518–20.

51. Lamormaini to the emperor, Sept. 18 and Oct. 14, 1630, published in Dudik, "Korrespondenz Kaiser Ferdinands," pp. 337–39.

52. Schoppe, "Philoteca," CS 243, ff. 441–46. These folios and the following up to f. 478 contain long and bitter criticism of Ferdinand, Lamormaini, and the Jesuits. They must be used with caution because of Schoppe's strong anti-Jesuit bias that will be discussed later.

53. D'Addio, *Il Pensiero Politico di Scioppio*, pp. 195–98.

54. See above, chap. 5, n. 37.

55. HHStA, Religion. 35ᴵⱽ, ff. 37–39v.

56. Emperor to Saxony, Aug. 23, 1630, HHStA, RTA 100aⁱⁱⁱ, ff. 70–74; BA, 5:677–678.

57. Emperor to Saxony, Sept. 19–20, 1630, HHStA, RTA 100aⁱⁱⁱ, ff. 66–71; Pallotto to Barberini, Oct. 5, 1630, cited in Repgen, 1:1:224, n. 128; BA, 5:679.

58. Bireley, *Maximilian von Bayern*, p. 135.

59. Vitelleschi to Lamormaini, Nov. 23, 1630, ARSJ, Aust. 4I, f. 355; he is responding to Lamormaini's of Oct. 5, 14, and 20.

60. This quotation and its context are taken from a manuscript prepared for the Elector of Trier in 1636 entitled "De praesentibus Sacri Romani Imperii calamitatibus earumque causis et remediis." It is cited in d'Addio, *Il Pensiero Politico di Scioppio*, pp. 197–98, n. 193, from Schoppe's "De Vita Sua," CS 223, ff. 60–71. A similar passage is found in Schoppe's "Philoteca," CS 243, f. 446; see also f. 450.

Despite his anti-Jesuit bias and the time lapse between the events he reports and his writing about them, Schoppe's account here is, in my opinion, essentially trustworthy. To be sure, he may have embellished a bit or telescoped events. From his account, it is not completely clear whether Maximilian and Tursi went to Lamormaini together or not. The more probable reading of the text is that they did, unlikely as this may seem.

61. "Discurs uber des Reichs statum" (after 1637), published in Albrecht, *Auswärtige Politik*, pp. 379–81; see below, n. 80.

62. Minutes, BA, 5:643–46.

63. The next day Rocci wrote Barberini, BL 6967, ff. 169–72, that he hoped the Catholics would not purchase peace by a suspension of the Edict. He had raised the matter and had been reassured that nothing would be done without proper consideration and consultation of the theologians. Repgen, 1:1:226, assumes it was Maximilian who reassured him. Rocci did not write this, but it is probable from the context.

64. Minutes, BA, 5:646–48.

65. Minutes of the meeting of the imperial councilors, BA, 5:648–49.

66. Minutes of the conference of the deputies of the Catholic electors, BA, 5:652–54; see also the minutes of the meeting of the Bavarian privy council, Oct. 28, 1630, BA, 5:654–55. In his instruction for the delegates to the Frankfurt Conference, Jan. 27, 1631, HHStA, RTA 101aⁱ, ff. 5–8, Ferdinand stated clearly he had approved contacts with the Protestants at Regensburg.

67. Bireley, *Maximilian von Bayern*, p. 137; see also the imperial instruction mentioned in the previous note.

68. Emperor to Franz Wilhelm von Wartenberg and Johann von Hyen, HHStA, Religion. 35ⁱᵛ, ff. 66–66v; see Klopp, "Restitutionsedikt," p. 125.

69. Pallotto (Vienna) to Barberini, Aug. 2, 1630, Repgen, 1:2:no. 15; see the discussion in ibid., 1:1:203–4.

70. *Status Particularis*, pp. 39–41. The author refers to an undated (final?) report of Pallotto for Urban VIII that I have not located. The author's treatment of Ferdinand is very positive.

71. Rocci to Barberini, BL 6967, ff. 39–48; see also above, n. 63.

72. See above, n. 7.

73. Albrecht, *Auswärtige Politik*, pp. 282–84.

74. Ibid., pp. 253–57, 303–4. Despite repeated French efforts to convince him to be a candidate for the imperial office, Maximilian never considered this seriously. See, for example, ibid., pp. 219–20.

75. Vitelleschi to Lamormaini, Dec. 14, 1630, ARSJ, 4I, f. 373.

76. Nov. 30 and Dec. 14, 1630, ibid., ff. 363–65, 373; these were responses to Lamormaini's of Oct. 28, Nov. 4 and 11.

77. Position paper of the imperial councilors, Oct. 18, 1631, BAGW, 1:no. 393. Though a list is given of those present at the privy council session that approved this paper, it is impossible to tell which individuals endorsed it, though a majority certainly did. See also Khevenhiller, *Annales Ferdinandei*, 11:1126–27, 1483.

78. Eggenberg did not leave Regensburg for good in early September, as Heydendorff, *Die Fürsten zu Eggenberg*, pp. 108–9, surmises. Minutes of a conference of Nov. 7–8 show that he was still there then; see BA, 5:663. Minutes of a meeting in Vienna on Jan. 11, 1631, show that he was present; see HHStA, RTA, 101aⁱⁱ, ff. 32–32v. A letter to Wallenstein, dated Mar. 28, 1631, and cited by Zwiedineck-Südenhorst, *Eggenberg*, p. 101, indicates he had retired to Graz by then.

79. Eggenberg to Ferdinand II, Apr. 20, 1631, printed in Zwiedineck-Südenhorst, *Eggenberg*, pp. 192–97.

80. "Discurs über des Reichs statum," published in Albrecht, *Auswärtige Politik*, pp. 379–81. This manuscript dates from 1637 or later, since it refers to Ferdinand as deceased. Corrections in Maximilian's own hand guarantee that it represents his thought. It is a short interpretation of the events between 1624 and 1635 that was probably drawn up as a background paper for some stage of the peace negotiations between 1637 and 1648 and was meant to justify concessions to the Protestants. See Bireley, *Maximilian von Bayern*, pp. 222–23.

81. The "Articuli Acatholicorum, welche sie zu Regenspurg ubergeben," or Hessian Points, are published in BA, 5:680–85; the "Gegenerclerung uf die proponirte mittel zur gutlichen vergleichung der religionsstrittigkeiten," or Catholic Response, in BA, 5:685–90; see Bireley, *Maximilian von Bayern*, p. 137.

82. Bireley, *Maximilian von Bayern*, p. 140.

83. For a more complete analysis of these papers as well as of a commentary of Laymann on both of them, see Bireley, *Maximilian von Bayern*, pp. 140–43.

84. Jan. 11, 1631, BL 7054, ff. 78–79.

85. "Consilium theologicum cuiusdam monachi Dominicani et celebris professoris," BH, Kriegs. 242, 22 folios. The probable author of this was Cosmas Morelles, a Spanish Dominican, professor of theology at the University of Cologne and apostolic inquisitor for Cologne, Mainz, and Trier. On Morelles, see Andreas Kraus, "Die *Annales Ecclesiastici* des Abraham Bzovius und Maximilian I von Bayern," *Reformata Reformanda: Festgabe für Hubert Jedin*, ed. Erwin Iserloh and Konrad Repgen, 2 (Freiburg, 1965): 262 ff., and "Morelles (Cosme Gil)," *Enciclopedia Universal Ilustrada*, 36 (Madrid, n.d.): 993–94.

86. Burckhardt, *Richelieu*, pp. 370–402; O'Connell, *Richelieu*, pp. 228–42.

87. O'Connell, *Richelieu*, pp. 243–49, 271–72, 351–53, 416–25.

Chapter 7

1. Günter, *Restitutionsedikt*, p. 144.

2. From the very beginning, Jesuit colleges were centers of pastoral activity as well as educational institutions. See Ladislaus Lukács, "De origine collegiorum externorum deque controversiis circa eorum paupertatem obortis," *Archivum Historicum Societatis Jesu*, 29 (Rome, 1960):189–245, and 30 (Rome, 1961):3–89, esp. 46–49 and 59–60; George E. Ganss, "The Origins of Jesuit Colleges for Externs and the Controversies about their Poverty, 1539–1608," *Woodstock Letters*, 91 (Woodstock, Md., 1962):126–27, 132–36, 140–41, 144–45, 148, 150–66. Ganss's article is a translation and condensation of that of Lukács.

3. "Vita Lamormaini," f. 47; cf. Lamormaini to Vitelleschi, Oct. 5, 1624, ARSJ, Aust. 23, ff. 28–28v.

4. The novitiates were in Vienna and Leoben in Styria, and the seminaries in Graz, Olomouc, Prague, and Klagenfurt.

5. "Vita Lamormaini," f. 55; Duhr, 2:1:323–24; Kroess, *Geschichte der böhmischen Provinz*, 2:1:285. On Althan, see Josef Sokoll, "Althan, Michael Adolf Graf v.," *Neue Deutsche Biographie*, 1 (Berlin, 1953): 219–20.

6. Lamormaini to Ferdinand III, Mar. 31, 1637, Benedictine Monastery of Pannonhalma (Hungary), Archives no. 16 (119 A2).

7. Carafa to Barberini, Feb. 16, 1628, BL 6951, ff. 36–38.

8. "Vita Lamormaini," ff. 56v–58; this is referred to in Vitelleschi to Lamormaini, Mar. 2, 1630, ARSJ, Aust. 4I, f. 240.

9. Vitelleschi to Lamormaini, Jan. 15, 1628, ARSJ, Aust. 3II, f. 954.

10. Vitelleschi to Lamormaini, Feb. 15, 1628, ARSJ, Aust. 3II, f. 976.

11. Vitelleschi to Lamormaini, Sept. 2, 1628, ARSJ, Aust. 4I, f. 15; see Duhr, 2:2:160.

12. See, for example, Tilly to Lamormaini, Stade, Nov. 30, 1629, BH, Jesuitica 648.

13. *Justa Defensio Sanctissimi Romani Pontificis, Augustissimi Caesaris . . . demum minimae Societatis Jesu . . .* , pp. 6–14; to bolster his case for the authority of the Holy See in such matters, Laymann gave eleven pages of examples in which Rome had transferred monasteries from one order to another, Appendix, pp. 10–21.

14. On the Bursfeld Congregation, see Paulus Volk, "Bursfeld, Abbey of," *New Catholic Encyclopedia*, 2 (New York, 1967):905–6. Laymann's argument also applied to the Premonstratensians and to the canons, or canonesses, regular of St. Augustine, who did not constitute a religious order and are not to be confused with the Augustinian Friars or Augustinians.

15. ASV, NG 118, ff. 36v–38, enclosure with Pallotto to Barberini, Jan. 6, 1629, Kiewning, 2:no. 8. This short paper points out that in dealing with the recovered monasteries in the Palatinate, the pope distinguished between monasteries that belonged to a congregation and those that did not. Nevertheless, the monastery went to Harrach; see Barberini to Pallotto, Feb. 3, 1629, ASV, NG 118, f. 44.

16. Günter, *Restitutionsedikt*, pp. 40–45.

17. Imperial decrees of Nov. 20, 1628 (Premonstratensians), Jan. 17 (Benedictines), and Feb. 15, 1629 (Cistercians), printed in Hay, *Astrum Inextinctum*, pp. 390–94. The references to the *Astrum Inextinctum* are to the first edition (n.p., 1636), a copy of which is in the Vatican Library. There is another first edition (Cologne, 1636), with a different pagination; a copy of it is in the Harvard Law Library. See also Günter, *Restitutionsedikt*, pp. 45–46.

18. BL 7054, ff. 70–70v.

19. Position paper of the committee of councilors, Feb. 1, 1629, HHStA, Religion. 34^i, ff. 21–23v; see Duhr, 2:2:116, and notes.

20. Mar. 27, 1629, ibid., ff. 96–100.

21. Printed in Hay, *Astrum Inextinctum*, pp. 388–89.

22. Emperor to Wilhelm Mundbrot (Jesuit provincial superior in Munich), May 9, 1629, printed in Laymann, *Justa Defensio*, pp. 546–47.

23. Emperor to the commissioners for the Swabian Circle, printed in Laymann, *Justa Defensio*, pp. 544–45; Duhr, 2:2:163–64. See the letter of Vitelleschi thanking Ferdinand effusively for his efforts on behalf of the colleges, Sept. 1, 1629, ARSJ, Germ. 113I, ff. 394–95.

24. Memorial for the Fathers Rector in Constance and Hall, BH, Jesuitica 649, f. 6. This is dated only Ingolstadt, Jul. 29, but the content points clearly to 1629.

25. Minutes of the Propaganda Congregation, Mar. 6 and 23, 1629, Tüchle, *Acta SC de Propaganda Fide*, pp. 227–28, 232.

26. Barberini to Pallotto, Jul. 21, 1629, Kiewning, 2:no. 146. A letter of Lamormaini to Barberini, Jul. 14, 1629, BL 7054, f. 74, refers to Barberini's response to the confessor's of Mar. 10 and 12 (!); this response has not survived.

27. Pallotto to Barberini, Sept. 22, 1629, with an enclosure, Pallotto to the emperor, undated, Kiewning, 2:no. 182. See also Laymann, *Justa Defensio*, Proemium, nos. 6–7 (unpaginated).

28. Printed in Hay, *Astrum Inextinctum*, pp. 385–87, and in P. L. Carafa, *Legatio Apostolica*, pp. 195–97. According to the letter of Lamormaini cited below in n. 31, copies of this letter were sent to "nearly all the bishops of Germany." See also Laymann, *Justa Defensio*, Proemium, nos. 7–10, and Günter, *Restitutionsedikt*, pp. 145–46.

29. Emperor to Savelli, printed in Hay, *Astrum Inextinctum*, p. 389; emperor to the imperial commissioners of the Swabian Circle, Dec. 12, 1629, printed in Laymann, *Justa Defensio*, p. 548.

30. Laymann, *Justa Defensio*, Proemium, nos. 10–13.

31. Lamormaini to Theodor Busaeus, Jan. 12, 1630, ARSJ, Boh. 94, ff. 262–63.

32. Lamormaini to the emperor (extract), undated, printed in Laymann, *Justa Defensio*, pp. 325–26.

33. Ibid., Proemium, nos. 14–15.

34. Lamormaini to P. L. Carafa, Nov. 21, 1629 (copy), ASV, Misc., Armarium 8, vol. 90, f. 183. Carafa was not indicated clearly as the addressee of this letter; that he was the addressee is shown by his letter to Barberini of Dec. 7, ibid., ff. 239–240v, with which Lamormaini's letter was enclosed. See also P. L. Carafa, *Legatio Apostolica*, pp. 67–74, and Duhr, 2:2:164–66.

35. Cosmas Morelles, OP, to the Elector of Cologne (extract), Rome, Jan. 26, 1630, enclosure with Elector of Cologne to Franz Wilhelm von Wartenberg, Bonn, Feb. 18, 1630, Forst, *Politische Korrespondenz des Grafen Franz Wilhelm von Wartenberg*, no. 376. The congregation's decision was reached on Jan. 22. On the Congregation of the Palatinate, see above, chap. 6, n. 8.

36. BL 2200, f. 84. Savelli to the emperor, Jan. 26, 1630, printed in Laymann, *Justa Defensio*, pp. 415–16, shows that Savelli himself thought the emperor wanted the monasteries returned to the former owners.

37. Vitelleschi to Lamormaini, Feb. 23, 1630, ARSJ, Aust. 4I, f. 237.

38. *De monasteriorum ab haereticis recuperatorum translatione disceptatio* (n.p., n.d.); see Günter, *Restitutionsedikt*, p. 167, who gives a much longer alternative title found also in Laymann, *Justa Defensio*, Proemium, no. 4, *Disceptatio seu quaestio.* . . .

39. *Ad sacram caesaream majestatem judicium duorum theologorum super translatione restituendorum in imperio monasteriorum ab antiquis ordinibus ad societatem Jesu* (n.p., n.d.).

40. Günter, *Restitutionsedikt*, pp. 145–46, 175.

41. Klopp, "Restitutionsedikt," pp. 123–24. The Propaganda Congregation discussed these plans and referred them to the Congregation of the Palatinate on May 21, 1630; see Tüchle, *Acta SC de Propaganda Fide*, p. 285.

42. Lamormaini to Busaeus, Regensburg, Jul. 22, 1630, ARSJ, Boh. 94, f. 276.

43. Sept. 30, 1630, BL 6937, ff. 117–22v.

44. For the Bishop of Würzburg's support of Lamormaini, see the "Vita Lamormaini," f. 56; for other bishops, see Duhr, 2:2:167, n. 1.

45. Günter, *Restitutionsedikt*, pp. 151–52, 161–64.
46. Ibid., pp. 151–52, 161–64; see esp. the letter from Mundbrot to Schönhainz, Regensburg, Aug. 18, 1630, cited on p. 152, n. 1.
47. Hay, *Astrum Inextinctum*, pp. 262–63, 270–75.
48. Lamormaini to the Abbot of Kaisheim, Oct. 7, 1630, printed in Hay, *Astrum Inextinctum*, pp. 267–68; for the intervening correspondence, see ibid., pp. 263–67.
49. Hay, *Astrum Inextinctum*, pp. 268–69; for Abbot Anton's later view, Hay cites a letter of R. P. Ernst Schmuter, presumably a Cistercian or Benedictine, to the Abbot of Kaisheim, May 7, 1631.
50. Lamormaini to the emperor, undated, HHStA, GK 25, ff. 518–19v; there is a German translation of this in Klopp, *Der dreissigjährige Krieg*, 3:1:428–31. From Lamormaini's letter of Oct. 7 to the Abbot of Kaisheim (see n. 48), it is possible to date Lamormaini's paper Oct. 4 or 5. Cf. Duhr, 2:2:166, who mentions but fails to analyze this document.
51. Emperor to Savelli, Apr. 25, 1630, printed in Hay, *Astrum Inextinctum*, pp. 389–90.
52. *Abbot-General* would have been the proper term. On the government of the Cistercians, see Louis J. Lekai, "Cistercians," *New Catholic Encyclopedia* 3 (New York, 1967): 118–19.
53. Emperor to the pope, ARSJ, Germ. 119, ff. 314–16; emperor to Savelli, Oct. 16, 1630, ibid., ff. 316–17v, with enclosure, ff. 318–18v, listing the foundations the emperor desired to be transferred to the Society. See also the "Vita Lamormaini," ff. 55v–56, and Duhr, 2:2:167.
54. ARSJ, Germ. 119, ff. 318v–319. This copy was notarized on Nov. 27, 1641, and was sent to Rome on Feb. 9, 1642, along with a number of other documents including the letters from Germ. 119 cited in n. 53; see the covering letter of Emperor Ferdinand III to Duke Federigo Savelli (successor to his father as imperial ambassador in Rome), ibid., ff. 296–98. The occasion was an attempt by Vitelleschi to determine precisely what lands the German colleges owned and especially to settle a disagreement with Count Johann Ludwig von Nassau-Hademar (1590–1643). Johann Ludwig converted from Calvinism to Catholicism in Vienna in 1629 under Lamormaini's direction, and later as an aulic councilor he undertook diplomatic missions for the emperor. See Joachim, "Johann Ludwig," *Allgemeine Deutsche Biographie*, 14 (Leipzig, 1881):258–60.
55. Rocci to Barberini, Oct. 22, 1630, BL 6967, ff. 163–68.
56. BL 6967, ff. 163–68.
57. *Pro Sacra Caesarea Maiestate eiusdemque ad suum Oratorem instructione super impediendis antiquarum fundationum mutationibus, suscepta defensio contra Judicium duorum theologorum super translatione restituendorum in Imperio monasteriorum ab antiquis ordinibus ad Societatem Jesu* (n.p., 1630).
58. D'Addio, *Il Pensiero Politico di Scioppio*, pp. 211–12, attributes this to Schoppe; Günter, *Restitutionsedikt*, pp. 168–69, to Hay.
59. Günter, *Restitutionsedikt*, pp. 172–73. Copies of the *Amica Responsio cujusdam theologi e societate Jesu ad quaedam eidem objecta* (n.p., 1630) and the

Disceptatio placida super Famosa quaestione (n.p., 1630) are in the Bavarian State Library in Munich. Further evidence that Contzen was the author of these can be found in BH, Jesuitica 883/2, f. 207 ff., where there are notes of his for another contribution to the polemic. See also Vitelleschi to Mundbrot, Dec. 7, 1630, ARSJ, GS 6, f. 309.

60. Günter, *Restitutionsedikt*, p. 181; see also Duhr, 2:2:167.

61. Paul Laymann, *Censura Astrologiae ecclesiasticae et Astri inextincti, a Gaspare Scioppio in lucem editi*, 2d ed. (Cologne, 1638), p. 153. The preface of the *Justa Defensio* is dated Jan. 20, 1631.

62. Vitelleschi to Mundbrot, Jan. 25 and Feb. 2, 1631, ARSJ, GS 6, ff. 319–20.

63. Vitelleschi to Laymann, May 3, 1631, ARSJ, GS 6, f. 348.

64. *Astrologia Ecclesiastica, Hoc est Disputatio de Claritate ac multiplici Stellarum in Ecclesiae firmamento fulgentium, id est, Ordinum Monasticorum*, and *Astrum Inextinctum, id est, Causae Dictio ex divino humanoque iure pro veterum Ordinum honore ac patrimoniis adversus famosum volumen Pauli Laimanni Jesuitae in Monachos editum* (n.p.); see d'Addio, *Il Pensiero Politico di Scioppio*, p. 212.

65. See above, n. 61, where a second edition is cited.

66. See above, nn. 17 and 64. This edition was still called the first edition and carried an extended title different from the 1634 edition.

67. See, for example, the books of two Jesuits, Valentinus Mangioni, *Astri Inextincti Theoricae sive Jus Agendi antiquorum ordinum pro recipiendis Monasteriis quae non nemo male appellat sua, confutatum* (Cologne, 1639), and Johann Crusius, *Astri inextincti a Gaspari Scioppio et f. Romano Hay benedictino in orbem evulgata. Eclipsis seu deliquium propositis variis quaestionibus* (Cologne, 1639). For further contributions, see I. Gordon, "El sujeto de dominio de los colegios de la Compañia de Jesús en la Controversa alemana sobre la restitucion de los monasteros," pp. 17–19.

68. Günter, *Restitutionsedikt*, p. 167.

69. Printed in Hay, *Astrum Inextinctum*, pp. 267–68.

70. *Astrum Inextinctum*, pp. 338–39.

71. Pp. 110–23, esp. 121–22.

72. D'Addio, *Il Pensiero Politico di Scioppio*, pp. 213–14, 219. For a good assessment of Schoppe's attitude toward the Jesuits, see ibid., pp. 39–48, 110, 213–25.

73. *Actio perduellionis in Jesuitas juratos S.R. Imperii hostes* or *Flagellum Jesuiticum* (n.p., 1632), and *Anatomia Societatis Jesu* (n.p., 1633). The first was published under the pseudonym Philoxenus Melander, the second under the pseudonym "Sanctii Galindi e Societate Jesu." For a list of the titles of Schoppe's anti-Jesuit works, published or manuscript, see d'Addio, *Il Pensiero Politico di Scioppio*, pp. 211–14.

74. D'Addio, *Il Pensiero Politico di Scioppio*, 213–14. This suggests an area for future research.

75. Grenzinus to Vitelleschi, Jan. 29, 1628, ARSJ, Aust. 23, ff. 50–51; Vitelleschi to Grenzinus, Feb. 26, 1628, ARSJ, Boh. I, 1, ff. 223–24.

76. Vitelleschi to Dombrinus, Feb. 26, 1628, ARSJ, Aust. 3II, f. 977.

77. Vitelleschi to Lamormaini, Mar. 21 and Apr. 15, 1628, ARSJ, Aust. 3II, ff. 984–85, 993–94; see the "Vita Lamormaini," f. 66.

78. Feb. 16, 1630, ARSJ, Aust. 4I, f. 223.

79. Vitelleschi to Dombrinus, Jan. 13, 1629, ARSJ, Aust. 4I, f. 60.

80. Vitelleschi to Montmorency, Jul. 13, Aug. 24, and Sept. 7, 1630, ARSJ, Aust. 4I, ff. 299, 320, 324.

81. Vitelleschi to Lamormaini, Aug. 31, 1630, ARSJ, Aust. 4I, ff. 321–22.

82. Vitelleschi to Georg Forer, Apr. 13, 1630, ARSJ, Aust. 4I, ff. 255–56.

83. ARSJ, Aust. 4I, ff. 341–42.

84. Vitelleschi to Montmorency, Feb. 1, 1631, ARSJ, Aust. 4I, ff. 403–5; see also Vitelleschi to Montmorency, Mar. 22, 1631, ibid., f. 435.

Chapter 8

1. Roberts, *Gustavus Adolphus*, pp. 464–69, 481, 493, 511.

2. BL 7054, ff. 78–79.

3. Knöringen to Urban VIII, Dec. 12, 1630, Repgen, 1:2:no. 28; Vitelleschi to Contzen, Jan. 11, 1630, ARSJ, GS 6, f. 313. Wartenberg's views were communicated to Rome in a letter of P. L. Carafa dated Jan. 3, 1631; see Repgen, 1:1:239–45.

4. Rocci to Barberini, Nov. 15, 1630, BL 6967, ff. 211–15; Repgen, 1:1:244–57. The two reports of the congregation were drawn up by Francesco Paolucci and dated Jan. 31, 1631, Repgen, 1:2:nos. 30, 31.

5. All were dated Feb. 10, 1631, Repgen, 1:2:nos. 33–44; for the five bishops, see below, n. 82.

6. Barberini to Rocci, Feb. 8, 1631, Repgen, 1:2:no. 32; for the letter to P. L. Carafa, see the notes to no. 32; cf. the discussion of papal policy in Repgen, 1:1:254–60.

7. Albrecht, "Finanzierung des Dreissigjährigen Krieges," pp. 389–91.

8. Rocci to Barberini, Mar. 15, 1631, BL 6968, ff. 74–84; see Repgen, 1:1:260–61.

9. Emperor to Stadion, HHStA, RTA 101a^i, ff. 9–9v; instruction for the imperial delegates to the Frankfurt Conference, Jan. 27, 1631, ibid., ff. 5–8; on Stadion, see Schwarz, *Imperial Privy Council*, pp. 252–53.

10. HHStA, RTA 101a^{ii}, ff. 19–24; a reference to the convention to be held in February "of the coming year" shows that this draft was drawn up before Jan. 1, 1631; in the margins of these folios the draft was completely rewritten to serve as the register copy of the instruction for the Frankfurt Conference dated Jul. 8, 1631.

11. Minutes of the privy council session, Jan. 11, 1631, HHStA, RTA 101a^{ii}, ff. 32–32v.

12. See also Vitelleschi to Lamormaini, Mar. 29, 1631, ARSJ, Aust. 4I, ff. 439–40. Lamormaini had written on Feb. 1 indicating his satisfaction with the instruction.

13. On the whereabouts of Eggenberg, see above, chapter 6, n. 78. Suvanto, *Wallenstein und seine Anhänger*, pp. 68–76, argues that Eggenberg left court principally because he opposed the appointment of the King of Hungary to the command of the imperial army, a step that some in Vienna were advocating. This may have been an added reason for his departure, but it cannot have been the main reason. As Suvanto indicates himself, the emperor was not enthusiastic about his son's assuming the military command at this time.

14. HHStA, RTA 101aⁱ, ff. 10–13v.

15. See above, n. 10; Rocci to Barberini, Feb. 8, 1631, BL 6968, ff. 36–41, reported the postponement of the Frankfurt Conference.

16. On the Leipzig Conference, see Roberts, *Gustavus Adolphus*, pp. 458, 483–88; Ritter, *Deutsche Geschichte*, 3:481–84; Gebauer, *Kurbrandenburg*, pp. 148–75.

17. The Protestant Estates assembled in Leipzig to the Four Catholic Electors, Apr. 3, 1631, Londorp, *Acta Publica*, 4:134–35; the same to the emperor, Apr. 7, 1631, ibid., 4:136–43.

18. Resolution of the Protestant Estates assembled in Leipzig, Apr. 12, 1631, Londorp, *Acta Publica*, 4:144–46. This was sent to the emperor on Apr. 14.

19. Gebauer, *Kurbrandenburg*, pp. 174–75.

20. Undated, HHStA, RTA 100b, ff. 269–77. A notation on f. 278v shows that Breuner was the author of this paper and that it was drawn up at the time of the Leipzig Conference. Summarizing remarks in Latin in the margin appear to be in Lamormaini's hand. On Breuner, see Schwarz, *Imperial Privy Council*, pp. 210–12.

21. Roberts, *Gustavus Adolphus*, p. 446.

22. Ibid., pp. 466–67.

23. HHStA, Kriegs. 91 (March), ff. 41–44.

24. Günter, *Habsburgerliga*, pp. 33–36; Albrecht, *Auswärtige Politik*, pp. 232–40. Spain hoped to include the Catholic states in the alliance.

25. Mar. 19, 1631, HHStA, Kriegs. 91 (March), ff. 45–49.

26. May 4, 1631, ibid., 92 (May), ff. 44–47.

27. See above, chap. 3, n. 52.

28. Günter, *Habsburgerliga*, p. 47.

29. On Werdenberg, see Schwarz, *Imperial Privy Council*, pp. 122, 383–85.

30. For the Spanish evaluation of Dietrichstein, see Günter, *Habsburgerliga*, p. 79. He was given the honor of meeting the Infanta in Genoa in 1630 and conducting her to Vienna for her wedding with the King of Hungary.

31. On Hegenmüller, see Schwarz, *Imperial Privy Council*, pp. 246–47; on Dohna, Arno Duch, "Dohna, Karl Hannibal von," *Neue Deutsche Biographie*, 4 (Berlin, 1959): 51.

32. The instruction for Hegenmüller, dated May 6, 1631, is in HHStA, Traut. 101ⁱⁱ, ff. 161–78, with a secret supplementary instruction, ff. 179–80; the former is printed in Londorp, *Acta Publica*, 4:147. For the mission of Dohna, see Gebauer, *Kurbrandenburg*, p. 176.

33. May 14, 1631, Londorp, *Acta Publica*, 4:152–53.

34. Saxony to the emperor (given Hegenmüller), May 20, 1631, HHStA, Traut., 101ⁱⁱ, ff. 190–215, and a handwritten note, May 20, 1631, HHStA, Friedens. 9cⁱⁱ, ff. 3–4v. The position paper of a committee of councilors dealing with Saxony's response and Hegenmüller's oral report is in HHStA, Friedens. 9cⁱⁱ, ff. 18–27v.

35. Jun. 14, 1631, HHStA, Traut. 101ⁱⁱ, ff. 217–26v.

36. Roberts, *Gustavus Adolphus*, pp. 495–96.

37. On the Dinkelsbühl Conference, see Bireley, *Maximilian von Bayern*, pp. 149–53.

38. Kurz von Senftenau to the emperor, Dinkelsbühl, May 15, 1631, HHStA, Traut., 101ⁱⁱ, ff. 61–68. On Kurz von Senftenau, see Schwarz, *Imperial Privy Council*, pp. 260–63, who calls him "without question the ablest and most influential of the Imperial Vice-Chancellors of the seventeenth century." He succeeded Stralendorf in this post and retained it until 1659.

39. Kurz von Senftenau's report on the Dinkelsbühl Conference, undated, HHStA, Traut. 101ⁱⁱ, ff. 89–96; emperor to Maximilian and Mainz, Jun. 9, 1631, ibid., ff. 78–81.

40. Bireley, *Maximilian von Bayern*, pp. 159–60.

41. Mainz to the emperor, Jun. 7, 1631, HHStA, RTA 101aⁱ, ff. 76–79v; emperor to Stadion, ibid., ff. 84–85; Bireley, *Maximilian von Bayern*, pp. 153.

42. BH, Jesuitica 704, ff. 23–24.

43. Proposition of the Bavarian emissary (Johann Kütner), presented Aug. 7, 1631, BAGW, 1:no. 332; emperor to Maximilian, Aug. 9, 1631, ibid., 1:no. 333; Eggenberg to Maximilian, Sept. 1, 1631, BH, KSchw 131, f. 37; Albrecht, *Auswärtige Politik*, pp. 256–62; Bireley, *Maximilian von Bayern*, pp. 167–69.

44. On Quiroga, see de Carrocera, "El Padre Diego de Quiroga."

45. Ibid., pp. 81–84.

46. Khevenhiller, *Annales Ferdinandei*, 11:9–14; Duhr, 2:2:236–37.

47. Klopp, *Der dreissigjährige Krieg*, 3:2:18–22; Quazza, *Guerra di Mantova*, 2:245, 267.

48. Rocci to Barberini, Mar. 22, 1631, BL 6968, ff. 85–92.

49. Klopp, *Der dreissigjährige Krieg*, 3:2:35, 38; Leman, *Urbain VIII*, pp. 7–8. The text of the Peace of Cherasco (Apr. 6, 1631) is in Dumont, *Corps universel diplomatique*, 6:1:9–12.

50. Rocci to Barberini, Apr. 19, 1631, BL 6968, ff. 113–121v.

51. Emperor to Eggenberg, Apr. 18, 1631, published in Zwiedineck-Südenhorst, *Eggenberg*, pp. 191–92; see also pp. 94–95.

52. Rocci to Barberini, Apr. 26, 1631, BL 6968, ff. 122–130v.

53. Eggenberg to the emperor, Apr. 20, 1631, published in Zwiedineck-Südenhorst, *Eggenberg*, pp. 192–97.

54. Instruction for Kurz von Senftenau's mission to Paris, Jun. 8, 1631, HHStA, Staaten., Frankreich, Berichte und Weisungen 24.

55. Quazza, *Guerra di Mantova*, 2:303–5. The text of this second Peace of Cherasco is in Dumont, *Corps universel diplomatique*, 6:1:14–17.

56. Jul. 31, 1631, HHStA, Staaten., Frankreich, Berichte und Weisungen 23, ff. 49–56.

57. O'Connell, *Richelieu*, pp. 159, 203, 213.

58. Leman, *Urbain VIII*, pp. 21–22, 27, 34; O'Connell, *Richelieu*, pp. 259–61.

59. Jun. 19, 1631, Günter, *Habsburgerliga*, no. 48.

60. Philip IV to the Duke of Guastalla, Apr. 22 and Jun. 19, 1631, Günter, *Habsburgerliga*, nos. 43, 49; Philip IV to the Marquis of Cadereyta (second Spanish ambassador in Vienna), May 28, 1631, ibid., no. 47. See also pp. 75–77.

61. Apr. 22, 1631, Günter, *Habsburgerliga*, no. 43 (p. 278).

62. Philip IV to Pedro de Axpe, May 9, 1631, Günter, *Habsburgerliga*, no. 44.

63. Vitelleschi to Lamormaini, Jul. 12 and 26, 1631, ARSJ, Aust. 4I, ff. 488, 490; Vitelleschi to Ferdinand II, Jul. 26, 1631, ARSJ, Germ. 113II, f. 460.

64. For Spanish reluctance to oppose the Edict openly, see Philip IV to the Duke of Guastalla, Nov. 2, 1631, Günter, *Habsburgerliga*, no. 63.

65. See above, n. 63.

66. Vitelleschi to Cardinal Borja, Sept. 28, 1631, ARSJ, Hispaniae 70, f. 257; Vitelleschi to Ferdinand II, Oct. 25, 1631, ARSJ, Germ. 113II, f. 467; Vitelleschi to Ferdinand, King of Hungary and Bohemia, Oct. 25, 1631, ibid., ff. 466–67; Philip IV to Pedro de Axpe, Oct. 9, 1631, Günter, *Habsburgerliga*, no. 61.

67. ARSJ, Aust. 4I, f. 523.

68. Oct. 18, 1631, ARSJ, Aust. 4I, 532–34.

69. Heydendorff, *Die Fürsten zu Eggenberg*, pp. 114–16.

70. Philip IV to the Marquis of Cadereyta, Sept. 15, 1631, Günter, *Habsburgerliga*, no. 53; Philip IV to the Duke of Guastalla, Sept. 15, 1631, ibid., no. 55, 56; see also pp. 79–80, 86.

71. On Dietrichstein, see Schwarz, *Imperial Privy Council*, pp. 225–26; on Thun, see ibid., pp. 368–69.

72. Philip IV to the Duke of Guastalla, Sept. 15, 1631, Günter, *Habsburgerliga*, no. 55 (pp. 294–97).

73. Philip IV to Pedro de Axpe, Oct. 7, 1631, Günter, *Habsburgerliga*, no. 61 (pp. 314–15).

74. Rocci to Barberini, Jul. 26, 1631, BL 6969, ff. 23–29.

75. Ritter, *Deutsche Geschichte*, 3:488–96; Roberts, *Gustavus Adolphus*, pp. 512–26; Bireley, *Maximilian von Bayern*, 159–60.

76. Emperor to Savelli, May 7, 1631, HHStA, Staaten., Romana 53; Rocci to Barberini, May 10, 1631, BL 6968, ff. 145–151.

77. Albrecht, "Finanzierung des Dreissigjährigen Krieges," pp. 553–54; Repgen, 1:2:290–91.

78. Jun. 28, 1631, BL 2201, ff. 113v–114v.

79. Jul. 12, 1631, ibid., f. 123.

80. Rocci to Barberini, Aug. 9, 1631, BL 6969, ff. 34–39.

81. Stadion and Hildbrandt to the emperor, Aug. 5, 1631, HHStA, RTA 101aⁱ, ff. 70–71; on Hildbrandt, see Oswald von Gschliesser, *Der Reichshofrat*, p. 205. For a discussion of the Frankfurt Conference, see Bireley, *Maximilian von Bayern*, pp. 160–65.

82. The ecclesiastical princes represented in addition to the three electors were

the Archbishop of Salzburg and the bishops of Bamberg, Würzburg, Eichstätt, Constance, and Worms. (The Elector of Trier was also Bishop of Speyer, and the Elector of Cologne also Bishop of Münster, Paderborn, Hildesheim, and Liège.) In addition to Bavaria, the secular states with delegates were Anterior Austria and the Tyrol (the lands of Archduke Leopold), and the city of Cologne.

83. These are in HHStA, RTA 101a.

84. Because of a dispute over protocol, Carafa did not meet personally with Stadion but wrote him a letter, Frankfurt, Aug. 27, 1631, Repgen, 1:2:no. 48. Cf. the discussion of Carafa's visit in Frankfurt, Repgen, 1:1:268–72.

85. Gebauer, *Kurbrandenburg*, pp. 181–85, 188, 192–96.

86. HHStA, RTA 101a[iv], ff. 13–14v; this corresponded to their instructions.

87. Bireley, *Maximilian von Bayern*, p. 162.

88. Ritter, *Deutsche Geschichte*, 3:496–501; Roberts, *Gustavus Adolphus*, pp. 531–38.

89. HHStA, RTA 101a[iv], ff. 24–24v, 31; emperor to the delegates in Frankfurt, Oct. 8, 1631, ibid., ff. 64–64v.

Chapter 9

1. Leopold von Ranke, *Französische Geschichte*, ed. Willy Andreas (Wiesbaden and Berlin, 1957), 2:45.

2. Pazmany to Hmira Janos, Tyrnau, Dec. 5, 1631, *Epistolae Collectae*, 2:no. 697.

3. Rocci to Barberini, Feb. 7, 1632, BL 6970, ff. 62–71v.

4. Maximilian to the emperor, Sept. 26 and Oct. 3, 1631, BAGW, 1:nos. 365, 374; emperor to Maximilian, Oct. 8 and 11, ibid., 1:nos. 378, 380.

5. Position paper, BAGW, 1:no. 376.

6. Irmer, *Verhandlungen*, 1: xxviii.

7. Oct. 18, 1631, BAGW, 1:no. 393.

8. Bireley, *Maximilian von Bayern*, pp. 174–76.

9. Position paper, undated, HHStA, RTA 100b, ff. 142–47v; there are two versions of the paper here that dates from about Nov. 1.

10. Mainz and Maximilian to the emperor, Nov. 10, 1631, HHStA, RTA 100b (end); emperor to Mainz and Maximilian, Nov. 25, 1631, ibid.

11. This letter seems never to have been sent. Both drafts are found within an undated paper of the privy council, HHStA, Friedens. 46g, ff. 407–11. Schwarz, *Imperial Privy Council*, p. 51, calls attention to the fact that it is misplaced in the archives and dates it tentatively in 1633. In my opinion, it belongs here.

12. The four others were Joannes Lucas Struchius, a Jesuit who among other things had taught moral theology at the college in Vienna (see ARSJ, Aust. 26, ff. 13, 141v), the prior and lector of the Discalced Carmelite convent in Vienna, whose names were not given, and the Spanish Dominican, Juan de Valdespino, a doctor of theology and professor of scripture at the University of Vienna, whom Kink, *Geschichte der Universität zu Wien*, 1:1:377, calls the equal of the most

famous masters of earlier times. He had been a signer of the position paper of the imperial theologians on the Counterreformation in Bohemia (1627); see above, chap. 2, n. 48.

13. Repgen, 1:2:no. 49I.

14. Repgen, 1:2:no. 49II, ibid., 1:1:274–81. This was sent to Rome with Rocci's report of Nov. 22.

15. Repgen, 1:1:281–87. Repgen, in my opinion, does not recognize the degree of freedom Urban's position left the emperor.

16. Rocci to Barberini, Dec. 13, 1631, BL 6969, ff. 208–18v; Droysen, "Verhandlungen über dem Universalfrieden," pp. 234, 242–43, 257.

17. Instructions for Questenberg's mission to Ingolstadt, Dec. 6, 1631, HHStA, RTA 100b.

18. On Maximilian's negotiations with Charnacé, see Bireley, *Maximilian von Bayern*, pp. 170–75.

19. Emperor to Maximilian, Dec. 21, 1631, BAGW, 1:no. 473; emperor to Questenberg, Dec. 21, 1631, ibid., 1:no. 475.

20. Questenberg to the emperor, Dec. 22, 1631, and Jan. 1, 1632, HHStA, RTA 100b; emperor to Questenberg, Jan. 7, 1632, ibid. On the meeting at Ingolstadt, see also Bireley, *Maximilian von Bayern*, pp. 175–76.

21. Mann, *Wallenstein*, pp. 764–71; Diwald, *Wallenstein*, pp. 459–66; Ritter, *Deutsche Geschichte*, 3:525.

22. Mann, *Wallenstein*, pp. 773–75, 782–83.

23. Dec. 10, 1631, BAGW, 1:no. 450; Mann, *Wallenstein*, pp. 785–86; Ritter, *Deutsche Geschichte*, 3:525–26.

24. Leopold von Ranke, *Geschichte Wallensteins*, 3d ed. (Leipzig, 1872), p. 159, cited in Repgen, 1:1:288.

25. Mann, *Wallenstein*, pp. 814–15. There is evidence that Wallenstein was ready to go much further in making concessions at this time and actually gave the impression to Protestant contacts that freedom of religion in the Habsburg lands was acceptable to him. See Mann, *Wallenstein*, pp. 814–15, and Suvanto, *Wallenstein und seine Anhänger*, pp. 128–30. My interpretation follows Mann.

26. Mann, *Wallenstein*, p. 773.

27. Bireley, *Maximilian von Bayern*, pp. 172–74.

28. Position Paper, Jan. 28, 1632, BAGW, 2:no. 604.

29. Albrecht, *Auswärtige Politik*, p. 341.

30. Bireley, *Maximilian von Bayern*, pp. 179, 181–86.

31. Platzhoff, *Geschichte des europäischen Staatensystems*, p. 193.

32. Günter, *Habsburgerliga*, pp. 98–105.

33. See above, n. 28.

34. Vitelleschi to Lamormaini, Mar. 29, 1632, ARSJ, Aust. 4II, ff. 599–600.

35. Pazmany to the emperor, Pressburg, Feb. 10, 1632, *Epistolae Collectae*, 2:no. 712; Günter, *Habsburgerliga*, pp. 107–9. Important for understanding Vienna's conception of this treaty is a document in HHStA, Friedens. 18, ff. 3–12, entitled "Relatio Summaria, was an unterschidlichen Orthen ratione foederis ad defensionem Sacri Romani Imperii erecti vom 14 Feb. 1632 gehandelt

worden." It is undated and in Latin. Obviously drawn up in early April 1633, it outlines the purpose of the treaty and then traces the efforts to obtain the adherence of different states but especially of France and the pope.

36. Mar. 2, 1632, HHStA, Friedens. 18, ff. 19–27v, 29; see also Khevenhiller, *Annales Ferdinandei*, 12:310–12, and Leman, *Urbain VIII*, pp. 95, 112–14, who attributes part of the initiative for Schwarzenberg's mission to the new nuncio in Paris, Alessandro Bichi.

37. Günter, *Habsburgerliga*, pp. 99, 109–14; Ritter, *Deutsche Geschichte*, 3:524.

38. For a summary of the events under Philip II, see William V. Bangert, *A History of the Society of Jesus* (St. Louis, 1972), pp. 98–102, 110–13; for a fuller treatment, see Antonio Astrain, *Historia de la Compañia de Jesús en la Asistencia de España*, vol. 3, *1573–1615*, 2d ed. (Madrid, 1925).

39. Pra, "Philippe IV d'Espagne et la Compagnie de Jésus," pp. 208–15. Pra publishes in French translation the undated report of de la Palma. The account of these events in Astrain, *Historia de la Compañia de Jesús*, 5: 198–204, adds little beyond what is found in Pra.

40. ARSJ, Toletana 9, ff. 214–15; this is found in French translation in Pra, "Philippe IV d'Espagne et la Compagnie de Jésus," pp. 214–17. See also Vitelleschi to Francesco Aguado, Jan. 10 and May 4, 1632, ARSJ, Toletana 9, ff. 205, 221v. Aguado was a leading Spanish Jesuit who had recently become the confessor of Olivares. Vitelleschi's letters indicate he also wrote directly to Olivares, but I have not been able to find this letter.

41. Vitelleschi to Lamormaini, Feb. 25, 1632, ARSJ, Aust. 4II, f. 583.

42. Mar. 2, 1632, "Vita Lamormaini," ff. 62–62v; according to Vitelleschi to Lamormaini, Apr. 3, 1632, ARSJ, Aust. 4II, ff. 605–7, he also wrote Olivares, but I have been unable to locate this letter.

43. Vitelleschi to Francesco Aguado, Aug. 24, 1632, ARSJ, Toletana 9, ff. 255v–256. According to the "Vita Lamormaini," f. 62v, the king was satisfied with Lamormaini's letter.

44. Vitelleschi to Lamormaini, Apr. 3, 1632, ARSJ, Aust. 4II, ff. 605–7.

45. Feb. 25, 1632, ARSJ, Aust. 4II, f. 538.

46. Nicholas Jagniatorius to Vitelleschi, Jan. 3, 1632, ARSJ, Aust. 21, f. 55.

47. Jan. 10, 1632, ARSJ, Aust. 21, ff. 62–64.

48. Vitelleschi to Georg Forer (provincial superior in Vienna), May 1, 1632, ARSJ, Aust. 4II, ff. 626–27.

49. See above, n. 44.

50. Lamormaini to Vitelleschi, Apr. 3, 1632, ARSJ, Aust. 21, f. 118; Nicholas Jagniatorius to Vitelleschi, Jun. 12, 1632, ibid., f. 121.

51. "Vita Lamormaini," ff. 63–63v.

52. Published in Dudik, "Korrespondenz Kaiser Ferdinands," p. 275. Two other handwritten notes from Ferdinand to Lamormaini, dated Jan. 11 and 12, 1632, ibid., pp. 274–75, are too cryptic to be completely intelligible, but they point toward Lamormaini's involvement in the formation of policy toward France.

53. "Vita Lamormaini," f. 72v. It is impossible to date this statement, and it may well stem from another period of Lamormaini's tenure as confessor. In the margin of the Roman copy of the "Vita Lamormaini," there was written in an unidentified hand, "Caution here; better to omit this," presumably in any biography of Lamormaini or history of the Society using the "Vita."

54. Much has been written about the Göllersdorf agreement, but as Lutz, "Wallenstein, Ferdinand II, und der Wiener Hof," pp. 227–28, has remarked, modern research has not been able to establish what the terms were or whether they were written. Lutz's article is an extended review of Suvanto, *Wallenstein und seine Anhänger*. I have followed the interpretation of Mann, *Wallenstein*, pp. 826–34, rather than Diwald, *Wallenstein*, pp. 473–75, 478–80.

55. Rocci to Barberini, Feb. 14, 1632, BL 6970, ff. 78–88.

56. Jan. 2, 1632, published in Dudik, *Waldstein*, p. 194.

57. Apr. 9, 1632, ibid., p. 194.

58. Artur Goldmann, "Die Universität, 1529–1740," *Geschichte der Stadt Wien*, ed. Anton Mayer, 6:49.

59. Albrecht, *Auswärtige Politik*, pp. 339–40; Pastor, *Geschichte der Päpste*, 13:429–31.

60. Rocci to Barberini, Dec. 27, 1631, BL 6969, ff. 219–25; Albrecht, "Finanzierung des Dreissigjährigen Krieges," pp. 555–56.

61. Statement presented to the pope by Pazmany, Apr. 6, 1632, *Epistolae Collectae*, 2:no. 725; this was an enclosure with Pazmany to the emperor, Apr. 10, 1632, ibid., 2:no. 727, where Pazmany wrote that it was a nearly verbatim report of what he told the pope in his audience and later presented in writing.

On the mission of Pazmany, see Leman, *Urbain VIII*, pp. 146–66, and Pastor, *Geschichte der Päpste*, 13:441–48.

62. On this incident, see Leman, *Urbain VIII*, pp. 133–37, and Pastor, *Geschichte der Päpste*, 13:434–41.

63. See, for example, Girolamo Grimaldi (extraordinary nuncio in Vienna) to Barberini, Nov. 5 and 26, 1633, BL 6980, ff. 172–76v, 185–90v.

64. Pazmany to the emperor, Apr. 10, 16, 24, May 1, 1632, *Epistolae Collectae*, 2:nos. 727, 731, 734, 736; see also the "Relatio Summaria," cited above, n. 35.

65. Pazmany to the emperor, Apr. 10, 1632, *Epistolae Collectae*, 2:no. 727.

66. Emperor to Pazmany, Apr. 28, 1632, HHStA, Staaten., Romana 53.

67. Bireley, *Maximilian von Bayern*, p. 184; Pastor, *Geschichte der Päpste*, 13:440–41, 448–51.

68. Albrecht, "Finanzierung des Dreissigjährigen Krieges," pp. 400–406.

69. "Relatio Summaria," see above, n. 35; see also Leman, *Urbain VIII*, pp. 113–17.

70. Albrecht, *Auswärtige Politik*, pp. 320–22; Leman, *Urbain VIII*, pp. 217, 235–36; see also Weber, *Frankreich und das Reich*, pp. 112–13, 121–27, 146, 192–93.

71. "Relatio Summaria," see above, n. 35; report of the committee of coun-

cilors on negotiations with France, Jul. 18, 1632, HHStA, Friedens. 18, ff. 104–5, approved by the privy council, Jul. 19, ibid., f. 106v; Khevenhiller, *Annales Ferdinandei*, 12:317–22; Leman, *Urbain VIII*, pp. 116–18.

72. Grimaldi to Barberini, Jul. 17, 1632, BL 6978, ff. 33–45v.

73. Grimaldi to Barberini, Jul. 3, 10, Sept. 11, 1632, ibid., ff. 14–20, 22–32, 115–19. On Sept. 25, however, Grimaldi wrote that he thought Werdenberg had lost all hope for an understanding with France, ibid., ff. 132–36v.

74. Grimaldi to Barberini, Jul. 31, Sept. 11, 1632, ibid., ff. 59–67v, 115–19; Rocci to Barberini, Sept. 18, 1632, BL 6971, ff. 48–57.

75. Grimaldi to Barberini, Jul. 10, Aug. 14, 1632, BL 6978, ff. 22–32, 76–80.

76. Grimaldi to Barberini, Jun. 26, 1632, ibid., ff. 1–13.

77. Ritter, *Deutsche Geschichte*, 3:531–39; Mann, *Wallenstein*, pp. 835, 839–49, 854–60; Roberts, *Gustavus Adolphus*, pp. 694, 699–706, 710, 714–20, 726, 733.

78. Roberts, *Gustavus Adolphus*, p. 735.

79. Oct. 16, 1632, ARSJ, Germ. 111, f. 4.

80. Sept. 24, 1632, BAGW, 3:no. 1304.

81. Emperor to Wallenstein, Oct. 31, 1632, BAGW, 3:no. 1488; see Roberts, *Gustavus Adolphus*, pp. 748–50.

82. Mann, *Wallenstein*, pp. 875–93; Roberts, *Gustavus Adolphus*, pp. 739–48, 763–73.

83. *Virtutes*, p. 80. Writing from Vienna to Olivares on Jan. 3, 1632, Quiroga mentioned a plan formulated by a *"cierto personaje"* to assassinate Gustav Adolph. He had talked the matter over with the Queen of Hungary and other figures favorable to Spain, he indicated, and he recommended that the sum required by the concocter of the plan be set aside for him. In his response of Mar. 2, 1632, Günter, *Habsburgerliga*, no. 70, Philip IV refused to have anything to do with the plan, which was unbecoming a "rey grande y justo." Ferdinand's response, according to Lamormaini, was much the same; the plot was beneath both a Christian and an emperor.

84. *Virtutes*, pp. 26, 35; see Richard Müller, "Wiens räumliche Entwicklung und topographische Benennungen," *Geschichte der Stadt Wien*, ed. Anton Mayer, 4:378, and Ernst Tomek, "Das kirchliche Leben und die christliche Charitas in Wien," ibid., 5:257.

85. Dec. 11, 1632, BL 6978, ff. 212–18v.

86. Vitelleschi to Lamormaini, Jan. 1, 1633, ARSJ, Aust. 4II, ff. 733–34.

Chapter 10

1. Gebhardt, however, was not a privy councilor and is not listed in Schwarz, *Imperial Privy Council*. See above, chap. 4, n. 62.

2. Position paper with comments of the privy council, Dec. 5–9, 1632, BAGW, 3:no. 1637.

3. *Epistolae Collectae*, 2:no. 798.

4. Grimaldi to Barberini, Mar. 19, 1633, BL 6979, ff. 78–85v. The three "grandi e dotti Praelati" mentioned by Grimaldi can only be Pazmany, Bishop Anton, and Dietrichstein. Pazmany is named explicitly in Grimaldi to Barberini, Mar. 26, 1633, ibid., ff. 86–89.

5. Jan. 28–Feb. 4, 1633, BAGW, 3:no. 1801. From a draft much corrected in his hand in HHStA, Friedens. 9c^{ii}, I conclude that Stralendorf was the principal author.

6. See above, n. 4; see also Grimaldi to Barberini, Jan. 15, 1633, BL 6979, ff. 12–15.

7. Grimaldi to Barberini, Mar. 5, 1633, ibid., ff. 64–69.

8. Donnersberg to Maximilian, Mar. 16, 1633, BH, KSchw 132, f. 32.

9. Grimaldi to Barberini, Apr. 9, 1633, BL 6979, ff. 117–22; see also above, n. 4.

10. Albrecht, *Auswärtige Politik*, pp. 355–61; Baustaedt, *Richelieu und Deutschland*, pp. 74, 79–100, 103; Weber, *Frankreich und das Reich*, pp. 230–70.

11. Richelieu, *Mémoires*, 22:449–51; Baustaedt, *Richelieu und Deutschland*, pp. 72–73; Leman, *Urbain VIII*, pp. 272–73.

12. Position paper with remarks of the privy council, Mar. 31–Apr. 1, 1633, HHStA, Friedens. 18, 1633, ff. 8–14; the "Relatio Summaria," discussed above, chap. 9, n. 35, dates from this time. See also Leman, *Urbain VIII*, pp. 262–63, 292–93.

13. Albrecht, *Auswärtige Politik*, pp. 362–63; van der Essen, *Le Cardinal-Infant*, pp. 105–10; Günter, *Habsburgerliga*, p. 130.

14. Philip IV to Quiroga, Jan. 1, 1633, Günter, *Habsburgerliga*, no. 83 and pp. 127–28.

15. Philip IV to Castañeda, Feb. 10, 1633, Günter, *Habsburgerliga*, no. 90; Philip IV to the Count de Monterrey, Viceroy of Naples, Sept. 6, 1632, ibid., no. 78.

16. Mann, *Wallenstein*, pp. 919–21.

17. It is difficult to know precisely what different parties understood to be the state of affairs in a particular normative year unless they spelled it out. The years 1620, 1618, and 1612 all seem to have meant simply the prewar status for the Empire apart from the Habsburg lands. The differences lay in the Habsburg territories. The year 1618 meant the prewar status there. The year 1620 seems to have allowed for the changes in the Bohemian lands including Saxon occupation of the Lusatias, though this would depend upon the precise date within the year that was taken as normative. Matthias was elected emperor in 1612, thus ending a long conflict over the succession in the House of Habsburg; it was also a year of relative Protestant strength. Thus 1612 seems to have connoted a greater degree of religious freedom for the Protestants in the Habsburg lands than 1618 and a greater measure of stability even for the Empire.

18. Imperial instruction for the delegates to the conference at Breslau, Aug. 26, 1633, BAGW, 4:no. 2008, where there are many references to Leitmeritz; Donnersberg to Maximilian, Vienna, Apr. 27, 1633, BH, KSchw 132, ff. 127–28;

Mann, *Wallenstein*, pp. 921–23; Frohnweiler, "Friedenspolitik des Landgrafen Georgs," pp. 92–108. As Frohnweiler points out, p. 103, the special precautions taken to keep these negotiations secret may account for our present difficulty to determine exactly what proposals were made.

19. Rocci to Barberini, Apr. 9, 1633, BL 6972, ff. 98–103.

20. Vitelleschi to Lamormaini, Jan. 1, 1633, ARSJ, Aust. 4II, ff. 733–34; Vitelleschi to Wallenstein, Jan. 1, 1633, ARSJ, Germ. 113II, ff. 514–15.

21. Vitelleschi to Lamormaini, Mar. 26 and May 21, 1633, ARSJ, Aust. 4II, ff. 791–92, 807–8.

22. Vitelleschi to Contzen, Feb. 12 and Apr. 12, 1633, ARSJ, GS 6, ff. 521, 552; Vitelleschi to Lamormaini, Feb. 19 and Apr. 26, 1633, ARSJ, Aust. 4II, ff. 765, 799. On Wallenstein and astrology, see Mann, *Wallenstein*, pp. 669–73, 974–76.

23. Grimaldi to Barberini, May 14, 1633, BL 6979, ff. 170–75v.

24. Report of the Austrian provincial congregation, Apr. 17, 1633, ARSJ, Congregationes 62, f. 178v; Vitelleschi to Lamormaini, Jul. 2, 1633, ARSJ, Aust. 4II, ff. 832–33.

25. Hallwich, *Wallensteins Ende*, 2:xciv–xcv. See also Gerhard von Questenberg to Wallenstein, Vienna, Jun. 12, 1633, Toegel, *Documenta Bohemica*, 5:no. 504; Wallenstein's Deputy to Heinrich von San Julian (his emissary in Vienna), Jun. 15, 1633, Hallwich, ibid., 1:no. 476; Eggenberg to Wallenstein, Jun. 20, 1633, Hallwich, ibid., 1:no. 482. Cf. Mann, *Wallenstein*, pp. 948–51.

26. Rocci to Barberini, Jun. 18, 1633, Repgen, 1:2:no. 52; Grimaldi to Barberini, Jun. 18, 1633, ibid., 1:2:no. 50.

27. Rocci to Barberini, Jun. 25 and Jul. 2, 1633, Repgen, 1:2:no. 55, no. 57.

28. Emperor to Wallenstein, Jul. 9, 1633, Hallwich, *Wallensteins Ende*, 1:no. 518; Gerhard von Questenberg to Wallenstein, Jul. 15, 1633, BAGW, 4:no. 1976.

29. Hallwich, *Wallensteins Ende*, 2:xcv.

30. Rocci to Barberini, Jul. 2, 1633, Repgen, 1:2:no. 57.

31. Grimaldi to Barberini, Jul. 16, 1633, Repgen, 1:2:no. 62.

32. Grimaldi to Barberini, May 14, 1633, BL 6979, ff. 176–84v.

33. Trautmannsdorf to the emperor, Bischof-Teinitz, Oct. 29, 1633, BAGW, 4:no. 2102.

34. The three delegates to the emperor, Gross-Petrowitz, Sept. 10, 1633, BAGW, 4:no. 2021.

35. Urban VIII to Ferdinand II, Jul. 9, 1633, Repgen, 1:2:no. 59; see also Rocci to Barberini, Jul. 30 and Sept. 3, 1633, Repgen, 1:2:nos. 68, 79.

36. Rocci to Barberini, Sept. 10, 1633, BL 6973, ff. 97–103. I have followed here the interpretation of papal policy found in Repgen, 1:1:316–21, but I think he considerably underestimates the effect of the nuncios' remonstrances and those of Lamormaini on the emperor. This, of course, is not Repgen's primary concern.

37. Aug. 26, 1633, BAGW, 4:no. 2008.

38. Bireley, *Maximilian von Bayern*, p. 197.

39. Emperor to Trautmannsdorf, Nov. 26, 1633, BAGW, 4:no. 2139.

40. Bireley, *Maximilian von Bayern*, p. 197.

41. Emperor to Wallenstein, Sept. 25, 1633, Hallwich, *Wallensteins Ende*, 1:no. 708; Wallenstein to the emperor, Sept. 29, 1633, ibid., 1:no. 716; ibid., 2:xcvii; Mann, *Wallenstein*, pp. 963–76.

42. Emperor to Wallenstein, Oct. 18, Hallwich, *Wallensteins Ende*, 2:no. 793; Mann, *Wallenstein*, 977–79.

43. Mann, *Wallenstein*, p. 981; Hallwich, *Wallenstein Ende*, 2:ciii–civ.

44. Trautmannsdorf to the emperor, Bischof-Teinitz, Oct. 29, 1633, BAGW, 4:no. 2102.

45. Franz Julius to the emperor, undated, BAGW, 4:no. 2108; this clearly dates from mid-November. See also Hallwich, *Wallensteins Ende*, 2:ciii, and Mann, *Wallenstein*, pp. 982–84.

46. Philip IV to Castañeda, Oct. 4, 1633, Günter, *Habsburgerliga*, no. 115.

47. Philip IV to Oñate, May 18, 1634, Günter, *Habsburgerliga*, no. 137; Mann, *Wallenstein*, pp. 954–60, 1015–17; Ritter, *Deutsche Geschichte*, 3:565–68.

48. Maximilian to Richel, Dec. 18, 1633, Irmer, *Verhandlungen*, 3:no. 319.

49. Richel to Maximilian, Dec. 14, 1633, Irmer, *Verhandlungen*, 3:no. 318; Mann, *Wallenstein*, pp. 984–98; Ritter, *Deutsche Geschichte*, 3:568–71.

50. Richel to Maximilian, Jan. 18 and 25, 1634, Irmer, *Verhandlungen*, 3:nos. 361, 386.

51. Mann, *Wallenstein*, pp. 1001–18; Ritter, *Deutsche Geschichte*, 3:570–72.

52. Paper presented on Jan. 11, 1634, published in Mitis, "Gundacker von Liechtenstein," pp. 103–10. Liechtenstein was to be an important figure in the government of Ferdinand III. For a good discussion of his career, see ibid., esp. pp. 37–99.

53. Ferdinand to Lamormaini, Jan. 24, 1634, published in Dudik, "Korrespondenz Kaiser Ferdinands," pp. 276–77; Lamormaini to Vitelleschi, Mar. 3–4, 1634, published in Srbik, *Wallensteins Ende*, pp. 310–13.

54. For the events of the last three paragraphs I have followed Mann, *Wallenstein*, pp. 1057–85, 1095–1125, who relates them in great detail. See also Ritter, *Deutsche Geschichte*, 3:572–77.

55. See above, n. 53. This long and detailed letter is a major primary source for the last days of Wallenstein.

What Wallenstein's ultimate intentions were and whether he was involved in a conspiracy are questions that constitute the heart of the Wallenstein problem. A vast literature on the question exists that will probably never be resolved to the satisfaction of all. I have generally followed Mann's interpretation of Wallenstein, which I find most convincing because it takes into account the complexities and contradictions in the general's character. In my opinion, however, Mann does not show the same understanding for Wallenstein's antagonists that he does for the general. This is especially true of Maximilian of Bavaria. For the literature, see the extensive bibliography in Mann. For two evaluations of Mann's *Wallenstein*, see Press, "Zwei Biographien Wallensteins," and Nostitz, "Golo Manns 'Wallenstein.'"

The Jesuit Johannes Weingartner, the German court preacher in Vienna, was the author of a bitter anti-Wallenstein polemic entitled "Exhortatio Angeli Provincialis ad Imperatorem et Reges Austriacos," that appeared in the winter of 1633–34. Srbik has shown this in his *Wallensteins Ende*, pp. 93–97, 285–97, where he also discusses Weingartner at length. But Srbik greatly exaggerates Weingartner's influence at court in general and in the Wallenstein affair in particular. His name is scarcely found in the Vienna *Acta*, and there is no record of any request for his opinion, even at the time of the Peace of Prague when nearly twenty-five theologians were consulted. Nor did he figure in the nuncios' reports in any significant way. In the Jesuit correspondence with Rome the few times his name was mentioned it was usually questioning his unbecoming conduct at court; see Duhr, 2:2:235. As early as July 20, 1630, Vitelleschi wanted Weingartner removed from his post as soon as a suitable substitute could be found (see his letter of that date to Florence Montmorency, then making the visitation of the Austrian Province, ARSJ, Aust. 4I, ff. 301–3), and he dismissed him from the Society in 1642. There were, incidentally, two other court preachers, one for Latin and one for Italian.

56. Vitelleschi to Lamormaini, Apr. 1, 1634, Aust. 4II, ff. 923–24.

57. Philip IV to the emperor, May 18, 1634, Günter, *Habsburgerliga*, no. 137.

58. "Vita Lamormaini," f. 81; *Virtutes*, p. 12.

59. Rocci to Barberini, Apr. 15, 1634, BL 6974, ff. 148–58v.

60. Rocci to Barberini, Apr. 22, 1634, ibid., ff. 159–69v.

61. See, for example, the emperor's instruction for Franz Julius, Dec. 17, 1633, BAGW, 4:no. 2174.

62. May 24, 1634, HHStA, Friedens. 10v, ff. 36–39.

63. Minutes, ibid., ff. 1–6. The minutes of the talks were sent back weekly to Vienna along with the reports of the delegates.

64. Minutes of the talks at Leitmeritz, Jun. 16–17, 1634, ibid., ff. 31–40, 43–52; Saxon memoranda, presented Jun. 16–17, 1634, ibid., ff. 41–41v, 53–58, 59–61v, 63–65v, 68–70.

65. Imperial delegates to the emperor, Jul. 17, 1634, ibid., 10^{ii}, ff. 60–60v, 71–71v.

66. Imperial delegates to the emperor, Jun. 21 and Jul. 5, 1634, ibid., ff. 41–43, 50–56.

67. Minutes of the talks at Pirna, Jul. 29, 1634, ibid., 10^{v}, ff. 264–74v.

68. Trautmannsdorf to the emperor, Bischof-Teinetz, Oct. 29, 1633, BAGW, 4:no. 2102.

69. Imperial delegates to the emperor, Aug. 28, 1634, HHStA, Friedens. 10^{ii}, ff. 72–72v, 97.

70. Philip IV to Castañeda, May 18, 1634, Günter, *Habsburgerliga*, no. 138; Philip IV to Oñate, May 18, 1634, ibid., no. 140.

71. Albrecht, *Auswärtige Politik*, pp. 370–71; Ritter, *Deutsche Geschichte*, 3:577–80; Günter, *Habsburgerliga*, pp. 169–73. Spain and the emperor concluded an alliance on Oct. 31, 1634, but it appears it was never ratified by both in the same form; see Günter, ibid., pp. 190–95, 198, 210, and Leman, *Urbain VIII*, p. 522.

72. Ritter, *Deutsche Geschichte*, 3:585–86; Baustaedt, *Richelieu und Deutschland*, p. 103.

73. Grimaldi to Barberini, Oct. 8, 1633, BL 6980, ff. 151–57; the prescription (not strictly instruction) for Lustrier was dated Sept. 14, 1633, HHStA, Staaten., Frankreich, Berichte und Weisungen 24. On Lustrier's mission, see Leman, *Urbain VIII*, pp. 364–69, and on Lustrier himself, Tüchle, *Acta SC de Propaganda Fide*, p. 321. Lustrier was close to Cardinal Dietrichstein and later served as his chancellor and represented him in Rome.

74. Leman, *Urbain VIII*, pp. 360–70, 375–76.

75. Grimaldi to Barberini, Nov. 5, 1633, BL 6980, ff. 172–76v. The reference in Grimaldi's report to the *"intempestiva risoluzione"* of Pope Clement VII against Henry VIII and the parallel drawn with Richelieu reveals some interesting Roman attitudes on the English Reformation; see Leman, *Urbain VIII*, pp. 417–18.

76. Grimaldi to Barberini, Dec. 24 and 31, 1633, BL 6980, ff. 204–12v, 213–20v; Repgen, 1:1:325.

77. Instruction for Baglione, Jul. 2, 1634, Repgen, 1:2:no. 81; ibid., 1:1:325, 339–340.

78. Vitelleschi to Lamormaini, Apr. 29 and Jun. 3, 1634, ARSJ, Aust. 4II, ff. 934, 940–41.

79. Rocci to Barberini, Aug. 12, 1634, BL 6975, ff. 9–17v. On the renewal of the Franco-Dutch alliance, see O'Connell, *Richelieu*, pp. 295, 298, and Leman, *Urbain VIII*, p. 397. As a result of this new agreement with France, the Dutch broke off peace talks with Spain.

80. Ritter, *Deutsche Geschichte*, 3:579–81, 583, 586–87; Baustaedt, *Richelieu und Deutschland*, pp. 128–29, 142, 149.

81. Rocci to Barberini, Sept. 30, 1634, BL 6975, ff. 60–69.

82. Vitelleschi to Lamormaini, Oct. 14, 1634, ARSJ, Aust. 4II, ff. 983–84.

83. Heydendorff, *Die Fürsten zu Eggenberg*, pp. 136–38; see Philip IV to Oñate/Castañeda, Aug. 24, 1634, Günter, *Habsburgerliga*, no. 147.

Chapter 11

1. Imperial delegates in Pirna to the emperor, Nov. 23, 1634, HHStA, Friedens. 10[iii], ff. 128–128v; Repgen, 1:1:341.

2. There is a manuscript copy of the Pirna Points in HHStA, Friedens. 16, ff. 171–210; they are printed in the anonymous *Pirnische u. Pragische Friedens Pacten*. For a good summary, see Ritter, *Deutsche Geschichte*, 3:588–94; see also Repgen, 1:1:343–44.

3. Of the Lower Saxon (arch)bishoprics, only Magdeburg and Halberstadt were mentioned explicitly in the Points. According to the position paper of the privy council, Jan. 20, 1635, HHStA, Friedens. 11a, ff. 48–58, Vienna foresaw the return of Minden. Bremen and Verden were not mentioned, though the list was explicitly incomplete.

The same paper shows that Vienna considered the terms guaranteeing to the Catholics the return or retention of the following imperial church territories in the south and west: the (arch)bishoprics of Mainz, Cologne, Münster, Paderborn, Bamberg, Würzburg, Speyer, Worms, Strasbourg, Osnabrück, plus the lands of the Grand Master of the Teutonic Knights. According to the Pirna Points, Protestant holders of imperial church lands were denied the right to be present and to vote at imperial diets, but they held this right for circle assemblies (*Kreistage*).

4. Emperor to Maximilian, Dec. 13, 1634, HHStA, Friedens. 10^{iv}, ff. 21–24; see also the position paper of the privy council cited above, n. 3.

5. HHStA, Friedens. 10^{iv}, ff. 3–16.

6. Weber, *Frankreich und das Reich*, pp. 192–96, 245–46, 388. Sötern was captured by Spanish troops when they took the city of Trier on Mar. 26, 1635, and he spent most of the rest of the war in detention, first in the Spanish Netherlands and then in Vienna and Linz.

7. Emperor to Maximilian, Dec. 13, 1634, HHStA, Friedens. 10^{iv}, ff. 21–24.

8. Rocci to Barberini, Dec. 30, 1634, BL 6945, ff. 208–11.

9. Barberini to Rocci, Oct. 21, 1634, cited in Repgen, 1:1:335, n. 121.

10. Repgen, 1:1:337–38; Leman, *Urbain VIII*, pp. 345, 390–96.

11. Cologne and Mainz to the emperor, Oct. 2, 1634, KSchw 963, f. 301 ff.; Cologne's opinion regarding the peace negotiations at Leitmeritz and Pirna, enclosure with Cologne to Maximilian, Oct. 16, 1634, ibid., ff. 320–28. On Ziegler's mission, see Foerster, *Ferdinand von Köln*, p. 19, and n. 8.

12. See Cornelius Henry Mottmann to Count Thun, Jan. 20 and Feb. 10, 1635, HHStA, Staaten., Romana 52. Mottmann reported on the thinking of Francesco Barberini. He was an official of the Roman Rota who also served as an imperial agent in Rome. During late 1634 and early 1635 he wrote regularly to Count Thun.

13. Günter, *Habsburgerliga*, p. 182.

14. Baustaedt, *Richelieu und Deutschland*, pp. 149–51.

15. Philip IV to Oñate, Feb. 16, 1635, Günter, *Habsburgerliga*, no. 157; see also pp. 203–4.

16. Baglione to Barberini, Jan. 20, 1635, Repgen, 1:2:no. 94.

17. Justus Gebhardt to Nicholas von Miltitz (Saxon negotiator), Jan. 3, 1635, HHStA, Friedens. 11a, ff. 1–iv.

18. HHStA, Friedens. 11a, ff. 48–58. Wandruszka, *Reichspatriotismus*, pp. 23–25, discusses an undated German version of this Latin position paper, ibid., 10^{iv}, ff. 57–70v.

19. Usually those in favor of peace pointed to the precedent of Ferdinand I, not Charles V, who was believed to have abdicated largely because of his unwillingness to accept the concessions he knew would have to be made to the Protestants at Augsburg in 1555. Those opposed to concessions normally cited with favor the example of Charles V. Thus both sides claimed the support of the imperial tradition. On the abdication, see Heinrich Lutz, *Christianitas Afflicta*, (Göttingen, 1964), esp. pp. 412–15.

20. Jan. 20, 1635, HHStA, Friedens. 11a, ff. 62–63.

21. Though twenty-four theologians participated in the conference, some

wrote up no opinion and others combined on a joint effort. Hence only sixteen written opinions are in the HHStA, Friedens. 11a, ff. 214–87. Repgen, 1:1:355–56, discusses these briefly. Also important for the conference is the material found in D.A., Karton 90, which includes the proceedings, "Compendium Gestorum in Congregatione Theologorum" (henceforth Compendium), twenty-six closely written folios, signed by Basilio d'Aire (see below, n. 25), and dated Feb. 26, 1635. The participants were the following:

JESUITS
Lamormaini, Belgian, imperial confessor (no written opinion)
Heinrich Philippi, Belgian, confessor of the King of Hungary (no written opinion)
Ambrosio Peñalosa, Spaniard, preacher to the Queen of Hungary
Carl Musart, Belgian, pro tem dean of the faculty of theology at the University of Vienna
Michael Sumerckher, Austrian (Carniola), provincial superior of the Austrian Province
Blase Slaninus, Bohemian, rector of the academy at Olomouc
Ludwig Crasius, Belgian, professor of theology at Olomouc
Joannis Lucas Struchius, German (Nuremberg), teacher in the college in Vienna (no written opinion)

CAPUCHINS
Diego de Quiroga, Spaniard, confessor of the Queen of Hungary
Valeriano Magni, Milanese (see below, n. 25)
Basilio d'Aire, Belgian, adviser to Cardinal Harrach of Prague and his agent in Vienna

DOMINICANS
Juan de Valdespino, Spaniard, professor of theology in the University of Vienna (He first prepared a joint paper with his Dominican colleague and then submitted his own a day later.)
Sigmund Ferrarius, Neapolitan, superior of the convent in Vienna

CONVENTUAL FRANCISCANS (joint opinion)
Henry Dent, German (Cologne), superior of the convent in Vienna
Ambrose Hertt, German (Cologne), regent of the convent in Vienna

DISCALCED FRANCISCANS (joint opinion)
Bonaventure, Lorrainer
Vitus Ochsius, German (Cologne)
Michael Cumar, nationality unclear, commissioner general (present only at the later sessions)

DISCALCED CARMELITES (joint opinion)
Alexander of Jesus and Mary Wendt, Spaniard (sic), prior of the convent in Vienna
Stephen of St. Peter, Spaniard, reader in theology

BARNABITES
Joannes Maria Crassus, Milanese, superior of the house in Vienna
Vigilius Batocletus, Austrian (Trent), reader in theology

DISCALCED AUGUSTINIANS
Ignatius of Santa Maria, Portuguese (After the first session he replaced
Damasus, a Frenchman.)

DIOCESAN CLERGY
Stephan Zwieschlag, rector magnificus of the University of Vienna and cantor
in St. Stephen's Cathedral

22. Alessandro d'Ales to Barberini, Feb. 3, 1635 (two letters), Repgen, 1:2:nos.
104, 105.

23. Imperial decree for the theologians' conference, Jan. 20, 1635, HHStA,
Friedens. 11a, ff. 64–65v; questions for the theologians' conference, enclosure
with emperor to Dietrichstein, Feb. 9, 1635, D.A., Karton 90, f. 114; questions
for the theologians' conference, enclosure with emperor to Dietrichstein, Feb. 10,
1635, ibid., ff. 115, 120.

24. Compendium, D.A., Karton 90, ff. 42v–43, 46–47v, 64–64v; Dietrichstein to the emperor, Feb. 5 and 7 (with enclosure), HHStA, Friedens. 11a, ff.
148–48v, 165, 212; emperor to Dietrichstein, Feb. 7, 1635, ibid., f. 161. During
the conference Ferdinand was staying at Sopron.

25. Magni originally went to Poland at the request of the nuncio Grimaldi to
attempt to arrange for the mediation of the King of Poland in the conflict between
France and the House of Austria. But little came of this. See Leman, *Urbain VIII*,
pp. 295–96. Magni remained in Poland during most of the reign of King Ladislaus (1632–48); he returned to Bohemia and Germany in the 1650s, and died in
1661; see above, chap. 2, n. 32.

On Basilio d'Aire, see Winter, *Josefinismus*, p. 13, and Tüchle, *Acta SC de
Propaganda Fide*, p. 231, n. 27.

26. HHStA, Friedens. 11a, ff. 262–63, 247–49.

27. Baglione to Barberini, Jul. 7, 1635, BL 6992, f. 3.

28. Feb. 10, 1635, D.A., Karton 90, f. 110v.

29. Compendium, D.A., Karton 90, ff. 40–41. Lamormaini used the disagreement between the two imperial representatives on this and several other points as
the basis for his demand that the theologians be given more documentation about
the terms of the peace; see also ibid., ff. 43, 46.

30. Compendium, D.A., Karton 90, f. 63v; the concluding folios of the minutes
contain Lamormaini's final speech before the conference.

31. HHStA, Friedens. 11a, f. 218; Crasius to an unidentified correspondent in
Munich (Contzen?), Feb. 24, 1635, BH, Jesuitica 704, f. 14.

32. HHStA, Friedens. 11a, ff. 226–27.

33. Ibid., ff. 221–23. See Caramuel y Lobkowitz, *Romani Imperii Pacis licitae
demonstratae Prodromus*, pp. 39–41; the source of his account of the conference
was Quiroga.

34. HHStA, Friedens. 11a, ff. 262–63.

35. Ibid., ff. 247–49, 258–61.

36. See above, n. 11.

37. HHStA, Friedens. 11a, ff. 247–49, 277–87.

38. See Wartenberg to Urban VIII, Altötting, Mar. 5, 1635, and Wartenberg to Barberini, Mar. 7, 1635, Repgen, 1:2:nos. 120, 121.

39. Alessandro d'Ales to Barberini, Feb. 17, 1635, Repgen, 1:2:no. 110.

40. Mainz to the emperor, Jan. 8 and 23, Apr. 2, 1635, HHStA, Friedens. 11a, ff. 13–14, 94–95, and Friedens. 11b, ff. 2, 9; Mainz to Trautmannsdorf, Mar. 26, 1635, ibid., ff. 3–4.

41. Maximilian to the emperor, Feb. 14, 1635, HHStA, Friedens. 11a, ff. 179–181v; Bireley, *Maximilian von Bayern*, pp. 213–20.

42. Cologne to the emperor, Dec. 24, 1634, BH KSchw 963, f. 63 ff. Cologne exhibited the rationale for his position in a set of "Considerations" drawn up by his theologians and sent to Maximilian and the emperor, undated, HHStA, Friedens. 10^{iv}, ff. 33–55v; see Foerster, *Ferdinand von Köln*, pp. 26–30, and Wandruszka, *Reichspatriotismus*, p. 33.

43. Bireley, *Maximilian von Bayern*, pp. 216–17, and Foerster, *Ferdinand von Köln*, pp. 40, 49–51; see also Maximilian to Richel and Paul Andreas von Wolkenstein (his emissaries to Vienna), May 4, 1635, BH, KSchw 965, ff. 208–9, where the elector comments on Wartenberg's minimal activity in Vienna.

44. Emperor to Mainz, Feb. 21, 1635, HHStA, Friedens. 11a, ff. 192–93; emperor to Cologne, Feb. 21, 1635, ibid., ff. 189–91v; Richel (who had presented Maximilian's letter to the emperor) to Maximilian, Feb. 28, 1635, BH, KSchw 377.

45. Undated, HHStA, Friedens. 15, ff. 329–65v.

46. See above, n. 31.

47. Position papers on the Pirna Points, Mar. 5 and 10, 1635, HHStA, Friedens. 11a, ff. 313–23, 325–43, 345–55. Folios 288–310v are miscellaneous minutes of the discussions held between Feb. 27 and Mar. 5. A paper of Pazmany, dated (incorrectly?) May 10, is published in *Epistolae Collectae*, 2:no. 951. This and the following paragraphs are based on this material unless otherwise noted. Also present at some of the meetings were Gebhardt and Johann Söldner, a court secretary.

48. Baglione to Barberini, Feb. 24 (two letters) and Mar. 3, 1635, Repgen, 1:2:nos. 113, 114, 117; Alessandro d'Ales to Barberini, Feb. 24, 1635, ibid., no. 115. See also Leman, *Urbain VIII*, pp. 453–54, 458, 465–66, 484–85.

49. The allusion here is not completely clear. It seems to refer to no one event but to the failure of Wallenstein both militarily and politically during the whole year 1633.

50. According to Alessandro d'Ales to Barberini, Feb. 3, 1635, Repgen, 1:2:no. 104, Trautmannsdorf reported that the French were putting great pressure on Saxony. See also the imperial delegates in Prague to the emperor, Mar. 21, 1635, HHStA, Friedens. 11a, ff. 517–17v, and Leman, *Urbain VIII*, p. 460.

51. The reference is to events in the reign of Amaziah, King of Judah.

52. The remarks of the emperor at this Mar. 5 session are found in HHStA,

Friedens. 11a, ff. 343v–44v, as well as in several annotations throughout the paper. Several other councilors joined the eight for this session. Another important session of Mar. 10, with the emperor present, dealt with more strictly political matters, including the Palatinate question.

53. HHStA, Friedens. 11a, ff. 383–94v, 433–87.

54. Questenberg to the emperor, Jan. 30, 1635, ibid., ff. 122–24; emperor to Ferdinand Kurz von Senftenau, Feb. 9, 1635, ibid., ff. 174–75; Gebhardt to Trautmannsdorf, Vienna, Mar. 14, 1635, HHStA, Traut. 102^{iii}, f. 173. Trautmannsdorf and Kurz were already under way; Gebhardt was soon to follow.

55. Mar. 28, 1635, HHStA, Friedens. 11a, f. 564.

56. Bireley, *Maximilian von Bayern*, p. 218; minutes of the privy council meeting, Mar. 30, 1635, HHStA, Friedens. 15^{ii}, ff. 6–8v; position paper of the committee of councilors, Apr. 30, approved by the emperor, May 1, 1635, ibid., 11b^{ii}, ff. 197–202v.

57. For the text of the Peace of Prague, see *Pirnische u. Pragische Friedens Pacten*. The principal text and three of the protocols are printed in Dumont, *Corps universel diplomatique*, 6:1:89–102; for an overview of the other protocols and where they can be found, see Bittner, *Verzeichnis der österreichischen Staatsverträge*, nos. 252–61.

I am indebted to Fraulein Doktor Kathrin Bierther, Munich, for several important clarifications regarding the Peace of Prague. She has been commissioned to edit the documentation of the Peace by the Historische Kommission bei der Bayerischen Akademie der Wissenschaften.

On Württemberg in particular, see Günter, *Restitutionsedikt*, pp. 269–70, 308–9.

58. Stetten, *Geschichte der Stadt Augspurg*, 2:360–61, 411–12.

59. Position paper of the committee of councilors, Apr. 28–29, 1635, HHStA, Friedens. 11b^{ii}, ff. 187–94; imperial delegates in Prague to the emperor, May 19, 1635, ibid., 12^{i}, ff. 69–73v, 88. See also Repgen, 1:1:379. Bremen was mentioned in the Peace (art. 6), but only with respect to a guarantee of the free exercise of religion.

60. Wandruszka, *Reichspatriotismus*, p. 60.

61. Baglione to Barberini, Jun. 9, 1635, BL 6991, ff. 121–23.

62. Repgen, 1:1:376–88, 393–94, 530.

63. My interpretation of the Peace of Prague follows Haan, *Kurfürstentag von 1636/1637*, pp. 4–6, 15–24, and 289–90, and "Ferdinand II und das Problem des Reichsabsolutismus," esp. pp. 210–13, 241–42, 260–64. Haan shows that both Wandruszka, *Reichspatriotismus*, pp. 45, 57–60, 66–67, 114, and Dickmann, *Westfälische Friede*, pp. 73–74, exaggerate the strength of the emperor's position after the Peace. Goetze, *Die Politik des Oxenstierna*, esp. pp. 148–51, 175–77, greatly exaggerates the position of the emperor created by the Peace of Prague.

64. The military reform called for by the Peace was calculated to provide a smoother functioning of the combined forces fighting for the emperor and was not promoted as a step toward a German monarchy; see Haan, "Ferdinand II und das Problem des Reichsabsolutismus," p. 261.

65. Haan, *Kurfürstentag von 1636/1637*, pp. 84–85.

66. Ibid., pp. 151–55, 172, 255; see Repgen, 1:1:391–401.

67. For the previous three paragraphs see Haan, *Kurfürstentag von 1636/1637*, pp. 1–24, 71–74, 83–87, 223, and Ritter, *Deutsche Geschichte*, 3:599–606.

68. Duhr, 2:2:177.

69. For imperial policy after 1635, see Haan, *Kurfürstentag von 1636/1637*, pp. 80–92, 114–16, 170–82, 224–51, 268–91; Bierther, *Reichstag von 1640/1641*, pp. 63–77, 179–97, 314–27; Dickmann, *Westfälische Friede*, passim; Hans Wagner, "Die Kaiserlichen Instruktionen."

According to Hurter, *Geschichte Ferdinands II*, 11:422, Ferdinand approved Christian of Denmark's postulation of Bremen for his son on Apr. 30, 1636, even though the archbishopric had been promised to Leopold William. This was on condition that he accept the Peace of Prague, which involved a commitment to support the emperor against Sweden and to allow in Bremen the Catholic religious practice of Nov. 12, 1627. Christian refused the offer.

70. Haan, "Ferdinand II und das Problem des Reichsabsolutismus," pp. 260–64. Schwarz, *Imperial Privy Council*, p. 95, asserts that there is no evidence in the records of the imperial privy council or the aulic council of an intent on the part of Ferdinand to establish an absolute hereditary monarchy in the Empire. This confirms my own experience in the archives. Stieve, "Ferdinand II," p. 662, also denies any such intent to Ferdinand.

71. Hantsch, *Geschichte Österreichs*, p. 343.

72. For the relationship of the Habsburg monarchy to the Empire after 1648, see Evans, *The Making of the Habsburg Monarchy*, pp. 274–308, and the literature cited there.

73. Hann, *Kurfürstentag von 1636/1637*, p. 95.

74. Ferdinand to Lamormaini, Jan. 25, 1636, published in Dudik, "Korrespondenz Kaiser Ferdinands," p. 278; Haan, *Kurfürstentag von 1636/1637*, p. 253; *Virtutes*, pp. 22–23.

75. Khevenhiller, *Annales Ferdinandei*, 12:2361; Hurter, *Geschichte Ferdinands II*, 11:560–65.

76. In the preface to the *Virtutes*, Lamormaini announced his intention to write a four-part biography of Ferdinand dealing with his youth, his government in Styria, his government in the Empire, and his virtues. The other parts have never been found and probably were never written.

77. For Lamormaini's career after 1635, see Duhr, 2:2:714–20; for his activity on behalf of Catholic claims in Württemberg, see ibid., 176–80, and Günter, *Restitutionsedikt*, pp. 287–93, 308.

78. Koch, *Geschichte des deutschen Reiches unter Ferdinand III*, p. 4; Steinberger, *Die Jesuiten und die Friedensfrage*, pp. 16–18.

79. Duhr, 2:1:473–78, 2:2:232–35; Steinberger, *Die Jesuiten und die Friedensfrage*, pp. 36, 39–40, 58–59, 61, 161.

80. *Annales Ferdinandei*, 11:427–30. Khevenhiller died in 1650. The volume here cited probably was not published until 1726; see Coreth, *Österreichische Geschichtsschreibung*, p. 70, n. 148.

Bibliography

Manuscript Sources

BRNO
Státní Archiv, Dietrichstein Archiv
  Karton 90, 435.
FLORENCE
Biblioteca Mediceo-Laurenziana
Codici Scioppiani 220, 223, 243.
GRAZ
Universitätsbibliothek
  Handschriften 1097, 1158, 1159:1, 2.
MUNICH
Bayerisches Hauptstaatsarchiv[1]
  Allgemeines Staatsarchiv
    Jesuitica 648, 704, 883/2.
    Akten zur Geschichte des Dreissigjährigen Krieges 212, 242.
  Geheimes Staatsarchiv
    Kasten Schwarz 69, 71, 131, 132, 377, 769, 777, 963, 965.
PANNONHALMA [Benedictine Monastery near Györ, Hungary]
Archives no. 37 (118 G30), no. 116 (119 A2).
ROME
Archivio Congregazione de Propaganda Fide
  Scritture originali riferite nelle Congregazioni Generali 67, 69, 70, 71, 72,
    214, 330.
  Istruzioni 1, 2.
Archivio Segreto Vaticano
  Segreteria di Stato
    Miscellanea, Armarium 8, vols. 89, 90, 91.
    Nunziatura di Colonia, 7, 8, 9, 10, 11, 13.
    Nunziatura di Germania 115, 116, 117, 118, 119, 120, 131M.
    Nunziature Diverse 9, 10, 11.
  Segreteria dei Brevi
    Epistolae ad Principes 44, 45, 46, 47.
Archivum Romanum Societatis Jesu
  Austriae Provincia 3I–II, 4I–II, 5I, 21, 23, 26, 135, 136.
  Bohemiae Provincia 1I–II, 11, 12, 93, 94, 95, 192, 201.

---

1. For a full list of the material in the Bavarian State Archives consulted as well as cited, see my *Maximilian von Bayern, Adam Contzen, S.J., und die Gegenreformation in Deutschland 1624–1635* (Göttingen, 1975).

Congregationes 59, 60, 62.
Franciae Provincia 4, 5, 32.
Germaniae Assistentia 111, 113I–II, 119.
Germaniae Superioris Provincia 5, 6, 7, 21.
Hispaniae Assistentia 70, 82.
Rheni Inferioris Provincia 6, 7I.
Rheni Superioris Provincia 1.
Toletana Provincia 9.
Vitae 139, 161.
Biblioteca Apostolica Vaticana, Fondo Barberini Latini
(These numbers indicate bound volumes containing almost exclusively papal
correspondence, in particular the correspondence of the secretariat of state, for
the pontificate of Urban VIII.)

2172	6200	6746	6937	6962	6978
2198	6201	6747	6938	6967	6979
2199	6217	6748	6942	6968	6980
2200	6218	6753	6944	6969	6988
2201	6223	6754	6945	6970	6989
2202	6224	6755	6948	6971	6990
2203	6253	6886	6949	6972	6991
2204	6254	6893	6950	6973	6992
2629	6260	6902	6951	6974	7054
	6261		6952	6975	7056
	6515			6976	

VIENNA
Österreichisches Staatsarchiv, Abteilung Haus-, Hof- und Staatsarchiv, Reichs-
    kanzlei
    Friedensakten 9c, 10, 11a, 11b, 12a, 12b, 13a, 13b, 15, 16, 18.
    Grosse Correspondenz 25, 27, 29a.
    Kriegsakten 76, 77, 78, 79, 82, 83, 86, 87, 88, 90, 91, 92, 93, 94.
    Mainzer Erzkanzleiarchiv, Reichstagsakten 119, 120, 121, 123, 124.
    Reichshofratsprotokolle 1625, 1628, 1629.
    Reichtagsakten 96, 97b, 98, 99, 100a, 100b, 101a.
    Religionsakten 32, 33, 34, 35.
    Staatenabteilungen
        Frankreich
            Berichte und Weisungen 23, 24.
            Varia 5.
            Noten, 1628–35.
        Romana 50, 51, 52, 53
            Varia 6.
            Hofkorrespondenz 9, 10.
        Spanien
            Varia 4.

Trautmannsdorffisches Familienarchiv 99, 100, 101, 102, 103, 104, 157, 171.
Österreichische Nationalbibliothek
Handschriftensammlung, no. 7378.

Sources and Literature Published before 1700

Carafa, Carlo. *Commentaria de Germania Sacra Restaurata*. Cologne, 1639.
Caramuel y Lobkowitz, Joannes. *Sacri Romani Imperii Pacis licitae demonstratae
. . . Prodromus et Syndromus sive additamentum*. Frankfurt, 1648.
Contzen, Adam. *Politicorum Libri Decem . . .* Mainz, 1620.
Gualdo Priorato, Galeazzo. *Historia delle guerre di Ferdinando II e Ferdinando
III imperatori, e del rè Filippo di Spagna contro Gustavo Adolfo . . . e Luigi,
rè di Francia, successe dall'anno 1630 sino all'anno 1640*. N.p., [ca. 1640].
Hay, Romanus. *Astrum Inextinctum sive Jus Agendi Antiquorum Religiosorum
Ordinum, pro recipiendis suis Monasteriis (quae nonnulli perperam Extincta
fuisse dicunt) et bonis Ecclesiasticis, per S.C. M^{tis} Edictum Generale . . .*
N.p., 1636.
Lamormaini, William. *Ferdinandi II Romanorum Imperatoris Virtutes*. Vienna,
1638.
Laymann, Paul. *Justa Defensio Sanctissimi Romani Pontificis, Augustissimi
Caesaris, S.R.E. Cardinalium, Episcoporum, Principum, et aliorum, demum
minimae Societatis Jesu . . .* Dillingen, 1631.
[————]. *Pacis Compositio inter Principes et Ordines Catholicos atque Augus-
tanae Confessionis Adhaerentes in Comitiis Augustae a. 1555 edita*. Dil-
lingen, 1629.
Londorp, Michael Casper. *Der romischen kayserlichen Majestät . . . Acta publica
und schriftliche Handlungen . . .* 4 vols. Frankfurt, 1668.
*Pirnische u. Pragische Friedens Pacten, zusampt angestelter Collation und An-
weisung der Discrepantz und Unterscheids* [sic] *zwischen denenselben*. N.p.,
1636.
Princeps in Compendio. Vienna, 1668.
[Schoppe, Kaspar]. *Actio perduellionis in Jesuitas juratos S.R. Imperii hostes*.
N.p., 1632.
[————]. *Anatomia Societatis Jesu*. N.p., 1633.
————. *Classicum belli sacri; sive Heldus redivivus*. Pavia, 1619.
Status Particularis regiminis S.C. Majestatis Ferdinandi II. Leiden, 1637.

Sources and Literature Published after 1700

Abgottspon von Staldenried, Germon. *P. Valeriano Magni. Sein Leben im
allgemeinen, seine apostolische Tätigkeit in Böhmen im besondern*. Olten,
1939.
Albrecht, Dieter. *Die auswärtige Politik Maximilians von Bayern 1618–1635*.

Schriftenreihe der Historischen Kommission bei der Bayerischen Akademie der Wissenschaften, vol. 6. Göttingen, 1962.

————. See *Briefe und Akten.*

————. "Zur Finanzierung des Dreissigjährigen Krieges." *Zeitschrift für bayerische Landesgeschichte* 19 (Munich, 1956): 534–67. Reprinted in Rudolf, ed., *Der Dreissigjährige Krieg*, pp. 368–412.

————. "Das konfessionelle Zeitalter. Zweiter Teil: Die Herzöge Wilhelm V und Maximilian I." *Handbuch der bayerischen Geschichte*, ed. Max Spindler. Vol. 2, *Das Alte Bayern: Der Territorialstaat vom Ausgang des 12 Jahrhunderts bis zum Ausgang des 18 Jahrhunderts*, pp. 351–409. Munich, 1969.

————. "Die Kurialen Anweisungen für den Nuntius Rocci zum Regensburger Kurfürstentag 1630." *Quellen und Forschungen aus Italienischen Archiven und Bibliotheken* 35 (Tübingen, 1955): 282–89.

Aldea, Quentin. *España, el Papado y el Imperio durante la Guerra de los Treinta años.* Comillas, 1958.

Aretin, Carl Maria von. *Bayerns auswärtige Verhältnisse seit dem Anfang des 16 Jahrhunderts.* Passau, 1839.

Astrain, Antonio. *Historia de la Compañia de Jesús en la Asistencia de España.* Vol. 5, *Vitelleschi, Carafa, Piccolomini, 1615–1652.* Madrid, 1916.

Avenel. *See* Richelieu.

Baustaedt, Berthold. *Richelieu und Deutschland. Von der Schlacht bei Breitenfeld bis zum Tode Bernhards von Weimar.* Berlin, 1936.

Bierther, Kathrin. *Der Regensburger Reichstag von 1640/1641.* Regensburger Historische Forschungen, vol. 1. Kallmunz, 1971.

Bireley, Robert. *Maximilian von Bayern, Adam Contzen, S.J., und die Gegenreformation in Deutschland, 1624–1635.* Schriftenreihe der Historischen Kommission bei der Bayerischen Akademie der Wissenschaften, vol. 13. Göttingen, 1975.

————. "The Origins of the '*Pacis Compositio*' 1629: A Text of Paul Laymann, S.J." *Archivum Historicum Societatis Jesu* 42 (Rome, 1973): 106–27.

Bittner, Ludwig. *Chronologisches Verzeichnis der österreichischen Staatsverträge.* Vol. 1, *Die österreichischen Staatsverträge von 1526 bis 1763.* Vienna, 1903.

Brandi, Karl, ed. *Der Augsburger Religionsfriede.* 2d ed. Göttingen, 1927.

Briefe und Akten zur Geschichte des Dreissigjährigen Krieges. N.s., *Die Politik Maximilians I von Bayern und seiner Verbündeten, 1618–1630.* Part 2. 5 vols. Edited by Walter Goetz and Dieter Albrecht. Leipzig and Munich, 1907–64.

Burckhardt, Carl J. *Richelieu: His Rise to Power.* Translated and abridged by Edwin and Willa Muir. New York, 1940.

Carafa, Carlo. "Relatione dello stato dell'imperio e della Germania, fatta dopo il ritorno della sua nuntiatura appresso l'imperatore 1628." Edited by Johann G. Müller. *Archiv für Kunde österreichischer Geschichtsquellen* 23 (Vienna, 1860): 101–449.

Carafa, Pier Luigi. *Legatio Apostolica Petri Aloysii Carafae, Episcopi Tricaricensis Ad Tractum Rheni et ad Provincias Inferioris Germaniae ab Anno 1624 usque ad Annum 1634.* Edited by Josephus A. Ginzel. Würzburg, 1840.

Chlumecky, Peter Ritter von. *Die Regesten der Archive im Markgrafthume Mähren*. Vol. 1, *Die Regesten oder die chronologischen Verzeichnisse der Urkunden in den Archiven zur Iglau . . . sammt den noch ungedruckten Briefen Kaiser Ferdinands des Zweiten, Albrechts von Waldstein und Romboalds Grafen Collalto*. Brünn, 1856.

Chudoba, Bohdan. *Spain and the Empire, 1519–1643*. Chicago, 1952.

Cordara, Jules Cesare. *Historiae Societatis Jesu Pars Sexta, 1616–1633*. 2 vols. Rome, 1750–1859.

Coreth, Anna. *Österreichische Geschichtsschreibung in der Barockzeit, 1620–1740*. Veröffentlichungen der Kommission für Neuere Geschichte Osterreichs, vol. 37. Vienna, 1950.

———. *Pietas Austriaca. Ursprung und Entwicklung Barocker Frömmigkeit in Österreich*. Munich, 1959.

Cuthbert, Father. *The Capuchins: A Contribution to the History of the Counterreformation*. 2 vols. London, 1929.

D'Addio, Mario. *Il Pensiero Politico di Gaspare Scioppio e il Machiavellismo del Seicento*. Milan, 1962.

De Carrocera, Buonaventura. "El Padre Diego de Quiroga, diplomatico y confessor de reyes, 1574–1649." *Estudios Francescanos* 50 (Barcelona, 1949): 71–100.

Dickmann, Fritz. "Das Problem der Gleichberechtigung der Konfessionen im Reich im 16 und 17 Jahrhundert." *Historische Zeitschrift* 201 (Munich, 1965): 265–305.

———. *Der Westfälische Frieden*. Münster, 1959.

Diwald, Helmut. *Wallenstein: Eine Biographie*. Munich, 1969.

Droysen, Gustav. "Die Verhandlungen über dem Universalfrieden im Winter 1631/1632." *Archiv für sächsische Geschichte*, n.s. 6 (Leipzig, 1880): 144–252.

Dudik, Beda. "Kaiser Ferdinand II und dessen Beichtväter." *Historisch-politische Blätter* 78 (Munich, 1876): 469–80.

———. "Kaiser Ferdinand II und P. Lamormaini." *Historisch-politische Blätter* 78 (Munich, 1876): 600–609.

———. "Korrespondenz Kaiser Ferdinands und seiner Familie mit Becanus und Lamormaini." *Archiv für österreichische Geschichte* 54 (Vienna, 1876): 219–350.

———. *Waldstein, von seiner Enthebung bis zur abermaligen Übernahme des Armee-Ober-Commando*. Vienna, 1858.

Duhr, Bernhard. *Geschichte der Jesuiten in den Ländern deutscher Zunge*. Vols. 1 and 2, parts 1 and 2. Freiburg, 1907–13.

———. "Neues Licht über Wallensteins Schuld." *Stimmen der Zeit* 107 (Munich, 1924): 175–88.

Dumont, Jean. *Corps universel diplomatique*. Vol. 5, 2, *1600–1630*. Vol. 6, 1, *1630–1650*. Amsterdam, 1726–28.

Eckhardt, Carl C. *The Papacy and World Affairs, as Reflected in the Secularization of Politics*. Chicago, 1937.

Eder, Karl. "Ferdinand II." *Neue Deutsche Biographie* 5 (Berlin, 1960): 83–85.

_____. "Rahmen und Hintergrund der Gestalt Ferdinands II (1619–1636)." *Festschrift für Julius Franz Schütz*, edited by Berthold Sutter, pp. 315–24. Graz and Cologne, 1954.

Engelbert, Karl. "Das Bistum Breslau im Dreissigjährigen Krieg." *Archiv für schlesische Kirchengeschichte* 25 (Hildesheim, 1967): 201–51.

Essen, Alfred van der. *Le Cardinal-Infant et le politique européene de l'Espagne, 1609–1641.* Vol. 1, *1609–1634.* Louvain and Brussels, 1944.

Eubel, Conrad. See *Hierarchia catholica.*

Evans, R. J. W. *The Making of the Habsburg Monarchy, 1550–1700: An Interpretation.* Oxford, 1979.

Fagniez, Gustav. *Le Père Joseph et Richelieu, 1577–1638.* 2 vols. Paris, 1894.

Fellner, Theodor, and Kretschmayr, Heinrich. *Die österreichische Zentralverwaltung.* Section 1, vol. 1. Vienna, 1907.

Fiedler, Josef, ed. *Die Relationen der Botschafter Venedigs über Deutschland und Österreich im 17 Jahrhundert.* Vol. 1, *Matthias bis Ferdinand III.* Fontes Rerum Austriacarum, Section 2, vol. 26. Vienna, 1866.

Fink, Karl A. *Das vatikanische Archiv. Einführung in die Bestände und ihre Erforschung.* 2d ed. Rome, 1951.

Foerster, Joachim F. *Kurfürst Ferdinand von Köln: Die Politik seiner Stifter in den Jahren 1634–1650.* Schriftenreihe der Vereinigung zur Erforschung der Neueren Geschichte 6. Münster, 1976.

Forst, Hermann. *See* Wartenberg.

Fouqueray, Henri. "Le Père Jean Suffren à la cour de Marie de Medicis et de Louis XIII, d'après Les Mémoires du temps et des documents inédits." *Revue des Questions historiques* 68 (Paris, 1900): 74–131, 445–71. Also published separately, Paris, 1900.

Franz, Günther. "Glaube und Recht im politischen Denken Kaiser Ferdinands II." *Archiv für Reformationsgeschichte* 49 (Gütersloh, 1958): 258–69. Reprinted in Rudolf, ed., *Der Dreissigjährige Krieg*, pp. 413–27.

Franzl, Johann. *Ferdinand II. Kaiser im Zwiespalt der Zeit.* Graz, 1978.

Frohnweiler, Karl-Heinz. "Die Friedenspolitik des Landgrafen Georgs II von Hessen-Darmstadt, 1630–1635." *Archiv für hessische Geschichte und Altertumskunde*, n.s. 29 (Darmstadt, 1964): 1–185.

Ganser, Irimbert. "Ferdinand II im Lichte der Geschichtsschreibung." Ph.D. dissertation, University of Vienna, 1949.

Gauchat, Patrick. See *Hierarchia catholica.*

Gebauer, Johannes H. *Kurbrandenburg und das Restitutionsedikt von 1629.* Hallesche Abhandlungen zur neueren Geschichte, vol. 38. Halle, 1899.

Gindely, Anton. *Geschichte der Gegenreformation in Böhmen.* Edited by Theodor Tupetz. Leipzig, 1894.

_____. "Die Maritimen Pläne der Habsburger und die Antheilnahme Kaisers Ferdinand II am Polnisch-Schwedischen Kriege während der Jahre 1627–1629." *Denkschriften der kaiserlichen Akademie der Wissenschaften, Philosophisch-Historische Classe* 39 (Vienna, 1891): 1–54.

_____. *Waldstein während seines ersten Generalats, 1625–1630.* 2 vols. Prague and Leipzig, 1886.

Goetz, Walter. See *Briefe und Akten.*

_____. "Wallenstein und Kurfürst Maximilian von Bayern." *Zeitschrift für bayerische Landesgeschichte* 11 (Munich, 1938): 106–20.

Goetze, Sigmund. *Die Politik des schwedischen Reichskanzlers Axel Oxenstierna gegenüber Kaiser und Reich.* Beiträge zur Sozial- und Wirtschaftsgeschichte, vol. 3. Kiel, 1971.

Gordon, I. "El sujeto de dominio de los colegios de la Compañia de Jesús en la Controversa alemana sobre la restitucion de los monasteros." *Archivo teologico granadino* 16 (Granada, 1953): 5–62.

Gross, Lothar. *Die Geschichte der deutschen Reichshofkanzlei, 1559–1806.* Vienna, 1933.

_____, and Bittner, Ludwig. *Gesamtinventar des Wiener Haus-, Hof- und Staatsarchivs aufgebaut auf der Geschichte des Archivs und seiner Bestände.* 5 vols. Vienna, 1936–40.

Gschliesser, Oswald von. *Der Reichshofrat. Bedeutung und Verfassung, Schicksal und Besetzung einer obersten Reichsbehörde von 1559–1806.* Veröffentlichungen der Kommission für Neuere Geschichte des ehemaligen Österreichs, vol. 33. Vienna, 1942.

Günter, Heinrich. *Die Habsburgerliga, 1625–1635. Briefe und Akten aus dem General-Archiv zu Simancas.* Berlin, 1908.

_____. *Das Restitutionsedikt von 1629 und die katholische Restauration Altwirtembergs.* Stuttgart, 1901.

Haan, Heiner. "Kaiser Ferdinand II und das Problem des Reichsabsolutismus: Die Prager Heeresreform von 1635." *Historische Zeitschrift* 207 (Munich, 1968): 297–345. Reprinted in Rudolf, ed., *Der Dreissigjährige Krieg,* pp. 208–64.

_____. *Der Regensburger Kurfürstentag von 1636/1637.* Münster, 1967.

Hallwich, Hermann, ed. *Briefe und Akten zur Geschichte Wallensteins, 1630–1634.* 4 vols. Fontes Rerum Austriacarum, Section 2, vols. 63–66. Vienna, 1912.

_____. *Fünf Bücher Geschichte Wallensteins.* 3 vols. Leipzig, 1910.

_____. *Wallensteins Ende. Ungedruckte Briefe und Acten.* 2 vols. Leipzig, 1879.

Hantsch, Hugo. *Die Geschichte Österreichs.* Vol. 1. 4th ed. Graz, Vienna, and Cologne, 1959.

_____. "Kaiser Ferdinand II (1578–1637)." *Gestalter der Geschicke Österreichs,* pp. 157–70. Edited by Hugo Hantsch. Innsbruck, Vienna, and Munich, 1962.

Heckel, Martin. "*Autonomia* und *Pacis Compositio.* Der Augsburger Religionsfriede in der Deutung der Gegenreformation." *Zeitschrift für Rechtsgeschichte* 76, kanonistische Abteilung 45 (Weimar, 1959): 141–248.

Heydendorff, Walther E. *Die Fürsten und Freiherren zu Eggenberg und Ihre Vorfahren.* Graz, 1965.

Hierarchia catholica medii et recentioris aevi. Vol. 3, *Saeculum XVI ab anno 1503 complectens*, ed. Conrad Eubel. Vol. 4, *A pontificatu Clementis PP. VIII (1592) usque ad pontificatum Alexandri PP. VII (1667)*, ed. Patrick Gauchat. Münster, 1910–35.

Holborn, Hajo. *A History of Modern Germany: The Reformation.* New York, 1964.

Hopf, Alexander. *Anton Wolfradt. Fürstbischof von Wien und Abt des Benediktinerstiftes Kremsmünster, Geheimer Rath, und Minister Kaiser Ferdinands II.* 3 vols. Vienna, 1891–94.

Hurter, Friedrich. *Friedensbestrebungen Kaiser Ferdinands II.* Vienna, 1860.

———. *Geschichte Kaiser Ferdinands II.* Vols. 8–11. Schaffhausen, 1857–64.

Institutum Societatis Jesu. Vol. 2. Florence, 1893.

Irmer, Georg. *Die Verhandlungen Schwedens und seiner Verbündeten mit Wallenstein und dem Kaiser von 1631–1634.* 3 vols. Publikationen aus den Preussischen Staatsarchiven, vols. 35, 39, 46. Leipzig, 1888–91.

Jedin, Hubert. "Eine Denkschrift über die Gegenreformation in Schlesien aus dem Jahre 1625." *Archiv für schlesische Kirchengeschichte* 3 (Breslau, 1938): 152–71. Reprinted in Hubert Jedin, *Kirche des Glaubens, Kirche der Geschichte, Ausgewählte Aufsätze und Vorträge.* Vol. 1, pp. 395–412. Freiburg, Basel, and Vienna, 1966.

Khevenhiller, Franz Christoph von. *Annales Ferdinandei, oder Wahrhaffte Beschreibung Kaysers Ferdinandi des Andern . . . Geburth . . . und vollzogenen hochwichtigen Geschäfften.* Vols. 9–12. Leipzig, 1724–26.

Kiewning, Hans. ed., *Nuntiaturberichte aus Deutschland nebst ergänzenden Aktenstücken.* Section 4, *Siebzehntes Jahrhundert, Nuntiatur des Pallotto 1628–1630.* 2 vols. Berlin, 1895–97.

Kink, Rudolf. *Geschichte der kaiserlichen Universität zu Wien.* Vols. 1, parts 1 and 2, and 2. Vienna, 1854.

Klopp, Onno. *Der dreissigjährige Krieg bis zum Tode Gustav Adolphs 1632.* Vols. 2 and 3, parts 1 and 2. Paderborn, 1893–96.

———. "Das Restitutionsedikt im nordwestlichen Deutschland." *Forschungen zur deutschen Geschichte* 1 (1862): 75–129.

Koch, Mathias. *Geschichte des deutschen Reiches unter der Regierung Ferdinands III.* Vol. 1. Vienna, 1865.

Koenigsberger, H. G. *The Habsburgs and Europe 1516–1660.* Ithaca, 1971.

Kollmann, Ignatius, ed. *Acta Sacrae Congregationis de Propaganda Fide Res Gestas Bohemicas Illustrantia.* Vol. 1, part 1, 1622–1623, part 2, *Index.* Vol. 2, 1623–1624. Prague, 1923–54.

Kornis, Jules. *Le Cardinal Pázmány (1570–1637).* Paris, 1937.

Kowalsky, Nicolo. *Inventario dell'Archivio storico della S. Congregazione "de Propaganda Fide."* Schöneck and Beckenried, 1961.

Kraus, Andreas. *Das päpstliche Staatssekretariat unter Urban VIII. 1623–1644. Römische Quartalschrift für christliche Altertumskunde und Kirchengeschichte*, Supplement 29. Rome, Freiburg, and Vienna, 1961.

Kroess, Alois. *Geschichte der Böhmischen Provinz der Gesellschaft Jesu*, Vols. 1

and 2, section 1. *Quellen und Forschungen zur Geschichte Österreichs und der angrenzenden Gebiete*, vols. 11 and 13. Vienna, 1910–27.

———. "Gutachten der Jesuiten am Beginne der katholischen Generalreformation in Bohmen." *Historisches Jahrbuch* 34 (Munich, 1913): 1–39, 257–94.

Krones, Franz von. *Geschichte der Karl Franzens Universität in Graz*. Graz, 1886.

Lecler, Joseph. *Toleration and the Reformation*. 2 vols. Translated by T. L. Westow. New York and London, 1960.

Leman, Auguste. *Urbain VIII et la rivalité de la France et de la maison d'Autriche de 1631 à 1635*. Lille and Paris, 1920.

Loserth, Johannes, ed. *Akten und Korrespondenzen zur Geschichte der Gegenreformation in Innerösterreich unter Erzherzog Karl, 1578–1590*. Fontes Rerum Austriacarum, Section 2, vol. 50. Vienna, 1898.

———. *Akten und Korrespondenzen zur Geschichte der Gegenreformation in Innerösterreich unter Ferdinand II*. Part 1, *1590–1600*. Part 2, *1600–1637*. Fontes Rerum Austriacarum, Section 2, vols. 58, 60.

Lutz, Georg. "Glaubwürdigkeit und Gehalt von Nuntiaturberichten." *Quellen und Forschungen aus Italienischen Archiven und Bibliotheken* 53 (Tübingen, 1973): 227–75.

———. *Kardinal Giovanni Francesco Guidi di Bagno: Politik und Religion im Zeitalter Richelieus und Urbans VIII*. Bibliothek des Deutschen Historischen Instituts zu Rom, vol. 34. Tübingen, 1971.

———. "Wallenstein, Ferdinand II, und der Wiener Hof. Bemerkungen zu einem erneuten Beitrag zur alten Wallensteinfrage." *Quellen und Forschungen aus Italienischen Archiven und Bibliotheken* 48 (Tübingen, 1968): 207–43.

Mann, Golo. *Wallenstein*. Frankfurt, 1971.

Mareš, Franz. "Beiträge zur Geschichte der Beziehungen des Fürsten Johann Ulrich von Eggenberg zu Kaiser Ferdinand II und zu Wallenstein." *Sitzungsberichte der kgl. böhmischen Gesellschaft der Wissenschaften, Classe für Philosophie, Geschichte, und Philologie, Jahrgang 1892*. Prague, 1893.

———. "Die maritime Politik der Habsburger in den Jahren 1625–1628." *Mitteilungen des Instituts für österreichische Geschichtsforschung* 1 (Innsbruck, 1880): 541–78 and 2 (1881): 49–82.

Mayer, Anton, ed. *Geschichte der Stadt Wien*. Vols. 4–6. Vienna, 1911.

Mecenseffy, Grete. *Geschichte des Protestantismus in Österreich*. Graz and Cologne, 1956.

Messow, Hans-Christoph. *Die Hansestädte und die Habsburgische Ostseepolitik im 30-Jährigen Kriege, 1627–1628*. Neue Deutsche Forschungen, vol. 3. Berlin, 1935.

Mitis, Oswald von. "Gundacker von Liechtensteins Anteil an der kaiserlichen Zentralverwaltung, 1606–1654." *Beiträge zur neueren Geschichte Österreichs* 5 (Vienna, 1908): 35–118.

Nischan, Bodo. "Reformed Irenicism and the Leipzig Colloquy of 1631." *Central European History* 9 (Atlanta, 1976): 3–26.

Nolden, Karl. "Die Reichspolitik Kaiser Ferdinands II in der Publizistik bis zum

Lübecker Frieden 1629." Ph.D. dissertation, University of Cologne, 1958.
Nostitz, Oswald von. "Golo Manns 'Wallenstein.'" *Stimmen der Zeit*, 190, 7 (Munich, 1972): 281–84.
O'Connell, D. P. "A Cause Célèbre in the History of Treaty Making. The Refusal to Ratify the Peace Treaty of Regensburg in 1630." *The British Yearbook of International Law* 42 (London, 1967): 71–90.
————. *Richelieu*. London, 1968.
Opel, Julius Otto. *Der niedersächsisch-dänische Krieg*. 3 vols. Halle, 1872–94.
Pagès, George. *The Thirty Years War, 1618–1648*. Translated by David Maland and John Hooper. New York, 1971.
Parker, Geoffrey. *The Dutch Revolt*. Ithaca, 1977.
Pastor, Ludwig von. *Geschichte der Päpste seit dem Ausgang des Mittelalters*. Vol. 12, *Leo XI und Paul V, 1605–1621*. Vol. 13, parts 1 and 2, *Gregory XV und Urban VIII, 1621–1644*. Freiburg, 1927–29.
Pazmany, Peter. *Epistolae Collectae*. Edited by Franciscus Hanuy. 2 vols. Budapest, 1910–11.
Pekař, Josef. *Wallenstein, Tragödie einer Verschwörung*. 2 vols. Berlin, 1937.
Petry, Ludwig. "Politische Geschichte unter den Habsburgern." *Geschichte Schlesiens*. Edited by Ludwig Petry and J. Joachim Menzel. Vol. 2, *Die Habsburgerzeit, 1526–1740*, pp. 1–136. Darmstadt, 1973.
Pieper, Anton. "Die Relationen des Nuntius Carafa über die Zeit seiner Wiener Nuntiatur, 1621–1628." *Historisches Jahrbuch* 2 (Munich, 1881): 388–415.
Platzhoff, Walter. *Geschichte des europäischen Staatensystems, 1559–1660*. Munich and Berlin, 1928.
Polišenský, Josef. *Documenta Bohemica Bellum Tricennale Illustrantia*. Vol. 1, *Der Krieg und die Gesellschaft in Europa, 1618–1648*. Prague and Vienna, 1971.
Posch, Andreas. "Guillaume Lamormaini, (1570–1648)." Translated by Alphonse Sprunck. *Biographie nationale du pays de Luxembourg depuis ses origines jusqu'à nos jours*. Fascicle 5 (Luxembourg, 1953): 265–97.
————. "Zur Tätigkeit und Beurteilung Lamormainis." *Mitteilungen des Instituts für österreichische Geschichtsforschung* 63 (Vienna, 1955): 375–90.
Pra, J. "Philippe IV, Roi d'Espagne et la Compagnie de Jésus, Episode Historique, 1631." *Précis Historique*, series 3, vol. 3 (Paris, 1894): 205–17.
Press, Volker. "Böhmischer Aristokrat und Kaiserlicher General. Zwei Biographien Albrecht von Wallensteins." *Historische Zeitschrift* 222 (Munich, 1976): 626–38.
Quazza, Romolo. *La guerra per la successione di Mantova e del Monferrato, 1628–1631*. 2 vols. Mantua, 1926.
Rabb, Theodore, ed. *The Thirty Years War*. 2d ed. Lexington, Toronto, and London, 1972.
Re, Nicolo del. *La Curia Romana; lineamenti storico-giuridici*. 3d ed. Sussidi eruditi, vol. 23. Rome, 1970.
Repgen, Konrad. "Lukas Holsteinius als politischer Gutachter in Rom. Eine

unbekannte Denkschrift aus der Zeit des Restitutionsedikts." *Quellen und Forschungen aus Italienischen Archiven und Bibliotheken* 39 (Tübingen, 1959): 342–52.

————. *Die römische Kurie und der westfälische Friede: Idee und Wirklichkeit des Papsttums im 16. und 17. Jahrhundert.* Vol. 1, *Papst, Kaiser und Reich, 1521–1644*, part 1, *Darstellung*, part 2, *Analekten und Register.* Bibliothek des Deutschen Historischen Instituts in Rom, vols. 24, 25. Tübingen, 1962–65.

Richelieu. *Lettres, instructions diplomatiques, et papiers d'état du Cardinal de Richelieu.* Edited by D. L. M. Avenel. Vols. 1, 3, 7, 8. Paris, 1853–77.

————. *Mémoires, 1629–1638. Nouvelle collection des mémoires pour servir à l'histoire de France depuis la xiiie siècle jusqu'à la fin du xviiie.* Edited by Joseph Michaud et Jean Joseph Poujoulat. Vols. 22, 23. Paris, 1857.

Richter, Karl. "Die böhmischen Länder von 1471–1740." *Handbuch der Geschichte der böhmischen Länder.* Edited by Karl Bosl. Vol. 2, *Die böhmischen Länder von der Hochblüte der Ständeherrschaft bis zum Erwachen eines modernen Nationalbewusstseins*, pp. 97–412. Stuttgart, 1974.

Ritter, Moriz. *Deutsche Geschichte im Zeitalter der Gegenreformation und des Dreissigjährigen Krieges.* 3 vols. Stuttgart, 1889–1908. Reprint. Darmstadt, 1962.

————. "Der Ursprung des Restitutionsedikts." *Historische Zeitschrift* 76 (Munich, 1896): 62–102. Reprinted in Rudolf, ed., *Der Dreissigjährige Krieg*, pp. 135–74.

Roberts, Michael. *Gustavus Adolphus. A History of Sweden, 1611–1632.* Vol. 2, *1626–1632.* London, 1958.

Rudolf, Hans Ulrich, ed. *Der Dreissigjährige Krieg: Perspektiven und Strukturen.* Wege der Forschung, vol. 451. Darmstadt, 1977.

Russo, Rosario. "La politica del Vaticano nella Dieta di Ratisbona del 1630." *Archivio Storico Italiano* 84 (Florence, 1926): 25–88, 233–85.

Schwarz, Henry F. *The Imperial Privy Council in the Seventeenth Century.* Cambridge, Mass., 1943.

Seppelt, Franz X., and Schwaiger, Georg. *Geschichte der Päpste.* Vol. 5, *Das Papsttum im Kampf mit Staatsabsolutismus und Aufklärung. Von Paul III bis zur französischen Revolution.* Munich, 1959.

Spiegel, Käthe. "Die Prager Universitätsunion (1618–1654)." *Mitteilungen des Vereins für Geschichte der Deutschen in Böhmen* 62 (1924): 5–94.

Srbik, Heinrich Ritter von. *Wallensteins Ende.* 2d ed. Salzburg, 1952.

Steinberger, Ludwig. *Die Jesuiten und die Friedensfrage in der Zeit vom Prager Frieden bis zum Nürnberger Friedensexekutionshauptrezess, 1635–1650.* Freiburg, 1906.

Stepischnegg, J. "Georg III Stobäus von Palmburg." *Archiv für österreichische Geschichtskunde* 15 (Vienna, 1856): 71–132.

Stetten, Paul von. *Geschichte der Heil. Rom. Reichs freyen Stadt Augspurg.* 2 vols. Frankfurt, 1743–58.

Stiegele, Rudolf. "Beiträge zu einer Biographie des Jesuiten Wilhelm Lamormaini." *Historisches Jahrbuch* 28 (Munich, 1907): 551–69, 849–70.

Stieve, Felix. "Ferdinand II, Deutscher Kaiser." *Allgemeine Deutsche Biographie* 6 (Leipzig, 1877): 644–64.

Sturmberger, Hans. *Adam Graf Herberstorff. Herrschaft und Freiheit im konfessionellen Zeitalter.* Munich, 1976.

————. *Aufstand in Böhmen: Der Beginn des Dreissigjährigen Krieges.* Munich and Vienna, 1959.

————. *Georg Erasmus Tschernembl: Religion, Libertät und Widerstand.* Forschungen zur Geschichte Öberösterreichs, vol. 3. Graz, 1953.

————. *Kaiser Ferdinand II und das Problem des Absolutismus.* Linz, 1967.

Suvanto, Pekka. *Wallenstein und seine Anhänger am Kaiserhof, 1631–1634.* Studia Historica, vol. 5. Helsinki, 1963.

Tapié, Victor-L. *The Rise and Fall of the Habsburg Monarchy.* Translated by Stephen Hardman. New York, 1971.

Toegel, Miroslav, ed. *Documenta Bohemica Bellum Tricennale Illustrantia.* Vol. 5, *Der schwedische Krieg und Wallensteins Ende.* Prague and Vienna, 1977.

Tomek, Ernst. *Kirchengeschichte Österreichs.* Vol. 2. Innsbruck and Vienna, 1949.

Treasure, Geoffrey R. R. *Cardinal Richelieu and the Development of Absolutism.* New York, 1972.

Tüchle, Hermann, ed. *Acta SC de Propaganda Fide Germaniam spectantia. Die Protokolle der Propagandakongregation zu deutschen Angelegenheiten, 1622–1649.* Paderborn, 1965.

Tupetz, Theodor. "Der Streit um die geistlichen Güter und das Restitutionsedikt 1629." *Sitzungsberichte der kaiserlichen Akademie der Wissenschaften, Philosophisch-Historische Classe* 102 (Vienna, 1883): 315–556.

Turba, Gustav. *Die Grundlagen der pragmatischen Sanktion.* Vol. 2, *Die Hausgesetze.* Wiener Staatswissenschaftliche Studien, vol. 11, book 1. Vienna and Leipzig, 1913.

Uhlirz, Karl. *Handbuch der Geschichte Österreichs und seiner Nachbarländer Böhmen und Ungarn.* Vol. 1. Graz, Vienna, and Leipzig, 1927.

Urban, Helmut. "Druck und Drucke des Restitutionsedikts von 1629." *Archiv für die Geschichte des Buchwesens* 14 (1974): 609–54.

————. *Das Restitutionsedikt: Versuch einer Interpretation.* Munich, 1968.

Vilar, R. Rodenas. *La politica europea de España durante la Guerra de Treinta años, 1624–1630.* Madrid, 1967.

Wagner, Hans. "Die kaiserlichen Instruktionen (1637–1645): Einleitung." *Acta Pacis Westphalicae.* Edited by Max Braubach and Konrad Repgen. Series 1, *Instruktionen,* vol. 1, *Frankreich, Schweden, Kaiser,* pp. 327–54. Münster, 1962.

Wandruszka, Adam. *Reichspatriotismus und Reichspolitik zur Zeit des Prager Friedens von 1635.* Graz and Cologne, 1955.

Wartenberg, Franz Wilhelm von. *Die Politische Correspondenz des Grafen Franz Wilhelm von Wartenberg Bischof von Osnabrück, 1621–1631.* Edited by Hermann Forst. Publikationen aus den Preussischen Staatsarchiven, vol. 68. Leipzig, 1897.

Weber, Hermann. *Frankreich, Kurtrier, Der Rhein und das Reich, 1623–1635.* Pariser Historische Studien, vol. 9. Bonn, 1969.

Wedgwood, Cicely V. *The Thirty Years War.* London, 1938.

Weech, Friedrich von. "Mitteilungen aus dem Vatikanischen Archiv: Verzeichnis des Inhalts der Akten der Congregazione sopra il Palatinato." *Zeitschrift für die Geschichte des Oberrheins,* n.s. 10 (Karlsruhe, 1895): 632–49.

Wiedemann, Theodor. *Geschichte der Reformation und Gegenreformation im Lande unter der Enns.* Vol. 1. Prague, 1879.

Winter, Eduard. *Barock, Absolutismus und Aufklärung in der Donaumonarchie.* Vienna, 1971.

————. *Der Josefinismus: Die Geschichte des österreichischen Reformkatholizismus, 1740–1848.* Berlin, 1962.

Woisetschläger, Kurt, ed. *Der innerösterreichische Hofkünstler Giovanni Pietro de Pomis.* Graz, 1974.

Zeeden, Ernst Walter. "Das Zeitalter der Glaubenskämpfe (1555–1648)." *Handbuch der deutschen Geschichte.* Edited by Herbert Grundmann. Vol. 2, *Von der Reformation bis zum Ende des Absolutismus*, pp. 119–239. 9th ed. Stuttgart, 1970.

Zwiedineck-Südenhorst, H. von. *Hans Ulrich Fürst von Eggenberg.* Vienna, 1880.

Index

Acquaviva, Claudio, S.J., superior general of the Jesuits (1581–1615), 11

Adolf Friedrich, Duke of Mecklenburg. See Mecklenburg, duchy

Agnelli-Soardi, Vincenzo. See Mantua, Vincenzo Agnelli-Soardi, Bishop of

Aguado, Francesco, S.J., 270 (n. 40)

Aldringen, Johann von, 202, 203

Alegambe, Philippe, S.J., 120

Alessandro d'Ales, Capuchin, 211, 212, 215, 216, 219

Alsace, 206, 207

Althan, Michael Adolf von, 134

Anselm Casimir von Wambold, Archbishop-Elector of Mainz (1629–47), 89, 93, 198; at the Electoral Convention of Regensburg, 114, 117, 123–26, 129, 130; and the Frankfurt Conference, 152, 159; and the Peace of Prague, 211, 218, 219, 226. See also Catholic electors; Catholic League

Anstruther, Robert, 114

Anterior Austria, 5, 6, 16, 155, 167

Anton Wolfradt, Abbot of Kremsmünster and Bishop of Vienna (1631), 36, 58–59, 158; life and career, 19, 157, 230; and Spain, 19, 158, 165, 194; and France, 121, 157, 177–78, 186, 207, 221–22; and negotiations with the Protestants, 126, 157, 172, 190–91, 192, 194–95, 197, 199, 208; and the monastery controversy, 137, 142, 143; and Lamormaini, 137, 157, 158, 190, 191, 208; and Wallenstein, 182, 202; and the Peace of Prague, 220–23, 225, 229

Aquileia, patriarchate, 42, 61, 69, 70–71

Aquinas, Thomas, 131

Argenti, Joannes, S.J., 10, 11

Arnim, Hans Georg von, 79, 94, 203; negotiations with Wallenstein, 171, 175, 176, 195–96, 199–200

Augsburg, Heinrich von Knöringen, Bishop of, 53, 74, 88, 142, 152, 174; and the Peace of Augsburg, 76–77, 92–93

Augsburg, city: Counterreformation in, 90, 92–94, 123, 124, 172, 224–25; Saxon intervention on behalf of, 123, 154

Augsburg, Peace of, 25–26, 52, 87, 125, 130, 220, 227, 228, 237 (n. 7); and the Edict, 75–76; as interpreted by Laymann, 86, 92–93; and Lamormaini, 88–89

August of Saxony, son of Elector John George, 64, 210

Aulic council: organization and role in government, 18. See also Judicial reform, imperial

Austrian lands, 46, 213; demand for free exercise of religion in, 194, 204, 210

Avigliana, 162

Axpe, Pedro de, 164

Aytona, Marquis of, 29, 68, 73; and Lamormaini, 72

Baden-Durlach, Margrave of, 212

Baglione, Malatesta, 207, 211

Bagno, Giovanni Francesco Guidi di, 96, 160

Baltic area: plans for Habsburg expansion in, 24, 47, 62, 65, 79

Bamberg, Johann Georg Fuchs von Dornheim, Bishop of (died 1633), 74, 152, 167

Bamberg, bishopric, 277 (n. 3)

Bandini, Giovanni, cardinal, 81

Baner, Johann, 205

Barberini, Francesco, cardinal, 42, 211; position in the Curia, 21; and Lamormaini, 69–70, 73, 82, 115. See also Urban VIII, pope

Barberini, Maffeo. See Urban VIII, pope

Barberini, Taddeo, 167

Bardi, 42

Bärwalde, Treaty of, 151, 156, 161, 162, 163

Basilio d'Aire, Capuchin, 186, 208; at the theologians' conference in Vienna, 216, 218, 219, 278 (n. 21)

Bavaria. See Maximilian, Elector of Bavaria